Collective Bargaining in Education

Negotiating Change in Today's Schools

Collective Bargaining in Education
Negotiating Change in Today's Schools

Edited by

Jane Hannaway

and

Andrew J. Rotherham

HARVARD EDUCATION PRESS
Cambridge, Massachusetts

Library of Congress Control Number 2005937616

Paperback 10-digit ISBN 1-891792-71-7
Library Edition 10-digit ISBN 1-891792-72-5

Paperback 13-digit ISBN 978-1-891792-71-7
Library Edition 13-digit ISBN 978-1-891792-72-4

Published by Harvard Education Press,
an imprint of the Harvard Education Publishing Group

Harvard Education Press
8 Story Street
Cambridge, MA 02138

Cover Design: Anne Carter

The typefaces used in this book are Berthold Akizdenz Grotesk and Sabon.

Table of Contents

INTRODUCTION 1
Jane Hannaway and Andrew J. Rotherham

CHAPTER ONE 7
The History of Collective Bargaining among Teachers
Richard D. Kahlenberg

CHAPTER TWO 27
Union Membership in the United States
The Divergence between the Public and Private Sectors
Henry S. Farber

CHAPTER THREE 53
Scapegoat, Albatross, or What?
The Status Quo in Teacher Collective Bargaining
Frederick M. Hess and Andrew P. Kelly

CHAPTER FOUR 89
The Costs of Collective Bargaining Agreements
and Related District Policies
Paul T. Hill

CHAPTER FIVE 111
The Effects of Collective Bargaining on Teacher Quality
Susan Moore Johnson and Morgaen L. Donaldson

CHAPTER SIX 141
Are Teachers Unions Good for Students?
Dan Goldhaber

CHAPTER SEVEN 159
Teachers Unions and No Child Left Behind
Paul Manna

CHAPTER EIGHT 181
The Educational Value of Democratic Voice
A Defense of Collective Bargaining in American Education
Leo Casey

CHAPTER NINE 203
The As-Yet-Unfulfilled Promise of Reform Bargaining
Forging a Better Match between the Labor Relations
System We Have and the Education System We Want
Julia E. Koppich

CHAPTER TEN 229
Union Power and the Education of Children
Terry M. Moe

CONCLUSION 257
Jane Hannaway and Andrew J. Rotherham

NOTES 267

ABOUT THE CONTRIBUTORS 301

INDEX 305

Introduction

JANE HANNAWAY
ANDREW J. ROTHERHAM

his volume had its beginnings in a casual sidebar conversation at a conference on what seemed to be an unrelated topic. Our discussion was wide ranging, but it ended up on teacher collective bargaining and the promise and perils it holds for advancing education in the United States. We came to realize that much about school reform is directly or indirectly related to teacher collective bargaining. We then compared notes about what we knew from research about collective bargaining and who was pursuing the topic in an analytic way. Despite the work of a few well-known figures, the landscape was sparsely populated. We could think of many critics and many apologists, but few objective analysts. We could also come up with the standard rhetorical arguments, claims, and counterclaims, but little in the way of reasoned arguments or solid empirical evidence. So we decided to bring together the people who had systematically studied the area, others who had well-articulated views about collective bargaining, and several more respected education researchers and analysts to produce this volume. We added to this mix some of the most well-respected thinkers in the American Federation of Teachers (AFT) and the National Education Association (NEA) as well as leading analysts, researchers, and practitioners, all of whom we convened in Washington, D.C., for a day-and-a-half discussion centered on the papers our experts produced.

This volume and the conference that preceded it show the disappointing polarization that characterizes discussion of these vital issues as well as the profound lack of relevant data, research, and analysis. However, this effort also serves as an important first step in greater examination of these issues and dialogue about them. The conference brought together scholars, partisans, and educators for discussion. Many of the participants had never been in the same room together, despite being longtime antagonists. There was much important and honest exchange of reasoned argument and a clear delineation of the important issues that give rise to debate.

The topic of this volume is timely. The labor movement in the United States is at a critical juncture because of dramatic changes in the U.S. economy—especially the move to a service economy, increased globalization, and increased household income. To be sure, organized labor will likely always be an important player in economic and social decisionmaking in this country, but its role will evolve to fit today's environment, just as the role of other societal institutions evolves over time. But what about public-sector unions, in particular the most powerful among them, the teachers unions? Are they subject to the same pressures? How are they similar to and different from private-sector unions? And how are professional unions and professional bargaining similar to and different from bargaining by other groups? These are some of the questions our contributors address.

Most importantly and most centrally, we are concerned here with describing the role that collective bargaining has played over the years for teachers and the influence it has had on education more generally. Like the economy, education is at a critical juncture. State and national accountability requirements, the poor performance of many U.S. students relative to students in other industrialized countries, and great academic achievement gaps among different student groups within the United States have combined to exert performance pressure on schools like never before. These are conditions far different from those 40 years ago, when teacher collective bargaining developed. It is vital that policymakers understand what role collective bargaining currently plays to advance or constrain reforms intended to promote student achievement, and what role it might play in the future.

We should be clear that our intent is not to play the role of advocate or antagonist. We do not know all the answers; indeed, we are first trying to sort out the relevant questions. What is apparent is that collective bargaining by teachers is a key part of the scaffolding of education in the United States. We attempt to lay out systematically what we know and what we do not know about its role and its effects on student performance and school reform efforts.

The first three chapters lay the groundwork for those that follow. In chapter 1, Richard D. Kahlenberg describes how the adoption of collective bargaining in the 1960s changed the AFT and the NEA from "sleepy organizations" to "the most powerful forces in education" as well as potent actors in the national political arena. He also discusses attempts, especially those of the AFT president Albert Shanker, to direct union and collective bargaining efforts beyond the standard working-condition issues that concern all unions to professional issues of practice and policy. In much of the volume, the teachers unions are referred to generically—and they do indeed have a great deal in common—but in fact the AFT and the NEA are different organizations that at times pursue different objectives or employ different strategies, as Kahlenberg demonstrates.

In chapter 2, Henry S. Farber shows the sharp divergence in the fortunes of private- and public-sector unions in recent decades. In the early 1970s about 1 in 4 public- and private-sector employees was a member of a union; today more than 1 in 3 employees in the public sector belongs to a union, but only about 1 in 12 employees in the private sector. A big part of the public-sector increase is among local government employees, especially teachers. Farber suggests this public/private divergence is likely due to the greater advantages that public-sector unions, representing services typically unconstrained by market pressure and more open to political activity, can offer their members. Farber also discusses essential differences between public- and private-sector unions that are key to making sense of the issues this volume addresses.

Chapter 3, by Frederick M. Hess and Andrew P. Kelly, provides an inside look into collective bargaining by analyzing the legal framework and dynamics of the bargaining process as well as the agreements themselves. The evidence the authors present suggests that claims that unions completely restrict district management may be overstated. Hess and Kelly point out that district management is also party to contract terms, and they further suggest that administrators and school board members may sometimes use the collective bargaining agreement "as an excuse for inaction" beyond constraints in the agreements themselves.

We commissioned the next four chapters to review research on the effects of collective bargaining. Chapter 4, by Paul T. Hill, looks at the cost implications of collective bargaining and who bears those costs. His conclusions do not paint a pretty picture, and, like Hess and Kelly, he suggests that school boards and district administrators are part of the problem, as well as the bargaining agreements themselves. Common terms of collective bargaining agreements—overall increases in teacher pay scale, raises linked to seniority, salary credit for continuing education, and limits on class size and student contact minutes—create natural cost escalators. Over time these built-in escalators have had dramatic effects on school district costs that become serious problems, especially when districts run into financial difficulties. But more worrisome is Hill's discussion of how collective bargaining agreements tend to short shrift struggling schools serving disadvantaged children in the most important in-school resource, high-quality teachers.

Chapter 5, by Susan Moore Johnson and Morgaen L. Donaldson, attempts to address the relationship between teacher quality and collective bargaining. The authors explain why it is difficult to sort out the connection, partly because of the tremendous variation in labor policies and practices from state to state and district to district, but they bring to bear the available research to shape and inform the important questions. Do pay policies, including the single-salary schedule, attract or drive out effective teachers? Do agreements include provisions that might support effective teaching, for example, class size and time for preparation? Do teacher assignment terms ensure "fair and wise assignment, or . . . give undue weight to teachers' preferences and seniority, thus limiting some students' access to experienced teachers?" Do contracts establish reasonable means for professional evaluation, or do they protect poor teachers? Do agreements limit the professional influence of teachers or promote it?

The ultimate question of interest, of course, is the effect of collective bargaining on student achievement. Dan Goldhaber reviews the available research literature in chapter 6. In short, the research is sparse at best, and firm conclusions are not warranted one way or the other. Chapters 5 and 6 make all too clear that collective bargaining has unfortunately not been the focus of much systematic inquiry by scholars and policy analysts, despite its centrality to education.

We noted earlier that the education policy context today is different from what it was when collective bargaining first took root. One major difference is the teacher labor market. When teacher collective bargaining was established, schools still had a largely captive labor market because few other careers were open to women. Today, by contrast, competition for high-quality teachers is strong. A second important difference is the emphasis today on holding schools accountable for student outcomes. Chapter 7, by Paul Manna, examines the relationship between teachers union interests and the federal No Child Left Behind Act (NCLB), which requires states to conduct annual testing of students and to hold schools accountable for results. It also requires that schools hire highly qualified teachers in core subjects. Manna's analysis of the union-NCLB relationship provides an early glimpse into the possible fault lines and points of convergence between teachers unions and the new policy environment.

To help readers understand the major contours of the debate about these issues, the authors of the last three essays were invited to argue particular points. In chapter 8 Leo Casey of the United Federation of Teachers in New York was asked to make the case for why collective bargaining by teachers is beneficial in American education. He argues that what is in the common interest of teachers as educators is also in the best interest of students; the working environment of teachers is the learning environment of students. Julia E. Koppich, one of the few scholars who has studied teachers unions systematically, takes a "mend it don't end it" position and focuses chapter 9 on the promise and pitfalls of what has become known as "reform unionism," in which unions are involved in negotiating professional issues and not just issues associated with traditional industrial unionism. Koppich argues that changes may be needed in collective bargaining laws to ensure effective reform unionism and to bring about labor-management relations better suited to the current demands of education. In chapter 10 Terry M. Moe, also a scholar of unions, argues that it is unreasonable to expect unions to reform themselves in ways that make education for children their priority. Unions should be expected to behave in the same way that other organizations behave—that is, to promote their own interests. If the education system is to evolve in ways that truly promote the education of children, union power over schools should be weakened or eliminated, Moe argues.

A significant part of our discussion in the concluding chapter focuses on the need for not only more analysis and research but also—perhaps even more importantly—the need for greater transparency and broader involvement in the negotiating process itself and the political process that surrounds it. The consequences of collective bargaining are important both in terms of the allocation of significant public dollars and in the effective operation of the public school system for children. The stakes are simply too high to continue to ignore this integral part of the daily operations of many public schools and school districts.

We have many people to thank for helping us put this volume together. The first thanks should go to the authors for their work, which forms the backbone of this undertaking. A major thanks is also due the discussants who participated in the conferences and critiqued the papers that were delivered. Their comments led to revisions of papers in ways that made them fuller, more nuanced, and more accurate. Their feedback and expertise also helped to guide the discussion and debate at the conference in fruitful ways. The discussants included Joan Baratz Snowden, AFT; Kate Walsh, National Council on Teacher Quality; Harry Holzer, Georgetown University; Michelle Rhee, the New Teacher Project; Janet Hansen, RAND; Martin West, Harvard University; Russlyn Ali, The Education Trust; William Raabe, NEA; Jennifer King Rice, University of Maryland; Chester Finn, Fordham Foundation; and Thomas Mooney, Ohio Federation of Teachers. We are also grateful to Alan Bersin, former superintendent of San Diego schools, for his forthright discussion of his frontline experiences with unions as he headed one of the most ambitious school reform efforts in the country. Bersin is now California's secretary of education. Charles

Kerchner, a noted scholar of teachers unions, commented on Bersin's discussion and provided additional insights into collective bargaining laws and their reform. Many other attendees were active in discussions, providing views and information to us and to authors both during and after the conference, and we are grateful to them as well.

Much behind-the-scenes support was necessary to produce this volume. Will Marshall, Sara Mead, and Renee Rybak of the Progressive Policy Institute provided valuable advice and support. At the Urban Institute, Irene Steward organized the logistics of the conference and kept all the trains running on time, and Danny Loss tied up all the loose ends for final production of this volume. Stu Kantor of UI's Communication Division provided helpful advice and support for the conference.

Finally, we gratefully acknowledge the support provided by The Broad Foundation and the Smith Richardson Foundation. This project would not have been possible without their willingness to provide philanthropic support to examine this important and controversial issue. We're also grateful to Harvard Education Press for its uncompromising professionalism and top-flight support.

CHAPTER ONE

The History of Collective Bargaining among Teachers

RICHARD D. KAHLENBERG

While the nation's two major teachers unions have been around quite some time—the National Education Association (NEA) was founded in 1857 and the American Federation of Teachers (AFT) in 1916—collective bargaining for teachers is a much more recent phenomenon, going back only a little more than four decades. The adoption of collective bargaining greatly enhanced the power of teachers, transforming the NEA and AFT from somewhat sleepy organizations to institutions widely regarded today as the most powerful political forces in education.[1]

Beginning in the second half of the twentieth century, organized labor as a whole saw its numbers (and, therefore, its influence) shrink from 35 percent of the workforce in the 1950s to just 12.5 percent—and just 7.9 percent of the private-sector workforce—50 years later.[2] The two teachers unions, by contrast, grew dramatically during this period, from a combined 750,000 members in 1960 (just before the advent of collective bargaining) to 4 million members today.[3] Almost 90 percent of public schoolteachers nationally are members of the NEA or AFT.[4] "After the post office," says the former education secretary Lamar Alexander, "schools are the most unionized activity in America."[5]

This chapter traces the remarkable history of teacher collective bargaining in the twentieth century and the beginning of the twenty-first. It reviews the formidable obstacles to bargaining through midcentury, which bumped up against the growing demand for teacher power in the 1950s. We then examine the watershed moment in the early 1960s when teachers won a major collective bargaining agreement in New York City. The chapter next turns to the ensuing fights over the scope of collective bargaining—the question of whether unions should be able to bargain over education policy as well as wages, hours, and working conditions—and the spread of collective bargaining as the NEA and AFT competed, district by district, to represent the nation's teachers.

As teachers unions gained power through collective bargaining, they grew highly controversial. Supporters argued that collective bargaining brought about higher teacher salaries, better benefits to recruit more qualified teachers, a reduction of class size, increased time for classroom preparation, and the like. Critics castigated unions for using collective bargaining agreements to protect incompetent teachers, oppose efforts to reward merit, and oppose greater school choice for parents, among other things. The chapter traces the reaction to these charges: the AFT's call for education reform in the 1980s and 1990s, led by its president, Albert Shanker, and the NEA's delayed response, culminating in NEA president Bob Chase's vision of a "New Unionism" in 1997. This chapter concludes with some analysis of the degree to which teacher unionism and collective bargaining adhere to these reform agendas today.

THE FOUNDING OF THE TWO MAJOR TEACHER ORGANIZATIONS: THE NEA (1857) AND THE AFT (1916)

The history of the nation's two leading teachers unions long predates the advent of collective bargaining. The NEA was founded in 1857 as an organization of teachers and school administrators. The group didn't think of itself as a union, and administrators soon came to dominate the organization, holding 90 percent of the leadership and staff positions. The NEA sought to shape education reform, and in 1893 its Committee of Ten on Secondary School Studies recommended a liberal arts education for all high school students, which had a major impact on high school curriculum in the United States.[6]

In 1886 the American Federation of Labor (AFL) was founded as a collection of private-sector unions. Although the AFL was a major supporter of public schools, the confederation of unions did not originally include teachers.[7] Early on the AFL had little interest in organizing any profession. In 1919 AFL president Samuel Gompers said flatly, "We don't need any college men in the labor movement."[8] Gompers didn't say anything about the college woman, though the AFL was generally hostile to women of any educational attainment.[9]

In 1897 Margaret Haley led a group of teachers in Chicago to organize a union outside of the NEA. But antiunion forces on the Chicago school board had union members fired, which severely undercut the effectiveness of the group.[10] Looking for greater strength in numbers, in April 1916 Chicago teachers joined with others to form the American Federation of Teachers, which was granted a charter by the AFL.[11]

John Dewey received the first AFT membership card and was considered the union's "intellectual guru."[12] Dewey wanted teachers to be in unions to help them identify with their working-class students, though at that time, collective bargaining for teachers was not a realistic option.[13] Instead, local teacher organizations would attend school board meetings and make requests for salary increases. They participated in what the AFT later called "collective begging."[14] While teacher organizations sought to elect teacher representatives to the school board, the political influence of the organizations was limited in the early part of the century, as the largely female teaching profession lacked the franchise.[15]

OBSTACLES TO COLLECTIVE BARGAINING (1916–1959)

In the early years several obstacles to collective bargaining required considerable effort to overcome. Perhaps the biggest barrier was that public school teachers, as public employees, were thought by virtually all parties to be outside the ambit of collective bargaining. The founding AFL president, Samuel Gompers, strongly opposed strikes by public employees.[16] Responding to striking police officers in Boston in 1919, then-Massachusetts governor Calvin Coolidge famously declared, "There is no right to strike against public safety by anybody, anywhere, at any time."[17] Although teachers pushed to be included in the landmark 1935 National Labor Relations Act, the legislation limited collective bargaining rights to the private sector.[18] Labor's champion, Franklin D. Roosevelt, opposed strikes by public employees, writing in a 1937 letter, "All government employees should recognize that collective bargaining as usually understood cannot be transplanted into public service. . . . Actions looking toward the paralysis of government by those who have sworn to support it are unthinkable and intolerable."[19] As late as 1959, AFL-CIO president George Meany said, "It is impossible to bargain collectively with government."[20] Moreover, both the NEA and AFT had no strike policies in place through the 1950s, which forfeited their only point of leverage in negotiations.[21] Because teachers did not have laws protecting the right to organize, they were open to retaliation for trying to form a union. Teachers faced termination by school boards merely for joining a union not only in Chicago but also in Cleveland, Seattle, and elsewhere.[22]

A second barrier came from within the profession: teaching was a white-collar endeavor, made up mostly of college graduates who considered unions to be for blue-collar workers of lesser educational attainment. Teachers told union organizers, "My mom and dad are union members. That's why they had enough money for me to go to college. But . . . what kind of professional joins a union?"[23]

Third, fighting within the teaching profession prevented the solidarity required for collective bargaining. In particular, elementary school teachers, who were largely female and less well paid, wanted a single salary schedule for all teachers, while secondary teachers, who were more likely to be male and to be paid more highly, wanted a large differential in salary based on level of teaching.[24] Administrators often exploited these differences to prevent cooperation.[25] In some places, like New York City, teachers also divided along lines of race, ethnicity, and region. In the late 1950s New York had 106 different teacher organizations.[26] Because of the disunity, each was powerless.

Finally, although elements within the AFT were sympathetic to collective bargaining, the teaching profession as a whole was dominated by the much larger NEA. In 1920 the AFT had 10,000 members compared to the NEA's 53,000; by 1940 the AFT had 30,000 compared to the NEA's 203,000; and in 1960 the AFT had 59,000 members compared to the NEA's 714,000.[27] The NEA, with its strong contingent of administrators, was adamantly opposed to collective bargaining.

THE GROWING DEMAND FOR COLLECTIVE BARGAINING (1950s)

Though there were formidable obstacles to the organizing of teachers, there were also certain facts that aided the push toward collective bargaining by the mid-twentieth century. First, by the 1950s the private-sector labor movement had become a powerhouse, representing more than one-third of workers and winning sizable wage increases through collective bargaining.[28] Unorganized teacher pay, by contrast, was poor. In 1952 the AFT president Carl Megel noted that "the average salary for teachers in the United States during the past year was approximately $400 less than the income for the average factory worker."[29] Since the vast majority of teachers had college degrees, the income disparity was particularly striking.[30]

Second, many teachers were frustrated with poor working conditions. For example, they had noneducational responsibilities such as removing snow on school grounds. Further, elementary school teachers often had no breaks for lunch and were required to monitor the cafeteria and bathrooms. Many were forced to punch a time clock, and when they were sick and had to miss work, they were required to bring a doctor's note. Teachers were also forced to stay for long staff meetings at the principal's whim. Administrators were all-powerful and could change the grades given to students by teachers. Sexist rules required that female teachers leave the classroom as soon as they became pregnant.

Finally, without a union or collective bargaining agreements providing for grievance proceedings, teachers were open to abuses by administrators. They could play favorites in class assignments, sticking outspoken teachers with tough classes containing the roughest kids. Some principals openly berated teachers in front of their students.[31]

THE BIG BREAKTHROUGH: NEW YORK CITY (Early 1960s)

The growing pressure for collective bargaining resulted in a few isolated examples of collective bargaining agreements in Montana, Illinois, and Rhode Island in the 1930s through the 1950s, but the watershed development came in New York City in the early 1960s.[32] Members of the Teachers Guild, the AFT local, which alone among New York teacher organizations supported collective bargaining, decided it was time to act. Charles Cogen, a high school social studies teacher, led the Guild. But the driving forces were the younger AFT organizers David Selden and Albert Shanker.[33]

Selden and Shanker insisted that there was no reason public employees should not bargain collectively. Teachers should not have to give up their rights to association just because their employer was the government, they contended. Although public employee strikes were illegal, Selden and Shanker, taking a page from the civil rights movement, argued that striking could be thought of as a form of civil disobedience, in which an oppressed group breaks the law on principle and then pays the penalty meted out. They noted that teacher strikes involve public inconvenience rather than an endangerment of public health and safety, as strikes among other public employees, like police or firefighters, might.[34]

In New York teachers also benefited from a serendipitous precedent. When the city took over the private subway system, it inherited the system's unionized workforce, which demanded to engage in collective bargaining with its new employer.[35] The argument for collective bargaining in New York also received a boost when Wisconsin legislators adopted the nation's first public employee collective bargaining law in 1959.[36]

Although many teachers said it wasn't "professional" to be in a union, Shanker asked: Was it professional to be poorly paid and bossed around by administrators? Professionalism, in law, medicine, and the like, is marked by good pay, autonomy, and freedom from arbitrary treatment by supervisors. What was professional about having to bring in a doctor's note for sick days? He said, "A professional is an expert, and by virtue of his or her expertise, is relatively unsupervised. And you are constantly supervised and told what to do."[37] Indeed, he argued, collective bargaining was essential to getting administrators to treat teachers like true professionals.

At the same time organized labor saw that the labor force was moving away from blue-collar occupations toward more highly educated professionals, and that it must jettison its bias against organizing professionals. Walter Reuther of the United Auto Workers saw that with automation, labor had to expand its base and begin organizing white-collar professionals. Reuther and other like-minded union leaders were convinced to invest in the New York teacher movement, providing critical funds to the fledgling organization.[38]

To address the issue of teacher disunity, Shanker and Selden, along with their colleague George Altomare, forged a compromise between warring elementary and secondary teachers. In New York City in March 1960, the Teachers Guild merged with high school teachers to create the United Federation of Teachers (UFT). The key to the merger was the adoption of the principle that pay differentials would be based not on the grade level taught (elementary versus high school) but on seniority and levels of teacher education. Because high school teachers were much more likely to have master's degrees, most kept their higher salaries, but the new rule meant that the differential between elementary and high school teachers was not automatic but based on a credential that all teachers could understand.[39]

With a newly united organization, the UFT approached the city and in May 1960 received a pledge from Mayor Robert Wagner to hold an election to see whether teachers wanted to bargain collectively.[40] But over the summer a city lawyer disputed the legality of the move, and Wagner backed off his promise.[41] The UFT considered its options. The risks to striking were high. In New York State, under the 1947 Condon-Wadlin Act, striking teachers would lose their jobs.[42] There was a split among the union strategy committee. Many of the older union members were radical in philosophy but conservative in action.[43] They noted that the UFT had only about 4,500 members—roughly 10 percent of the teaching staff—and the union might be crushed in a strike. But Shanker and others argued that the organization would be meaningless if it did not respond to the broken promise with a strike. And on November 7, 1960, the day before the Kennedy-Nixon presidential election, the UFT staged a one-day walkout.[44]

Only 5,000 teachers out of 50,000 struck, a small number, but still too many for firing them all to be practical, so they did not lose their jobs.[45] The strike worked: Mayor Wagner promptly agreed to form a committee of labor leaders to decide what to do. The committee, not surprisingly, recommended a collective bargaining election.[46] In June 1961 teachers voted 27,000 to 7,000 to pursue collective bargaining.[47] In December 1961 a collective bargaining election was held between the UFT and the Teacher Bargaining Organization (TBO), an NEA affiliate in New York (along with the nonaligned Teachers Union). The UFT prevailed over the TBO by a vote of 20,045 to 9,770.[48]

The vote was significant in its own right: New York City had more teachers than the 11 smallest states combined.[49] But it had broad implications for all of American labor. At the time *Business Week* magazine asked, "How long will the government clerk go on thinking a union is below her dignity when the teacher next door belongs?"[50] In January 1962 John Kennedy issued Executive Order 10988 allowing federal employees to bargain collectively.[51] Although teachers were not directly affected by the executive order, Kennedy's move helped validate the entire notion of public employee bargaining.

Meanwhile, in New York, having won collective bargaining rights, the UFT pushed for higher pay and free lunch periods for teachers, among other things. When the school board balked, teachers struck on April 12, 1962, and this time, 20,000 teachers stayed out.[52] The NEA criticized the strike as unprofessional and said the use of illegal tactics taught a bad lesson to American schoolchildren.[53] But once again, the strike worked, and New York's governor Nelson Rockefeller managed to "find" $13 million in state money for the city's schools.[54] In June 1962 the UFT forged the nation's first major teacher collective bargaining contract, including a $995 pay increase and a duty-free lunch period. Over time union negotiations also eliminated indignities like the requirement of a doctor's note for illness and the need to punch a clock.[55]

EARLY FIGHTS OVER THE SCOPE OF COLLECTIVE BARGAINING (1960s)

Once collective bargaining rights were won, unions pressed to expand the scope of bargaining beyond the issues of wages, hours, and working conditions to include educational quality. In 1963 the UFT pushed for a reduction in class size and the establishment of a special enrichment program for ghetto schools, which the union helped design, called More Effective Schools.[56] The school board responded that it was opposed to including in the contract anything that had to do with school improvement, saying, "Now you're trying to dictate policy to us."[57]

Opponents argued that it is undemocratic to negotiate public policy with one special-interest group.[58] The teacher-unionist-turned-critic Myron Lieberman, for example, argued that it is "nonsense" to expand the scope of bargaining, saying it is like the United Auto Workers negotiating over "the price of cars, their color, and safety features."[59] Supporters of broad bargaining responded that teachers have special expertise that should be employed.[60] Shanker said that unlike autoworkers, teachers are blamed when things go wrong: "No one dreams of going to Ford or General Motors and saying, 'Ralph Nader says my car is unsafe; I demand that you fire the following workers.' In the schools it's very different. The parent marches in and says, 'This class is behind in reading: fire the teacher.'"[61] Others noted that it is difficult to draw a clear line between what is an issue of wages, hours, and working conditions and what is educational policy. The budget implications of a decision about the salaries, for example, can effectively determine what education policies can be pursued with remaining dollars.[62]

In its contract negotiations, the UFT, at the urging of parents and civil rights groups, pushed hard to include education reform. In a 1966 address to the annual convention of the AFT, the civil rights leader Bayard Rustin urged teachers unions to bargain for quality education and get policy "written into their contracts."[63] In 1967 the UFT went on strike for 14 days, mostly over nonwage issues: a tougher school discipline policy, reduced class size, and a call for expansion of the More Effective Schools program for disadvantaged schools. The union slogan was "Teachers Want What Children Need." The board was able to come to agreement on wage issues but refused to "delegate the making of policy . . . to the union and exclude participation of parents and the public."[64] This issue was never fully resolved and would resurface again in later years.

THE SPREAD OF COLLECTIVE BARGAINING AND GROWTH IN POLITICAL INVOLVEMENT (1960s–1970s)

The breakthrough for collective bargaining in New York in the early 1960s led to "an explosion of teacher unionism" in the late 1960s, according to the Swarthmore historian Marjorie Murphy.[65] Following on the victory in New York, the AFT won bargaining elections in Detroit in 1964 and in Philadelphia in 1965. By 1968 AFT membership reached 175,000, up from 60,000 in 1960.[66] "The AFT threatened to surpass the NEA" in membership, Murphy says.[67]

Threatened by the AFT's ascendancy, the NEA, led by teacher activists in Michigan, reversed its opposition to collective bargaining in the late 1960s.[68] In 1969 the NEA officially recognized the right to strike.[69] As the NEA transformed itself from an education association to a teachers union, supervisors and administrators were spun out of the organization.[70] Don Cameron, the longtime executive director of the NEA, says that in the decade from 1965 to 1975, the NEA changed "from a tea-and-crumpets organization" into a union.[71] The competition between the NEA and AFT over collective bargaining was intense, and bargaining probably spread more quickly than it would have had there been just one union. (Once a school district elected a union as a representative, it was difficult, though not impossible, for the opposition to dethrone the incumbent union.)[72]

With pressure from the AFT and NEA and other unions representing government employees, legislators began to follow Wisconsin's lead in adopting public employee collective bargaining laws. By 1966 seven states had such laws on the books.[73] Over time this number grew to 34 states and the District of Columbia.[74] Most state laws prohibited strikes, but in practice teachers often violated the laws and succeeded in having penalties waived as part of the settlement of the strike.[75]

Thanks to the effectiveness of teacher strikes in New York, the phenomenon spread. Shanker argued in 1967 that while teachers do not wish to strike, "the city has convinced us that striking brings us gains we need and cannot get any other way." He said, "There would be no teachers' union today if we did not defy the law."[76] In 1964 there were 9 teacher strikes; in 1966, 30; and in 1967, 105.[77] By the 1975-76 school year, there were 203 teacher strikes, a record number.[78] The strikes gave unions the power to disrupt the everyday lives of a district's public school students and parents and put tremendous political pressure on public officials to come to an agreement. Over time, however, as unions became more firmly established, the political climate toward unions changed, and as both management and unions realized strikes were detrimental to their images, the number of teacher strikes declined.[79]

As a direct consequence of collective bargaining, union membership skyrocketed. NEA membership rose from 766,000 in 1961, before the first major collective bargaining agreement, to 2.7 million today. The AFT went from 70,821 to 1.3 million during the same period.[80] In percentage terms, Murphy notes, unions represented "only a small fraction of school teachers" in 1961, but with the advent of collective bargaining, the proportion of public school teachers who were in unions that represented them in bargaining shot up to more than half by 1971, and to 72 percent by the late 1970s.[81] (The percentage of teachers who are members of the AFT and NEA is somewhat higher today—nearly 90 percent—because teachers in districts and states without collective bargaining are sometimes still members of the union in order to receive certain benefits and to lobby on behalf of teachers.)[82] The revenue of the AFT and NEA tops $1 billion annually.[83]

Alongside the growth in collective bargaining came an increase in teacher involvement in political affairs. During the presidency of Lyndon Johnson, a former schoolteacher, Congress passed the Elementary and Secondary Education Act of 1965, providing significant federal funds for low-income students. In the early 1970s lawsuits seeking equalization of school funding triggered a substantial rise in the proportion of education spending provided at the state level. Both developments led teachers to go beyond collective bargaining with local school boards to lobby for state and federal funds and to shape state and federal education policies that inevitably accompanied education spending.

Teachers unions became major political players, particularly within the Democratic Party. The NEA gave only 4 percent of donations to the Republican Party, while the AFT—although considered more centrist on education reform—gave less than 2 percent to Republicans.[84] Among major Democratic donors, the AFT ranked 7th and the NEA 12th.[85] The NEA routinely had more delegates to Democratic National Conventions than any state except California.[86]

Some conservatives argued that the unions' close ties to the Democratic Party inhibited Democrats' ability to call for creative education reform. Some liberals responded that conservative attacks on teachers unions were likewise testament to the connection between teachers unions and the Democratic Party.

CONTROVERSY OVER THE GROWING INFLUENCE OF COLLECTIVE BARGAINING AND TEACHERS UNIONS (1970s–Today)

When collective bargaining catapulted the NEA and AFT to positions of power over education policy, they quickly become objects of controversy. They engendered a heated debate within political and academic circles about whether teachers unions and collective bargaining have a positive or negative effect on education. The debate continues to this day and is the subject of several papers in this volume.

Supporters of teachers unions cited an array of positive educational developments that grew out of collective bargaining. Some argued that bargaining increased teacher salaries and fringe benefits significantly, thereby attracting a higher quality of teacher to the profession. In 1982 the researchers William H. Baugh and Joe A. Stone found that the teachers union pay premium amounted to 12 percent for wages and that the premium for fringe benefits was probably larger.[87] Overall, between 1961 and 2001, the average annual salary of public school teachers (in current dollars) rose from $5,264 to $43,262.[88] In addition, by giving union members a voice in how they are treated, collective bargaining appears to have reduced employee turnover, though turnover still remains high among teachers.[89]

Many commentators have pointed out that the unions' role in raising wages (and with it, teacher quality) was especially important given the declining role of gender discrimination in the workforce. For many years schools had received a discrimination subsidy because highly able women entered teaching as bias shut them out of other professions like law, medicine, and architecture.[90] As equal-opportunity laws were passed and attitudes changed, salary increases were required just to stay even in attracting quality teachers, so the role of unions, supporters argued, was more important than ever.

Unions also bargained for reduced class size, a condition that appears to benefit students. One study in the 1970s found that 34 percent of collective bargaining agreements for teachers included a maximum class size.[91] Between 1960 and 2001 student-teacher ratios were reduced from 25.8 students for every teacher to 15.9.[92] A study by Randall Eberts and Joe Stone in the 1980s found that the student-teacher ratio is nearly 12 percent lower in bargaining than in nonbargaining districts.[93] The evidence from several studies suggests that reduction in class size raises academic achievement, particularly for children in the early grades, though this finding is not without controversy.[94]

Teachers unions bargained for other benefits that supporters said improved education. By ensuring that teachers had less responsibility for noneducational tasks like bathroom supervision and had time set aside specifically for classroom preparation, collective bargaining increased the quality of instruction, supporters argued.[95] Eberts and Stone found that teachers in unionized districts had 4 percent greater preparation time than those in nonunionized districts.[96] Likewise, many bargaining agreements earmarked funding for professional development.[97] Research finds that well-designed staff development, such as that used by teachers in New York City's Community School District 2, can boost student achievement.[98]

Teachers unions also bargained and lobbied for tougher discipline policies for students, which supporters argued was good for education. The AFT was a leading force in the passage of legislation to reduce student disruptions in Texas and West Virginia. And in Minneapolis, New York City, and elsewhere, unions have written into collective bargaining contracts provisions for better student discipline. Better discipline has also been associated with higher student academic achievement.[99]

Other benefits of collective bargaining may be more subtle. Some argued that by gaining better treatment of teachers from principals and administrators, collective bargaining helps promote the democratic message of public education. If children see their teachers being mistreated and demeaned in an arbitrary fashion—as occurred with some regularity before collective bargaining—they are taught a harmful lesson. "For teachers," said Shanker, being treated with dignity is "especially important because they're models for all the kids in our society."[100]

Critics countered that the growing power of teachers unions was detrimental to education because the needs of children often diverged from the narrow self-interest of teachers. Opponents argued that union contracts reduce flexibility and thwart innovative education reforms. In the early days teachers unions were often accused of showing little concern for promoting educational achievement. Shanker, who would later become an innovative education reformer, quipped in his earlier days that he would start representing the interests of kids when they started paying union dues.[101]

Union critics first pointed to the frequency of teacher strikes. Unions were more concerned with gaining raw power through illegal strikes than with the harm incurred by children from lost instruction time, it was argued. In the 1973 film *Sleeper*, Woody Allen satirized UFT president Shanker's penchant for engaging in illegal and lengthy teacher strikes, depicting him as a madman. Allen's character awakens in the year 2173 to find that civilization was destroyed when "a man by the name of Albert Shanker got hold of a nuclear warhead."[102]

Union critics were even more vexed by provisions in collective bargaining agreements that made it time consuming at best, and virtually impossible at worst, for administrators to fire incompetent teachers.[103] In Florida, for example, the involuntary rate of dismissal for teachers was 0.05 percent in a recent year, compared with 7.9 percent in the Florida workforce as a whole.[104] The average cost of dismissing a teacher in New York State during the 1990s was reportedly $200,000.[105]

Supporters of pay for performance or systems of merit pay for teachers criticized collective bargaining and unions for thwarting those policies. Under the single salary schedule, seniority and an accumulation of credits were rewarded, not actual teacher quality or merit as reflected in student achievement, critics said. The salary structure, they charged, made it difficult to reward (and retain) great teachers, who often left the classroom for higher paying jobs in school administration.[106]

Unions were also criticized for opposing efforts to empower parents through greater school choice, either within the public system or through a system of private school vouchers. And collective bargaining agreements, which gave experienced teachers the first chance at desirable jobs within a district (often at schools with affluent populations), meant that low-income students who needed the best teachers most often ended up with the worst.[107]

Finally, some criticized unions for allegedly resisting efforts to impose accountability measures. Teachers unions, critics said, were frequently calling for the public to spend greater and greater amounts of money on education but were unwilling to have these investments measured against results in educational achievement.

The criticism of teachers unions and collective bargaining probably reached its zenith in August 1996, when the presidential candidate Bob Dole accepted his nomination at the Republican National Convention. Dole excoriated teachers unions: "If education were a war, you would be losing it. If it were a business, you would be driving it into bankruptcy. If it were a patient, it would be dying."[108]

REINVENTING TEACHER UNIONISM AND COLLECTIVE BARGAINING (1980s–1990s)

Long before Dole's speech, however, a few key leaders within the teachers union movement argued that the time had come for unions to embrace a new kind of collective bargaining that not only was concerned with traditional teacher interests but also would respond to the attacks from critics and offer a set of constructive compromises that met the legitimate complaints about the unions without giving up on fundamental principles.

For Shanker and the AFT, the need to engage in reform was underlined by the conservative ascendency in the late 1970s and early 1980s. In 1978 teachers unions dodged a bullet when a plan for tuition tax credits came very close to passing the U.S. Congress. In 1980 came the election of Ronald Reagan, who was openly hostile to unions and supportive of private school vouchers. If public schools weren't performing, they couldn't be moved to Mexico, like auto plants, but they could be put out of business by private schools.

The AFT's key move came in the spring of 1983, with the release of the seminal report *A Nation at Risk* from the National Commission on Excellence in Education. The report, which warned of a "rising tide of mediocrity" in American education, was roundly attacked by much of the education establishment, including the NEA. Sponsored by the Reagan administration's Department of Education, the report was considered suspect by most in the teachers union movement, given Reagan's antiunion and anti–public education reputation. But Shanker took a different view, arguing that the report's critique of public schools was sound and that the best way to save public education was to embrace the recommendations. The executive director of the National Commission, Milton Goldberg, recalled that the report might have been crippled if there had been unanimous opposition in education circles. "It was vital that someone with stature step up," he said. "Al Shanker never wavered on that issue and the rest of the education community and public finally caught up to him."[109] As the reform agenda stemming from the *Risk* report moved forward, the AFT began forming partnerships with the business community and others for various changes.

In 1985 Shanker made a series of three widely noted speeches outlining a new notion of teacher unionism based on teacher professionalism.[110] Just as the

AFT had revolutionized teaching by introducing collective bargaining 25 years earlier, Shanker called for "a second revolution" in which teachers would bargain for improved education. Shanker declared, "Collective bargaining has been a good mechanism, and we should continue to use it. But now, we must ask whether collective bargaining will get us where we want to go." He argued, "I am convinced that unless we go beyond collective bargaining to the achievement of true teacher professionalism, we will fail in our major objectives: to preserve public education in the United States and to improve the status of teachers, economically, socially, and politically."[111]

In a departure from the early days when Shanker said he would represent children when they started paying union dues, Shanker now said a key element of all professions is that members are concerned not only with their own interests but also with those of their "clients."[112] He advocated what Susan Moore Johnson and Susan M. Kardos would later call "reform bargaining" rather than "industrial bargaining."[113] Among other things, the speeches offered creative compromises on the three key issues about which collective bargaining was under attack: protection for incompetent teachers, resistance to merit pay, and opposition to school choice. To answer the longstanding complaint that unions protected unworthy teachers, Shanker endorsed a controversial program, used in Toledo, Ohio, under which experienced lead teachers would police their peers, sometimes advocating termination of employment. The notion was revolutionary at the time. For years a clear line had been present: it was management's job to weed out bad teachers, and the union's job to ensure they received due process to guard against unfair dismissal. The procedure was adversarial, in which the union played the role of defense lawyer, making the state prosecution prove its claim. Peer review obliterated the line and undercut the principle of worker solidarity so central to industrial unionism. Dal Lawrence, the author of the Toledo plan, explained, "Here we were, a teachers union, and we were evaluating and even recommending the non-renewal and terminations of teachers."[114]

The plan also involved a dramatic departure from the traditional fiduciary responsibility of unions to equal representation of members. Indeed, some argue the plan is legally suspect because courts have held that a union must "exercise fairly the power conferred upon it in behalf of all those members for whom it acts, without hostile discrimination among them."[115] In practice, teachers are tougher on colleagues than are administrators: peer review results in more dismissals than when administrators evaluate teachers.[116] Interestingly, in places like Cincinnati and Rochester, it was management, rather than unions, that resisted peer review most fiercely.[117]

On the issue of merit pay, or pay for performance, Shanker offered another compromise. He continued to oppose plans in which principals reward certain teachers, because it might lead to favoritism and might discourage teachers within a school from cooperating with one another on how to improve instruction. But he said it was time for unions to recognize that the issue of merit must be honored. "Most people in this country believe hard work and better work ought to be rewarded, and opposing this makes us look like we are not interested in quality. So we ought to think about ways of handling the issue while avoiding the pitfalls," he argued.[118]

In a speech, Shanker called for the creation of an organization (which later became the National Board for Professional Teaching Standards) to provide for teachers the equivalent of board certification for doctors, with extra pay to those who qualified. Today more than 30 states provide bonuses for board-certified teachers, as do many localities, providing a way for high-quality teachers to get extra money without moving into administration and leaving the classroom.[119] North Carolina Governor Jim Hunt, who chaired the board of the NBPTS, argues, "More than any other single person, Al Shanker was the founder of the [group]."[120] As with peer review, Shanker believed the NBPTS involved a sensible exception to union principles of solidarity.

On the issue of school choice, Shanker always argued that private school vouchers would undermine American unity and lead to greater stratification between rich and poor, but he said that unions needed a response to proponents of vouchers who attacked unions for trapping poor kids in bad schools. Although unions have an interest in opposing even public school choice, because choice strengthens the hands of parents against teachers, in April 1985 Shanker became the first national teachers union leader to back public school choice, declaring that the country should provide "the greatest possible choice among public schools."[121]

Most importantly, Shanker became a strong proponent of the standards, testing, and accountability movement in education. In 1996 the *New York Times*' Sara Mosle identified Shanker as one of three leading advocates for standards—along with Diane Ravitch and E. D. Hirsch—and said Shanker was "the one who has pushed the longest and hardest for standards."[122] Shanker and the AFT used the bully pulpit on behalf of standards, lobbied for tough legislation that included consequences, and issued reports evaluating state standards. In places like Cincinnati, key tenets of the standards movement, such as ending social promotion, were written into the union contract as part of a Bargaining for Better Schools effort.[123] In 1997 Hirsch said, "If any single person could be said to be responsible for the astonishing shift in public sentiment that recently prompted the president of the United States to call for national educational standards—a proposal that would have been unthinkable a few years back—that person would be Al Shanker."[124]

All these new union approaches were controversial within the AFT. In the summer of 1996, when Shanker told union delegates, "It is as much your duty to preserve public education as it is to negotiate a good contract," there was applause, but not everyone in the union agreed.[125] Recalls Shanker's successor, Sandra Feldman, "There was a good deal of resistance among the stalwarts, who felt we should stick to unionism and leave education to the boards of education."[126]

The resistance led some to question how far local union leaders, who actually negotiate collective bargaining contracts, went in implementing Shanker's ideas. Chester Finn, for example, argued that Shanker was "one of the authentically insightful and imaginative figures in American education," but that "the AFT locals are simultaneously going on strike, battling reforms, and defending the status quo as if everything were hunky dory."[127] Finn told Sara Mosle, "Look, I agree with Al Shanker four days out of every five. But he's not representative of his union. He is way ahead of his membership."[128] Myron Lieberman also alleged a "disconnect between Shanker's rhetoric and AFT practice."[129] Reforms have often been slow to catch on in local districts.[130] In 1996 Shanker expressed frustration to *U.S. News and World Report*'s Thomas Toch: "Convincing people to change has been a damn difficult thing to do. I would go into a state, talk up reform and as soon as I left, the union attorney would come in and say, 'We've got a great tenure law, let's keep it.'"[131]

To the foot draggers, Shanker argued that his reform agenda was not selling out teachers, but rather recognizing their enlightened self-interest. True, unions have a legal "duty of fair representation" just as a corporation has a fiduciary duty to maximize shareholder profits.[132] But just as corporations engage in philanthropy with the argument that goodwill ultimately benefits shareholders, a union president can argue—as Shanker did—that reforms were necessary to preserve public education and union jobs.

Throughout most of the Shanker era (which ended with his death in 1997), the NEA resisted his reform ideas. On *A Nation at Risk*, peer review, extra pay for board-certified teachers, public school choice, standards and assessments, and charter schools, the NEA dragged its feet.[133] Time and again, it was the smaller AFT that outthought the NEA. "Over the years," wrote Ted Fiske in the *New York Times*, "David has consistently outwitted Goliath."[134]

But just as the NEA ultimately followed the lead of the AFT in the adoption of collective bargaining, so the NEA eventually moved in the direction of embracing a new form of collective bargaining, at least at the leadership level, and at least for a time. On February 5, 1997, in a widely noted speech at the National Press Club, then–NEA president Bob Chase said the NEA had to change its course. He argued for a New Unionism, which puts "issues of school quality front and center at the bargaining table." Chase conceded, "In some instances, we have used our power to block uncomfortable changes, to protect the narrow interests of our members, and not to advance the interests of students and schools." But he said the union must now embrace such reforms as peer review, or America would end up with a system of private school vouchers. "We must revitalize our public schools from within, or they will be dismantled from without," he declared.[135] Thomas Toch notes, "It was exactly the same message that Albert Shanker had delivered . . . 12 years earlier."[136] In 1999 Chase made waves when he endorsed experimentation with teacher pay for performance.[137]

NEW UNIONISM TODAY

With Shanker gone and Bob Chase having retired in 2002, what are the prospects for New Unionism today? The current record is mixed, and the outlook for the future is uncertain, both at the local and national levels of the NEA and AFT.

Both unions have important pockets of reform. Charles Taylor Kerchner highlights several districts where significant reform has taken place, including Minneapolis, Rochester, Columbus, Cincinnati, Denver, Toledo, New York, Seattle, and Poway, California.[138] Today, for example, some 50 districts are using peer review.[139] To address the criticism that seniority rules meant that experienced teachers rarely taught in high-poverty schools, the UFT has agreed to a 15 percent pay premium for teachers who teach in New York City's low-performing schools.[140] And in 2004 the UFT proposed to cut the time required to terminate incompetent teachers to six months.[141] Perhaps most significantly, an NEA local in Denver has a contract that includes a revolutionary provision under which teachers receive bonuses in part based on student achievement. Incentives are also provided to teachers who work in high-poverty schools.[142]

Having said that, the New Unionism has not been embraced as widely as supporters had hoped. Julia Koppich, a leading authority on reform bargaining, asks in her chapter in this volume, "Why has reform unionism not spread more broadly?"[143] Is the industrial model adopted by teachers unions in the 1960s simply too difficult to change once put in place?

Innovative districts are not necessarily receiving the support from their national leadership that they once did. The current AFT president, Edward J. McElroy, supports many education reforms but says, "If someone gets elected to be a union leader, they didn't get elected to be dean of education."[144] McElroy has also been more critical of the No Child Left Behind Act (NCLB) than his predecessor, Sandra Feldman, which some (though not all) observers worry may be a sign that he will yield to members who are disgruntled with accountability measures.

The new NEA president, Reg Weaver, is considered more of a traditional unionist and is unenthusiastic about reforms like the Denver pay-for-performance experiment.[145] The NEA also has been increasingly outspoken in its opposition to NCLB. The union is on record as resisting the use of testing "as an indicator of school success."[146] The NEA Representative Assembly has supported a resolution to allow students to opt out of standardized tests.[147] In 2005 the NEA ratcheted up its opposition to NCLB by filing a lawsuit complaining of unfunded mandates.[148] Likewise, within the NEA nationally, the local Denver pay-for-performance plan has been received coolly, and the NEA national convention rejected a pay-for-performance resolution by a substantial margin.[149]

In recent years reform presidents of local unions have suffered electoral defeats in Los Angeles, Chicago, San Francisco, Hartford, and Cincinnati, suggesting to some a trend away from the New Unionism. But both liberals like Tom Mooney of the Ohio Federation of Teachers and conservatives like the union critic Mike Antonucci note that local union elections are complicated and shouldn't necessarily be viewed as referenda on education reforms. Adam Urbanski, president of the innovative Rochester Teachers Association and director of the Teacher Union Reform Network (TURN), also rejects the notion that large trends can be deduced from individual district results.[150] At this point it is too early to know whether recent elections portend a crippling of the New Unionism or a temporary and reversible setback.

The history of teacher unionism suggests the importance of strong leaders who were willing to tell their members things they sometimes did not want to hear—initially, that they should embrace collective bargaining, and later, that they needed to reform it. Urbanski says that in Rochester and elsewhere, Albert Shanker's speeches gave local leaders indispensable political cover to push education reforms they believed important.[151] Political science 101 suggests it is easier to be a statesman the more insulated one is from voters, so bold leadership must generally come from the very top.

Are we likely to see inspired leadership in the coming years? On the one hand, each new generation of union leadership will be further removed from the original fights establishing collective bargaining, will be less likely to have gone to jail for teacher unionism, and will therefore have less political capital to draw on to push unpopular but necessary reforms. On the other hand, teachers unions are more firmly ensconced in the political landscape than ever, which should free leaders to take risks that were impossible to pursue when teachers unions were fledgling organizations fighting for survival. Internal AFT and

NEA polling suggests younger members are comparatively more concerned about school-quality issues than about wages and benefits compared with their older counterparts.[152]

It is difficult to know how these countervailing pressures will play out. Will the new leadership of the AFT and NEA revert to a more traditional unionism of an earlier era or continue down the course set by adherents of the New Unionism? Given the power of teachers unions, the answer will have significant ramifications for the future of public education in the United States.

CHAPTER TWO

Union Membership in the United States
The Divergence between the Public and Private Sectors[1]

HENRY S. FARBER

INTRODUCTION

In 1974, one in four workers in both the private and public sectors were members of labor unions. Two quite different tales unfold since that time. By 2004 only 8.2 percent of workers in the private sector were members of unions. In stark contrast, the union membership rate among public-sector workers increased to 37.1 percent over the same period. Figure 1 contains plots of the time series of private- and public-sector union membership rates from 1973 to 2004 derived from tabulations of the Current Population Survey (CPS), and it illustrates these trends.[2] The union membership rate in the private sector has declined steadily since 1973, with a particularly sharp rate of decline in the 1980s. The union membership rate in the public sector increased sharply during the 1970s to about 38 percent in 1979 and has been largely steady since.

The public sector is not homogeneous. It is composed of three substantial, distinct subsectors: (1) federal government employees, (2) state government employees, and (3) local government employees. Since 1983 the CPS has identified type of public employee, and Figure 2 contains plots of total employment by subsector and the share of overall employment in each subsector for the 1983-2004 period. Federal government employment was virtually unchanged over this period at about 3 million workers, and, because the labor force grew substantially over this period, the federal government's share of total employ-

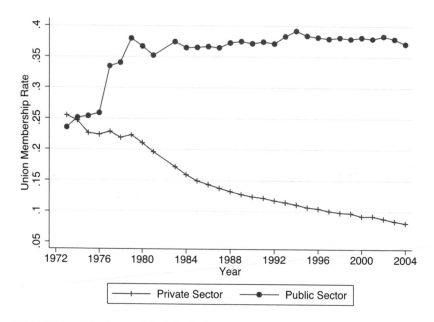

FIGURE 1: **Private- and Public-Sector Union Membership Rates, 1973–2004**

ment fell substantially. State government employment rose from 3.7 million in 1983 to 5.6 million in 2004, for a growth rate of 2 percent per year, implying a slight increase in employment share. Local government is by far the largest subsector, and its employment rose from 8.3 million in 1983 to 10.6 million in 2004, for a growth rate of 1.2 percent per year. However, local government's share of total employment fell steadily from almost 10 percent in 1983 to under 9 percent by 2004.

Figure 3 contains plots of the time series of public-sector union membership rates by subsector. These show steady union membership rates in each of the three sectors at levels that far exceed the private sector. The highest union membership rate is in the local government sector, where more than 40 percent of workers belong to unions. Union membership rates in the state and federal government sectors are approximately 30 percent.

Given the size and importance of the local government sector, it is worth examining more closely different categories of local government employees. Panel A of Figure 4 contains plots of employment of local government workers in three important categories: teachers, police, and firefighters.[3] The largest category by far is teachers, whose numbers increased from 2.4 million in 1983 to

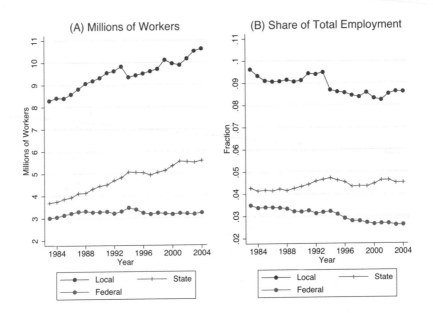

FIGURE 2: Public-Sector Employment, 1983–2004

3.1 million in 2004. Numbers of police and firefighters are relatively small (800,000 and 270,000 respectively in 2004). Panel B of Figure 4 contains plots of the share of local government employment for each of the three types of workers. Teachers make up fully 30 percent of local government employees, and their share has been roughly fixed since 1983. While there are many fewer police, their share increased from about 5.3 percent to 7.8 percent of local government employment since 1983.

All three of these groups of local government employees are highly unionized. Panel A of Figure 5 contains plots of the union membership rate for three important groups of local government employees: teachers, police, and firefighters. Interestingly, the union membership rate of firefighters has fallen dramatically in the last two decades, from 82 percent in 1983 to 69 percent in 2004, while the union membership rates of police and teachers have been roughly constant over this period.

Perhaps a more realistic picture of the importance of unions in local government considers not only union members but also nonmembers who are covered by collective bargaining agreements (free riders). Toward this end, panel B of Figure 5 contains plots of the union coverage rate for the three groups of local

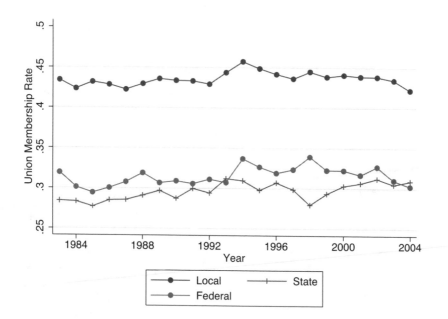

FIGURE 3: Public-Sector Union Membership Rates, 1983–2004

government employees.[4] The striking result is that union coverage rates have fallen substantially over time for all three groups of local government workers. The coverage rate for firefighters fell from 86 percent to 70 percent between 1983 and 2004. Over the same period the coverage rate for teachers fell from 74 percent to 66 percent. There was a smaller decline for police, from 64 percent to 59 percent. On balance, while the incidence of collective bargaining among local government employees has declined, unions remain a very important factor in public-sector labor markets.

These bare facts suggest important differences among labor markets within the public sector as well as between those in the public and private sectors. These differences serve as the starting point for my analysis of unions in the two sectors. In the next section I present more detailed evidence on employment growth and union membership rates in the two sectors. I also present a decomposition of changes in union membership in each sector into components due to changes in union and nonunion employment. In the third section, Does Public Policy Matter?, I narrow my focus to the public sector and consider interstate variation in the legislative environment governing public-sector collective bargaining and how these laws affect the unionization rate. Section 4,

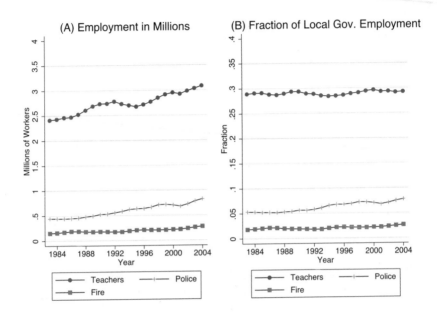

FIGURE 4: **Local Government Employment, 1983–2004 (Three-Year Moving Average)**

Public-Sector Bargaining Laws and Wages, extends this analysis to wages, and in the fifth section, I conclude.

EMPLOYMENT GROWTH AND UNION MEMBERSHIP

Employment in the private sector of workers age 18-65 increased from 71 million in 1983 to 104 million in 2004.[5] This is an average annual employment growth rate of 1.8 percent. Employment in the public sector increased from 15 million in 1983 to 19.4 million in 2004, for an average annual employment growth rate of 1.2 percent. Thus, public-sector employment has grown more slowly than private-sector employment in the last two decades.

Employment Growth and Union Membership in the Private Sector

There is substantial disagreement about reasons for the sharp decline in the private-sector union membership rate. Many observers have argued that the legal and political support for organizing new union members in the private sector deteriorated through the 1970s and 1980s. Richard B. Freeman and Paul C. Weiler focus on the intensified opposition to unions by employers.[6] Paul Alan

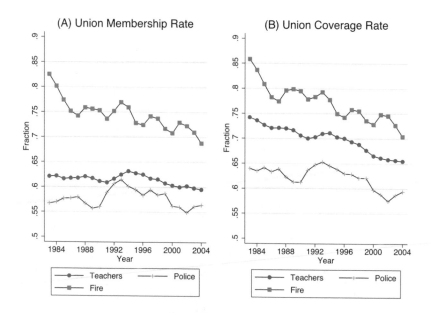

FIGURE 5: Local Government Unionization Rates, 1983–2004 (Three-Year Moving Average)

Levy emphasizes changes in the administration of the National Labor Relations Act (NLRA) due to changes in composition of the National Labor Relations Board (NLRB).[7] Still others claim that changes in the U.S. economic environment substantially reduced the attractiveness of unions to workers and the acceptability of unions to employers. In this view the economic environment became increasingly open to foreign competition in product markets, and capital became more mobile internationally. Consequently, unions could no longer guarantee their workers higher wages while maintaining reasonable levels of job security.

In some earlier work Henry S. Farber and Bruce Western present evidence contrasting two explanations for the decline of union membership in the private sector.[8] The first emphasizes legal and institutional factors affecting union organizing activity. The second is based on differential employment growth rates in the union and nonunion sectors. Farber and Western present a simple accounting framework to decompose the decline in the private-sector union membership rate into components due to the level of union organizing and the differential in the rates of employment growth between the union and nonunion sectors.[9] They conclude that union organizing activity in the private sector was an inconsequential factor in the period studied (1973-1998). Since 1983 less than 0.2 percent of the nonunion workforce was organized each year through successful NLRB-supervised representation elections.

Panel A of Figure 6 contains the time series of measured private employment growth rates in the union and nonunion sectors between 1973 and 2004.[10] There is a substantial differential in growth rates, with union employment shrinking by an average of 1.6 percent per year and nonunion employment growing at an average of 2.5 percent per year. The growth rate of private-sector union employment was much more volatile than the growth rate of nonunion employment. The standard deviation of the union growth rate was 3.1 percentage points, while the standard deviation of the nonunion growth rate was only 1.8 percentage points. The relatively high volatility of the union growth rate is due to large fluctuations prior to 1984. Since 1984 both sectors have had comparable variability in growth rates, with standard deviations of about 1.5 percentage points.

Panel B of Figure 6 contains the relative private-sector employment growth rate, computed as the difference between the nonunion and union employment growth rates. This plot verifies the consistently higher employment growth rate in the nonunion sector. In fact, there are only three years in the sample in which the union growth rate exceeded the nonunion growth rate (1975, 1977, and 2001). On average, the relative employment growth rate was 4.1 percent between 1974 and 2004, and it averaged 3.3 percent since 1990. Thus, there is a consistent, though declining, differential in employment growth rates over the entire period.

Growth (or decline) in employment comes from two sources. First, there is change in employment in existing establishments. The extreme case of decline in employment is when a firm dies or an establishment closes. Second, there is the creation of new establishments through either the birth of a new firm or the opening of a new establishment in an existing firm. The dynamic nature of the U.S. economy is such that there are substantial deaths of existing firms and establishments and substantial births of new firms and establishments. Even if union establishments and firms did not die at a disproportionate rate, all new firms are born nonunion. The result is that the union membership rate in the private sector has a tendency to decrease unless there is significant ongoing new organization activity. The observed union new organization rate through elections of about 0.2 percent of the nonunion workforce each year is trivial relative to the differential in employment growth rates since 1990 of more than three percentage points. It is no surprise that the private-sector union membership rate continues to fall, and, without a dramatic and unlikely turnaround in organizing activity, this decline will continue.

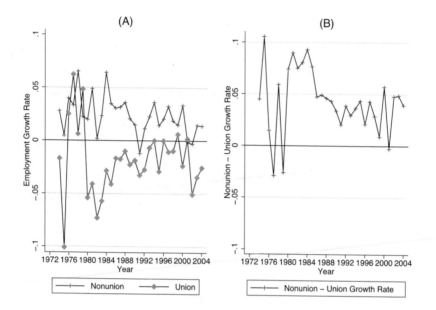

FIGURE 6: Private-Sector Employment Growth Rates, 1973–2004

Employment Growth and Union Membership in the Public Sector

The situation in the public sector is quite different. The same analysis of employment growth that I used in the section entitled Employment Growth and Union Membership in the Private Sector can be carried out for the public sector. I start this analysis in 1983 for three reasons:

- A rapid change in legislation occurred at the state level in the 1970s that caused a tremendous spurt in organizing nonunion public-sector workers.
- There was an important change in the wording of the key question on union membership in the CPS in 1977 that inflated the union membership rate, particularly in the public sector.[11]
- The CPS did not start to distinguish between local, state, and federal employees until 1983.

To this end, panel A of Figure 7 contains plots of union and nonunion employment growth rates in the public sector between 1984 and 2004. The average growth rates are comparable, at about 1 percent per year. In contrast to the private sector, the nonunion segment of the public sector has a slightly more volatile growth rate than does the union segment (a standard deviation of

2.2 percentage points in the nonunion segment versus a standard deviation of 1.7 percentage points in the union sector).

The striking difference is that employment growth in the private sector has been strongly positive among nonunion workers and strongly negative among union workers. In contrast, employment growth in the public sector has been balanced and positive among both nonunion and union workers.

Why the Contrast between the Private and Public Sectors?

The difference in experience between the public and private sectors since 1980 reflects many factors, but four stand out.

Differences in the dynamics of employment

While employment has grown at roughly comparable rates in the two sectors, the character of that growth is very different. Employment growth in the private sector is the result of both the growth of existing firms and the creation of new firms, while some older firms shrink and die. Since new firms are born nonunion and require fresh organization if they are to become unionized and since some of the death and shrinkage is among unionized firms, there is a natural tendency for union membership in the private sector to shrink.

In contrast, employment in the public sector tends to grow along with population as the demand for public services increases. There is very little death of jurisdictions, and most governmental units continue to exist. While some new jurisdictions are created, most growth is accommodated through expansion (sometimes dramatic) in existing jurisdictions. Since public employees in many of these jurisdictions are already unionized, new employment will be unionized even without new organization. Thus, unions in the public sector can maintain membership levels with less new organizing than is required in the private sector.

Another contrast related to employment dynamics is that job security is much higher in the public sector. Tabulations of supplements to the CPS with information on job tenure (time with the current employer) from 1983 through 2001 show that private-sector workers averaged 6.5 years of tenure, while public-sector workers averaged 9.7 years. Tabulations of the Displaced Workers Surveys (DWS), biannual supplements to the CPS since 1984, show that the job loss rate in the private sector was 2.5 times higher than in the public sector on average (10% vs. 4% in three years). Thus, workers in the public sector can expect to remain in their jobs longer than workers in the private sector. Since workplace public goods like labor unions require investment by workers, the longer time horizon of public-sector workers relative to private-sector workers makes unions more attractive to workers in the public sector.

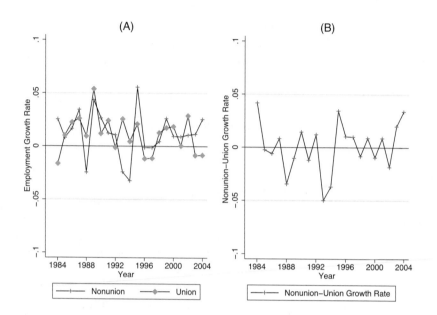

FIGURE 7: Public-Sector Employment Growth Rates, 1984–2004

Differences in the nature of the products produced

Part of the reason for the decline of unions in the private sector is that the set of goods and some services produced in the private sector face substantial competition from goods and services produced in other countries. Unions in the private sector thrive when they can "take wages out of competition" by ensuring that all firms in an industry face the same wage structure. Within the United States, this can be done through a vigorous effort to organize all firms, a strategy that is not feasible in the global economy. The public sector tends to produce goods that are not tradable. For example, public education and public safety (police and fire protection) cannot be provided overseas. This makes it easier for unions in the public sector to take wages out of competition.

One caveat to this seemingly simple strategy is that there is an increasing tendency for public-sector employers at all levels to outsource the provision of some services to private-sector firms. This ranges from outsourcing of janitorial services in public buildings to the contracting of prison operation to private firms. Public-sector employers can use the threat of outsourcing to private-sector firms to win wage concessions in the same way that private-sector firms can use the threat of outsourcing to foreign firms to win wage concessions.

On balance, however, the difference in the products produced implies that public-sector unions can raise wages with less loss of employment than would occur in the private sector. As a result, and other things being equal, unions will be relatively more attractive to workers in the public sector.

Differences in the roles that unions can play

Unions in the private sector focus on workplace issues. These include primarily (1) collective bargaining for wages, benefits, and other conditions of employment and (2) the administration of the workplace with regard to seniority rules for bidding on jobs, promotions, and layoffs and with regard to settling of workplace disputes through the administration of a grievance mechanism. Aside from broad lobbying activities that can affect public policy, private-sector unions do not play a political role that affects the wages and other benefits of members in any direct fashion.

Unions in the public sector have additional incentives and functions. In particular, the payoff to unions in the public sector of involving themselves in the political process can be substantial. Allocation of funds that can be used to pay public employees is in the hands of local and state government officials. Lobbying and working for the reelection of union-friendly officials can have a direct payoff in contract terms. A strong public-sector union can increase the amount of funds available for union members. The resulting increase in membership benefits will, other things being equal, make unions relatively more attractive to workers in the public sector.

Differences in the incentives employers face

Private-sector employers generally face stiff market discipline. If they are producing at higher cost due to paying union workers a premium, then competition from nonunion firms, either domestic or foreign, can undercut their price and reduce demand for their product. To the extent that workers in the private sector understand this dynamic, they understand that unions may not be able to deliver significant improvements in compensation without risking a loss of employment.

Public-sector employers are not in this situation. Their products are not sold in a market, so there is no standard market discipline. What discipline there is comes from the political process. When compensation increases in the public sector, the increase in costs can be met through an increase in taxes. While there might be some cut in employment, it is not likely to be as severe as in the private sector, where other firms can provide the same output. The employers and unions in the public sector can work together through the political process to push through tax increases. Essentially, governmental taxing authority allows the financing of union compensation in a way that is not possible in a competitive market. Again, this will make unions relatively more attractive to workers in the public sector.

DOES PUBLIC POLICY MATTER?

Prelude: The Situation in the Private Sector

Collective bargaining in the private sector is governed primarily by the National Labor Relations Act (NLRA), passed in 1935 as the Wagner Act. The NLRA protects and de?nes the rights of workers to organize into labor unions and to bargain collectively with their employers regarding the terms and conditions of employment. The law provides an election procedure for determining whether a majority of the workers in a potential bargaining unit desire to be represented by a particular union and for certifying the union as the exclusive representative of the workers. After certification, employers and unions are required to "bargain in good faith." It is difficult to determine the effect of the NLRA on union membership rates and on labor market outcomes, such as wages, because there is little variation in the legal environment geographically or over time.

One exception is due to amendments to the NLRA passed in 1948 as the Taft-Hartley Act. Among other things, the Taft-Hartley Act allowed states to pass laws, called right-to-work (RTW) laws, that make it illegal for unions and firms to negotiate union security provisions in their contracts. Union security provisions include union shop clauses, which require employees to become dues-paying members of the union within a fixed period of time after hiring, and agency shop clauses, which require employees to either become dues-paying members of the union or to support the union financially through payment of fees in lieu of dues within a fixed period of time after hiring. As of 2004, 22 states have passed right-to-work laws.[12] These states are located primarily in the South and Mountain regions of the Unites States, which historically have been inhospitable to union organizing.

Based on tabulations of the 2004 CPS, the private-sector union membership rate was 14.4 percent in states without RTW laws and 3.8 percent in states with RTW laws. However, it is inappropriate to draw the conclusion from this contrast that RTW laws have a causal effect in reducing union membership. Right-to-work laws are more likely to exist in states where there is little interest by workers in unions or particularly strong employer opposition. To the extent that RTW laws reflect lower worker demand, the laws simply prevent coercive support of unions by workers who do not want them. However, to the extent that RTW laws reflect employer opposition, the laws provide a mechanism that makes successful organization more difficult.

A substantial older literature attempts to determine the causal mechanism through which union membership is lower in states with RTW laws, and the results are inconclusive. In earlier work I present an analysis that attempts to separate the lower level of union membership in RTW states into components due to differences in worker demand for union representation and differences in employer opposition.[13] He finds that the differences are consistent with lower worker demand for union representation in RTW states. Another example is by David T. Ellwood and Glenn Fine, who examine changes in union organizing activity within states after the passage of RTW laws.[14] They find a substantial short-run decline in union organizing that lessens over time.

Public-Sector Variation in Regulation

Collective bargaining by state and local government employees is governed by legislation passed at the state level between the late 1950s and the 1970s.[15] This legislation covers many dimensions of union activity, including the right to bargain collectively, the scope of issues that can be bargained, union security provisions, and dispute settlement mechanisms.[16] This legislation has been fairly stable since 1980. With this legislation in place, public-sector workers were able to organize, largely because the political process gives employers neither the tools nor the incentives to resist organization effectively.[17]

My central source of information on these laws is the NBER Public Sector Collective Bargaining Law Data Set developed by Richard B. Freeman and Robert G. Valletta.[17] This data set contains information on various dimensions of state-level public-sector collective bargaining laws collected annually from 1955 to 1984 for five distinct categories of public employees: (1) state, (2) local police, (3) local firefighters, (4) local school teachers, and (5) other local employees. Some measures included in these data were updated through 1996.[18] For measures not updated, I carried forward the 1984 values. I carried forward the 1996 values through 2004 for the updated measures.

Panel A of Figure 8 illustrates the development of these laws by counting the number of states in each year that had laws in place allowing collective bargaining by public-sector workers in four categories (state workers, local police, local firefighters, and local teachers). The total increased from one state in 1955 to more than 40 states for firefighters and teachers and to more than 30 states for police and state workers by 1979. Panel B sets a higher bar by counting the number of states in each year that had laws in place implying or explicitly stating a duty to bargain on the part of public-sector employers in each of the four

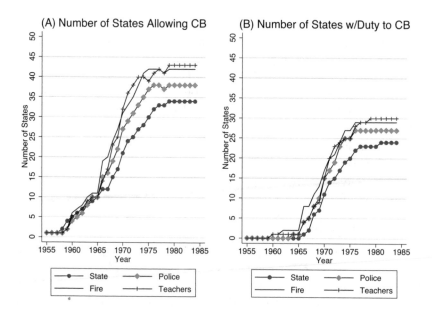

FIGURE 8: Public-Sector Bargaining Laws, 1955–1984

categories. The total here increased from no states in 1955 to more than half the states for police, firefighters, and teachers (local government employees) and 23 states for state workers by 1979. Relatively little change has occurred in the legislative environment since 1980.

In my analysis I exploit variation in these laws across types of workers within a given state and variation in these laws over time within states to identify the effect of these laws on union membership and labor market outcomes.

I focus on two measures of these laws as they relate to their favorableness to union organization. The first is a single index of union security provisions in the laws. This index can take on five values:

1. Agency shop prohibited or right-to-work law covering public employees

2. No legal provision

3. Agency shop negotiable

4. Union shop negotiable

5. Agency shop compulsory

These are arranged in increasing order of favorableness to the union as indicated by Freeman and Valletta.[19] There is very little variation over time in these

TABLE 1: **Distribution of Union Security Law Index, 1983–2004**

Group	Prohibited	No Provision	Agency Shop Negotiable	Union Shop Negotiable	Agency Shop Compulsory
State	0.498	0.203	0.179	0.040	0.080
Police	0.498	0.242	0.180	0.060	0.020
Fire	0.498	0.222	0.180	0.080	0.020
Teachers	0.508	0.202	0.250	0.000	0.040
Other Local	0.478	0.262	0.180	0.060	0.020
All	0.496	0.226	0.194	0.048	0.036

Note: These are fractions of state/year observations in each worker group with the specified value of the union security law index. The data are from the NBER Public Sector Collective Bargaining Law Data Set as updated.

laws. Defining an observation as a type of worker in a given year in a given state, between 1983 and 2004 there were a total of eight changes in union security law levels in three states, and five of these relate to the adoption of a right-to-work law in Idaho in 1985. However, there is more variation within states across types of workers. In 1983 there was at least one difference in union security provisions among the five types of workers within a state in 14 states, and in 2004 there were differences in 13 states. Table 1 contains a breakdown of type of law for each worker group between 1983 and 2004.

An analysis of variance of the union security index illustrates that most of the variation is accounted for by state. The analysis of variance is carried out by ordinary least squares (OLS) regression of the index in each state/year/type cell on a complete set of state (50), year (22), and worker type (5) indicators (omitting one of each). Since this is a balanced design with one observation in each cell, the three dimensions are orthogonal and the variance decomposition is unique. The regression accounts for 83.6 percent of the overall variation in the union security index. State alone accounts for 83.4 percent of the variation, year none, and type 0.2 percent. This is not surprising, given that a central component of the union security index is the existence of an RTW law, that RTW laws cover all categories of workers, and that there was almost no variation in RTW laws over time.

The second measure of the laws that I use is an index of the strength of collective bargaining rights used by Freeman and Valletta's study.[20] This is an eight-category classification as follows:

1. Collective bargaining prohibited

2. No provision

TABLE 2: Distribution of the Collective Bargaining Rights Index, 1983–2004

Group	Prohib.	No Prov.	CB Permit	Meet & Present	Duty	Duty FF/Med	Duty Strike	Duty Arb.
State	0.160	0.134	0.120	0.068	0.221	0.101	0.156	0.040
Police	0.080	0.142	0.172	0.040	0.338	0.081	0.047	0.100
Fire	0.060	0.082	0.152	0.100	0.290	0.109	0.047	0.160
Teachers	0.080	0.060	0.187	0.020	0.315	0.121	0.196	0.020
Other Local	0.100	0.162	0.162	0.060	0.199	0.101	0.196	0.020
All	0.096	0.116	0.159	0.058	0.273	0.103	0.129	0.069

Note: These are fractions of state/year observations in each worker group with the specified value of the union collective bargaining rights index. "Duty" denotes "duty to bargain." The data are from the NBER Public Sector Collective Bargaining Law Data Set as updated.

3. Collective bargaining permitted

4. The right to meet and present offers

5. Employer duty to bargain, express or implied, with no specific dispute settlement mechanism

6. Duty to bargain with fact finding or mediation required

7. Duty to bargain with strikes allowed

8. Duty to bargain with arbitration required

These are arranged in order of increasing favorableness to the union as indicated by Freeman and Valletta.

Table 2 contains a breakdown of type of law for each worker group over the period 1983-2004. Provision of collective bargaining rights is much more common than the allowance of union security provisions. Overall, collective bargaining rights are prohibited in 10 percent of the state/year/group cells, and there is no provision in another 12 percent. Some form of duty to bargain is required in fully 57 percent of cells, with almost half of these a duty to bargain without specification of a dispute settlement mechanism. Police, firefighters, and teachers are more likely to have a duty to bargain than state workers or other local workers. For example, fully 65 percent of state/year cells for teachers require a duty to bargain. Not surprisingly, police and firefighters are rarely allowed the right to strike, but this is compensated for by a higher level of availability of arbitration.

Once again, there is not much time-series variation in this index. Between 1983 and 2004 there were a total of 20 changes in the value of the collective bargaining index in seven states, and all of these reflected the imposition of a duty to bargain of some kind. There is substantial variation in collective bargaining rights within states across types of worker. In 1983 there was at least one difference in collective bargaining rights among the five types of workers within a state in 31 states, and in 2004 there were differences in 29 states. There is no straightforward way to summarize the patterns of differences across types of workers, and there is no obvious pattern (e.g., with more or less favorable laws for certain types of workers).

An analysis of variance of the collective bargaining index once again illustrates that most of the variation is accounted for by state. The regression accounts for 76.3 percent of the overall variation in the collective bargaining index. State alone accounts for 74.9 percent of the variation, year 0.05 percent, and type 1.4 percent.

It is clear from the analysis of variance that intertemporal variation will not be useful in identifying the effect of the laws on outcomes. The bulk of the variation in laws is interstate and common across worker type, but this will not be useful either, since there are likely important state-specific unmeasured factors that are correlated with both the legislation and with the outcomes of interest.

I rely on the variation within states across different types of workers (after accounting for common interstate differences across worker types) to identify the effects of the law. While only a small fraction of the overall variation is from this source, it is an empirical question as to whether there is sufficient variation to identify the effects.

Public-Sector Bargaining Laws and Union Coverage

I define union coverage as the fraction of workers who report either being a union member or being a nonmember covered by a collective bargaining agreement. It is clear that there is a strong relationship between union coverage and public-sector bargaining laws. Table 3 contains average union coverage across all 50 states and the 22 years from 1983 to 2004 by the category of union security law and type of worker. Union coverage is strongly increasing with the favorableness of the law for all types of workers. Overall, 28.9 percent of state and local government employees are unionized when union security provisions are prohibited, while 65 to 70 percent are unionized where agency shops are allowed or compulsory.

A similar pattern is found with regard to collective bargaining rights. Table 4 contains average union coverage across all 50 states and the 22 years from 1983 to 2004 by the category of collective bargaining rights law. Union coverage is strongly increasing in the favorableness of the law for all types of workers. For example, 17 percent of state and local government employees are

TABLE 3: Union Coverage by Union Security Law and Type of Worker

Law Type	State	Police	Fire	Teacher	Other	All
Prohibited	0.206	0.410	0.636	0.546	0.219	0.289
No Provision	0.259	0.602	0.808	0.688	0.302	0.375
Agency Shop Negotiable	0.532	0.887	0.909	0.849	0.582	0.654
Union Shop Negotiable	0.489	0.762	0.771	–	0.505	0.511
Agency Shop Compulsory	0.720	0.954	0.943	0.892	0.789	0.728
All	0.347	0.620	0.766	0.697	0.380	0.446

Note: Data from CPS merged outgoing rotation group files from 1983 to 2004. Weighted by CPS final sample weights. N=512,982.

unionized when collective bargaining is prohibited, while half to three-quarters are unionized when there is a duty to bargain.

The substantial differences in union density by type of law likely reflect large differences across states in the political, social, and economic environments as they relate to labor unions. In order to account for unmeasured differences across states, I estimate a linear probability model of union coverage using these same data. The model includes fixed effects for state and year along with indicator variables for type of worker where appropriate. The model also includes measures of individual worker characteristics that could affect the likelihood of union membership or coverage, including age, education, race, sex, and marital status.

Column 1 of Table 5 contains estimates of the coefficients of the union security law index from a linear probability model of union coverage where the omitted category is "No Provision." This model includes the demographic measures and fixed effects for year and for type of worker. No controls for state are included. Thus, these estimates are contaminated by unmeasured state-specific characteristics that are correlated with union coverage. As in Table 1, these estimates show a substantial positive relationship between the likelihood of union membership and the union security law index. Compared to there being no legal provision, union coverage is 20 to 40 percentage points more likely where an agency or union shop is either negotiable or compulsory. Legislation requiring an agency shop is relatively rare but is associated with a particularly large increase in the probability of union coverage.

Column 2 of Table 5 contains estimates of a similar model that differs only by including state fixed effects. Thus, these estimates account for unmeasured fixed state-specific factors that are correlated with both public-sector union density and the laws governing union security provisions for public-sector workers. These estimates, which are based on variation within states across

TABLE 4:   Union Coverage by Collective Bargaining Law and Type

Law Type	State	Police	Fire	Teacher	Other	All
Prohibited	0.143	0.220	0.434	0.412	0.127	0.170
No Provision	0.188	0.411	0.766	0.474	0.213	0.241
Permitted	0.142	0.405	0.634	0.463	0.163	0.269
Right to Meet and Present	0.299	0.408	0.511	0.677	0.178	0.280
Duty to Bargain	0.535	0.756	0.855	0.806	0.585	0.633
Duty to Bargain w/FF or Med	0.405	0.605	0.799	0.772	0.427	0.508
Duty to Bargain w/Strike	0.517	0.741	0.823	0.848	0.450	0.564
Duty to Bargain wi/Arb	0.625	0.866	0.915	0.863	0.568	0.743
All	0.347	0.620	0.766	0.697	0.380	0.446

Note: Data from CPS merged outgoing rotation group files from 1983 to 2004. Weighted by CPS final sample weight. N=512,982.

types of workers in the legislation, show much smaller differentials in the probability of unionization relative to the case where there is no legal provision. Where an agency shop is negotiable, the differential is about 10 percentage points. The differential is about 15 percentage points where an agency shop is compulsory. Interestingly, there is no significant differential where a union shop is negotiable. On balance, it appears that union security provisions in the state law play a significant role in the level of union density in the public sector.

Table 6 contains the results of the same analysis for the index of collective bargaining rights rather than for the index of union security provisions. Column 1 of the table contains estimates of the coefficients of the collective bargaining rights index from a linear probability model of union coverage where the omitted category is "No Provision." As before, these models include the demographic measures and fixed effects for year and type of worker. No controls for state are included, and these estimates are contaminated by unmeasured state-specific characteristics that are correlated with union coverage. As in Table 4, these estimates show a substantial positive relationship between a legally required duty to bargain and the likelihood of union coverage. Compared to there being no legal provision, union coverage is 23 to 40 percentage points more likely where the employer has a duty to bargain.

Column 2 of Table 6 contains estimates of a similar model that differs only by including state fixed effects. These estimates rely on within-state variation in the laws governing collective bargaining rights across types of workers. The magnitudes of the estimates are attenuated relative to those obtained relying on both within- and between-state variation in the first column, but there remains a statistically significant positive relationship between the probability of union coverage and an employer's duty to bargain. On average, an employer's duty to

TABLE 5: Effect of Union Security Laws on Union Coverage

Law Type	(1)	(2)
Prohibited	-0.087	0.032
	(0.002)	(0.007)
No Provision	–	–
Agency Shop Negotiable	0.253	0.095
	(0.002)	(0.006)
Union Shop Negotiable	0.191	0.019
	(0.004)	(0.011)
Agency Shop Compulsory	0.419	0.156
	(0.004)	(0.007)
State Fixed Effects	No	Yes

Note: The reported coefficients of law type indicator are from OLS regressions of individual union status that include controls for education category (4), sex, marital status, the interaction of sex and marital status, race (nonwhite), age, and age squared along with fixed effects for calendar year and controls for worker type. The omitted category is "No Provision." Data are from the CPS merged outgoing rotation group files from 1983 to 2004. The estimates are weighted by CPS final sample weights. Standard errors are in parentheses. N=512,982.

bargain results in a 5 to 7 percentage point increase in the overall probability of union coverage.

Public-Sector Bargaining Laws and Wages

Laws governing collective bargaining in the public sector can have important effects on the wages paid to employees. Union workers may earn more where legislation makes unions stronger and more secure. Nonunion workers may earn more as well if nonunion public-sector employers attempt to forestall union organization (the threat effect of unions).[21] In order to investigate this, I estimate OLS regression models of log real hourly earnings separately for union and nonunion workers. The model includes fixed effects for state and year along with indicator variables for type of worker where appropriate. The model also includes measures of individual worker characteristics that could affect earnings, including age, education, race, sex, and marital status.

Column 1 of Table 7 contains estimates of the coefficients of the union security law index from this regression model estimated over the sample of union workers. This model includes the demographic measures and fixed effects for year and for type of worker. No controls for state are included. Thus, these estimates may be contaminated by unmeasured state-specific characteristics that are correlated both with the legislation and with earnings. These estimates show

**TABLE 6: Effect of Laws Defining Collective Bargaining Rights on Union
Coverage with Within- and Between-State Variation**

Law Type	(1)	(2)
Prohibited	-0.071	0.009
	(0.003)	(0.005)
No Provision	–	–
Permitted	-0.040	-0.007
	(0.003)	(0.005)
Right to Meet and Present Offers	0.061	0.004
	(0.004)	(0.006)
Duty to Bargain	0.347	0.058
	(0.002)	(0.005)
Duty to Bargain with Med/FF	0.228	0.067
	(0.003)	(0.010)
Duty to Bargain with Strike	0.293	0.062
	(0.003)	(0.006)
Duty to Bargain with Arbitration	0.394	0.048
	(0.006)	(0.008)
State Fixed Effects	No	Yes

Note: The reported coefficients of law type indicator are from OLS regressions of individual union status that include controls for education category (4), sex, marital status, the interaction of sex and marital status, race (nonwhite), age, and age squared along with fixed effects for calendar year and controls for worker type. The omitted category is "No Provision." Data are from the CPS merged outgoing rotation group files from 1983 to 2004. The estimates are weighted by CPS final sample weights. Standard errors are in parentheses. N=512,982.

a substantial positive relationship between the union security law index and earnings. Compared to there being no legal provision, earnings of union workers are about 10 percent higher where an agency or union shop is either negotiable or compulsory. Where agency and union shops are prohibited, largely through the existence of RTW laws, earnings are about 7.5 percent lower. The second column of Table 7 contains estimates from the same model, this time estimated over the sample of nonunion workers. These estimates also show a substantial positive relationship between earnings and the likelihood of union membership that is similar in magnitude to the relationship for union workers. This suggests that low-wage states are more likely to have RTW laws.

The estimates in columns 3 and 4 of Table 7 include state fixed effects to account for omitted state-specific factors that are correlated with both the union security law index and earnings. These estimates are more plausibly interpreted as the causal effect of the law on earnings. Column 3 of Table 7 contains

TABLE 7: Effect of Union Security Laws on Log Real Wages

Law Type	(1) Union	(2) Nonunion	(3) Union	(4) Nonunion
Prohibited	-0.075	-0.017	0.070	0.015
	(0.003)	(0.003)	(0.009)	(0.012)
No Provision	–	–	–	–
Agency Shop Negotiable	0.111	0.101	0.037	0.001
	(0.003)	(0.003)	(0.008)	(0.013)
Union Shop Negotiable	0.075	0.158	0.133	0.093
	(0.006)	(0.007)	(0.012)	(0.027)
Agency Shop Compulsory	0.109	0.098	0.012	0.032
	(0.005)	(0.009)	(0.009)	(0.015)
State Fixed Effects	No	No	Yes	Yes

Note: The reported coefficients of law type indicator are from OLS regressions of log real hourly earnings that include controls for education category (4), sex, marital status, the interaction of sex and marital status, race (nonwhite), age, and age squared along with fixed effects for calendar year and controls for worker type. The omitted category is "No Provision." Data are observations with unallocated wages from the CPS merged outgoing rotation group files from 1983 to 2004. The years 1994 and 1995 are not included due to problems identifying observations with allocated wages. The estimates are weighted by CPS final sample weights. Standard errors are in parentheses. N=376,646.

these estimates for union workers, and they show a small statistically significant effect of 3.7 percent of the ability to negotiate agency shop provisions on earnings. The ability to negotiate a union shop implies a larger increase in earnings of about 13 percent. Column 4 of the Table contains these estimates for nonunion workers, and they show no statistically significant effect of the laws on nonunion earnings other than for the ability to negotiate a union shop provision. On balance, these estimates suggest that laws allowing the negotiation of agency and union shops have a small positive effect on earnings of union workers and very little effect on earnings of nonunion workers.

Table 8 contains the results of the same analysis for the index of collective bargaining rights rather than for the index of union security provisions. The first two columns of the table contain earnings function regression estimates of the coefficients of the collective bargaining rights index for union and nonunion workers respectively. As before, these models include the demographic measures and fixed effects for year and type of worker. No controls for state are included, and these estimates are contaminated by unmeasured state-specific characteristics that are correlated with earnings. The estimates in column 1, for

TABLE 8: **Effect of Laws Defining Collective Bargaining Rights on Log Real Wages**

Law Type	(1) Union	(2) Nonunion	(3) Union	(4) Nonunion
Prohibited	-0.063	0.031	-0.014	0.019
	(0.006)	(0.004)	(0.009)	(0.007)
No Provision	–	–	–	–
Permitted	-0.070	-0.005	-0.077	0.019
	(0.006)	(0.004)	(0.008)	(0.008)
Right to Meet and Present Offers	0.088	0.017	0.030	0.006
	(0.007)	(0.005)	(0.009)	(0.010)
Duty to Bargain	0.140	0.126	-0.039	0.011
	(0.005)	(0.004)	(0.007)	(0.008)
Duty to Bargain with Med/FF	0.087	0.070	-0.074	-0.033
	(0.005)	(0.004)	(0.013)	(0.022)
Duty to Bargain with Strike	0.049	0.050	-0.045	0.005
	(0.005)	(0.004)	(0.008)	(0.010)
Duty to Bargain with Arbitration	0.173	0.093	-0.062	-0.042
	(0.007)	(0.013)	(0.011)	(0.019)
State Fixed Effects	No	No	Yes	Yes

Note: The reported coefficients of law type indicator are from OLS regressions of log real hourly earnings that include controls for education category (4), sex, marital status, the interaction of sex and marital status, race (nonwhite), age, and age squared along with fixed effects for calendar year and controls for worker type. The omitted category is "No Provision." Data are observations with unallocated wages from the CPS merged outgoing rotation group files from 1983 to 2004. The years 1994 and 1995 are not included due to problems identifying observations with allocated wages. The estimates are weighted by CPS final sample weights. Standard errors are in parentheses. N=376,646.

union workers, show a substantial positive relationship between the legislation requiring a duty to bargain and earnings. Compared to there being no legal provision, earnings are 5 to 17 percent higher where the employer has a duty to bargain. The estimates in column 2, for nonunion workers, show a very similar pattern.

Columns 3 and 4 of Table 8 contain estimates of a similar model that differs only by including state fixed effects. These estimates rely on within-state variation in the laws governing collective bargaining rights across types of workers. The estimates in column 3, for union workers, show, surprisingly, that earnings are substantially *lower* for union workers where the employer has a duty to bargain. Clearly, the duty to bargain is required in states where union workers are relatively well paid. But within states and within type of worker across states, union workers whose employers have a duty to bargain tend to earn 4 to 8 percent less than otherwise similar workers where there is no legal requirement. This is a puzzling finding. Finally, the estimates in column 4 of the Table, for nonunion workers, show virtually no relationship between the collective bargaining rights index and earnings.

CONCLUDING REMARKS

In this study I documented the dramatic divergence between the fortunes of unions in the public and private sectors in the United States since the 1970s. While the union membership rate in the private sector fell from 25 percent in 1975 to 8.2 percent in 2004, the rate in the public sector increased from the same level in 1975 to more than 35 percent in 2004. In the private sector, nonunion employment grew by an average of 2.5 percent per year between 1973 and 2004, while union employment fell by an average of 1.6 percent per year. Average employment growth rates in the public sector were about 1 percent per year for both the union and nonunion sectors between 1983 and 2004.

I proposed four reasons for the divergence in union membership rates between the private and public sectors. These focus on differences in (1) employment dynamics, (2) the nature of products produced, (3) the role that unions can play, and (4) incentives faced by employers. Each of these makes public-sector union jobs more stable or increases the value of unions to workers.

Next I turned to an analysis of the role of public policy regarding collective bargaining in the public sector on union coverage and earnings. Legislation at the state level governs collective bargaining by state and local government employees, and the regulations can differ by group of worker (state, police, fire, teacher, other local). There are large differences across states in the policies embodied in these laws, and this interstate variation in the legislation is contaminated with observed state-specific factors that are correlated with the outcomes of interest. My solution was to exploit within-state variation in laws by type of worker. I found that union coverage is significantly higher where unions are allowed to negotiate union security provisions (e.g., agency shop) and where employers have a legal duty to bargain with labor unions. With regard to earnings, I found there is a small positive effect on earnings of legislation allowing union security provisions and a surprising negative effect on earnings of a legal duty to bargain.

On balance, unions in the public sector have thrived relative to unions in the private sector for important structural reasons. Lack of market competition for the products of the public sector and lack of fiscal discipline through the political process make the value of unions to public-sector workers relatively high. Public policy governing labor relations in the public sector, working in conjunction with those structural factors, has provided an environment in which unions can thrive.

CHAPTER THREE

Scapegoat, Albatross, or What?
The Status Quo in Teacher Collective Bargaining

FREDERICK M. HESS
ANDREW P. KELLY

T eacher collective bargaining agreements generate many impassioned claims. Critics assert that teacher contracts usurp managerial authority, stifle creative staffing, protect ineffective educators, prevent rewarding talent, and produce massive inefficiencies.[1] Such critics point to studies like a 2005 review of collective bargaining agreements in ten Rhode Island districts that found that the contracts focused on "adult entitlement," severely limited "school autonomy," and increased the cost of schooling.[2] Union advocates counter that collective bargaining has helped deliver teachers from unacceptable treatment and that the provisions in question were earned in fair negotiations, were agreed to by district negotiators, are essential to protecting teachers from cavalier or incompetent management, and are sufficiently flexible to permit sensible reforms.[3] Reform unionists also suggest that collective bargaining can be a powerful tool for improving teacher quality, allowing unions and school districts to collaboratively promote teacher "professionalism," peer review, differentiated compensation, and professional development.[4]

This chapter examines collective bargaining and the contracts it produces. While teachers unions clearly play an important role in state and national politics, this chapter does not assess the political role of unions or attempt to determine the impact of unions on student achievement or the daily operations of schools. By focusing on collective bargaining, the essay concentrates on where unions affect district policies and operations most directly.

We review the formal landscape of teacher collective bargaining, sketch the dynamics of the bargaining process, and consider the content of collective bargaining agreements (CBAs). Perhaps most intriguing, we ask whether contracts constrain district management as much as some ardent union critics have suggested or whether these constraints result in part from the arbitration process, operational routines, timid district leadership, or contract implementation.

Unions and the agreements they negotiate are instruments of commerce. Contrary to how they are often characterized, teachers unions exist neither to defend children nor to plunder the public treasury. Rather, they are commercial entities created to serve the needs of members, who seek (among other things) job security and compensation. Member demands sometimes coincide with those of students but may also conflict with the interests of students, parents, taxpayers, and district leaders. It is vital to keep that inevitable tension in mind when examining the world of teacher collective bargaining. At the same time, Howard Nelson, a senior researcher with the American Federation of Teachers (AFT), argues, "Bad education hurts our members. We explicitly have a keen interest in children."[5] It is also important to remember that contracts are mutual agreements between the local union and the district.

Teacher CBAs have taken on a new salience recently as management reforms, structural change, and federal No Child Left Behind (NCLB) requirements run up against the collective bargaining process. Superintendents in cities like San Diego, New York City, and Los Angeles have faulted the collective bargaining agreement for impeding school improvement.

In a nationally discussed negotiation, the Philadelphia superintendent Paul Vallas set out in fall 2004 to revise the rules governing teacher transfer and assignment, primarily by reducing the role accorded teacher seniority.[6] Vallas sought to leverage the NCLB mandate that bargaining agreements not contravene "corrective action" or "restructuring" measures in schools needing improvement.[7] Although Philadelphia's revised agreement ultimately involved only minor policy changes, how the NCLB mandates will alter collective bargaining remains uncertain. Answering that question requires a better understanding of existing agreements and how they are reached.

Here we summarize bargaining across the country and contract negotiations at the district level. To do so, we interviewed more than 50 national, state, and local district and union officials; systematically analyzed sample contracts from 20 districts; and examined how the press covered recent contract negotiations in those districts. We randomly selected 20 districts from the 199 with collective bargaining agreements on file at the Bureau of Labor Statistics (BLS) in January 2005. We drew ten contracts from states with mandatory collective bargaining and ten from states without mandatory collective bargaining. We analyzed the content of these contracts and the negotiations that produced them. We sought to interview officials from the local union and the district administration in all 20 districts, though some district or union personnel were unavailable for comment. We also collected local press coverage to supplement the responses of local interviewees.

UNDERSTANDING THE STATUS QUO

Largely absent amid the debates about teachers unions is a clear understanding of what teacher collective bargaining looks like today. CBAs are the contracts that govern the relationship between any group of employees and its employer. In the case of teacher collective bargaining, the two parties are the local teachers union and the school district.

In nearly all states, teacher collective bargaining is regulated at the state level. In states with mandatory collective bargaining, employers must collectively bargain with organized employees. Unorganized employees may seek to organize as a bargaining unit as follows: an organization seeking to represent the employees must petition the state agency, be approved by the agency, and win a majority vote of employees in a certified election. If the organization fails to win a majority vote, no collective bargaining agent is created.

Thirty-three states require districts to collectively bargain with organized teachers, and another 6 allow collective bargaining but do not require it.[8] About 75 percent of the nation's 14,500 school districts are in the 33 states requiring districts to collectively bargain with organized bargaining units.[9] Of the 17 states without mandatory collective bargaining, 11 have school districts with CBAs. Those 11 include the 6 states that have legislation authorizing—but not requiring—school districts to bargain.[10]

In most states without mandatory collective bargaining, teachers may still organize and pursue collective bargaining, but the school district is not obliged to deal with the selected representative. In a few states, such as Texas, state law stipulates that districts may *not* collectively bargain. In Texas districts where teachers have organized and selected a representative, districts typically negotiate with teachers through a process called "exclusive consultation."

The courts have ruled that states may regulate collective bargaining but may not prevent public employees from joining unions, deeming such restrictions a violation of the First Amendment right to free association.[11] Consequently, all 50 states have teachers unions and more than 80 percent of all teachers are union members.[12] But collective bargaining enjoys no such constitutional protection. The school law scholar Louis Fischer explains, "While the First Amendment protects the rights of teachers to associate and advocate, it does not guarantee that their advocacy will be effective or that government bodies must bargain with them."[13]

Collective bargaining was largely unknown in K-12 schooling until the 1960s. Before then, school districts enjoyed a free hand in setting compensation and work conditions. In 1960 the United Federation of Teachers (UFT) chose to strike in New York City over these issues. The following spring the UFT won a generous CBA, fanning faith in the "powerful tool" of collective bargaining and sparking a rise in union membership.[14] In 1966 the UFT's parent, the American Federation of Teachers (AFT), had 125,000 members; by 1981 it had grown to 580,000.[15] Faced with the AFT's explosive success, the larger, more pedigreed National Education Association (NEA) also embraced collective bargaining. During the 1970s collective bargaining became the norm in teacher-district relations.

How Does Collective Bargaining Work?

In addition to defining whether bargaining is "authorized, allowed, or prohibited," state teacher bargaining laws generally cover several other subjects. The laws define which employees will be bound by the contract, how teachers who wish to collectively bargain can choose a representative, how bargaining takes place, how disputes will be resolved, the legality of teacher strikes, the legality of payroll deduction of union dues or agency fees, and the scope of the bargaining process. The "scope" refers to whether bargaining on certain issues is mandated, permitted, or prohibited. In practice, the scope of negotiations is structured by what state law permits and how state law regulates district operations. Many regulations governing teacher compensation, teacher tenure, the school year, and class size are enshrined in state law or the state code (often at the behest of teachers, the union, and their allies). In such cases negotiations are limited both by what the "scope" law permits and by state regulations outside the purview of the collective bargaining process.

A CBA is a legal contract laying out the rights and obligations of teachers and the school board. The agreement establishes "the terms and conditions of employment of employees, places limitations on the ability of the employer to change those terms and conditions, and specifies certain kinds of duties or requirements of employees."[16] Agreements range from simple, short documents to long, detailed, and complex contracts. The BLS has 199 teacher collective bargaining contracts on file covering districts with 1,000 or more contracted employees. The average length of the contracts in this sample is 105 pages, ranging from 25 pages in Worcester, Massachusetts, to 387 in Chicago.

Conceptually, bargaining tends to fall along a continuum of two general approaches, typically referred to as traditional bargaining and collaborative (or "interest based") bargaining.[17] Traditional bargaining assumes that labor and management have clear-cut and opposing positions and that each party makes some concessions. Sometimes termed "zero-sum bargaining," it aims to allocate limited resources. Interest-based bargaining (IBB) focuses on increased communication, flexibility, joint problem solving, and identifying common ground.[18] In IBB, the two parties sketch out their concerns to identify areas of mutual interest. "New unionists" have suggested that, since both teachers and the district benefit from high-performing schools, interest-based bargaining allows the two sides to tackle shared concerns regarding professional development, teacher evaluation, teacher quality, and working conditions.[19] In reality, of course, most negotiations tend to encompass some collaborative bargaining and some that is more "zero-sum."

During the bargaining process, the two sides seek an agreement for a set period, frequently three or four years. If the parties are unable to reach an agreement, they enter into the conflict resolution process set out by the existing contract or by state law. Most contracts are settled before initiative procedures become necessary. However, when district management and the union cannot agree, states furnish procedures for one side or the other to declare itself at an impasse. In many cases districts extend the terms of the existing contract when this happens. Such a course satisfies district officials worried about work stoppages (because teachers are prohibited from striking as long as the contract is in effect) while assuaging union members by leaving existing contract language in place. In many states, including Connecticut, Massachusetts, New York, Rhode Island, and Washington, the law stipulates that some or all of the terms of an expired contract remain in effect after the contract expires. The provisions remain valid either for a set period (one year in the case of Washington) or until a new agreement is reached.

When one or both parties determine an impasse has been reached, state laws provide various methods for resolution, including mediation, fact finding, and binding arbitration. In mediation, the most widely used impasse procedure, both parties present their positions to a third party. The third party makes recommendations, suggests compromises, and attempts to bring both sides together. Mediation is nonbinding and confidential. If mediation is unsuccessful, the parties frequently enter fact finding. The two sides document their positions at length to a fact-finding team composed of one member appointed by the union, one by the district, and one acceptable to both sides. The fact-finding team judges the relative claims, though its determination is typically only advisory. Fact finding is conducted formally; one union official noted that "it feels like a different process from negotiations."[20] Unions and districts are often leery of fact finding. As one national AFT official explained, "Fact finding is very costly for unions and school boards because it's a semijudicial process. Preparing is labor intensive for both sides."

Union critics argue that unions enjoy advantages in mediation and fact finding owing to their institutional resources and specialized expertise. Union officials reject such claims and argue that districts have more legal and budgetary resources at their disposal. A lack of data on mediation, fact finding, and their outcomes makes it difficult to weigh these competing claims.

Binding arbitration is the method of last resort. It is rarely used in contract negotiations and is a mandated component of the bargaining process in only a few states. In binding arbitration, both sides submit their proposed contracts, and the arbitrator decides on a final contract. District and union officials prefer to avoid arbitration because it puts the agreement in someone else's hands. As one NEA official explained, in a sentiment echoed by both district staff and AFT officials, "The best settlement is the one that is negotiated at the table. . . . The one guarantee in arbitration is that you'll have a settlement, but it is not in the hands of the participants. . . . The threat of arbitration can be an effective tool: if it's the last best offer it can force the parties to come closer together to avoid arbitration."[21]

The methods of impasse resolution and the rules for entering into one process or another vary substantially from state to state. In Illinois and Indiana, for instance, state law provides that after a set period either party can declare an impasse and request mediation. In Colorado and Louisiana, which do not have collective bargaining laws, impasse procedures are less formalized. In Rhode Island and Vermont, state law calls for fact finding if a mediator is unable to resolve an impasse within a fixed time. New York and Ohio also provide explicit guidelines for fact finding, while Maryland law calls for mediation but not fact finding. Connecticut recently repealed the section of state law providing for fact finding.

To streamline impasse procedures and manage conflict, state collective bargaining laws frequently establish a body to deal with labor relations. These boards range from administrative overseers to very powerful and influential organizations. In California, for instance, the Public Employee Relations Board (PERB) is a quasijudicial organization charged with administering public employee contracts.[22] While PERB's rulings can be appealed to the courts, the board makes the first determination in a dispute, and its decisions carry great weight in monitoring and influencing contract implementation.[23] In states with no entity to deal with labor relations, disputes are routed to the courts or to other quasijudicial arrangements.

Once the two parties agree to terms, the contract is sent to the school board and the teachers for ratification. Contracts range in duration from one to six years or longer, though long contracts often specify salaries for only a year or two and then provide for the parties to reopen the salary question.[24]

Contracts are sometimes reopened before their expiration, in a process commonly called "impact bargaining." When changes in state or federal law, district policy, or district fiscal circumstances call for management actions that conflict with the existing agreement, the district can renegotiate specific elements of the contract with the union. In the words of one union official, "In recent years, impact bargaining is playing a much, much bigger role than it ever did. When layoffs are occurring, with proposals like small school or the Chicago 2010 initiative, with NCLB and IDEA, the role of impact bargaining has grown."[25] The results of impact bargaining are not formally ratified like the full contract is but are subject to approval by the district school board and the governance body stipulated in the union's constitution.

How Much Do Collective Bargaining Laws Matter?

How do state collective bargaining statutes affect contract outcomes? Intuitively, teachers unions should have a stronger bargaining position in states that mandate collective bargaining than in states that do not. While research generally supports this statement, the variation between contracts negotiated in states with mandatory collective bargaining and those negotiated in other states should not be overstated. A 1979 study of teacher bargaining by Lorraine McDonnell and Anthony Pascal found that, though districts often bargained with little attention to state laws, the presence of such a law "makes a difference." The authors pointed out that teacher organizations in states with collective bargaining laws "are at least guaranteed some minimal success as a result of the protection afforded by the statute" and that the scope provisions of a state law were "significant predictors" of what contracts included.[26]

While state laws are related to variations in contract language, local conditions often prove more influential than statutes. McDonnell and Pascal suggested, "Local attitudes and the relationship the two parties create with each other are far more significant [than collective bargaining laws] in determining the tenor of the negotiations process and the quality of the final contract."[27] Their 1988 follow-up study found that the "state legal environment" did not help explain whether district contracts contained "professional teaching" provisions restricting the number of subjects teachers could be asked to teach, class size, or permissible paperwork.[28] Remember, the presence of a state collective bargaining statute does not guarantee all districts will collectively bargain. In California, for instance, 63 school districts with fewer than 500 students have no collective bargaining contract; one district with enrollment of more than 10,000 (Clovis) also does not collectively bargain.[29] Teachers in hundreds of districts across the mountain, plains, and border states have similarly opted not to collectively bargain, even when state law empowers them to do so.[30]

Scholars have sought to calculate the "union pay premium," the effect of unionization on teacher salaries. These findings are less ambiguous than those on contract language and show that teachers under a CBA have higher salaries than those without a CBA. Analyses from the early 1980s found that unionization raised salaries by between 3 and 9 percent,[31] with some researchers finding as much as a 12 percent increase.[32] A more recent examination found the union pay premium was about 5 percent in collective bargaining districts where 50 percent or more of teachers were union members.[33] Regarding unionism's effect on total district expenditures, a 2000 literature review found conflicting estimates ranging from no effect to a 12 to 15 percent increase.[34]

Researchers have also used contract length as a crude metric of how much contracts restrict management flexibility. Some have suggested that larger, more complex contracts are a product of union success at the bargaining table. A 2000 study documented the growth of the CBA in Milwaukee from 18 pages in 1964 to 174 pages by the early 1990s (not counting the 1,700 memoranda of understanding appended to the contract).[35] An examination of the 199 CBAs at the BLS, however, shows no obvious variation in contract length between districts in states with and without mandatory collective bargaining.[36] The average contract length is 105.3 pages for sample districts in states with mandatory collective bargaining and 101.3 pages for districts in other states. It is unclear what to make of this result. The consistency in length may have more to do with district size than with any statutory condition; all larger districts might tend to have longer contracts.

Moreover, several union officials argue it is a mistake to imagine contract length is a proxy for union success. Said one, "Management sometimes tries to add language to add commitments for teachers or to promote their reforms. Contract length doesn't tell you who wanted these provisions."[37] An AFT officer who has negotiated several contracts said, "Page lengths are a misleading way to discuss contract provisions. For instance, in one negotiation we had a negotiation subcommittee that crafted a 50-page-plus document on teacher evaluation. Management was ready to write the whole thing into the contract. . . . I said, 'Let's just reference the document.' So we did. So the evaluation language applies, but it's not in the pages of the contract."[38]

A NATIONAL PICTURE OF BARGAINING DYNAMICS

Existent research has done little to separate the effects of varying state statutes, local political and economic conditions, and personal dynamics in union-management relationships. No scholarly analysis explains why some union-district negotiations are more peaceful than others or why conflict may surge and fall from one contract negotiation to the next within a given district. Nonetheless, conventional wisdom holds that interest-based bargaining is popular when districts are flush with resources and can offer generous raises, while scarce resources make bargaining more contentious. However, many who observe district bargaining firsthand are dubious that such a simple relationship exists.

Sally Klingel of Cornell University's School of Industrial and Labor Relations has suggested that interest-based bargaining can represent a collaborative strategy to hammer out an agreement in tough times.[39] Districts may also employ a more collaborative approach when the parties in an adversarial environment are frustrated by the lack of progress. Survey data from Oregon hint that a shift toward collaborative bargaining may result from various factors, including personnel changes, a history of exceptionally contentious negotiations, or tight financial times.[40] Likewise, a 1991 survey of Illinois districts revealed that districts that had undergone a work stoppage and those that had been involved in collective bargaining the longest were more likely to adopt an interest-based approach.[41] In a case study of Medina, Ohio, rising health-care costs and a poor economic climate prompted the Medina teachers union to issue a strike notice in 1990, inducing the union and district to create a "labor-management governance team" and pursue interest-based bargaining. The approach was successful, and by 2002 the district had used collaborative bargaining through three negotiation cycles.[42]

Recent negotiations in the Denver public schools highlight the fluidity of these two models. Denver has been held up as a paradigm of progressive collaborative bargaining and willingness to explore innovative policies. Its pay-for-performance experiment, set to commence in 2006, was approved by a majority of union members, endorsed by Denver's mayor, and hailed as nationally significant. That agreement, ratified in 2004, resulted from a joint union-district effort to survey teacher attitudes, which revealed a willingness to consider a pay-for-performance system. The new ProComp system determines teacher salary based on four criteria: learning gains, evaluation, "battle pay," and credentials; it has been heralded as an example of how unions and districts can partner to advance reform.[43]

Even in Denver, however, negotiations have been collegial and contentious at different times. In 2003 the school board rejected the union's request for a salary increase, instead reducing the teacher school year by three days. Though teachers were disappointed, the president of the Denver Classroom Teachers Association (OCTA) said the members "accepted" that it was a difficult year for the district.[44] The 2004 negotiations, however, were much more heated, featuring "four months of bitter exchanges, a three-day mediation session and seven hours of talks."[45] After several protest rallies, the members ratified a contract that included a 1 percent raise. The 2005 negotiations had a rocky start when the DCTA issued a strike warning in mid-March after negotiations over salaries and benefits broke down.[46] Tight economic times eventually pushed the union toward a more combative stance, though its initial response to tight budgets was more conciliatory. Denver also illustrates how districts may collaborate on some issues (pay for performance) and not on others (benefits).

No comprehensive national data are available on the prevalence of various bargaining approaches. Based on anecdotal evidence from the states, Klingel estimates that less than 10 percent of districts in most states use interest-based bargaining.[47] However, an annual survey of Oregon school boards portrays a different landscape. The percentage of districts using "alternative" bargaining models (generally understood to mean collaborative or interest-based bargaining) increased from 50 to 61 percent between 1994 and 2000.[48] Currently, 31 of 34 NEA state associations report some districts are using interest-based bargaining. Klingel notes, "Each negotiation occurs in a particular economic, legislative, and social environment, which can make the selection of bargaining tactics complex, and subject to change."[49]

THE BALANCE OF POWER

The relative strengths of local unions and local school boards vary substantially across districts. The National Education Association has approximately 2.7 million members, 50 state affiliates, and local affiliates in more than 14,000 school districts. The American Federation of Teachers is slightly smaller, boasting 1.4 million members, 43 state affiliates, and 3,000 locals. While the massive national organizations provide advice and support to their affiliates, local unions are responsible for negotiating their contracts. The question of how effectively the AFT and NEA are able to wield their organizational strength to assist individual locals in collective bargaining provokes sharp disagreement. Union critics and many district officials argue that unions enjoy significant advantages in resources, institutional memory, and coordination. Union officials dismiss such claims as propaganda and argue that their resources and the ability of the national organizations to support local affiliates are massively overestimated.

Ron Wilson, executive director of the North American Association of Education Negotiators, a national group composed of school board representatives and negotiators, explains, "There is a definite difference in expertise, and state associations attempt to make up for that, but not every school board can provide those kinds of services. Districts often utilize labor relations consultants to close the gap, but small districts have to rely on associations to provide them the resources they need."[50] His organization, the only national organization that offers guidance to district negotiators, has 560 members in the United States and Canada (20 percent are from Canada), while the National School Boards Association has no arm focused on supporting districts in negotiations.

Union officials dismiss the notion that unions enjoy advantages in negotiations. They argue that districts have professional staff, are able to secure high-priced legal talent, and can access district resources and information that the union cannot. The AFT researcher Howard Nelson explained, "There are thousands of contracts negotiated every year. The national NEA and AFT do not negotiate contracts. Union negotiators often negotiate as many as ten contracts [while] school districts negotiate just one."[51] Another national union official argued, "Every time I've been in a negotiation, there's a very well paid expert attorney sitting on the management side of the table. It's that attorney that takes the lead in bargaining and strategizing for the district."[52]

To illustrate the gap, unions and their critics disagree about the significance of the NEA's UniServ system for collective bargaining. UniServ is a nationwide network of 1,650 full-time and 200 part-time employees who provide local affiliates with guidance on various matters, including negotiations, grievance resolution, and school change. The UniServ program, now 34 years old, has consistently been the NEA's most expensive budget item, costing the organization approximately $50 million in 2001. The NEA employs one UniServ representative for every 1,300 NEA members.[53] The UniServ representative, according to one NEA official, is "essential to the bargaining process" because he or she can serve as "a guide, trainer, and coach who can provide members with comparative bargaining data and train locals in new bargaining techniques."[54] UniServ staff do not set bargaining priorities for the locals or get involved in union elections, but they usually occupy one of the union seats at the bargaining table and work with local union leaders to identify issues and discuss strategies. Union leaders, however, downplay the significance of UniServ, noting that employees have multiple responsibilities, work with five districts, and have information and expertise that pale beside the staff that districts can readily hire. Here, as with so much else regarding unions and collective bargaining, we lack research to resolve the matter.

Accounts of the professionalism, engagement, and institutional memory of the union relative to the district are also conflicting. A 2001 National School Boards Association survey found that most board members have served fewer than five years, that two-thirds receive no compensation for their board service, and that 69 percent spend less than 25 hours a month on board-related duties.[55] There are no comparable data on local union leadership, but an observer noted, "When you get somebody in as an officer, they are usually there for a long time. Even when they leave, a like-minded vice president usually takes over."[56]

NEA and AFT union officials argue that local unions may suffer from the same turnover and instability that plague districts. For example, Chicago's teachers union has had a tumultuous past two years, culminating with a disputed election in July 2004. Rather than hand over power to the victor, the outgoing president Deborah Lynch changed the locks at the main AFT office and announced that she would remain president until a new election was held.[57] Lynch's allegations of fraud were eventually dismissed by the national AFT, and the presidency was transferred. Such leadership instability, according to a national observer, has made for a "totally green" union in Chicago that "needs some time before it can be strong."[58]

School board elections offer teachers unions the unusual opportunity to influence the makeup of the management team they will face at the bargaining table. School board elections are typically low-turnout and amateur affairs, so organized and energized interests—like teachers unions—can exert significant influence. Teachers unions are reportedly the most active interest group in board elections; almost 60 percent of board respondents say the teachers unions are "very active" or "somewhat active" in their local elections.[59] While such efforts do not themselves ensure any particular outcome, the ability of unions to influence the composition of management and to elect sympathetic board members has obvious implications for negotiations.

The teachers unions have actively supported preferred candidates in national and state elections. The teachers union critic Myron Lieberman has argued that the NEA and AFT have "thousands of full-time union staff who participate in local campaigns; also, [they have] an enormous expansion of data, facilities, and equipment that can be used in such campaigns."[60] How much of this infrastructure is actually used in local board elections is not clear, though the Stanford political scientist Terry Moe has asserted, "No other political group in the country can claim such a formidable combination of weapons, whether in education or any other field of public policy."[61] Using electoral outcome data, Moe documents the teachers unions' success in getting prounion candidates elected. He finds that school board candidates endorsed by the union win 76 percent of the time, while those whom the union does not endorse win 31 percent of the time. Even among incumbents, who are generally more likely to win than are first-time candidates, candidates endorsed by the union win 92 percent of the time, while those not endorsed win just 49 percent of the time. Not surprisingly, the union-endorsed candidates are much more positive than other candidates about collective bargaining and the impact of contracts on schools.

Unions thus shape the membership of school boards and possibly influence how candidates behave once elected. Board members concerned about reelection have incentives to step cautiously when challenging the union on collective bargaining, interpreting language, or grievance mediation. More generally, whether on the school board as a form of civic service, to address concerns about specific policies, to promote reforms, or to further political ambitions, board members generally find themselves better able to serve their desired ends by minimizing labor-management conflict.

The district's management team, composed of the superintendent and the district central office staff, thus finds itself in a delicate position. It is charged with enhancing performance and efficiency, but it works for school board members who have good reason to avoid labor-management conflict. Moreover, district superintendents and members of the management team are typically former teachers and principals who know they need the support of the district's teachers to implement instructional reforms or improve student achievement. The former Milwaukee superintendent Howard Fuller, regarded as hard-charging during his term in office, explains, "You don't want to be antagonistic to the teachers. At the end of the day you need effective teachers, so you have a mindset to really do the best you can for them."[62]

Believing themselves well served by maintaining labor peace, school board members and superintendents may prefer to interpret contract language in routine, accepted ways and hesitate to aggressively pursue changes. Consequently, the "high-powered" attorneys whom districts hire may shape a negotiating strategy that emphasizes getting a deal done, controlling the cost of the agreement, and managing political and public relations considerations. When it comes to nonmonetary provisions of a contract, the negotiating attorneys have no cause to be more aggressive than their clients. Attorneys will seek new flexibility on measures like teacher transfer or compensation only if their clients wish them to do so. How effectively attorneys advocate for managerial flexibility and how avidly district officials push for the contractual freedoms they claim to desire are open questions requiring more exploration.

District and union officials agree that often the best scenario for "win-win" collective bargaining is to have a strong union and a strong district negotiating team. Strong district and union leaders are able to make concessions calculated to advance their long-term interests and political legitimacy, while weak unions or union leaders are under more pressure to pursue short-term benefits to shore up rank-and-file support and forestall challenges. As a negotiator for 11 districts in New York State notes, "A strong union leader that has the authority and the support of their members [is] often not bad. They can sell a contract to the membership."[63] On the other side, a national union leader explains, "Ironically, when both sides are equally organized, that's when you get the collegial bargaining. It's disorganization on either side that can lead to chaos and traditional bargaining."[64]

NEW ISSUES IN CONTRACTS AND NEGOTIATIONS

In their 1979 study of teacher collective bargaining from 1970 to 1975, McDonnell and Pascal hypothesized that "teacher organizations first bargain over and obtain increases in salary and fringe benefits; they then move on to working conditions and job security and only lastly, to issues of education policy."[65] A 1988 follow-up study supported this analysis, showing that teachers unions had made much headway in improving working conditions in the years leading up to 1980. According to Pascal and McDonnell, union progress slowed in the late 1980s: "Not only did the rate of gain for our sample slow in the 1980s as compared with the previous decade, but a majority of unions still cannot obtain key provisions such as strong class size limits, curbs on teachers having to teach outside of their fields, and clear criteria for involuntary transfer."[66]

More recently, one national union observer argued that "there's been a general bent in legislatures to give management more rights than the unions."[67] The high-profile battle in Michigan in the mid-1990s illustrates how statutory change at the state level can reshape collective bargaining statewide. In 1994 the Michigan legislature sought to limit the power of the teachers unions at the bargaining table by removing issues from the current scope of bargaining law. The new law prohibited unions from bargaining on the policyholder of employee insurance, the date the school year starts, the decision to privatize noninstructional support personnel, and other issues.[68] The law also allowed the district to impose its "last best offer" if the two parties reached an impasse, with or without union approval.

In states that have narrowed or maintained the scope of bargaining via legislation, unions have found it more difficult to obtain concessions on contract language. One NEA official explained that unions find themselves with limited demands: "Because the scope is so narrow, they've bargained everything they can bargain."[69] An AFT official offered a different take, explaining, "A lot of times, given the narrow scope of what the state [collective bargaining] law says is negotiable, locals find themselves trying to get management to agree to things that are really beyond the scope of collective bargaining—things like curriculum, hiring, class size, and peer evaluation."[70]

Districts try to avoid yielding on management prerogatives. As a New York negotiator put it, "Our contracts have all the leave time that teachers are going to get and all the benefits that teachers are going to get. Salaries will move incrementally, [but] we're not going to move on [noncompensation benefits or working conditions] because we need to have as much flexibility as possible. If we can't lay people off in the manner that we need to, assign people the way we want, we're shooting ourselves in the foot."[71] As a district official noted, "We've been doing this for over 30 years. Contracts are quite long and complex—any concessions have to be carefully considered."[72]

The biggest issue at the bargaining table in recent years has been the rising cost of health care. As one national observer said, "The hottest button issue is health insurance because we've had a five-year period where we've had double-digit inflation in the cost of health care. At the same time that revenue has been going down for school districts, making it a huge issue at the bargaining table."[73] Statisticians at the National Health Statistics Group estimate that the "health benefit share" of compensation grew to 7.1 percent in 2003, above the previous high of 6.9 percent in 1993-94. As a result, employers have sought to pass more costs on to the employees through higher copayments and insurance deductibles.[74] The BLS estimates that the amount teachers paid for health coverage rose 13 percent from 2001 to 2003, while the average salary increased 3.3 percent (as calculated by the AFT) during that same period.[75]

TEACHER STRIKES ON THE DECLINE

Striking, or a "work stoppage," is typically the last resort when negotiations have reached an impasse. In an op-ed written during a 2003 negotiation, the president of the St. Louis teachers union likened the threat of striking to the desperate long pass in football: "The 'Hail Mary' pass that many community activists are urging is a boycott of the first day of school Sept. 8th. We believe it would be wise to wait and see what can be accomplished at the bargaining table."[76]

Forty states have passed legislation prohibiting teacher strikes, though many of these statutes list no penalties. Even in states with no-strike laws, teachers occasionally strike. However, union leaders generally regard the threat of a strike as a deterrent that can force the district back to the table. One NEA observer explained, "The best thing about the right to strike is that it gives you a reason to avoid the right to strike. You want to know that you have the right to strike if you need to but that we'll do whatever we can to avoid that."[77]

McDonnell and Pascal noted in 1979 that "the growth in teacher strikes has been phenomenal," citing that in 1960-61 there were 3 teacher strikes nationwide, and by 1975 there were 241 involving more than 175,000 teachers.[78] Since then the incidence of teacher strikes has declined dramatically. The number of strikes nationwide fell to 99 by 1991 and to 15 in 2003.[79] Experts attribute this decline to both sides having greater bargaining experience, state laws prohibiting strikes or requiring arbitration, and the rise of collaborative bargaining approaches.[80] Or, in the pithy formulation of one AFT official, "Simply put: strikes don't work very well."[81]

The nationwide decline in striking is due in part to a 1994 change in Michigan law. Before the 1994 law, which also limited the bargaining scope and gave districts "last best offer" power, Michigan had averaged about 35 teacher strikes a year, or 454 total strikes between 1967 and 1980. In 1991-92 alone, about 20 percent of the teacher strikes in the country occurred in Michigan. The 1994 law imposed stiff penalties if teachers opted to strike, including steep fines for teachers and the unions for classroom time missed.[82]

Pennsylvania was the other major source of teacher strikes, with 23.2 percent of strikes from 1971 to 1987.[83] In 1992 Pennsylvania passed Act 88, establishing impasse procedures to encourage more settlements. In 1998 then-governor Tom Ridge signed Act 46, which allowed the state to take over school districts. Teachers in a district under state control under Act 46 are not allowed to strike; those who continue to strike after state takeover will have their teaching certificates revoked.[84] Teacher strikes in Pennsylvania dropped from 34 in 1991 to 8 in 2003. Having fewer strikes in Pennsylvania and Michigan has fueled the dramatic reduction in the national figures.

Another explanation for the decrease in strikes is the maturation of bargaining relationships. Said one union official, "Over time, you come to know what to expect. In the 1970s and even into the 1980s, many districts and locals were still feeling their way."[85]

Obviously, however, teacher strikes still occur. As an NEA official remarked, "Striking is an option that you want to exercise with caution, but it can be effective."[86] Interestingly, like board or union turnover, a strike can cut both ways for future collective bargaining negotiations. A contentious strike can haunt labor-management relations for years. As one journalist observed, "Teachers' strikes are a feared feature of the education landscape," risking the "long term relationship . . . without achieving the goals sought by the union."[87] Middletown, New Jersey, endured two teacher strikes between 1998 and 2001; in one, 228 union members were led off to jail. The strikes damaged the teachers' reputations and prompted nearly 10 percent of the teaching force to defect to nearby towns. The community has now taken steps to ensure that future negotiations go more smoothly, and the state has passed "Middletown Legislation" that bolsters mediation procedures and prevents districts from imposing a contract.[88]

A MORE FINELY GRAINED PICTURE

To better understand how the broad strokes above apply at the district level, we examined the context and politics of collective bargaining in a stratified, random sample of 20 districts. Half the districts in the sample were from states with mandatory collective bargaining and half from states without mandatory collective bargaining. The sample was split because of speculation among policymakers and researchers about the impact of collective bargaining laws on collective bargaining and school district governance.

All 20 sample districts had their most recent contracts on file at the Bureau of Labor Statistics. However, neither the contract nor public records contained the necessary data on the length of negotiations, the degree of controversy, the scope of media coverage, the ratification vote, or the other contextual variables we wanted. Consequently, we sought to interview a district and a union representative in each district and examined all state newspaper accounts of the most recent contract negotiation during the year or years in which it was negotiated. The description of district context is presented in Table 1.

In the districts studied, 3 of the local unions were affiliated with the AFT and the other 17 with the NEA. According to figures collected from local union officials, in 17 of 20 districts, 86.2 percent of all teachers in the sample were union members; the percentage was slightly higher among districts in states with mandatory collective bargaining than among those in states without mandatory collective bargaining (Table 1). Among districts in states with mandatory collective bargaining, 91.6 percent of teachers were union members. The equivalent figure was 80.1 percent among districts in states without mandatory collective bargaining.

The effects of law and environment on membership size matter because larger local unions are able to exert more influence on the state organization and the district. In Kentucky, for instance, a newspaper reported in 2004 that "Jefferson County's 5,000-member teachers union was the driving force in pushing the Kentucky Education Association to call for . . . a strike starting Oct. 27 unless the state backs off high premiums, deductibles for all workers, and replacing co-pays with paying a percentage of doctor bills."[89]

Every district ratified a new contract between 1998 and 2004, with 70 percent doing so between 2002 and 2004. The average contract was 2.5 years long, varying from 6 years in Livonia, Michigan, to 1 year in six different districts. The typical contract in a state with mandatory collective bargaining spanned 2.8 years, about half a year longer than contracts in states without mandatory collective bargaining laws.

According to the union officials interviewed, the most recent contract negotiations took an average of 5 months. Negotiations took more than twice as

TABLE 1: Contract Information

District	Total teachers in district	Percentage of teachers who are members of union	Total students in district	National affiliation	When latest contract was ratified	Length of new contract (years)	Months of negotiation leading up to latest contract	Grievances that reach arbitration per year
Districts in Mandatory CB States								
Anne Arundel County, MD	4,511	93.1%	74,787	NEA	July 2004	1	5	4
Appleton, WI	975	100.0%	14,948	NEA	July 2001	2	12	0
Columbus, OH	4,289	100.0%	64,175	NEA	Dec. 2003	1.5	2	0
Indianapolis, IN	2,790	71.7%	40,731	NEA	June 2003	2	4	5
Livonia, MI	1,020	100.0%	18,423	NEA	July 1999	6	NA	3
Oklahoma City, OK	2,529	63.3%	40,856	AFT	Sept. 2004	1	3	1
Paterson, NJ	2,338	100.0%	26,193	NEA	July 2000	3	15	5
Portland, OR	2,760	NA	51,654	NEA	Sept. 1998	4	8	0
Springfield, MA	2,378	98.8%	26,594	NEA	July 1998	3	9	5
Wicomico County, MD	1,013	97.1%	14,395	NEA	Aug. 2003	4	8	0
AVERAGE	**2,460**	**91.6%**	**37,276**			**2.8**	**7.3**	**2.3**

TABLE 1: Contract Information (continued)

District	Total teachers in district	Percentage who are members of union	Total students in district	National affiliation	When latest contract was ratified	Length of new contract (years)	Months of negotiation leading up to latest contract	Grievances that reach arbitration per year
Districts in Nonmandatory CB States								
Aurora County, CO	1,830	NA	32,183	NEA	July 2002	3	3	NA
Colorado Springs, CO	1,918	99.1%	32,368	NEA	July 2004	1	1.5	4
Davis County, UT	2,658	79.8%	60,367	NEA	June 2004	1	1.5	0
Denver, CO	4,472	69.3%	72,361	NEA	Aug. 2004	1	4	1
Jefferson County, CO	4,857	100.0%	87,925	NEA	Sept. 2003	4	2	10
Jefferson County, KY	5,329	95.7%	95,651	NEA	July 2002	2	2	5
Kansas City, MO	2,643	60.5%	38,521	AFT	June 2002	3	7	1
Little Rock, AR	1,744	NA	25,526	NEA	Feb. 2000	3	2	2
Parkway, MO	1,218	85.7%	20,354	NEA	July 2002	3	3	10
St. Louis, MO	3,520	51.1%	45,480	AFT	Aug. 2002	1	3	0
AVERAGE	**3,019**	**80.1%**	**51,074**			**2.2**	**2.9**	**3.7**
OVERALL AVERAGE	**2,740**	**86.2%**	**44,174.6**			**2.5**	**5.0**	**2.9**

Note: Union membership was collected from the union in 15 cases, from the union website in one, and from newspaper accounts in one. Length of negotiation and number of grievances were collected from the union where available and from the district office in the other five districts. In cases where the data were available from both union and district officials on length of negotiation or number of grievances, the figures were in agreement.

long in states with mandatory collective bargaining as in other states, requiring an average of 7.3 months rather than 2.9 months. Despite this disparity, the length of negotiation appears unrelated to the combativeness of the bargaining process as measured by the number of protests, amount of media coverage, or the likelihood of a threatened strike in a given district (see Table 2).

How conflict-ridden are local negotiations? Striking and staging a sick-out are illegal in many states, and even the threat of these activities was rare in the sample districts. As Table 2 shows, the union threatened a strike or sick-out in 20 percent of districts both in states with and without mandatory collective bargaining. In no districts was a strike or sick-out reported. Brent McKim of the Jefferson County, Kentucky, Teachers Association explained, "The last thing that we want is a strike. But sometimes right is right . . . and the law is not." A Jefferson County district official agreed, noting, "We're aware that teachers have talked about a strike, so we are concerned. But we're hoping this evening's session can bring if not a resolution then very close to it."[90]

Union protests were reported in 7 of the 20 sample districts, including 20 percent of districts in states with mandatory collective bargaining and 50 percent of districts in states without mandatory collective bargaining. Where reported, protests were typically moderate, with no more than four in any district. Often, district and union officials discussed protests or the threat of protests in terms that suggested they were relatively unexceptional, low-impact occurrences. As a district official in Oklahoma City said, teachers "certainly have the right to [picket]. We'll respect their rights because we know they'll respect our right to conduct an orderly meeting."[91] Less common was the tension of a hostile negotiation in Paterson, New Jersey, where district officials expressed "surprise" and "disappointment" at an unanticipated teacher protest.[92]

There was little evident relation between the length of negotiations and the number of protests held. While both measures might be imagined as measures of bargaining "contentiousness," local context and personalities appeared more significant. For example, Jefferson County, Kentucky, had a quick, two-month negotiation in 2002 but endured four protests and one threatened strike or sick-out. One AFT official observed that the Jefferson County experience is "very common. [Threats] are usually just saber rattling [and] 'protests' help organize teachers for future action."[93] Meanwhile, Appleton, Wisconsin, took 12 months to negotiate its 2001 contract, but with no protests or threats; the union leader termed it a peaceful bargaining process in which "we didn't have to make noise."[94]

A largely unexamined element of collective bargaining is how it is covered in the media. Using the LexisNexis database, we searched how often local newspapers published articles that included the name of the local teachers union and the term "contract," and that featured some discussion of the contract or contract negotiations. For each district, we searched all daily newspapers in the state for the year in which the most recent contract was negotiated. Op-eds were counted separately from news articles. Newspaper coverage of the collective bargaining process was surprisingly limited, given that almost all sample districts were large and had daily local newspapers.

Eight districts had no news articles written about the most recent contract negotiations, and another four had no more than 1 newspaper article published. In other words, 60 percent of districts had no more than 1 newspaper story on the entire process, including 60 percent of districts in both states with and without mandatory collective bargaining. Three districts, Denver, Indianapolis, and Anne Arundel County (Maryland), had more than 10 articles written about their unusually contentious or nationally significant negotiations. Only one other district had more than 3 articles written about its negotiations and contract. Overall, 4.2 news stories on average were written about the negotiations and contract for districts in states with mandatory collective bargaining; the average was 2.1 for districts in other states.

There is little evident relationship between threatened actions or protests and media coverage. Only one of the four districts that threatened a strike or sick-out had even a single news story written about the negotiations or the contract, although the contract in that district was the subject of 20 stories. Just three of the seven districts with protests had more than two articles written about the negotiations or the contract. In several districts, when asked why no newspaper articles were written about the negotiations, union and district officials stated that the reporters didn't bother to pursue stories even when sent information. One union representative captured the surprisingly routine lack of media attention, observing, "I don't know [why they don't write about the contract]. We give them press releases but they never print any."[95]

Commenting on the limited newspaper coverage of collective bargaining, a national union official explained, "Bargaining is conducted behind closed doors. Neither side 'goes public,' even to its own members, until the entire contract is done. This is necessary because there is so much 'horse trading' that nothing is final until the entire contract is done."[96] Richard Colvin, a veteran education reporter and the director of Columbia University's Hechinger Institute on Education and the Media, notes that this reality should not excuse journalistic inattention. Colvin argues, "The fact that parties to one of the most important negotiations in any community choose to keep them private doesn't absolve reporters of the responsibility to dig and find out what both sides are proposing and whether it would contribute to or serve to undermine student achievement. It also doesn't absolve reporters of the responsibility, once negotiations are com-

TABLE 2: Conflict and Coverage during Negotiations

District	Was there a threat of a strike or a sick-out?	Was there a strike or a sick-out?	Were there any union protests?	Number of protests held	Number of newspaper articles on the contract	Number of newspaper op-eds on the contract
Districts in Mandatory CB States						
Anne Arundel County, MD	No	No	No	1	11	0
Appleton, WI	No	No	No	0	1	0
Columbus, OH	No	No	No	0	6	0
Indianapolis, IN	Yes	No	Yes	4	20	0
Livonia, MI	No	No	Yes	1	2	3
Oklahoma City, OK	No	No	No	0	0	0
Paterson, NJ	Yes	No	No	0	0	0
Portland, OR	No	No	No	0	1	2
Springfield, MA	No	No	No	0	1	0
Wicomico County, MD	No	No	No	0	0	0
AVERAGE	**20% yes**	**0% yes**	**20% yes**	**0.6**	**4.2**	**0.5**

TABLE 2: Conflict and Coverage during Negotiations (continued)

District	Was there a threat of a strike or a sick-out?	Was there a strike or a sick-out?	Were there any union protests?	Number of protests held	Number of newspaper articles on the contract	Number of newspaper op-eds on the contract
Districts in Nonmandatory CB States						
Aurora County, CO	No	No	No	0	0	0
Colorado Springs, CO	No	No	No	0	0	0
Davis County, UT	Yes	No	Yes	3	0	0
Denver, CO	No	No	Yes	2	11	1
Jefferson County, CO	No	No	No	0	3	0
Jefferson County, KY	Yes	No	Yes	4	0	0
Kansas City, MO	No	No	Yes	1	3	0
Little Rock, AR	No	No	No	0	3	0
Parkway, MO	No	No	No	0	0	0
St. Louis, MO	No	No	Yes	4	1	1
AVERAGE	**20% yes**	**0% yes**	**50% yes**	**1.4**	**2.1**	**0.2**

Note: Protest and strike data were collected from local union sources. In the five districts where union information could not be obtained, the data were collected from district staff. Newspaper coverage is for all articles that mentioned "teachers union" and "contract," and which actually discussed the contract or contract negotiations, in all daily newspapers in the state during the year the contract was signed.

pleted, to go beyond the press release and ferret out the details of the contract and to ask what that means for the community's children."[97]

Of the seven op-eds published, four supported the local union and three criticized the union stance. Two of the four prounion articles were written by members or officials of the teachers union. A quotation from a typical prodistrict op-ed reads, "The Denver Classroom Teachers Association needs a remedial course in 'working and playing well with others.'"[98]

TABLE 3: Ratification Vote Information

District	Number of union members voting on ratification	Percentage of total union membership voting on ratification	Total number of votes for ratification	Percentage of total votes for ratification
Districts in Mandatory CB States				
Anne Arundel County, MD	NA	NA	NA	NA
Appleton, WI	450	39%	428	95%
Columbus, OH	918	17%	821	89%
Indianapolis, IN	1,200	60%	1,116	93%
Livonia, MI	NA	NA	NA	NA
Oklahoma City, OK	NA	NA	NA	NA
Paterson, NJ	2,309	87%	2,059	89%
Portland, OR	NA	NA	NA	NA
Springfield, MA	220	95%	209	95%
Wicomico County, MD	590	60%	584	99%
AVERAGE		**60%**		**93%**
Districts in Nonmandatory CB States				
Aurora County, CO	NA	NA	NA	NA
Colorado Springs, CO	NA	NA	NA	NA
Davis County, UT	1,632	77%	1,322	81%
Denver, CO	2,434	79%	1,740	71%
Jefferson County, CO	3,250	65%	2,763	85%
Jefferson County, KY	4,437	87%	4,304	97%
Kansas City, MO	100	6%	99	99%
Little Rock, AR	NA	NA	NA	NA
Parkway, MO	731	70%	512	70%
St. Louis, MO	NA	NA	NA	NA
AVERAGE		**64%**		**84%**

Note: Ratification votes were available through a union representative or from newspaper coverage for 12 of the 20 districts. In the other 8 districts, the information was not available. Some local unions indicated they could not estimate the ratification vote or refused to disclose that information.

Ultimately, when contracts are finally agreed on, how active are union members in the ratification and how united are their votes? Ratification vote totals were available from the union or from news accounts in 12 districts, with 6 of the districts in states with mandatory collective bargaining (see Table 3). Similar percentages of union members participated in ratification votes in both types of districts: an average of 60 percent in districts in states with mandatory collective bargaining and 64 percent in districts where collective bargaining is not mandatory. The lowest turnout for a ratification vote was in Columbus, Ohio, where only 17 percent of union members voted. These numbers seem to be primarily a consequence of local union activism and the method of voting. In Columbus, for instance, the union holds a meeting to take the ratification vote, which depresses participation, while many other districts use a ballot or online voting system. Consequently, the president of the Columbus Education Association was "disappointed" but unsurprised when just 17 percent of members voted in the most recent contract ratification.[99] All contracts in the sample districts were ratified by hefty margins. The typical contract in a collective bargaining state received 93 percent support, with a low of 89 percent; the typical contract in a state without mandatory collective bargaining received 84 percent support, with a low of 70 percent.

THE CONTENT OF COLLECTIVE BARGAINING AGREEMENTS

Let us turn to the question of the contracts themselves. The few recent efforts to analyze the content of teacher collective bargaining contracts have generally focused on a single state and on particular provisions of the contracts. Such studies exist only in the cases of Michigan, Washington, Massachusetts, California, and Rhode Island.

The Michigan and Washington studies, conducted by two advocacy groups highly critical of teachers unions—the Makinac Center for Public Policy and the Evergreen Freedom Foundation, respectively—more closely resemble advocacy briefs than data analyses and focus on providing policy recommendations. The Makinac Center report examined the 583 CBAs in the state of Michigan in 1998 and offered recommendations for how provisions might be revised to increase management autonomy.[100] The Evergreen Freedom Foundation examined about 260 Washington CBAs and offered policy recommendations regarding exclusive representation, agency shop, and reduction in force provisions.[101] Both include their data in extensive appendices but fail to analyze them in the text of the report.

The California study, published by the Pacific Research Institute in 2002, presents data on the variation of contract strength across 460 districts. The study assigned each contract a "restrictiveness" score on a scale of 1 to 20 on five contract areas, including grievance procedures, teacher evaluation, and transfer and assignment provisions. The researchers found that the state's 10 largest districts had the most restrictive contracts and asserted that almost 75 percent of the contracts surveyed "contain numerous restrictions on the ability of school boards and district staff to manage."[102] Most recently, a 2005 Education Partnership study of ten teacher contracts from Rhode Island examined seven contract clauses and concluded that bargaining agreements severely restrict managerial freedom.[103] The study looked in particular at teacher evaluation, salary, seniority, and health insurance, offering recommended contract language in each case.

The most scholarly of the five single-state studies was a 2000 analysis of contracts in Massachusetts. The economist Dale Ballou examined contract provisions governing compensation, teacher evaluation, transfers, layoffs, and length and structure of the school day for 40 districts.[104] Ballou found that most districts operated under strict salary schedules, that districts varied considerably on teacher evaluation and transfers, that layoffs are typically based on seniority, and that contracts limit teacher workloads by restricting class size, the length of the school day and year, and the number of classes. He also found that while most contracts included some flexibility on at least one issue, administrators typically failed to take advantage of such flexibility.

While now dated, the McDonnell and Pascal studies of 1979 and 1988 remain the most comprehensive scholarly studies of teacher collective bargaining, drawing on both quantitative analyses of contract language and qualitative interview data from districts. The 1979 study examined 151 teacher contracts from a representative sample of districts and conducted fieldwork in 15 school districts and five state capitals. The 1988 effort looked at the same sample of contracts to examine outcomes over time and conducted fieldwork in 22 districts. Both studies present useful statistical findings, but they also reveal the limits of explaining contract outcomes based on empirical variables. As the 1988 study notes: "Based on our earlier research, we also believe that the explanation for strong contracts lies in variables necessarily missing from our current analysis. The nature of the relationship between union leadership and school management; a teacher organization's history with respect to strikes, grievances, and arbitration; and the preferences of rank and file members play a strong role in determining who gets what."[105]

THE LENGTH OF CONTRACT PROVISIONS

To extend and update this existing research on CBAs, we examined the negotiating context and CBAs for the same districts in which we previously considered the political context through interviews, analysis of media coverage, and collection of additional documents. We also coded the contracts, as was done in the Michigan, California, and Massachusetts studies.

When it comes to the length of the contract or its various provisions, it makes little difference whether a state has mandatory collective bargaining (Table 4). In both groups of states, the typical contract ran about 75 pages— though the dispersion seemed slightly greater in districts in states with mandatory collective bargaining. Both sets of contracts devoted a similar proportion of their attention to leaves of absence (13 percent), teacher evaluations (4 percent), teacher transfers (5 percent), and grievance procedures (6 percent). The contracts from districts in states without mandatory collective bargaining included a larger number of salary steps, an average of 20.2 rather than 15.2.

THE SUBSTANCE OF THE CONTRACTS

How explicit is the contract language on items such as the length of the school day, class size, and teacher transfers?

Contract restrictiveness on each issue is gauged on a 0 to 2 scale, where a 0 signifies that a clause is nonexistent or very vague, a 1 that the issue is addressed but in flexible or ambiguous language, and a 2 that the clause is clearly restrictive.

Table 5 documents the level of specificity used by the 20 contracts regarding four particular issues: length of school day, class size, transfer policy, and teacher input in curriculum. The scale spans from 0 to 2, with 0 signifying a clause was either nonexistent or exceptionally vague and 2 signifying extremely specific, perhaps restrictive, language. A rating of 1 signifies the issue is explicitly addressed but in flexible or ambiguous language.

The most significant finding is that the restrictiveness of these contract provisions, both in districts in states with mandatory collective bargaining and in those without it, was much less clear-cut than the conclusions from the California, Washington, Rhode Island, and Michigan studies would suggest. Contract provisions frequently included both flexible and more restrictive language in the same section, leaving formal guidance ambiguous. The contract language from districts in states with mandatory collective bargaining appeared moderately more restrictive, by about 26 percent on our simple scale, than that from districts in states without mandatory collective bargaining. That difference was the result of significantly more prescriptive language about the school day and curricular input; districts in states without mandatory collective bargaining were more restrictive on transfer policy and class size. Across the four issues examined, the language on the length of the school day was typically the

TABLE 4: Length of Contract Provisions

District	Total articles in contract	Total pages in contract	Pages on leave	Pages on teacher evaluation	Pages on teacher transfers	Pages on grievance procedure	Total salary steps
Districts in Mandatory CB States							
Anne Arundel County, MD	24	50	8 (16%)	3 (6%)	5 (10%)	3 (6%)	13
Appleton, WI	5	100	14 (14%)	4 (4%)	1 (1%)	4 (4%)	14
Columbus, OH	NA	96	12 (12.5%)	5 (5.2%)	3 (3.1%)	4 (4.2%)	25
Indianapolis, IN	20	36	7 (19.4%)	1 (2.7%)	–	3 (8.3%)	11
Livonia, MI	62	88	12 (13.6%)	2 (2.2%)	4 (4.5%)	5 (5.7%)	14
Multnomah, OR	23	75	12 (16%)	5 (6.6%)	10 (13.3%)	8 (10.5%)	17
Oklahoma City, OK	16	67	9 (13.4%)	3 (4.4%)	3 (4.5%)	6 (9%)	16
Paterson, NJ	30	156	15 (9.6%)	3 (1.9%)	5 (3.2%)	10 (6.5%)	9
Springfield, MA	34	73	10 (13.6%)	5 (6.8%)	3 (4.1%)	4 (5.4%)	18
Wicomico, MD	17	24	5 (20.8%)	2 (8.3%)	2 (8.3%)	3 (12.5%)	
AVERAGE	**25.6**	**76.5**	**10.4 (13.6%)**	**3.3 (4.3%)**	**4.0 (5.2%)**	**5.0 (6.5%)**	**15.2**

TABLE 4: Length of Contract Provisions (continued)

District	Total articles in contract	Total pages in contract	Pages on leave	Pages on teacher evaluation	Pages on teacher transfers	Pages on grievance procedure	Total salary steps
Districts in Nonmandatory CB States							
Aurora County, CO	48	65	13 (20%)	3 (4.6%)	3 (4.6%)	3 (4.5%)	42
Colorado Springs, CO	19	88	10 (11.3%)	4 (4.5%)	3 (3.4%)	5 (5.7%)	10
Davis County, UT	8	47	10 (21%)	2 (4%)	4 (8.5%)	4 (8.5%)	25
Denver, CO	32	62	6 (9.6%)	5 (8%)	4 (6.4%)	4 (6.4%)	13
Jefferson County, CO	44	83	9 (10.8%)	3 (3.6%)	7 (8.4%)	3 (3.5%)	25
Jefferson County, KY	33	73	10 (13.6)	4 (5.5%)	6 (8.2%)	7 (9.5%)	25
Kansas City, MO	13	63	9 (14.2%)	1 (1.5%)	4 (6.3%)	5 (7.9%)	13
Little Rock, AR	41	90	9 (10%)	3 (3.3%)	2 (2.2%)	5 (5.5%)	16
Parkway, MO	39	102	8 (7.8%)	2 (1.9%)	4 (.9%)	6 (5.8%)	13
St. Louis, MO	16	67	14 (21%)	1 (1.4%)	3 (4.4%)	3 (4.4%)	NA
AVERAGE	**29.3**	**74.0**	**9.8 (13.2%)**	**2.8 (3.8%)**	**4.0 (5.4%)**	**4.5 (6.1%)**	**20.2**
OVERALL AVERAGE	**27.6**	**75.3**	**10.1 (13.4%)**	**3.1 (4.1%)**	**4.0 (5.2%)**	**4.8 (6.4%)**	**17.7**

Note: The figures in the tables reflect the number of pages devoted to each topic of interest in the district contract. The percentages refer to the total proportion of each contract devoted to the topic in question.

TABLE 5: Explicitness of Contract Language

District	Length of school day	Class size	Transfers	Curriculum	Overall average
Districts in Mandatory CB States					
Anne Arundel Cty., MD	2	0	2	2	1.5
Appleton, WI	2	0	2	1	1.3
Columbus, OH	2	2	1	0	1.3
Indianapolis, IN	2	0	0	0	0.5
Livonia, MI	2	2	0	2	1.5
Multnomah, OR	2	0	1	1	1.0
Oklahoma City, OK	0	0	1	1	0.5
Paterson, NJ	2	0	0	2	1.0
Springfield, MA	1	2	0	2	1.3
Wicomico County, MD	2	0	2	1	1.3
AVERAGE	**1.7**	**0.6**	**0.9**	**1.2**	**1.1**
Districts in Nonmandatory CB States					
Aurora County, CO	2	0	0	0	0.5
Colorado Springs, CO	2	0	1	2	1.3
Davis County, UT	2	0	2	1	1.3
Denver, CO	1	2	0	0	0.8
Jefferson County, CO	1	1	1	0	0.8
Jefferson County, KY	1	2	2	1	1.5
Kansas City, MO	2	0	1	1	1.0
Little Rock, AR	0	0	2	1	0.8
Parkway, MO	0	0	1	0	0.3
St. Louis, MO	0	2	1	2	1.3
AVERAGE	**1.1**	**0.7**	**1.1**	**0.8**	**0.9**
TOTAL AVERAGE	**1.4**	**0.7**	**1.0**	**1.0**	**1.0**

most restrictive. On this count, one union official cautioned, "State law is sometimes incorporated into a contract. It is not really bargained."[106] Consequently, highly restrictive language on the school day or class size may, in some cases, reflect state statutes. Whether this explains the findings is unclear.

It is instructive to examine the language of contracts. Based on his study of Massachusetts teacher contracts, Ballou concludes that contract clauses are less restrictive than district officials often claim. He reports, "On virtually every issue of personnel policy there are contracts that grant administrators managerial prerogatives they are commonly thought to lack. . . . Yet, . . . administrators do not take advantage of [this flexibility]."[107]

The contracts studied here yield a similar finding. For example, while most contracts are relatively explicit about the length of the teacher workday, many allow for some discretion on the part of the administration. Paterson's relatively rigid contract gives administrators little operating room, setting the number of hours teachers must work and determining the time schools open and close. The contract states that "the total, in-school workday shall consist of not more than 7 hours," and that "sessions at the elementary and primary schools . . . shall begin at 8:20 a.m. and end at 2:55 p.m."[108] The Parkway, Missouri, contract, by contrast, does not mention a specified start or end time, stating simply that "school hours for teachers will be defined as beginning twenty (20) minutes before the opening of school each day and ending twenty (20) minutes after the scheduled dismissal of pupils."[109]

Some contracts include both ambiguous language and strict prescriptions within the same article. Denver's contract, for example, sets the teacher workweek at 40 hours and states that "the principal shall have authority to permit teachers to diverge from the regular school day." This clause is directly followed, however, by one that asserts that "the District's scheduled student contact day will not be extended without applying the due process of collective bargaining."[110] How the "student contact day" relates to the 40-hour work week, or how much discretion the principal has to shape the teacher workday, is unclear. Likewise, Appleton's contract states, "Because of the professional approach to this agreement, a work day with specific hours has not been established," but then includes the following: "The normal day for instructional purposes shall be from 7:40 a.m. until 3:10 p.m. However, in order to show flexibility without having to submit a waiver, a building may start as early as 7:29 and/or end as late as 3:20 p.m. provided that the total time students are in school for instructional purposes . . . and professional educators' maximum workload times . . . are not changed."[111] Both contracts contain language that appears flexible but then—in the same section of the document—include additional language that appears to constrain significantly or eliminate this flexibility. As a result, how much discretion the district actually has is ambiguous.

The pattern is largely the same with district transfer policy. Principals' ability to effectively staff their schools is related to how a contract defines the criteria for voluntary transfer. The question is how much discretion the contract grants principals in selecting a candidate versus how explicitly the contract uses seniority as a selection criterion. The sample contracts included some in which teacher transfer is based strictly on seniority, others in which the criteria are left to a principal or a selection committee, and others in which seniority is one factor considered alongside others.

Little Rock's contract, for instance, states that senior employees will be given priority when seeking to transfer. In the event of a vacancy, the contract stipulates, "Existing employees will be given preference for position, and senior district employees will be given preference in order of seniority."[112] By contrast, Springfield, Massachusetts's, seemingly more flexible contract reads, "In the determination of reassignments and transfers, the convenience and wishes of the individual teacher will be honored to the extent that these considerations do not conflict with the instructional requirements and best interests of the school system and the pupils."[113] Whether Springfield's language translates to more flexible policies depends, of course, on how language like "given preference," "wishes of the individual teacher will be honored [when possible]," "instructional requirements," and "best interests of the school system" is implemented in practice.

The transfer procedures in other contracts are more ambiguous. The St. Louis contract first declares, "In making assignments and transfers of employees, consideration shall be given to the following: grade level and subject matter areas (where applicable); position for which the employee is best suited by qualification and experience; available vacancies, staff balance, school/work and locality preference. The Superintendent of Schools may deny or institute any transfer for the good of the system." However, the same article states, "System-wide seniority will be given due consideration in making transfers" and provides that, if two employees are equally qualified, "transfers or promotion of the employee shall be made on the basis of system-wide seniority."[114] What constitutes "due consideration" and how to tell when two employees are equally qualified are left unaddressed.

Oklahoma City's contract strikes a similarly nebulous tone. The contract states that "transfers shall be granted to best meet the educational program of the school and best meet the needs of the students of that school," before asserting that "the granting of a transfer shall be based upon seniority when individual qualifications are equal."[115]

The contract for Kansas City, Missouri, sketches simple, three-part criteria for teacher transfer: fulfillment of court-ordered requirements, specialized academic needs of the district, and length of service in the district. The contract wording appears to suggest the three criteria are ranked in order, with legal concerns coming first, educational concerns second, and seniority last, or at least that they are of equal importance. However, the article proceeds to emphasize seniority, stating that if the length of service (seniority) "is equal or within sixty (60) days of being equal, the teacher possessing the greatest professional preparation as measured by the district's degree code . . . shall prevail."[116] In short, it is not at all clear how heavily considerations other than seniority may be weighted in making transfers.

In the end, given that union contracts are faulted for many of the rigidities of school governance, the substantial ambiguity in contract language governing issues like the school day, class size, and teacher transfers may be surprising. This finding echoes the results of Ballou's earlier study of CBAs in Massachusetts. One possible explanation for the disparity between what contracts say and how their language is often perceived is that district leaders may be reluctant to exploit contract language or aggressively pursue greater managerial freedom. One prominent urban superintendent—himself often at odds with the union—argued, "Districts tend to be far less aggressive in asserting management prerogatives than the language of their contracts arguably permits."[117]

What might explain this reluctance? First, in public education, management and labor share a common work history. "Trustees and superintendents who have been teachers and members of teachers unions end up negotiating contracts with the bargaining representatives of teachers," mused the same superintendent. "Fresh eyes and bold views typically are neither present nor welcome." As a result, district leaders may be skittish of provoking conflict and hesitant to upset the status quo. Other observers, like the Stanford political scientist Terry Moe, have argued that school board members are often union sympathizers or are hesitant to act aggressively due to the fear of union reprisals at the ballot box and in local affairs.

Second, district leaders know that pressing on contract language will almost certainly lead to grievance arbitration, a costly, time-consuming process that antagonizes teachers and that administrators would rather avoid. Grievance arbitration is a quasilegal, poorly understood process. Because arbitration is not part of the formal legal system, the role of precedent, the rules of evidence, and other legal principles employed by arbitrators may apply differently than in formal judicial proceedings. Despite the importance of arbitration, the process has largely escaped either scholarly or journalistic attention. How arbitration operates, how the process affects the decisions of district and union officials, and the outcomes of arbitration are questions deserving more systematic consideration.

A third possible explanation relates the presence of "past practice" clauses, which stipulate that contract provisions should be interpreted to be consistent with past practices. Myron Lieberman, author of *The Teacher Unions: How They Sabotage Educational Reform and Why*, suggests that this explains apparent inconsistencies in contract language and makes ambiguous provisions more prescriptive than they appear. However, others question that interpretation. Leo Casey, a veteran official with the New York City United Federation of Teachers, says it is hard to generalize from contract to contract, but that past practice clauses typically "codify existing regulations. A lot of times, it's a way to keep the district from unilaterally changing contracts and for unions to make sure that the district [pays] attention to its own written regulations in areas like class size. It doesn't privilege informal practices . . . maybe if it's something chiseled into state practice, but it would have to be a pretty high burden of proof. I've never seen a union local or a district just say in a grievance [arbitration] or anywhere that it was established practice to do something and get away with it."

In fact, many contracts feature language like that in the agreement between the Columbus Education Association and the Columbus, Ohio, Board of Education, which stipulates, "To the extent that any provision of the Administrative Guide, other Board policy, regulation or procedure, or building level policy, regulation or procedure conflicts with an expressed provision of this Association/Board Agreement, the provisions of the Association/Board Agreement shall have precedence." In short, with past practices as with so much else, our inquiry raises more questions than it answers. The nature, import, and effect of past practice clauses are more elements of collective bargaining that call out for additional examination and research.

Finally, contract length and language appear relatively similar in structure and content across districts. This is consistent with an observation that McDonnell and Pascal made in 1979: "There seems to be a convergence of collective bargaining outcomes over time. As more and more school systems follow the lead of flagship districts, there is less variation among individual contracts."

CONCLUSION

Union critics have suggested that teachers unions in states with mandatory collective bargaining laws often help write school district policy, that CBAs are highly prescriptive, and that school boards and school leaders find themselves excessively constrained by contract provisions. In practice, these claims may be accurate. However, our examination of collective bargaining processes and contracts suggests that such claims are at best an incomplete account, and at worst a misleading characterization of how collective bargaining affects district management.

Even in large districts, most negotiations over CBAs appear relatively moderate affairs. Threats of strikes are unusual, few union protests are reported, little media attention is devoted to negotiations or to the teacher contract, and contracts are ratified by wide margins. Moreover, on their face, some contract provisions are not as prescriptive as some accounts would suggest. Instead, consistent with previous research, potentially restrictive contract language is often ambiguously couched or paired with potentially contradictory language.

Many critical accounts of district governance and reform efforts suggest that unions have interpreted and implemented contracts far more successfully than have school administrators. But that issue is distinct from the collective bargaining process or from the contracts themselves. The findings here question whether some administrators and board members may be using the local CBA as an excuse for inaction. Our analysis asks how much responsibility district leadership, implementation, and execution should bear for various examples of operational inflexibility habitually attributed to the teachers unions.

Arbitration and its effects on contract implementation and district reluctance deserve further inquiry. How often do arbitrators find in favor of the union? How often in favor of the district? More generally, scholars need to examine the nature of the bargaining process. Of particular interest is how negotiations are affected by economic cycles, political developments, and statutes. Finally, the role that No Child Left Behind will play in collective bargaining negotiations remains to be seen. Whether district leaders will be eager or able to leverage NCLB's collective bargaining mandates, and how the unions will respond to such efforts, is unclear.

Reforming collective bargaining may alter some dimensions of the negotiating process and limit the subjects eligible for collective bargaining. Ultimately, however, altering the impact of teacher contracts on district management may turn as much on the willingness of district leadership to exploit existing contract language as on changing the formal provisions in contracts.

The authors would like to express our appreciation to Morgan Goatley, Tamarah Shuer, Richard Gioia, Michael Ruderman, and Juliet Squire. We would also like to thank those individuals in the sample school districts, at the National Education Association, and at the American Federation of Teachers, who graciously shared their time and expertise.

CHAPTER FOUR

The Costs of Collective Bargaining Agreements and Related District Policies

PAUL T. HILL

C omplaining about the impact teachers unions have on public education is like decrying today's weather. Unions are here, they are legal, and teachers have the right to join them. But that does not mean unions are pure forces of nature. Like the weather, teachers unions respond to human interventions in the long run. Political and economic activity can inexorably heat up the atmosphere or cool it down. Public officials in particular can make a big difference via the collective bargaining agreements they make with teachers unions.

Consider the evolution of collective bargaining agreements over the last 40 years. Local school boards have gradually given unions control over teacher placements, performance evaluations, working conditions, and work assignments within the schools.[1] In so doing, school boards have narrowed the options of principals—who have virtually lost the ability to choose teachers, make work assignments, fire ineffective teachers, and manage budgets—and parents—whose ability to affect student placements is limited by teachers' rights to jobs. These arrangements emerged over time, as school boards made conscious trade-offs between labor peace on the one hand and school shutdowns on the other. School boards might have made different decisions but they did not, generally placing greater weight on the short-term cost of a teacher job action than on the long-term cost of lost capacity to manage schools and adapt programs in light of performance.

As with growing evidence of global warming, the long-term costs of teacher collective bargaining agreements are now becoming clear. They are starting to bankrupt school districts and render them unable to adapt education to the needs of a changing population and a more demanding economy. This is so especially in the big northern and western cities where unions are best organized and collective bargaining agreements are most extensive.

This conclusion—which subsequent parts of the chapter will document in detail—does not amount to blaming the results of collective bargaining on the unions. It takes two parties to make a collective bargaining agreement, and as Terry Moe observes, when a union gets money, privileges, and job protection for teachers, it is only doing its job. However, a school board is not doing its job when it enters agreements that put the district into a permanent deficit position, or eliminate the district's capacity to make changes required for higher performance, or ensure that the neediest students will get inequitably small shares of funds and teaching talent.

One reason school boards have not done their job is that the long-term consequences of teacher collective bargaining agreements were hard to see.[2] As is now evident, school boards have little understanding of their districts' budgets, and no real capacity to judge whether a commitment made today is sustainable in the long run. Similarly, erosion of flexibility and district manageability came on slowly, and increments were difficult to observe. Only now, with increasing numbers of big districts running structural deficits, and schools unable to respond to new performance pressures, are the long-term consequences of collective bargaining agreements evident. This chapter will identify and quantify the long-term costs of collective bargaining and suggest how the costs can be mitigated. All the costs identified can be represented in dollar terms, but cost data are not always available; in those cases I will identify costs in looser ways, such as lost opportunity to students.

Though it says many harsh things about collective bargaining agreements, this essay does not try to weigh the costs they impose against the benefits. Collective bargaining could produce many desirable outcomes beyond higher pay for teachers and power for unions, such as creating conditions more conducive to student learning, making teaching a more desirable occupation, and supporting continuous improvement of the teacher labor force. Other chapters in this volume cast doubt on whether those potential benefits are realized. Future research might show some measurable benefits, but at present only the costs are clear. One-sided collective bargaining—in which unions are well informed, have strong agendas, and exercise political control over the school boards nominally negotiating with them[3]—apparently does not benefit students or strengthen schools. School boards that care only about the here and now, and have no way to project the consequences of an agreement made today into the future, are not competent negotiating parties. I hope this chapter will help elected officials and concerned citizens assess collective bargaining agreements and hold school boards accountable.

HOW COLLECTIVE BARGAINING AGREEMENTS IMPOSE COSTS

Like other unions, teacher associations normally bargain about wages, hours, and working conditions. Because the meaning of "working conditions" is elastic, the range of issues covered by collective bargaining agreements is enormous. Working conditions can include methods and standards for hiring, assignment to schools, duties within the school, job tenure, and limits on supervisors' authority. Many teacher contracts also include limits on the numbers of minutes a teacher may be in contact with students, and maximum numbers of students taught in a day. These requirements are well known, and each one is intended to impose some costs. Districts seldom count the costs explicitly. However, as I will show below, some of these costs are serious and may be the core cause of structural deficits evident in many big-city school systems.

What is even less obvious is how the costs of collective bargaining agreements are distributed within districts. Some costs of collective bargaining might affect all schools in the same way, but others might impose major costs on some schools or groups of students and have neutral or even positive financial effects on others. I will show how collective bargaining provisions distribute key costs and benefits, and provide evidence that disadvantaged students and the schools that serve them lose the most.[4]

How Collective Bargaining Affects Districts

Several features of collective bargaining agreements affect districts' overall costs. Since districts' incomes are determined independently of their costs—and timely increases in income are difficult if not impossible to arrange—many districts struggle to meet the costs imposed by collective bargaining agreements. The following are the main cost drivers related to collective bargaining:

> overall increases in teacher pay scale;
>
> automatic raises linked to seniority coupled with districts' inability to manage workforce composition;
>
> salary point credits linked to continuing education;
>
> limits on class size and student contact minutes; and

requirements that all tenured teachers be placed before new teachers can be hired.

The first four features work together to escalate districts' costs.[5] Overall salary scale increases happen only once every four or five years and often amount to just a little more than cost of living adjustments. However, when combined with teachers' longevity step increases (annual or semiannual automatic raises established in the standard teacher pay scale), total salaries can increase much more dramatically—in some analyses, at twice the announced rate of increase. In addition, teachers who gain graduate credits at a set rate— usually amounting to a year's progress toward a graduate degree, which takes teachers on average three or four years to attain—gain another increment similar in size to one annual longevity increase.

Michael Podgursky shows how this works for Chicago teachers:

> For example, a new teacher with a bachelor's degree hired in Chicago in the fall of 1999 earned $32,561. Between the fall of 1999 and the fall of 2002, the average starting pay for Chicago teachers rose a modest 6.1 percent. However, by the fall of 2002, that teacher hired in 1999 is now in her fourth year of teaching and her pay will have increased to $40,071, or 23.1 percent in three years. If the 2003–04 salary schedule again rises by 2 percent, as it has over the past several years, then at the start of the 2003 school year her salary will have grown by 31.1 percent. If she earns a master's by that time, as many teachers do, her pay will have increased by 38.6 percent in four years—an average annual growth rate of 8.5 percent.[6]

Limits on class size directly increase the numbers of teachers hired. Reducing class sizes by 15 percent from an average of 26 to 22 requires hiring one new teacher for every seven currently in the classroom. The impact on the overall salary bill is likely less than 15 percent, since new teachers are hired in at relatively low salaries and some members of the district teaching force do not work in the classroom. However, annual salary growth is especially fast for new teachers.

Limits on student contact time also increase salary costs. In the early 1980s high schools in Chicago had to maintain a student-teacher ratio of 14:1 in order to maintain a class size of 28. The number of daily student contact minutes allowed was much lower than the number of minutes students were required to be in class.[7] Districtwide, Chicago's student-teacher ratio is now 17:1.[8] Cost cutting has reduced Chicago teacher redundancies somewhat, but the current contract still says high school teachers must teach only five of eight 45-minute periods. Thus, to provide instruction in every classroom all day, a school must employ 1.6 times as many teachers as classrooms.[9]

Even in less aggressive union environments, individual teachers are required to teach less than 70 percent of the time students are in school, implying that a school would need 1.4 times as many teachers overall than would be teaching at any one time.[10] Seattle maintains a student-teacher ratio of 15:1 in order to maintain an average class size of 22.

In contrast, the New York Archdiocesan school system, which has union contracts but much less controlling ones, maintains a high school student-teacher ratio of 14:1 to maintain an average class size of 18, and an elementary ratio of 23:1 in order to maintain an average class size of 25.[11]

Of course, teachers work during the time they are not in direct student contact. Most teachers spend time preparing for class and attending meetings. Some extra teachers cover for teachers who are ill or taking part in professional development. However, not all schools or school systems employ such large numbers of excess teachers. Charter and parochial schools, which must function within fixed budgets, employ only the numbers of teachers required to meet classes, and double up classes when someone is ill. Substitutes are used for long-term absences, often when the regular teacher is paid via disability insurance.

Can all these differences be attributed to collective bargaining? Perhaps not. Big-city school systems that do not have collective bargaining also employ large numbers of extra teachers. They might do so because the logic of civil service leads to such redundancies, or because they try, like nonunionized companies, to avoid unionization by granting employees many of the benefits they would have gained through collective bargaining.

Of all the factors listed above, the first two are the most important. In cities with stable or falling school populations, total spending can be fixed at specific dollar levels. Since most districts' teacher salary bills are near or slightly above 50 percent of their operating budgets, a steady escalation of salary costs can create a major deficit. That is the main reason why some big districts outside the Sunbelt—Baltimore, Cleveland, Oakland, San Francisco, Seattle, and others—must deal with recurring annual deficits.[12] Unfunded mandates like special education also contribute to the structural deficit, but they involve much less money and their annual costs escalate much less.

In the past, combinations of student population growth, escalation in state spending, and new categorical program spending have hidden the deficits caused by teacher salary escalation. But when these growth factors all disappear, especially as fewer and fewer students attend city schools, the day of reckoning is there for all to see.

Just like a pyramid scheme collapses when its base ceases to grow, school districts run into big trouble when they must go years without spending increases.

Teacher job protections, aging teacher forces, guaranteed annual step increases, pay sweeteners for teachers who take graduate courses, and overstaffing all derive ultimately from collective bargaining. Unlike private organizations, which can cut their expenses when times are bad, school districts must continue paying for job commitments made when times were good.

Even in the rare case of a reduction in force for teachers, districts must release their lowest-paid teachers and keep the most expensive ones. Small dollar savings thus have exaggerated bad effects on class size and student services. Though no district has literally gone out of business due to such a cycle of decline, some give every appearance of being in it. Dayton public schools now serve only one-third the number of students enrolled in the 1960s, and Seattle less than one-half. Other big-city districts, such as New York, Los Angeles, and Miami, continue growing rapidly, so the base of their pyramids is expanding quickly enough to keep them out of trouble.[13] But all major urban districts have the same cost drivers, and any district can fall into the cycle of financial decline.

In addition to the factors explained above, measures needed to preserve tenured teachers' placement rights can cost big-city districts money and lower the overall quality of their teaching force. The cost implications of tenure are straightforward: it forces districts to keep some teachers whose performance does not correspond to their pay level. Expensive tenured teachers can keep their jobs as long as their performance is not egregious, not worse than that of brand new (and much cheaper) teachers. It is difficult to quantify this added expense, though some administrators think it exceeds 1 percent of the overall district salary budget.

The larger cost of protecting tenured teachers is harder to measure but easy to see: it can adversely affect the quality of new recruits to teaching jobs in city schools. Tenured teachers displaced from their jobs, whether at their own initiative, at that of a principal, or due to school closure or enrollment decline, have first claim on jobs that become available. Experienced teachers displaced by even more senior ones must also find jobs. Schools that have vacancies due to retirement or teachers transferring to other schools cannot hire teachers new to the district until all tenured teachers are placed.

Though some principals willingly hire from their district's internal labor market, many want to avoid hiring senior teachers whom they do not know and who might have done badly in their last jobs. Principals who expect vacancies might prefer to take their chances with a brand new teacher. Others might have identified a teacher they want—a substitute who performed well, a newly minted teacher who interned in the school, or an experienced but not highly senior person from another school. Such principals have a strong incentive to hide vacancies (e.g., by urging departing teachers to delay submitting their retirement papers) in hopes that all unattached senior teachers will get placed. Then principals can hire the teacher they want.[14]

This ploy works in individual cases, but it has bad implications for the district as a whole.[15] Big-city districts, where it takes a long time to place all the experienced teachers in search of jobs, often cannot hire new teachers until after school closes in the spring. Then principals stop hiding their vacancies and the district can offer jobs to newcomers. Unfortunately, simpler suburban districts also have vacancies and their senior placement processes take little time. They can offer jobs in the spring, when most new teachers are looking. Big-city districts start hiring after the surrounding districts have taken their pick and creamed off the most outstanding applicants. In some cases teachers who prefer working in urban schools choose suburban schools instead, feeling forced to go with a sure thing. This reduces the average quality of new hires, with enduring bad effects on the quality of the city district's teaching force.[16]

These factors come together to prevent big-city districts from competing effectively in the metropolitan-wide teacher labor market. A 2000 report on Boston drew out all the connections:

> Approximately 200 BPS teachers changed schools last spring, filling vacancies through a contractual process that bars schools from considering new teachers or experienced teachers from other districts. Because the contractual and administrative processes are so drawn out, BPS was advertising 285 open positions in June 1999, after many suburban districts had already completed most teacher hiring. In mid-August, BPS was still listing 105 vacancies. This year (as happens every year) the district's 417 first-year teachers will have their positions offered to senior teachers as "vacancies" for transfer as required in the Contract, unless the first-year teachers are given expedited tenure—a virtual lifetime job guarantee—after four or five months on the job.[17]

Some reviewers have commented that the cost escalation described might be attributed to the "cost disease" identified by William Baumol.[18] In an environment where most organizations can become more productive by creating new mixes of labor and technology, wages rise. People-driven organizations, whose staffing is fixed due to the character of the work they do, cannot become more productive, but they must compete in an ever more expensive labor market. Thus, as Baumol notes, costs for organizations like a string quintet rise continuously. Baumol includes higher education, and implicitly K-12 schools, in the group of cost disease–ridden organizations.

The salary scale increases discussed above might fit the cost disease hypothesis, but most of the cost drivers do not. Reductions in the teacher-pupil ratio, limits on teacher-student contact, protections for low-performing senior teachers, and restraints on new hiring go beyond increasing wages for a fixed group of people. They protect incumbents without respect to productivity, and they increase the number of people employed beyond the numbers previously considered necessary. Collective bargaining, not the cost disease, turns a string quintet into a group of eight.

Collective bargaining also forces districts into perverse internal spending patterns, which can exacerbate the problems of schools serving disadvantaged children, as the next section will show.

How Collective Bargaining Imposes Unequal Costs on Schools

Collective bargaining agreements could have severe consequences for district financial solvency without having any particular short-run consequences for schools. Schools could at least temporarily benefit from having a large teaching force, an expensive pay escalator, and teachers who are well paid for noninstructional duties. This could be the case for any district now currently in financial crisis. However, when districts discover that collective bargaining agreements have put them in a situation of structural deficit, schools can suffer. Hiring freezes, school closures, and abrupt reductions in central office services can all have negative effects on schools and students. The inevitable superintendent firings and school board turnover can also affect schools negatively.

However, collective bargaining agreements and the policies districts adopt to implement them can harm some schools, even in districts where structural budget deficits are currently hidden. This section will explain how collective bargaining provisions and the policies school boards adopt to implement them

limit poverty area schools' access to good new teachers;

make it impossible for schools to choose and keep teachers on the basis of fit;

make poverty neighborhood school teaching staffs unstable; and

ensure that poverty neighborhood schools have less money to spend than other schools.

Limiting the quality of teachers available to struggling schools

Few seasons have gone by in the past ten years without another report on the relatively low quality of teachers in schools serving low-income students. Kati Haycock and The Education Trust have led the way in this work, calling attention to the fact that teachers of poor and minority students are much less likely to be certified or have college training in the areas they teach, and less likely to have degrees above the bachelor of arts.[19] Neild et al. have also shown that middle schools, notoriously difficult places to teach, have particular trouble attracting qualified teachers.[20]

Some of these differences are due to urban districts' uncompetitive hiring practices and working conditions. But more recent research makes it clear that teacher qualifications are not evenly distributed within districts. Julian Betts and others at the Public Policy Institute of California have shown that poor children get less-qualified teachers, both statewide and within individual districts.[21] The Education Trust West has just published a report on teacher salaries within the 50 largest urban districts in California. In 42 of those 50 districts, the average teacher salary difference between schools ranked in the highest and lowest quartile on family income is $2,576. The average teacher salary difference between top and bottom quartile schools based on minority enrollment is $3,014.[22] (Statewide average teacher salary is just under $50,000.) This could amount to as much as a 12 percent difference in teacher salary spending between the highest and lowest quartile schools. As the Education Trust authors conclude, if a student "attended the highest-poverty schools from the time of kindergarten through high school, California will have spent a total of $141,714 less on all of her teachers (K-12) than on the K-12 teachers serving the most affluent students."

Collective bargaining agreements do not affect all schools in a district equally; schools that do not hire new teachers or get their new teachers outside the regular placement system are not directly affected. For example, schools that have special relationships with high-quality training institutions or can employ new teachers who once worked there as interns can hire early. These schools are almost always considered the best in the district, with excellent teaching staffs and long-term principals. However, struggling schools in low-income neighborhoods depend on the district's routine intake. If the district as a whole hires from the bottom end of the metropolitan teacher market, schools in poverty neighborhoods are directly hurt.[23] In Philadelphia more than half of all new middle school teachers have no certification at all.[24]

Principals who depend on new teachers complain about the good ones who got away because the district could not offer a contract when other potential employers demanded an answer, and about district human resource offices' poor performance at getting teachers who schools need.

The New Teacher Project study of teacher transfers in San Diego revealed that, due to a byzantine transfer process, the city district hired teachers months later than suburban districts.[25] Though the city received nearly 20,000 applications for teacher vacancies in 2004, 30 to 50 percent of applicants withdrew to take other jobs. Of those who withdrew, half were in crucial subject areas like special education, mathematics, and science. The New Teacher Project study of teacher contracts in five urban school districts shows that:

- Principals reported that they were forced to hire transfer teachers whom they did not want in their schools.
- Principals rated those teachers, after having them for a year in their school, as worse than the average teacher in their building.
- The transfer process hit needy schools the hardest, with high-poverty schools receiving teachers with the lowest-quality rankings.
- The transfer process minimizes the need for and use of an effective teacher evaluation system. Transferring the teacher out of a school relieves the principal of the need to defend a negative evaluation, and keeps the teacher's record clean.

It is hard to measure the joint impact of all the actions taken to preserve teacher transfer privileges. Insofar as the teacher labor market is able to judge quality, the teachers still available at the end of the hiring season are not likely to be the best. New teachers who are still around after most others have been hired and start in troubled schools are also more likely to leave the profession early. Some would attribute these outcomes to the qualities of the school and district rather than to teacher preferences.[26]

Limiting schools' control over their teaching force

In collective bargaining agreements, school boards generally let school staffing be driven by rules, not the judgment of school leaders. When job vacancies occur, interested teachers apply and the most senior applicant with the right paper qualifications gets the job. Moreover, senior teachers who are displaced from jobs in other schools can "bump" less senior teachers out of their jobs. Taken together, these provisions make it extremely difficult for school leaders to assemble the teaching staffs they need for their schools or to stabilize groups of teachers that work well together.

Collective bargaining treats teachers as commodities that can be fully described as packages of training and prior experience. School leaders, by contrast, see teachers as parts of teams, whose functioning depends on personalities, work habits, and specific skills whose presence or absence is not obvious on a standard teacher resume. These teams can be broken up at any time, often against the wishes of school leaders and the teachers involved.

Business leaders are often incredulous to learn that school principals cannot choose the people whom they supervise. They know that good staff members in any organization can be lured away by attractive jobs, but business unit leaders have some capacity to influence results by offering pay and work assignment incentives. Not so school leaders: the single salary scale and work rules leave them with no way to keep a valuable person.

Principals with good reputations have an advantage: they can attract highly senior teachers and can often pick among good alternatives. This is seldom so for schools in troubled neighborhoods, which often get as few as two applicants for a posted vacancy, compared to dozens of applicants for jobs in schools considered more desirable.

However, even schools able to attract many applicants can still be forced to take senior teachers rather than a younger person whom they would prefer. The result, from the most to least attractive school in a district, is that principals must often oversee teaching staffs that they did not hire, cannot fire, and that are perfectly free to cooperate with or oppose any effort to improve instruction.

Most school superintendents recognize this problem, and some have worked with union leaders to address it. New York City, Philadelphia, Boston, and Seattle have amended their collective bargaining agreements to allow a school leadership team to fill a vacancy with a teacher other than the most senior qualified applicant. However, schools that want to hire outside seniority must follow demanding procedures and create selection committees on which the majority is drawn from the ranks of union members, and the principal has only one vote among many. The United Federation of Teachers explains the New York City process, called the School Based Option (SBO), as follows:

> An SBO is the process whereby you and the UFT chapter leader agree to propose to the UFT represented school staff deviations from certain requirements of the various UFT contracts, such as staffing, class size, rotation, etc. After you and the UFT chapter leader reach agreement on the SBO proposal the UFT chapter leader arranges for a vote. The proposal must be approved by fifty-five percent (55%) of the staff who vote and the SBO must specify which provisions of the contract will be altered. The proposal must be approved by the UFT district representative and president, the LIS, and the Chancellor. (Source: Teachers' Contract, Article 8B)[27]

Not surprisingly, fewer than one-third of New York City schools have adopted the School Based Option,[28] and the numbers of teachers selected outside the seniority order is very small. In Seattle, despite union and district leaders' claim to have eliminated seniority as a factor in teacher hiring, there is no evidence about how many schools have instituted the prescribed procedures or how many teachers have been hired out of seniority order. Plenty of evidence suggests that seniority-based "bumping" continues in both districts.

Thus, despite some contrary efforts, seniority-based hiring continues to work against schools' ability to build compatible teaching forces and keep well-functioning teams together. A recent Philadelphia study illustrates the importance of site-level hiring: of teachers hired at the school level, 53 percent reported understanding the school's approach to education before taking the job, compared to only 18 percent of teachers who were assigned to schools by the central office.[29]

Destabilizing poverty neighborhood schools

Senior teachers' placement privileges mean they can pick the best jobs. Though senior teachers do not all have identical preferences, the vast majority would prefer to work in neighborhoods where parents are supportive, students are easy to manage, the environment is safe, and their cars are not vandalized. These preferences lead senior teachers overwhelmingly to prefer working in schools in the nicer middle-class neighborhoods. This is so even in poor districts serving an overwhelmingly minority population: there is always a difference between the nicest and most troubled schools, and senior teachers care about it.

Concentrations of senior teachers are often blessings for schools, but not always: some all-senior staffs are virtually unleadable due to ingrained habits and tenure-based individualism. But concentrations of senior staffs always eliminate options for schools in poor neighborhoods. The supply of experienced teachers is by definition limited: aside from raiding other districts, the only way a school system can increase its stock of senior teachers is to wait. Given teachers' incentives to retire when they have maxed out their pensions, experienced teachers can leave as often as new ones emerge.

If the supply of experienced teachers is fixed and they cluster in certain schools, other schools have no access to them. This means that some schools—usually the ones in the least attractive neighborhoods and serving the most challenging students—have no access to experienced teachers. In Philadelphia, for example, 70 percent of open positions in high-poverty schools are filled by brand new teachers, compared to less than 50 percent for high-income schools in the same district.[30]

Though attractive schools can have dozens or even hundreds of applicants for each teaching vacancy, troubled schools in the same district can have only one or two applicants, and sometimes none.[31] These applicants are seldom people who have options elsewhere. Thus, schools in the most challenging circumstances must often make do with teachers no one else wants, brand new teachers—and not necessarily the brilliant new ones who have just graduated at the top of their class in a respected education school—and experienced teachers whom other schools that have options do not want. Moreover, after new teachers serve a year or two in the bottom-of-the-barrel schools, they too use their seniority to claim posts in slightly more attractive schools. This leads to great turbulence in the schools shunned by senior teachers—teacher turnover rates between 30 and 70 percent per year, year after year.

A few poverty neighborhood schools overcome these problems, maintaining stable staffs and attracting enough good applicants to maintain quality after experienced teachers retire. These schools often have something special—an excellent principal, or some senior teachers who have stayed in the school despite having many opportunities elsewhere. These individuals are rare, however, and their career choices ignore strong incentives in the teacher placement system.

Defenders of seniority placement privileges make two arguments: first, that seniority is poorly correlated with teacher performance, and second, that some excellent principals prefer to hire junior teachers. Consequently, they claim, schools forced to hire all-junior staffs are at no real disadvantage. It is true that seniority is weakly correlated with performance at the individual level, but as Marguerite Roza has shown, there is a definite correlation between a school's average teacher salary (a measure of seniority) and student performance. This is because schools that can attract a highly senior staff are good places to work, and so can hand-pick the best among all applicants. Similarly, there are productive schools with many junior staff members, but these are usually schools that can pick the best among many applicants and know how to support vibrant young teachers and channel their energies effectively. Schools that cannot attract senior staff members and hire newcomers only after more attractive schools have creamed the applicant pool live in the worst of all worlds.

Some defenders of the system also say that teacher turnover can be good, citing examples of schools where a new principal has "cleaned house" and brought in a dedicated and compatible new staff. However, such examples do not demonstrate that turnover in general is good. Planned turnover is one thing: it can ultimately stabilize a school and improve teaching and learning. Constant turnover, especially when school leadership has no leverage about who stays and who goes, is a very different thing. As Neild et al. have shown, 40 percent of new teachers in poverty neighborhood middle schools leave the district after one year of teaching.[32]

Kacey Guin has shown that schools with chronic teacher turnover are chaotic, fail to make connections with parents, and cannot sustain an improvement strategy from one year to the next.[33] In one urban district, she found schools whose annual rate of teacher turnover over a seven-year period ranged from 14 to 35 percent. Moreover, teacher turnover rates were negatively correlated with overall school climate, teachers' perception of working conditions and influence over professional practice, and student achievement. Guin concluded:

> It is critical for school districts and school boards to recognize that high rates of teacher turnover may result in significant costs at both the school and district level. While turnover is normally associated with discrete questions of teacher supply and quality, it is important to acknowledge that teacher turnover may have a negative impact on schools as organizations. Based on the case studies in this report, schools with high rates of turnover do face serious organizational challenges, including the failure to establish a coherent instructional program and a lack of trust among teachers. Unfortunately, these high turnover schools are most likely to serve the students in most need of help. District and school level policies, including tracking turnover and providing incentives for teachers, will help identify and aid these turbulent schools in establishing the stable teaching staff necessary for building the personal relationships and organizational capacity needed for school improvement and student achievement gains.

Few analysts have tried to calculate the financial costs for rapid turnover, which would have to include the time principals spend recruiting new teachers, the adjustment period during which at least some new teachers are lost and unable to teach effectively, the demands imposed on other teachers, and the professional development expenditures wasted when teachers trained one year leave the next. One advocacy-oriented effort by a local ACORN unit makes a first effort at measuring some related costs.[34]

Underfunding poverty neighborhood schools

Though collective bargaining agreements do not expressly control the ways districts spend money, they set up a difficult challenge for school budgeting. If school budgets were set on a real dollar basis—a per-pupil amount times the number of students enrolled—and if schools paid the actual salary costs of their teachers, schools could not afford to pay the salaries of an all-senior teaching staff. If teachers were randomly distributed among schools, this would be no problem. But because some schools employ disproportionate numbers of senior teachers (and others consistently have very low-paid teaching forces), something must be done to allow schools to spend very different amounts of money.

The solution, evident in virtually every school district with a teachers union, is to ignore the actual cost of teachers by charging schools as if all teachers made the same salaries. Thus, districts charge schools the average districtwide salary cost of teachers, not the actual cost. This avoids making schools with all-senior teaching staffs look like they spend disproportionate amounts of money, and conversely overstates actual spending in schools with lower-cost junior teachers.

This practice hides a real transfer of resources from schools with junior teachers to schools with senior teachers. A school whose average teacher salary is 10 percent below the districtwide average does not get the difference in cash to spend on other things. Instead, the shortfall in that school's spending is transferred to other schools to pay for their above-average teacher salaries.

Marguerite Roza has documented this phenomenon in eight urban districts. All have the same pattern, though some (Houston, Cincinnati, and Seattle) are working to soften its effects on schools serving the disadvantaged. Salary cost averaging can distort spending patterns even in districts that have adopted weighted per-pupil funding. Poverty neighborhood schools can get above-average budgets, but if they are charged extra for their teachers (while other schools with smaller official budgets pay for their teachers at a discounted rate), they can still have below-average purchasing power.

Some district officials justify this arrangement, saying, "We don't want to discourage schools from hiring senior teachers just to save money." This view is sensible only if one ignores the essential competition among schools for teacher talent. Given that money and outstanding teachers are in limited supply, a policy that ensures one group of schools consistently more of a scarce resource ensures that others will get consistently less.

These arrangements move significant amounts of money around. The amount varies by district, depending on the size of the senior teachers cohort and how radically misallocated they are. In the cities Roza studied first—Seattle, Cincinnati, and Baltimore—the typical impact on a school's budget was to raise or lower it by 5.9 percent,[35] meaning that in a district that spends $100 million on teacher salaries, $6 million is reallocated to maintain senior teachers' privileges.

Later studies showed that consequences for the poorest and highest-minority schools can be even greater—they can lose as much as 20 percent of their schools' budgets due to salary disadvantages. At the other end of the distribution, the richest and whitest schools can benefit by more than 20 percent.[36]

The financial implications of the combined policy of seniority-based placement and salary cost averaging are not easy to see with the naked eye. Even after it was known for years that poor children got the least qualified teachers, nobody traced it to a deliberate policy of budgetary distortion until Roza started building school budgets up from the raw data in the late 1990s. School budgets never revealed the real spending pattern: cost averaging hid real spending differences and transferred money among schools, away from those in poverty neighborhoods and toward schools in more affluent parts of the district.

The Education Trust and other education groups have made it obvious that low-income children get the worst teachers.[37] This is often attributed to a moral weakness and lack of political will. But what is seldom acknowledged is that it is a direct result of teacher placement policies rooted in collective bargaining agreements, plus district policies made to enable implementation of those agreements. Districts have adopted salary averaging for one reason only: to enable implementation of the seniority placement provisions of collective bargaining agreements. There is no question who is responsible for this; school boards are, both for implementing the policy in the first place and for ensuring that they and the public are blind to its consequences.

Of course, teacher preferences underlie everything. If senior teachers did not prefer to avoid poverty area schools, neither senior placement privileges nor cost averaging would have the effects they do. However, if school districts handled money transparently—allocating real dollars to schools on the basis of enrollment and charging schools the actual salary and benefits costs of the teachers they employ—it would be harder for senior teachers to avoid challenging schools entirely. All schools would have salary cost constraints, and no school could afford an entire teaching staff paid at the top of the salary scale. Even the schools most attractive to teachers would be forced to hire mixes of senior, intermediate, and new teachers. Schools in poverty neighborhoods would have more money than their current teachers earn and would be able to bid for some of the experienced teachers who became available. This would not completely equalize teacher quality across the district—the most attractive schools would still be able to choose the best teachers at all experience levels—but it would make a start.

SUMMING UP: WHAT WE KNOW SO FAR AND WHAT WE STILL NEED TO KNOW

Though the costs of collective bargaining are becoming clearer, there is still a great deal more to learn. No one has tried to count up all the costs of collective bargaining for a particular district, and what we know about within-district spending distortions depends on the work done by Marguerite Roza, Karen Hawley Miles, and groups adopting their methods. A more thorough inquiry would need to be larger, better funded, and based on common metrics for counting the costs of collective bargaining. Table 1 identifies the sources of evidence about each kind of cost discussed above and suggests the form more

TABLE 1: Available Evidence on Collective Bargaining Effects and Measures Needed

	Available Measures	Measures Needed
Districtwide salary escalation	Now measured only as increases in the whole salary scale	Increases in actual teacher compensation for big-city districts
District structural deficits	Number of districts now acknowledging deficits	Comparative rates of total district budget growth and of teacher salary growth
Lower-quality recruits in big-city districts	Anecdotes, some comparison of teacher quality in city, metropolitan labor markets	Comparisons of measured ability and preparation for new teachers placed in all districts in a metro area
Concentration of low-quality recruits in poverty schools	National and statewide averages for poverty schools, local measures available for only a few places	Comparisons of measured ability and preparation for new teachers placed in all schools in a district
Schools' inability to control hiring and staff composition	Only one local study— Guin's	District-based studies of applicants and hires for high- and low-poverty schools, effects on instructional quality and continuity, family-school ties
Lower-quality staff in poverty schools	Moe's forthcoming analysis of effects of transfer rights in California	Comparison of teachers hired with and without collective bargaining constraints—e.g., hiring by charter and public schools in same neighborhoods
Staff instability in poverty schools	One study of staff turnover rates and educational consequences	Studies of staff turnover and educational consequences in every major city
Underfunding poverty schools	Rigorous dollar-based evidence on 6-8 districts	Real-dollar school spending data for all schools, all districts

definitive evidence should take. Beyond tracking the costs associated with individual factors, it is necessary to ask how these factors complement or oppose one another.

A serious investment in studies of how districts spend money, and how much collective bargaining agreements distort its use, would open up many new possibilities for school improvement. The first priority is good real-dollar-spending numbers for each school in a city, with real salaries used in a method like the one provided by Miles and Roza.[38]

Possible Remedies

Collective bargaining provisions and the actions districts have taken to implement them are major burdens on urban districts and on schools that must serve the most challenging students. At the district level, these burdens are serious enough to plunge many large districts into a permanent deficit position. Moreover, districts' struggles to stay within budget without violating collective bargaining agreements force them to take actions that accelerate the departure of families that can afford to move or pay private school tuition. In 2005 debate rages in Seattle about whether closing low-enrollment schools will save a significant amount of money since the district will have to reassign all teachers and administrators and continue paying their salaries.[39] Some analysts, moreover, fear that closing small schools will accelerate enrollment decline and worsen the district's deficit.

Districts whose populations grow rapidly can hide these deficits, in part because overcrowding in immigrant settlement neighborhoods holds down the unit costs of serving them. In the long run, however, even districts like Los Angeles, Dade County, and New York will have to come to terms with the shear between constant per-pupil funding and escalating teacher costs.

Have big-city school districts become like major airlines that can survive financially only if they get occasional big rescue packages from the government and move in and out of bankruptcy protection? The answer is probably yes, unless they imitate the big airlines by creating subsidiaries that can operate on a more sustainable cost structure. That is exactly why some districts are starting to charter and contract for schools, and why unions regard those measures as direct challenges to gains made via collective bargaining.

States and localities have other options. The Boston Plan for Excellence, the local public education fund, organized a coalition of poor and minority parents and related interest groups to demand a seat at the table during collective bargaining. They argued that the district was trading away their children's educational opportunities in a closed forum where the only interests represented were the union's—to get more for senior teachers—and the school board's—to avoid labor strife.[40] The result was a collective bargaining agreement that significantly curtailed teacher transfer rights and stabilized the poorest schools.[41] This kind of action is possible elsewhere, but only if organizations like local public education funds and business coalitions abandon their habit of happy talk, maintaining that all is well until there is unmistakable evidence to the contrary. It is hard to escape the conclusion that those groups' desire to maintain a united front with teachers unions, all together in the interests of children, is the unions' greatest political asset.

Such local actions as these are much likelier now that the real numbers on school spending, the costs of teacher transfers, and the consequences for the most challenged schools can be demonstrated. However, with few exceptions, school districts have not taken the initiative to assemble or report the necessary data. Independent researchers, funded by national foundations like Annie E. Casey, Gates, and Annenberg, have done all the heavy lifting here. However, local school boards could get it done if they wanted the facts, as could local business coalitions and public education funds.[42]

State governments could make the same sorts of demands, based on their constitutional responsibility for public education and well-grounded concern that major districts have bargained themselves into untenable positions. Local school boards and unions, of course, could take the initiative, suggesting ways they can gradually abandon the costliest artifacts of collective bargaining. Under former Houston superintendent Rod Paige and deputy superintendent Susan Sclafani, Houston proposed to eliminate distortions in school-level funding by taking advantage of senior teacher attrition: when senior teachers retired from schools whose per-pupil budgets were above the district average, those schools would replace them with newcomer teachers, and the freed funds would be reallocated to schools with below-average budgets.[43] Sclafani calculated that spending could be equalized in seven years via this method, without displacing any incumbent teachers. Houston was in a stronger position to propose this method, given Texas's relatively weak teacher labor laws, but even so, successive administrations abandoned the idea as too difficult politically. School districts could gradually introduce real-dollar school budgets as Cincinnati has done, and try to make poverty neighborhood schools more attractive by placing admired principals in them, as Seattle has done.

As Mary Beth Celio has suggested, school boards could better fulfill their basic responsibilities to the public if they routinely tracked information about teacher costs and transfers.[44] Data about rates of teacher turnover and real-dollar expenditures could identify schools in trouble and enable boards to intervene in schools on a downward spiral. Information about the numbers of applicants for vacancies could be another indicator of school health, and comparative data on neighboring districts could be used as a sign of a district's competitive position in the local professional labor market. Teacher choices are one of the few market-style indicators available to school boards, and school boards serious about school performance should use, not bury them.

Incumbent union leaders are unlikely to publicize such data or suggest remedies for problems they reveal. Senior teachers are the main supporters of local unions, and as the recent firings of reformist union leaders in Cincinnati and Seattle illustrate, those teachers punish leaders who put seniority-based advantages at risk. However, insurgents in local union elections could attract junior teacher support by attacking seniority privileges, and national union offices could help by providing data and suggestions for new collective bargaining provisions.

Parents and ordinary citizens also have options. One possibility is to demand that collective bargaining negotiations include parent and public-interest groups, as was done in Boston.

Another option is to formulate lawsuits and civil rights complaints based on the inequitable consequences of teacher transfer policies. For decades civil rights law firms have brought suits against state funding schemes for public education, claiming that lower funding for high-poverty school districts was a denial of the equal protection and primary state interest clauses of state constitutions.

The inequities *within* districts are much larger than the ones between districts on which school finance litigation has traditionally been founded.[45] Why the same rights-oriented litigators have not pursued the same arguments against public policies—including collective bargaining agreements and actions districts take to implement them—is anybody's guess. In part, the traditional alliance between unions and civil rights attorneys might have made litigators blind to the inequities caused by their friends. But regardless of what explains past inaction, the facts that could generate strongly founded claims of unequal protection are now on the table. From this nonlawyer's perspective, it seems only a matter of time before collective bargaining agreements face strong constitutional challenges.

Litigation might be a good thing if it gives school boards and unions incentives to fix the problems they have caused. Judicially imposed remedies to such problems are not always desirable—vide the perverse consequences of the *Hobson v. Hansen* order in the District of Columbia,[46] which distributed teachers immediately on the basis of salary, depleting some schools of needed specialists and doubling up certain skills in others, thus disrupting virtually every school. However, one successful lawsuit in a big city, followed by a sensible court order that took advantage of senior teacher attrition as Houston had planned to do, could transform the climate for collective bargaining nationwide.

But what is needed first is serious research estimating how much it costs districts to employ a more senior teaching staff than they would choose solely on the basis of productivity, how much the hidden escalations in the teacher salary scale cost, and how much professional development investment is wasted when teachers leave for other districts or quit teaching entirely due to searing experiences in troubled schools. Such research would make it possible to estimate how much—denominated in money and teaching talent—big-city districts lose as a result of being the weakest competitors in the local teacher labor market.

Though researchers in the field are familiar with the many ways collective bargaining agreements burden the most challenged schools, policymakers and the public generally are not. This is due in part to the complexity of the agreements and the opaqueness of school district recordkeeping and reporting. To calculate real-dollar school budgets, it is necessary to combine databases that districts keep separate, and often to conduct on-site counts of people actually working in schools.

There is no question that many of the facts laid out above are deliberately hidden. Local unions and school boards, the parties to collective bargaining agreements, only risk criticism if they make these results public. In addition, the very research community that has publicized the facts about disadvantaged students getting the worst teachers has been shy about naming its causes. Even after Roza and others showed how these phenomena are rooted in collective bargaining agreements, reports decrying inequitable distributions of teachers have blamed poor supply or a general lack of moral concern and political will.

Collective bargaining agreements are public policies knowingly endorsed and implemented by elected officials. School board members and district officials are responsible for the consequences. They have no right to plead ignorance of the costs imposed on schools and children. Citizens who question and challenge these agreements, and hold public officials accountable for making them, are acting to preserve public education.

CHAPTER FIVE

The Effects of Collective Bargaining on Teacher Quality

SUSAN MOORE JOHNSON
MORGAEN L. DONALDSON

Researchers finally have demonstrated what parents long have known: teachers differ in effectiveness, and those differences can have long-lasting effects on students' learning and life chances.[1] Although debate rages about how best to prepare teachers,[2] the need for good ones is now obvious. With increasing scrutiny of students' performance on standardized tests, concern grows that the quality of teachers today—as defined by subject-matter knowledge, commitment to students, and instructional success—is lower than it should be.

At the same time, there is increasing consensus about goals and strategies for improving teacher quality. If all students are to be taught by effective teachers, public education needs to attract many knowledgeable individuals with an interest in students and a promise for teaching. These teachers must work in the classrooms and schools where they are most needed, to ensure all students are taught by strong teachers. Schools have to provide sufficient resources and support so teachers can do their best work, increase their skills, and extend their influence. Over time schools should retain those who are effective in the classroom and best exercise leadership for improved teaching and learning throughout their school. Thus, teacher quality is about who enters and who stays, how their talents and skills are used, and how their growth is supported over time.

There is little agreement about what role, if any, teachers unions and collective bargaining should play in moving public education toward those goals. Maggie Haley, the founder of the Chicago Federation of Teachers, campaigned for better pay and working conditions in schools by asserting that "there is no possible conflict between the interest of the child and the interest of the teacher."[3] Although few would contest that some of what teachers unions pursue also benefits students—for example, the guarantee of a safe, well-ventilated classroom—many doubt that other union gains—such as limiting the length of a teacher's in-school workday—take account of students' interest. Teachers have a different relationship to students than assembly line workers to the products they make; thus, the industrial model for labor relations, which prioritizes basic union gains in wages, hours, and working conditions, may not be appropriate for professional teachers today. Moreover, teachers entering schools today may be less likely than their predecessors to look to unions for conventional protections, although they still expect support to do their job.[4] As school reformers focus on improving teacher quality, it is important to examine evidence about the roles of teachers unions and collective bargaining in determining who teaches, how teachers are assigned, the support they receive, and how they are assessed.

THE CHALLENGE OF CONDUCTING RESEARCH ON THIS TOPIC

Given the importance of this topic, surprisingly little research is available. Several factors make collective bargaining difficult to study and the effects of unionism hard to trace. First, collective bargaining is a process rather than a predetermined set of outcomes. Negotiations may be adversarial in one place and collaborative in another. Some bargained agreements constrain administrators from responsibly managing the schools, while others create opportunities for progressive change. A 1999 longitudinal analysis of 11 contracts revealed that almost half were decidedly "industrial in tone, form, and content."[5] They "set forth procedures for layoffs and transfers, class size limits, preparation time, and teaching loads, with little allowance for school-based decision making." By contrast, three contracts in this sample were "reform" in character, "recogniz[ing] the shared interests of labor and management; affirm[ing] the importance of flexible, nonstandardized practice; and defin[ing] differentiated professional roles for teachers." The remaining three contracts "contained new elements of reform that seem to have been appended to the old agreements without changing their overall purpose or character."[6] Given such variety, generalizing about the effects of unionism is imprecise and often uninformative.

Second, collective bargaining for teachers in the United States is highly decentralized. Each state decides whether its teachers have the right to bargain. State laws give teachers in Michigan and 33 other states the right to bargain, but do not grant this right to teachers in Texas and 15 other states. In states where teachers can bargain, statutes and case law establish the issues about which the sides must or may bargain. For example, in Illinois, management is required to negotiate with teachers about class size, while in Indiana it may choose whether to do so. Contracts also differ widely within the same state. Thus, the New Haven and Bridgeport contracts limit the number of preparations a teacher may be assigned, while the Hartford contract makes no such guarantees, even though all three districts bargain under Connecticut law. Within the constraints of state law, district labor and management may write and sign any agreement they choose. What the agreements include results from several factors: the state and local labor contexts, the history of labor-management relations within the district, prior contracts, current reforms, and the personalities and priorities of the participants. Understanding the impact of collective bargaining on teachers and their work necessarily involves examining and explaining such differences. Thus, given the range of possible outcomes from collective bargaining, findings reporting its average impact offer little of use to policymakers and practitioners.

Third, because unions and school boards in many states have been negotiating and signing contracts for more than 35 years, researchers today face daunting methodological problems as they try to establish the effects of collective bargaining. It might have been possible in the late 1960s, when bargaining was introduced, to collect and compare data about teacher quality or student performance in unionized and nonunionized states and districts before and after unionization. However, because education officials did not systematically collect such data, researchers today find it virtually impossible to make meaningful retrospective comparisons. This problem is further complicated by the fact that, in the decades following the institution of collective bargaining, nonunion states and districts tended to copy the policies and practices of unionized settings. In an effort to ward off union organizing among their teachers and ensure their schools would attract prospective teachers, school officials offered salaries and working conditions comparable to those recently won in nearby unionized settings. These so-called "spillover effects" quickly made it very difficult to isolate the effects of collective bargaining in different settings.

Fourth, collective bargaining was only one of many policies that changed public schools beginning in the late 1960s. Programs such as ESEA Title I and PL 94-142 fundamentally altered the responsibilities and practices of school officials and teachers. Simultaneously, expanded career opportunities for women transformed the labor market for public school teachers. Over the next two decades, many women, who in the past would have routinely chosen teaching, instead sought work in other fields, such as engineering, banking, and law. It became nearly impossible for researchers to isolate the role of collective bargaining during this rapid change. Thus, those intent on studying unions' effects on teaching must take all such changes into account and, as Samuel Johnson cautioned, not mistake "subsequence" for "consequence."[7]

THE ISSUES OF UNIONS AND TEACHER QUALITY

Given these limitations, what can be learned about the role of teachers unions and collective bargaining in matters of teacher quality? In the following discussion, we first consider evidence about pay and working conditions. Does collective bargaining increase pay and improve working conditions, thus making teaching attractive to individuals who might choose different careers? Or does the teachers' single salary scale dissuade promising candidates and drive out effective teachers? We then consider two working conditions, class size and preparation time. Do contracts address these issues and, if so, do they establish conditions for better teaching?

We then move to the issue of teacher assignment. Do union contracts ensure teachers have fair and wise assignments, or do they give undue weight to teachers' preferences and seniority, thus limiting some students' access to experienced teachers? We then consider contract language about teacher evaluation. Do contracts frame sound and constructive performance evaluations, or do they block schools from dismissing poor teachers? Finally, we explore professional growth. Do unions and collective bargaining limit teachers' opportunities for development, or do they create new possibilities for improvement and influence?

As will become clear, few answers to these questions are certain, and evidence often supports both sides of an issue. Ambiguity often is due to the limits of research. More frequently, however, it stems from the tremendous variation in labor policies and practices from state to state and district to district that precludes meaningful generalizations about how unions and collective bargaining reduce or improve teacher quality. Nonetheless, the available empirical evidence and current practices can provide insight into the possible outcomes of collective bargaining.

PAY

Pay, which in U.S. society is tied to social status, influences individuals' decisions about whether to enter and stay in teaching. Although other factors, such as working conditions, may be as important in teachers' career choices, pay has commanded the greater share of research attention, in part because data about salaries are readily available and have been reliably recorded over time. Researchers have studied whether collective bargaining affects overall pay levels and the structure of pay scales, as well as whether pay influences a school district's ability to attract and retain high-quality teachers.

The Effect of Collective Bargaining on Pay

It is widely agreed that pay affects individuals' career decisions and that an employer who can offer higher pay can select from a larger, stronger pool of candidates.[8] Thus, if collective bargaining has led to higher salaries, it also has helped school districts attract better teachers. In empirical studies designed to examine whether collective bargaining leads to higher pay, analysts have repeatedly found a positive effect. David Lipsky and John Drotning compared data from 696 unionized and nonunionized school districts in New York during the first year of negotiations under the Taylor Law. They found that collective bargaining had a "positive and highly significant" effect on salary changes after it was introduced in 1967, "adding about 15 percent to salary increases."[9] William H. Baugh and Joe A. Stone compared individual teachers' salary gains for 1974-75 and 1977-78.[10] Although they found relatively small wage gains during the early 1970s, they concluded that by the late 1970s, the union-nonunion wage differential among teachers reached 12 percent.

Unfortunately, these estimates fail to control for other developments contemporaneous with increased union activity that might also have boosted teacher salaries. For example, districts might have received increased federal funding at the same time they unionized. In this instance it would be impossible to determine whether salary increases were due to unionization or increased district funds. Recently researchers using more refined methods have concluded that the wage premium introduced by collective bargaining is lower than earlier estimates. For example, Caroline M. Hoxby compared the change in districts' salaries between 1972 and 1982 and between 1982 and 1992 and identified a union wage premium of 5.0 to 5.1 percent.[11] Hoxby's methods are the most advanced of those reviewed here and come closest to an unbiased estimate of the union wage premium. However, they rely heavily on assumptions that require further substantiation.[12]

Teachers' Pay Levels

Surveys indicate that pay plays a large role in a person's decision about whether to enter the classroom. Prospective teachers surveyed by Public Agenda reported that low pay was an important factor in their decision not to teach. Seventy-eight percent agreed that "teachers are seriously underpaid."[13] Respondents wanted to be "financially 'comfortable,'" which, according to them, teaching would not allow. As such results indicate, teachers are widely perceived to be paid less than comparable workers.

Researchers generally have concluded that teachers' pay compares unfavorably with compensation in fields that require similar preparation and time, although this point has been debated. For example, Sylvia Allegretto, Sean Corcoran, and Lawrence Mishel compared teachers' overall salaries to those earned by people in similarly skilled professions and concluded that teachers' weekly earnings were, on average, 12 percent less than those of architects, nurses, and accountants.[14] However, Richard Vedder compared the hourly wages of teachers and nonteachers, counting teachers' in-school, contractual hours and excluding after-school preparation time.[15] He concluded that teachers fared better than, for example, architects and civil engineers.

Although the debate about whether teachers are well paid is unresolved, scholars agree that teachers are paid relatively less today than they were in the 1980s. Comparing trends in teachers' wages to those of other professions, Allegretto, Corcoran, and Mishel concluded that relative wages for teachers declined through the 1970s, rose slightly in the 1980s, and then declined again in the 1990s.[16] During the 1990s the pay gap between teachers with a master's degree and their nonteacher counterparts nearly doubled, from $12,918 to $24,648.[17] A recent study based on a nationally representative sample revealed that between 1994 and 2004, teachers' salaries declined 3.4 percent, while the salaries of principals and superintendents rose.[18] No studies are available that compare these trends in unionized and nonunionized states or districts. Several studies that focus on teacher quality report that at the same time salaries decreased, the test scores of college graduates who became teachers declined.[19]

Economists have found that adequate pay is one factor that enables those who have chosen to teach to continue in that role.[20] Similarly, interview studies with current teachers suggest that, although adequate pay makes teaching affordable, it is not an attractor in its own right. Most teachers enter the classroom for the work they can do there, not the money they can earn. However, when poor working conditions make it hard to succeed in the classroom, teachers express more dissatisfaction with low pay.[21]

The Effect of Pay on Teacher Quality

Even if experts agree that collective bargaining leads to increased wages for teachers, the subsequent question is whether better pay leads to better teachers. Susanna Loeb and Marianne Page found that states offering their teachers higher pay than female college graduates could earn in other occupations had more students enroll in college and lower student dropout rates.[22] The researchers found that, adjusting for labor market and nonmonetary factors, raising teachers' salaries 10 percent was associated with a 3 to 4 percent reduction in high school dropout rates. These positive student outcomes may reflect higher teacher quality.

However, other researchers have found that higher pay has failed to attract and retain better teachers. According to Dale Ballou and Michael Podgursky, increases in teachers' salaries between 1979 and 1989 did not induce college students with higher SAT scores to become education majors.[23] A review of pay by Allegretto, Corcoran, and Mishel revealed mixed evidence about whether increased salaries attracted teachers from more selective colleges in the short run.[24] Overall, estimates of the effect of pay increases on teacher quality differ according to the methods and measures researchers have used.

For at least three reasons, empirical studies have not clearly linked increased pay and improved teacher quality. First, as Ballou and Podgursky argue, higher pay likely attracts and retains high-quality and low-quality teachers.[25] It is up to districts to select the strongest candidates and decide to rehire the best teachers. In previous research, Ballou concluded that such decisions were not made.[26] Second, as Loeb and Page explain, teacher labor markets are local, so research that fails to consider pay increases relative to the salaries offered by a district's neighbors or other employers may fail to identify the true effects of salary increases.[27] Accordingly, Dominic J. Brewer found that the higher the salaries offered by a district's neighbors, the greater the attrition from that district.[28] In a particularly puzzling set of findings, David Figlio concluded that, as a nonunionized district's salaries increased, it could recruit teachers from more selective colleges.[29] However, this relationship did not hold for unionized districts. Figlio theorized that, among nonunionized districts, pay increases were associated with increased teacher quality because such schools had more flexibility and could pay particularly promising or effective teachers substantially more than their less-stellar counterparts. However, Figlio's data permit only speculation, not verification, that this was the case.

A third reason that short-run estimates of the effect of pay on teacher quality have been mixed is that districts with poorer working conditions may offer higher salaries, or "compensating wage differentials," to draw teachers into these districts despite particularly difficult conditions.[30] As Susan Moore Johnson, Richard Ingersoll, and others have found, working conditions factor heavily in teachers' job decisions.[31] In these instances higher salaries may fail to attract and retain high-quality teachers.

The Structure of Pay

The single salary scale, often mistakenly considered the product of collective bargaining, was introduced decades earlier in 1921 in Denver and Des Moines.[32] By paying all teachers wages based solely on years of experience, the single salary scale was intended to end patronage and discrimination between black and white teachers and between lower-paid elementary teachers (mostly women) and higher-paid high school teachers (disproportionately men). Subsequently, the single salary scale was expanded with columns that rewarded teachers who earned academic degrees beyond the bachelor's. However, within each column on the pay scale (for example, bachelor's, bachelor's plus 30 hours, or master's), a teacher's upward movement still depended on experience, with every year bringing an automatic raise (or step increase) until the teacher reached the top of the scale.

Although the single salary scale was not the product of collective bargaining, unions largely have sought to preserve and reinforce it. Hoxby and Leigh report that collective bargaining has reduced the variation in starting salaries earned by first-year teachers, thus compressing the pay scale.[33] The authors conclude that, over time, this compression of starting salaries has led female teachers with higher aptitude to reject teaching as a career. However, because the researchers restrict their sample to individuals who graduated from undergraduate institutions in the previous year, they examine only a small subsample of each year's beginning teachers.[34] The authors do not explore the possibility that high-ability women may delay entry into teaching, which may be the case as liberal arts graduates complete a master's degree in education before beginning to teach. Thus, claims that teaching attracts lower-caliber candidates today than in the past must account for growing numbers of new teachers who enter the classroom five or more years after they graduate from college. Recent surveys of new teachers revealed that between 28 and 46 percent of respondents reported entering teaching after a substantial period working in another field.[35]

Clearly, however, teachers with greater opportunities outside education are more difficult to attract and retain in the classroom. Evidence that mathematics and science teachers are more likely to leave teaching than others suggests they are attracted to higher-paying jobs in other sectors and might remain in teaching if they could be paid more than their counterparts with less attractive alternatives.[36] Some analysts recommend a flexible wage scale that allows districts to offer more money to teachers in fields of shortage (e.g., mathematics, science, special education, and foreign languages) and might efficiently use limited resources to improve the quality of the teaching force. This strategy assumes that pay can induce individuals to remain in teaching despite poor working conditions. However, the nation's dramatic attrition rates among special education teachers suggest that working conditions may be at least as important as pay, since these individuals exit in large numbers even though, unlike science or math teachers, they cannot easily find jobs outside education.[37] Overall, unions have resisted efforts to pay higher wages to teachers in high demand, although local unions often informally allow districts to place individuals at a higher step on the salary scale than the step at which teachers would normally enter.[38]

Districts differ in how they distribute pay increases on the scale. In unionized districts, such decisions are reached through collective bargaining. A bargained pay increase of 4 percent applied across the scale gives more experienced teachers higher raises, since they begin with a higher base salary. In contrast, a district seeking to attract new teachers may want to frontload the salary scale, committing a larger share of resources to less-experienced teachers at the lower steps of the pay scale. However, union leaders are typically more experienced teachers and are thus likely to support wage increases that give greater benefit to senior members. The few studies examining the effects of pay distribution have found that higher starting salaries are associated with greater teacher retention.[39] With the retirement of many experienced union presidents, leadership in the union will likely shift to younger members, who may negotiate wage settlements that assign a higher percentage of the overall raise to initial steps on the salary scale.

Pay as an Incentive to Increase Teacher Quality

Only a small number of districts nationwide (including unionized and nonunionized settings) have explored alternative approaches to compensation. Enthusiasm about merit pay waned in the 1970s and 1980s when districts encountered philosophical, political, and logistical challenges to identifying and rewarding high-quality teachers.[40] Unions widely opposed these plans. Few programs that were instituted could reliably distinguish excellent teaching, and many suffered from inconsistent funding. As a result, most merit pay plans faltered and disappeared in the 1980s.[41]

Despite the poor record of merit pay, there is growing interest today in performance-based pay for teachers. This effort assumes that such an approach would attract individuals who seek opportunities to prove their worth and increase their pay more quickly than they could on the single salary scale. Also, advocates believe such an approach would induce current teachers to do better work. New teachers express more interest than their veteran counterparts in experimenting with alternative pay plans, although they, too, raise concerns about how assessments of their performance can be evenhanded.[42] Even experienced teachers are beginning to express more interest in alternative forms of pay than veterans did in previous decades.[43]

The American Federation of Teachers endorsed experiments with teachers' compensation in 2002, although the National Education Association narrowly rejected a similar position in 2000. However, the issue is not simply one of union endorsement or opposition; creating a plan to pay teachers on the basis of their performance is challenging. Even advocates of performance-based pay find it difficult to devise a fair and effective strategy for rewarding successful individual teachers without introducing unwanted competition within schools or discouraging teachers from working with the students who are least likely to show rapid improvement. Faced with such challenges, public schools experimenting with performance-based pay have tended to rely more on school-based rewards than individual rewards. Some reports indicate that such incentives have encouraged teacher collaboration and, by implication, the quality of instruction.[44]

Denver currently is experimenting with a knowledge- and skills-based pay structure, which includes rewards for teachers based on their formal evaluations and their students' achievement.[45] Conceived in the 1999-2000 collective bargaining sessions, ProComp was developed by the Denver Public Schools and the Denver Classroom Teachers' Association. Approved by the DCTA in 2004, ProComp offers teachers opportunities to increase their earnings by completing relevant coursework, earning satisfactory or distinguished evaluations, and demonstrating student attainment of objectives set by teachers and principals. Teachers with unsatisfactory evaluations have their salaries frozen until they receive a satisfactory evaluation.

Additionally, teachers may receive bonuses for working in underperforming schools and in fields with a shortage of licensed teachers. There is no limit on the number of teachers who may receive rewards, the number of bonuses teachers may qualify for in a given year, or the salary level that teachers may attain over their career. Moreover, student growth is not judged solely or even primarily on the state-mandated Colorado Student Assessment Program (CSAP) but on a wider range of objectives established by teachers and administrators.

ProComp offers substantially more earning opportunity to teachers and thus costs the district more. Therefore, full implementation of ProComp depended on voters' passing a mill-levy override in November 2005. Questions about its implementation remain, such as how objectives will be calibrated across grades and schools and how busy administrators will conduct evaluations and evaluate student growth. However, Denver teachers appear optimistic about this reform. In 2003, 89 percent of them supported awarding bonuses to teachers working at schools with high-need students, a practice that most other local unions still oppose. Moreover, ProComp is supported by a nine-year collective bargaining agreement rather than the customary three-year agreement, thus reducing the chance that this reform will be discarded in subsequent negotiations with new and perhaps less-invested participants.[46] The Denver ProComp pay plan is the first in recent years to be introduced in a large U.S. school district. It could improve the quality of the teaching force by attracting and retaining stronger and more effective teachers. Significant challenges to its establishment exist, although organized opposition by the union is not one of them.

Research, therefore, suggests that collective bargaining somewhat influences teacher quality through pay. Studies have shown that collective bargaining leads to modest wage increases. Observational analysis reveals that pay raises have had an inconsistent effect on teacher quality, but surveys of prospective and current teachers indicate that sufficient pay is necessary to attract and retain them in the classroom. By offering beginning teachers wages that are reasonably competitive with those offered by other employers, schools are likely to attract more candidates to teaching. Whether schools will select the highest-quality candidates in that pool is unclear. However, by ensuring that current teachers have an adequate salary, given local costs, collective bargaining may play an important role in providing high-quality teachers the means to remain in their job. Current enthusiasm for incentive pay suggests that new forms of compensation may motivate teachers to increase their skills once in the classroom, and several local unions have been active in devising such performance-based pay plans. As Denver's case demonstrates, such innovations will likely require the joint effort of management and unions, at the bargaining table and during implementation.

WORKING CONDITIONS

Although pay is important, it does not function alone in either drawing teachers into today's classrooms or retaining them once they are there.[47] Working conditions for teachers also affect who enters teaching and who stays.[48] Moreover, extensive research in schools demonstrates that the workplace can spur or impede the development of effective teaching and increase or decrease the possibilities for school improvement.[49]

Prospective teachers consider various working conditions in deciding to take a job. Some are directly addressed in collective bargaining, such as whether the school building is sound and functional, whether teaching assignments and workload are reasonable, and whether time is set aside to prepare for classes and work with colleagues. Some who might become excellent teachers never consider this career because schools—particularly those in large, urban districts—are widely portrayed as inhospitable workplaces. However, those who have chosen to teach recognize how working conditions differ from school to school and district to district, and they often seek out a setting where they can do their best work. In a national study of teacher attrition and mobility, researchers found that almost a third (32.1 percent) of teachers who changed schools cited working conditions as a prime reason for the move.[50] However, much of what matters to teachers, such as the quality of the principal's leadership, lies beyond what the union can effectively address.

All state laws that provide for collective bargaining include some version of "conditions of work" among topics that must be negotiated; thus, many working conditions that matter to teachers are addressed directly or indirectly in collective bargaining. However, those who bargain do not always agree about which topics are legitimate for negotiations and which should be reserved for management. Sometimes school officials resist conceding on certain topics because they think the resulting contract provisions will tie their hands, making it impossible to use educational resources efficiently. However, even when the union wins assurances about more favorable working conditions, the gains may be difficult to enforce and ultimately not provide what the teachers expect.

Facilities and Resources

In deciding whether to teach, prospective teachers factor in the quality of school facilities. In reporting about influences on the quality of their work, current teachers routinely mention whether their school buildings are safe and well maintained, and whether they have the resources they need to teach well. In fact, the evidence of deficiencies is considerable. The General Accounting Office documented serious deterioration of public school facilities, especially in urban school districts.[51] However, collective bargaining has only modestly improved these working conditions, in part because it is so costly to maintain buildings, upgrade equipment, and regularly replenish resources for instruction. But contract provisions about facilities, equipment, and resources also tend to be general and, thus, difficult for teachers unions to enforce.

Teachers are known to spend their own money on resources for their classroom. Based on survey data collected in 2001, the NEA concluded that, on average, teachers that year spent $443 on instructional resources.[52] Another study reports that first-year elementary teachers spend an average of $701 out of pocket for classroom materials.[53] Recently researchers reported that teachers in four school districts (Chattanooga, Tennessee; New York; Seattle; and Washington, D.C.) and the state of West Virginia listed the "lack of resources and materials" among the top five negative influences on their efficacy with students. This led researchers to conclude that "the physical condition of schools and the quality of instructional resources made a tremendous difference in the sense of efficacy that teachers felt."[54]

Moreover, the condition of schools signals to prospective and current teachers the level of regard the public holds for them and their work. Researchers who recently analyzed survey data from K-12 teachers in Washington, D.C., concluded that "facility quality" is an important predictor of teachers' decisions to leave their current position, and that "the benefits of facilities improvement for retention can be equal to or even greater than those from pay increases."[55]

Little evidence suggests that unions and collective bargaining have improved the physical aspects of teachers' work. Some local contracts offer general guarantees. For instance, the Lawrence, Massachusetts, contract stipulates that "whenever possible, the Superintendent will provide" basic services such as "storage space" and "well-lighted lavatories." In other districts management has agreed to provide annual stipends for teachers to equip and restock their classrooms. The Cambridge, Massachusetts, contract provides that teachers be reimbursed up to $450 annually for money spent on instructional materials. However, even in such cases, contract provisions do not guarantee a teacher will have all she needs to teach well.

Class Size

Class size is a contentious issue mandated for bargaining by some states but not others. Teachers and their unions have long sought classes of fewer than 20 to 25 students, arguing that smaller classes enable them to maintain better order, respond to students' work in more detail, and differentiate instruction in response to individual students' varied learning needs.[56] Class size became a growing focus of early bargaining. Lorraine McDonnell and Anthony Pascal found that 20 percent of the districts they studied had class-size provisions in their contracts in 1970; by 1975, 34 percent had them.[57]

Researchers have found evidence that larger class size is associated with increased teacher turnover, suggesting schools may lose their best teachers if their classes are large.[58] However, reducing class size across a school district, even by one or two students, is very costly, and until recently there was no evidence that such reductions lead to better student outcomes.[59] Moreover, some school officials oppose efforts to reduce class size as a union strategy to increase its membership or protect jobs.

Local contracts vary in their approach to class size limits. Some require that a new class be formed when there are even one or two students beyond the negotiated maximum. The Branford, Connecticut, contract, for example, sets strict limits for class size at the elementary (28 students), middle (28 students), and high school (30 students) levels and requires a new class be formed if the size exceeds the limit by two students. Other districts set general goals for class size. The school board in Lawrence, Massachusetts, agrees that it will "work in good faith to reduce class size when facilities become available." In other contracts, management promises to maintain an average class size within a school but sometimes even such guarantees have exceptions. According to the

Coventry, Connecticut, contract, "isolated deviations" from the mandated average of 27 students may occur, but classes are capped at 30 "insofar as possible." The details of class size provisions determine how they will affect classroom teaching, in some cases making it manageable, in others unwisely limiting the flexibility of teachers and administrators to make the best possible use of teaching resources.

Because they can be very specific, contractual guarantees of class size are more likely to be enforced than less specific assurances, such as a pledge to provide sufficient instructional resources. However, bargaining about a topic does not necessarily lead to advances for teachers. Charles Perry's 1979 study reported that, although all nine districts studied had bargained about class size, the unions had "made relatively little concrete progress in achieving definite, enforceable limits on class size or in reducing those limits where they exist." Perry concluded that the "relative weakness" of these provisions resulted from the "substantial economic costs of reducing or even standardizing class size."[60] Subsequent research has concluded that collective bargaining has lowered student-teacher ratios by approximately 12 percent.[61] Public Agenda reports that 86 percent of new teachers say that reducing class size would be a "very effective" way to increase teacher quality.[62] However, there is still no consensus about whether or how such changes benefit teacher quality. Proponents argue that smaller classes attract more job candidates and permit better instruction, while opponents contend that spending money to reduce class size is not the best use of scarce financial resources.

Preparation Time

Many districts bargain about whether to provide nonteaching time for teachers to prepare for class, grade papers, and meet with colleagues or parents. Because of their teaching schedule, secondary school teachers routinely have had "prep" periods for such work; elementary teachers have more recently won the right to such nonteaching time. As with class size, an argument can be made that preparation time leads to improved instruction, although opponents sometimes charge the time is unnecessary or misused.

Unionized teachers have, on average, 4 percent more preparation time than nonunionized teachers,[63] although this difference would likely be greater without the spillover effects mentioned earlier. Some contracts guarantee regular nonteaching time for all teachers, while others offer no such assurance. For example, the Malden, Massachusetts, contract specifies that teachers will have one preparation period per day "when scheduling permits." Some contracts specify how preparation time can or must be used. The Stonington, Connecticut, contract emphasizes that individual and group preparation should occur during this period and permits the principal to tell teachers how to use this time if she or he deems that necessary. Other districts place few constraints on teachers' preparation time. The Philadelphia collective bargaining agreement gives teachers the right to "exercise their professional judgment" in determining how to use their time. Virtually no research exists, however, about whether or how preparation time is used to support effective teaching.

Therefore, despite the obligation to bargain about working conditions that might attract and retain high-quality teachers, local contracts often fail to address those issues. Or, if they do, the contracts provide only general assurances of efforts to improve, which are hard to enforce. Guarantees that teachers will work in clean, maintained, and well-ventilated classrooms are standard in many union contracts, but the realities of decrepit facilities and depleted resources suggest that budget cuts or ineffective bureaucracies limit the implementation of these provisions. Similarly, assurances that teachers will have a role in school-site governance or that they will be assigned to teach within their field of license cannot be taken at face value.

TEACHING ASSIGNMENTS

Unions often are criticized for limiting school officials' right to hire and assign the best-qualified teachers to the schools and students that most need them. This is a particular concern in low-income, low-performing schools, which often experience repeated annual turnover as teachers exercise their transfer rights and move to higher-performing, more affluent schools. These teachers' vacated positions are often filled by inexperienced teachers hired late in the summer. Since virtually all teacher contracts call for layoffs in reverse order of seniority, these same schools are likely to lose the most teachers when enrollment declines or budget cuts reduce a school's teaching positions. In this case, seniority requires that the most recently hired teachers be released first.

Mimicking practices in industry, unionized districts that negotiated about teacher assignment in the early years of collective bargaining typically relied on seniority to determine not only how layoffs would proceed but also which teacher could transfer to another school or, in some cases, claim a junior colleague's position. Those who support using seniority as a criterion in job decisions note that it is objective, beyond the influence of favoritism or patronage. Those who oppose it contend that seniority-based decisions ignore the needs of schools and can undermine ongoing instructional programs. Administrators, such critics argue, should decide who will teach what and where.

Seniority has a prominent role in many union contracts—particularly those in large districts—but many other teacher contracts do not mention seniority as a criterion in teacher assignments, or use it only in conjunction with other factors, such as formal qualifications or programmatic needs of the school. However, reliance on seniority is rooted deeply in school culture, and even when they are not obliged to do so, administrators in bargaining and nonbargaining states use seniority to make difficult decisions that pit teacher against teacher. Teachers with more experience have traditionally been given priority in selecting the most sought-after schools, grades, subjects, and even classrooms. Sometimes such seniority rights are ensured by contract, but often they are not.

Annual Staffing Decisions

In staffing their schools each year, administrators in unionized districts typically complete three separate but related processes. First, they handle the voluntary transfer applications of permanent and provisional teachers who seek reassignment to another school. Second, they place teachers who lack a current position because they are returning from leave or have lost their position because of program cuts. Third, they hire new teachers to fill remaining vacancies. Some contracts specify the order and the schedule by which each process must occur, as well as the role that seniority and qualifications play in how these assignments are made. Usually schools cannot hire new teachers from outside the district until all current teachers have been assigned.

Transfers

In deciding who will be allowed to transfer from one school to another, contracts often say that seniority is to be considered along with other factors, such as qualifications or experience in the position. In some districts the most senior applicant for a position automatically receives the job. In the extreme, contracts grant a senior teacher the right to "bump" any junior teacher from her position, although very few districts currently permit bumping except in the case of layoffs. Rather, they allow senior teachers to transfer only to open positions. When such sequential bumping is permitted it has a cumulative effect; as teachers exercise their bumping rights over time, the most experienced teachers tend to move to the most attractive assignments—the wealthiest schools in a district or the most advanced classes in a department or school—leaving unwanted schools and classes with higher proportions of inexperienced teachers.[64] To the extent that teaching experience is positively related to effectiveness,[65] this practice is unlikely to serve students in underperforming schools and classes well. Some districts have recognized the deleterious effects of seniority-based transfers; in the current Philadelphia contract, labor and management agreed to cap at 50 percent the openings that any school may fill according to seniority.

Many local contracts allow transfers only to open positions and afford seniority little or no weight in transfers. Some contracts leave it to management to decide where teachers applying for transfer will be placed; they can base their decisions on the needs of the schools, without regard to seniority. Often the role of seniority, as specified in the contract, is ambiguous. Toledo, Ohio's, contract states that "seniority . . . shall be the sole determining factor in granting transfers if qualifications are relatively equal," but the agreement does not define relevant "qualifications." Similarly, the contract in Pinellas County, Florida, states that voluntary transfers will be determined by seniority, although "it is understood that each position shall be filled by the best qualified applicant."

A contract may explicitly allow a central office administrator, principal, or school-site committee to choose from among qualified applicants already employed by the district. For example, in Harrisburg, Pennsylvania, the board must post all vacancies and any teacher may apply, but "the selection of the person to fill any vacancy . . . shall be made by the Board and its decision shall be final and not subject to the grievance process." In Rochester, New York, teachers seeking to transfer must file an application to the particular school with an opening that interests them. Each school's planning team then reviews the applications and decides whom to interview. They then rank the candidates and can offer the position to the highest-ranking candidate(s). Although seniority plays no role in voluntary transfers, seniority may be the decisive factor in subsequent placements of teachers who have been transferred involuntarily.

In Montgomery County, Maryland, seniority has little prominence. The contract asserts that it is "in the best interest of the school system and the union" to allow teachers to "seek positions that are the best matches with skills and abilities" and to give administrators and school staff the "most simplified, timely, and open access to the pool of internal and external candidates." As in Rochester, teachers in Montgomery County may not bump colleagues from their positions. However, an individual who has completed at least three semesters of teaching and has "all effective ratings on his/her most recent evaluation" can seek a transfer by attending a job fair and interviewing with school representatives. According to the contract, a school's interviewing team may consider an applicant's seniority but should not give it priority over other criteria. Once the candidate and principal agree to the move, it still must be approved by the district's department of staffing. Although seniority need not be considered in selecting transfers, external candidates cannot be placed in schools until the first round of voluntary transfers, involuntary transfers, and returnees from leave have been assigned.

Assigning teachers who have no position

A second group of teachers to be placed include tenured teachers who have no current position due to a leave of absence, enrollment decline, or changes in their school's program. Sometimes these teachers have been forced to accept an involuntary transfer by their principal. Often placement is determined by seniority. Because school officials are legally obligated to these tenured teachers, they must find them a position. This can pose a serious challenge for schools in districts where teachers are routinely tenured, rarely dismissed for cause, or shuffled from school to school when they do not perform well.

Low-performing, low-income schools, which are most in need of strong teachers, experience many transfers out each year, as teachers vie for positions in other, less difficult schools. At the same time, few teachers are likely to request to transfer into such a school because it is seen as a poor place to work. (Notably, there is tentative evidence that, holding the socioeconomic status of a school's students constant, teachers are less likely to leave low-income schools if they are high-performing or have especially strong leadership and a collegial climate.)[66] Given the relatively large number of openings in unwanted schools, these schools are likely to receive more than "their share" of weak tenured teachers. Meanwhile, prospective teachers from outside the district who would eagerly accept difficult assignments cannot yet be hired.

The role of seniority and other factors

Strict, seniority-based transfers and reassignments can disrupt school improvement efforts and delay hiring new teachers. Notably, however, researchers have found factors beyond collective bargaining that contribute to this delay in large, urban districts.[67] First, state and municipal budgets often are not approved until midsummer, making it hard for districts to predict how many positions they will have and, thus, how many teachers they can hire. As a result, they cannot compete with nearby suburban districts for the most qualified job applicants. Second, antiquated, dysfunctional human resource offices often fail to carry out the transfer and placement of current teachers on schedule, thereby further limiting their chances to compete for the best teachers. Some school districts are currently overhauling their staffing process by renegotiating certain provisions of the collective bargaining agreement and revamping the human resource department. School-site hiring teams are being trained to make efficient and effective staffing decisions on behalf of their school. At the same time, district officials are requiring principals to take greater responsibility for evaluating and dismissing poor teachers, rather than transferring their problems to other schools. The Boston Public Schools provides a good example of the changes underway in some large, urban districts.

The Boston Public Schools

Since they organized to bargain in 1966, teachers in the Boston Public Schools (BPS) have been represented by the Boston Teachers Union (BTU), an affiliate of the American Federation of Teachers. From the start teachers held strong seniority rights. In the mid-1970s, a more experienced teacher could bump a less senior teacher from any position for which she was certified. Before 1952 teachers in Massachusetts were broadly licensed to teach all grades and subjects, and thus, in the early days of collective bargaining, a kindergarten teacher rightfully claimed a physics position at the highly competitive Boston Latin School.

However, since 1985 BPS and BTU officials have gradually reduced the prominence of seniority in staffing decisions. As a first step, they restricted bumping rights so that senior teachers could displace only non-tenured junior teachers. In 2000 negotiations, which nearly led to a strike, principals were given the right to offer letters of "reasonable assurance" to their first-year provisional teachers, protecting them from being bumped.

Formerly, when teachers applied to transfer, the individual with more seniority would automatically get the position. Through bargaining, principals gained the right to interview the three most senior applicants to their schools, thus having the chance to discourage inappropriate transfers. Later, school-site councils gained the right to select from among the three most senior teacher applicants for transfer. Today councils may choose among all tenured applicants. The current contract permits a school to post a position for outside hiring by February 15, when transfers are to begin, if 60 percent of its teachers agree. Also, the school-site council may reject any transfer applicant who has received two unsatisfactory evaluations between September and February. Thus, through negotiations, a teacher's qualifications and fit with a position have become central to all transfer decisions, while the role of seniority and the rights of senior teachers in the voluntary transfer process have diminished.

The assignment process for tenured teachers who lack positions (those returning from leave or those whose positions have been eliminated) also has changed dramatically in Boston. In a process called the "excess pool," such teachers once stated their preferences and were assigned to jobs in order of seniority. Schools welcomed well-qualified applicants returning from leave, but they regarded many participants in the excess pool as leftovers whom the district was obliged to place.

Several problems plagued this process, and both principals and teachers gamed the system to achieve their ends. First, teachers who had been rated unsatisfactory and thus were in danger of dismissal could place themselves in the excess pool and claim a fresh start in a new school. Meanwhile, principals who were unwilling to conduct the formal evaluations needed to dismiss incompetent teachers could assign them to the excess pool through an involuntary transfer. Sometimes a principal persuaded a teacher to enter the excess pool and avoid an unsatisfactory evaluation. This process, informally called "the dance of the lemons," meant that the least attractive schools were routinely staffed by ineffective teachers. Because such receiving schools often had weak principals, they typically became the repository of incompetent teachers.

Recognizing this problem, labor and management in Boston agreed in a subsequent contract that teachers could no longer volunteer for the excess pool. If they failed to find a school that was ready to hire them through the transfer process, they could not change positions. Meanwhile, principals were prohibited from getting rid of teachers by assigning them to the excess pool, unless the teacher's position had been eliminated due to declining enrollments or a change of program. Seniority still plays a role in placing Boston teachers in the excess pool, in that teachers bid on openings in order of seniority and are guaranteed to receive one of their three bids. However, principals and school-site councils can interview the applicants and submit their preferences to the human resource department, which makes the final assignments.

In 2001 Boston's human resource office began to improve its operations substantially and met the schedule for transfer and assignment it had negotiated with the union. However, in 2002 budget approval was delayed, and hundreds of positions remained unfilled when school started in September. Neither the union nor school officials could intervene.

Delayed hiring

Approving voluntary transfers and placing teachers who have no current position can take months to complete in large, bureaucratic districts. When the staffing schedule is further slowed by sluggish personnel practices or protracted budget approval, schools can lose their chance to compete with smaller, suburban districts for new teachers. Even though school officials in nearby suburban districts also must comply with their teachers' contract, it is less likely to include seniority as a prominent criterion for transfers. Personnel offices in the suburbs also tend to be smaller and more nimble, while funding and enrollment are more certain from year to year.

Boston's experience over time is confirmed by Elizabeth Useem and Elizabeth Farley's research on 14 districts, including 6 of the 8 largest districts in the country and 9 suburban Philadelphia districts.[68] Based on interviews and document analysis, Useem and Farley concluded that labor and management can work together to complete transfers early, thus enabling urban districts to compete with suburban neighbors for the most qualified candidates. Therefore, effective staffing of schools—particularly low-performing schools that serve low-income communities—depends on timely transfers, an open hiring process, an efficient human resource department, and attention to the needs of individual schools. If schools are to be well staffed, however, not only must the contract language and central office practices support good assignments, but principals also must evaluate teachers carefully and move to dismiss those who are unsatisfactory.

EVALUATION AND DISMISSAL

Even in unionized districts, teacher evaluation remains the province of management, although many negotiated agreements lay out how teachers are to be observed and assessed. It is the process of evaluation, rather than the substantive judgments that an administrator makes about a teacher's performance, that can be grieved and subsequently reviewed by arbitrators or the courts. State laws generally set a higher standard for dismissing tenured than nontenured teachers because the courts have determined that tenured teachers have a vested property right to a job under the 14th Amendment. Thus, districts must provide due process for all tenured teachers who are dismissed. Some states set the higher standard of "just cause" for dismissal, which generally requires the district to have documented a teacher's failure, provided adequate notice of the dismissal, followed the principles of progressive discipline, and proceeded in good faith.

Given that legal context, local contracts and unions can limit management's success in dismissing weak teachers and improving the performance of others. First, school officials may find the negotiated procedures for reviewing teachers' performance either reasonable or burdensome. Second, contracts may include a rating scheme that provides detailed feedback for all teachers about their performance or distinguishes only among the competent and incompetent. Third, union officials may decide to aggressively defend all members who receive negative evaluations, or they may do no more than protect the procedural rights of their members, as the collective bargaining laws require. Depending on how these factors add up in a district, they can create a situation in which principals regularly assess all teachers and move to dismiss those who are ineffective, or one in which teacher dismissal is a contentious, politically charged event that principals rarely undertake.

Contracts and unions differ markedly in how they treat the evaluation process. Some require that the principal or designee conduct a set number of observations by established dates, hold preobservation and postobservation meetings with the teacher, and submit a written evaluation within a specified period. An administrator's failure to adhere to such a provision, no matter how minor the infraction, could later become the basis of a grievance. These systematic requirements are meant to ensure that teachers will not be subjected to arbitrary or uninformed assessments, although some critics contend they are intended to hamstring administrators.

Other agreements lay out only the general outlines of the process and reinforce the rights of management to determine how it will take place. For example, the Unionville-Chadd's Ford, Pennsylvania, contract does not detail the evaluation process, instead stating, "If the employer makes any change from the evaluation system in place . . . the employer will inform and provide in-service training to the professional staff prior to the implementation." Depending on a principal's view of mandated deadlines, the number of teachers to be reviewed, and the quality of advice and assistance provided by district administrators, he or she may find these requirements fair or burdensome. In all cases, though, management has participated in negotiating them.

Some contracts specify the details of the observation and evaluation instrument itself, although it usually is the product of administrators' work or a joint labor-management committee in the district, rather than the give-and-take bartering of negotiations. The Minneapolis contract includes an extensive, detailed form for conducting classroom visits and reporting information. Nevertheless, Minneapolis administrators clearly retain the right and responsibility to make formative and summative judgments about a teacher's performance. Seattle's contract allows administrators to consider student achievement data in teachers' evaluations. Other contracts simply reference the district's evaluation instrument, including in the agreement only the procedures for evaluating a teacher's work.

Unions with an industrial rather than a reform orientation are likely to insist on having only two ratings—satisfactory and unsatisfactory—in order to discourage more nuanced judgments by administrators. Philadelphia is one such district. However, with increasing use of supervision and evaluation to improve all teachers' practice, some unions have advocated for exchange of information and more rating options. In 2003 Paul Toner, the union president in Cambridge, Massachusetts, initiated a plan to revise the district's evaluation instrument to include five ratings (from "unsatisfactory and lack of satisfactory progress" to "high satisfactory").

Although unions often participate in establishing procedures and shaping the format of evaluations, they are widely thought to have their greatest influence on teacher quality when they defend any and all teachers who receive negative evaluations. In doing so, they not only incur legal costs but also anger members who expect their leaders to hold higher professional standards. Districts that pursue dismissals also must hire lawyers and commit precious administrative time to prepare for an arbitration or court case. Even so, they may ultimately lose the case because of a procedural error—a missed observation, an unsigned evaluation report.

Few critics of teachers unions realize that a union may refuse to defend one of its members. In exchange for the right to bargain on behalf of a district's teaching staff, a local union accepts a legal duty to fairly represent all teachers in the district. However, the AFT and NEA cite case law from the private sector in explaining that this duty of fair representation "does not restrict a union from taking 'a good faith position contrary to that of some individuals whom it represents' or supporting 'the position of one group of employees against that of another.'" The union, they explain, must take an approach that is "well reasoned, fair, and in the best interests of its membership." Thus, "a union has the discretion to refuse to process or pursue a member's grievance, even a dismissal grievance, without violating its duty of fair representation."[69]

Privately, union leaders often explain that they have agreed not to defend members they know to be weak unless these teachers' procedural rights are violated. In exchange, they expect principals to evaluate teachers fairly and responsibly. Although few union leaders make this position public, Paul Toner explained it to the Cambridge Massachusetts Teachers Association in writing: "Grieving the content of an evaluation is difficult unless it is pure fabrication or the administrator makes reference to things that are not properly part of the evaluation process. An arbitrator is not going to rewrite an administrator's evaluation."[70]

Peer Assistance and Review

One of the most successful union initiatives regarding teacher evaluation is Peer Assistance and Review. Initiated in Toledo in 1983, this program engages teachers in the support and review of all teachers new to the district as well as experienced teachers judged to require intervention. Created with management and adopted through collective bargaining, this program selects and trains a group of experienced teachers who leave their classrooms for two years to mentor and evaluate novice teachers. After one year of closely supervising new teachers' work and modeling expert practice, the peer reviewers recommend to a joint committee of labor and management whether each new teacher should be reemployed or dismissed.

The program, which received the Innovations in American Government Award from Harvard University's John F. Kennedy School of Government in 2001, has been shown to yield higher retention rates and more dismissals than comparable districts where administrators are the sole evaluators. Over time Toledo's union and management decided to include in the process experienced teachers about whom administrators and colleagues had concerns. An independent cost-benefit analysis concluded that the Toledo Plan "streamlin[es] contract non-renewal and termination," thus saving $170,991 to $207,214 by the "most conservative estimates."[71] The program proved so successful that it served as the model for comparable efforts in other districts such as Cincinnati, Rochester, and Columbus. The NEA endorsed Peer Assistance and Review programs at its national convention in 1999.

PROFESSIONAL GROWTH

Traditionally, teaching has been a "flat" profession, offering few milestones beyond tenure and little variety in work tasks over the career.[72] When teachers had few professional options outside teaching, this structure worked. Since the mid-1980s, however, teachers and policy analysts have called for more differentiation in the teaching career. Educated women and people of color, traditionally drawn to teaching because they were excluded from other lines of work, now have expanded opportunities. Compared to law or even nursing, the flat structure of teaching offers few goals and leadership roles to strive for. Research on new teachers indicates that the flat structure of teaching is not likely to satisfy and retain them.[73] In today's labor market, teachers want variety in their workplace and are willing to look elsewhere if their school does not provide opportunities for professional development and growth.[74] Collective bargaining may play a role in retaining teachers and increasing their quality as the parties negotiate provisions regarding professional development, induction and mentoring, and career ladders.

The Effect of Professional Development on Teacher Quality

The quality of professional development and its effect on teacher quality have been uneven at best. However, 99 percent of teachers participate in professional development,[75] which aims to increase teacher quality. Thus, it presents an opportunity to improve teaching. Recent research suggests that professional development can promote increased teacher quality when it is embedded in teachers' ongoing classroom practice or focuses on content knowledge for considerable blocks of time over a lengthy period.[76]

Collective bargaining agreements do not specify the content of professional development, but they often restrict the amount of time schools and districts may require teachers to attend. Indeed, school leaders experimenting with reform models are often frustrated by contract provisions that limit how often professional development sessions may occur or how long they may last. Thus, collective bargaining may impede efforts to improve the quality of teachers' instruction by restricting how professional development is carried out. However, considerable dissatisfaction also exists among many teachers about the poor quality of much that passes for professional development.[77] Therefore, when teachers urge their union leaders to limit the time required for professional development, they may be voicing objections to the quality of the training rather than to spending time to improve their practice.

Collective bargaining may also influence teacher quality when it affects the daily schedule for teachers' work. Collaboration among teachers has been shown to facilitate growth in student learning,[78] but sometimes contracts interfere with the flexible scheduling necessary to foster collaboration. For example, some districts strictly limit the number of consecutive classes a teacher may teach. Such restrictions make it more difficult to schedule common planning time for collaboration.

However, collective bargaining has given certain school sites more autonomy in designing professional development. For example, Boston's within-district charter schools, or pilot schools, which were created through collective bargaining in 1994, often require teachers to work four longer days per week so they can release students early on the fifth day and hold intensive, two- or three-hour professional development sessions.

Induction and Mentoring

In response to the influx of new teachers and growing concern about their readiness and ultimate retention, collective bargaining has recently addressed issues of induction and mentoring. Like professional development, the quality of induction and mentoring programs varies widely.[79] Yet recent research has shown that comprehensive induction programs that include time for collaboration and a mentor who teaches the same subject decrease new teacher turnover,[80] although little is yet known about whether these programs lead to improved teacher quality and elevated student performance. Although some induction programs operate at the state level, certain districts have bargained to establish induction and mentoring for new teachers, often designating the criteria for selecting mentor teachers, setting stipends, and defining mentors' responsibilities.

Minneapolis is one such district, having created the Achievement of Tenure Process for New Teachers (A of T) in 2002, outlined in the current collective bargaining agreement. After attending a district orientation, new teachers meet with their mentor and administrators to set professional development goals. One such goal is to develop the professional portfolio required to attain tenure in the district. The district supports this work, releasing new teachers from two days of teaching, with pay, so they can observe effective colleagues. They also receive free professional development for course credit and can enroll in a peer-coaching class that qualifies them for a bonus. They can lease a laptop for three years before tenure, and after receiving tenure, may purchase the computer for $1. These details have been negotiated and established in Minneapolis's collective bargaining agreement and, thus, are the joint responsibility of management and labor.

Career Ladders

Efforts to establish career ladders for teachers were common in the late 1980s, after the 1986 release of *A Nation Prepared* by the Carnegie Commission on Education and the Economy. At the time many districts experimented with new roles that were linked to modest pay increases. However, career ladders languished and disappeared much as merit pay did during the same period.

As with performance-based pay, there is increased interest today in the possibility of career ladders. Research conducted during that time suggested that career ladders might improve teacher quality. Hart and Murphy found that new teachers who were characterized as "high-ability" by their college GPA and principals' ratings favored career ladders more than their lower-ability counterparts.[81] More recently Henke, Chen, and Geis found that about a third of all new teachers and 50 percent of new black teachers wanted to move into school leadership positions.[82] Thus, career ladders may provide recognition and status, which help schools dissuade high-quality teachers from leaving teaching for fields where the incentives and rewards of career advancement are more readily available.

Currently some districts are exploring the possibilities of career ladders in collective bargaining. Rochester was one of the first districts to establish a career ladder that offers roles for lead teachers. Since the late 1980s the Career in Teaching (CIT) program has differentiated teachers into four subgroups: interns, resident teachers, professional teachers, and lead teachers. Lead teachers are released from the classroom part-time to mentor interns (beginning teachers) and coach veteran colleagues whom administrators identify as struggling. Lead teachers evaluate interns and veteran colleagues. In fact, interns cannot move into the resident teacher category without the lead teacher's approval. Resident teachers are required to pursue a master's degree and are reimbursed for their studies. Once they receive tenure, teachers attain "professional" status. As professional teachers they may sit on the CIT panel, which selects and evaluates lead teachers, handles appeals regarding the CIT program, and makes employment recommendations to the school board. Professional teachers may also apply to become lead teachers, who qualify for additional compensation and leadership roles. The CIT receives favorable reviews from new and experienced teachers in Rochester's public schools.

Today the presence of career ladders may influence prospective teachers' job choices more heavily than in the past. In a recent survey of recent college graduates, 70 percent felt that teaching did not offer adequate "opportunities for advancement" while their current jobs provided such prospects.[83] Given the greater mobility of younger workers in today's economy,[84] it may become increasingly important for districts to create new roles if they are to retain high-quality teachers. Unlike their predecessors, today's teachers appear less inclined to stay in the classroom or the teaching profession in general.[85] If collective bargaining can establish new roles and career ladders for teachers, it may attract high-quality teachers to the profession and decrease the likelihood that such teachers abandon the classroom for other lines of work. However, with the exception of a few flagship districts, neither unions nor management has initiated such differentiated career paths.

The National Board of Professional Teaching Standards, proposed by the AFT president Albert Shanker and subsequently supported financially by the AFT and NEA, recognizes outstanding teachers on the basis of their demonstrated skills and knowledge and often rewards them with salary supplements. Recently Daniel Goldhaber and Emily Anthony concluded on the basis of student outcomes that National Board–certified teachers are more effective than applicants who do not receive this certification.[86] In districts such as Compton, Rhode Island, labor and management have collaborated to encourage teachers to apply for National Board certification and have developed specialized roles for those who succeed. Other districts, such as Boston, have relied on the board's intensive selection process to identify teachers who will be mentors or peer reviewers. Such efforts can promote improvement among teachers while recognizing and retaining high-quality individuals. Recent research indicates that National Board–certified teachers also have greater professional mobility and a sense of confidence and authority, which may enhance opportunities for instructional improvement in teachers' districts and schools.[87]

Overall, collective bargaining seems to play an important role in promoting or discouraging greater effectiveness among teachers by setting the parameters within which professional development, induction, and the development of new roles and recognition can occur. Districts and local unions that, through bargaining, sign contracts that restrict professional development and limit the supports and opportunities available to new and experienced teachers may reduce their ability to recruit and retain promising and productive teachers and limit teachers' growth. Collective bargaining that allows for flexible scheduling to facilitate better professional development, encourages investments in new teachers' induction and mentoring, and institutionalizes specialized roles and recognition for high-quality, experienced teachers may well increase teacher quality.

CONCLUSION

Assessing the impact of collective bargaining and unions on teacher quality is especially challenging, given so little research on the subject. No consistent evidence shows that the quality of the teaching force has either improved or diminished as a result of collective bargaining. In part, this is because conducting research about this topic is difficult. However, the findings also are inconclusive because collective bargaining practices and local teacher contracts vary widely. As a result, beliefs about the relationship between teachers unions and teacher quality are shaped far more by rhetoric and ideology than by disinterested, thorough inquiry.

Based on the research conducted, collective bargaining modestly increases teachers' pay. If higher wages lead to higher-quality teachers, then one might conclude that bargaining has a positive effect. Collective bargaining also leads, on average, to decreases in student-teacher ratios. Since smaller class size has been shown to improve student learning, at least in the early grades, one might also infer that this affects teachers' work positively. Further, researchers have found a positive relationship between collective bargaining and increased preparation time for teachers, which many educators believe is essential.

Beyond those basic findings, however, little can be said about the relationship between collective bargaining and teacher quality, except that policy and practice vary widely. Some outcomes of local bargaining, such as those that reinforce the single salary scale, strengthen the district's reliance on seniority, reject differentiated roles for teachers, or guarantee dogged defense for competent and incompetent teachers alike, likely compromise the quality of teaching. Other policies and practices, however, develop when those bargaining the contract recognize that certain features of teaching cannot be addressed with conventional labor approaches. Such approaches support experiments with performance-based pay, create incentives for teachers to work in hard-to-staff schools, limit seniority-based bumping, or create career ladders and differentiated roles for teachers. Provisions like these are likely to attract enterprising individuals who seek opportunities for growth and influence. In the first case, one might argue that collective bargaining negatively affects teacher quality. In the second case, collective bargaining might be credited with improving teachers' skills, understanding, and effectiveness.

What might create the conditions in which bargaining could promote teacher quality? Case studies of progressive reforms suggest that they result from steady, productive labor-management relationships developed over time, not from dramatic, one-time changes in contract language.[88] Often such districts have continuity of leadership on both sides of the bargaining table. The participants have a long-term allegiance to the district, its community, and its students and recognize that respect, candor, and trust are essential in their joint enterprise. Their work is about solving tough problems, not splitting the difference between extreme positions.

However, much can disrupt productive labor relations. Rapid turnover among superintendents or union leaders can derail promising initiatives. Sudden, deep budget cuts can lead to extensive layoffs of teachers and distrust of management. An authoritarian superintendent or a hostile union president can suddenly halt districtwide efforts to improve schooling. A reform approach to collective bargaining requires labor and management to recognize that, if teachers are to work as professionals, they must be treated as professionals. All too often management treats teachers like "hired hands,"[89] and labor treats teachers like factory workers. Neither attitude will lead to enhanced teacher quality.

Many of today's local union leaders have been teaching in their districts since the first collective bargaining agreement was signed in the late 1960s or early 1970s. They remember why particular provisions were bargained and may be reluctant to relinquish hard-won protections. Schooled in adversarial labor tactics, they may distrust innovative approaches to resolving differences, such as interest-based bargaining,[90] and avoid unconventional subjects, such as peer review or professional development. However, this generation of union leaders is about to retire and a new cohort of leaders—without the tie to the past—may emerge.

Whether union leaders a decade from now will be more progressive than their predecessors depends on what teachers want from their unions and how management acts. Teachers entering schools today hold different views about unions than do the veteran teachers they are replacing.[91] These new entrants are less concerned about job security and more interested in career development. They are less certain that unions are essential and more likely to believe that schools should decide, one by one, how to operate. As the center of gravity in the teaching force shifts toward less-experienced teachers, the kind of union leader these teachers prefer may also shift. It is not yet clear whether a new, progressive union leader will emerge to match the views of these teachers.

In part, the outcome will depend on what management does. Unions first gained strength among teachers because school officials were perceived as arbitrary, punitive, and politically influenced. Today a superintendent who acts with disrespect and disregard for the professional and personal needs of teachers can easily drive them to believe they need a hard-line union leader. When teachers perceive that school administrators are acting high handed, they often support, however reluctantly, the personalities and principles of conventional labor. Thus, although turnover in the teaching force could lead to flexible and creative labor-management relations serving students and teachers, this outcome is by no means certain.

Some union critics are impatient with the slow and unpredictable course of change. They contend that unions introduce undue barriers for administrators seeking to improve teacher quality, and argue that decisions about teacher pay, hiring, assignment, working conditions, professional support, and dismissal should be in the hands of management. However, collective bargaining is a well-established policy that could not easily be repealed. Moreover, schools will not improve without teachers' dedicated efforts. Even if collective bargaining were eliminated immediately and administrators were solely in charge, there is no guarantee that teacher quality would improve. There is no evidence that school management was more effective before collective bargaining or that schools in nonunionized states have improved teacher quality. Ensuring that better teachers are hired, that they are assigned sensibly, and that they are supported in their work will require far more than changes in the states' collective bargaining laws.

On the whole, it appears that collective bargaining can influence teacher quality. By focusing on what induces strong candidates into the classroom, what helps teachers become more effective on the job, and what sustains them over a career, collective bargaining could play a central role in increasing teacher quality. Prospective and current teachers today entertain a range of career options outside teaching. If they are dissatisfied, they may leave the classroom without looking back. To support and retain high-quality teachers, unions and districts may have to bargain about new ideas and new approaches in new ways.

The authors thank John Papay, who contributed to the contract analysis presented in this chapter.

CHAPTER SIX

Are Teachers Unions Good for Students?

DAN GOLDHABER

This chapter's title is a fundamental and much-debated question. The question also generates a great deal of political controversy: some education reformers point toward unions and the contracts that they strike with school systems as impediments to educational reform and improvement, while others suggest that teachers unions not only are essential to the improvement of teaching as a profession but also directly benefit students by providing teachers with a stronger collective voice. As it turns out, the rhetoric on both sides of this issue rests on rather shaky empirical grounds. Relatively little empirical work directly links unionization and student achievement. Furthermore, the causal impacts of teachers unions on students are difficult to establish since unions do not arise randomly. Consequently, findings from research that directly links unionization to student outcomes are open to interpretation.

The mission statements of the two large teachers unions—the National Education Association (NEA) and the American Federation of Teachers (AFT)—explicitly address the issue of educational improvement, not just the well-being of their members. The NEA mission states that one goal of the union is to "advance the profession of education," while the AFT mission includes the goal of "strengthen[ing] the institutions in which we work."[1] Moreover, the rhetoric used in debates over teacher contract issues is frequently tied up in discussions about what is best for students rather than what employees (teachers) value. A recent statement by a union representative discussing a labor dispute in Wisconsin aptly illustrates this point:

> What we see is a steady erosion of support for the people who have made our school system one of the very best in the nation. These declin-

ing salaries will cause the best of our teachers to leave the state or leave the profession, and will deter the best and brightest of our young people from choosing the education profession. If the quality of our teachers declines, so will the quality of the education this state provides its children.[2]

Of course, the view that teachers unions are primarily interested in promoting student achievement is not universally held; for example, the former education secretary Rod Paige referred to the NEA as a "terrorist organization" when criticizing it for obstructing key education reforms.[3] Some contend that public schools are impervious to reform in the absence of outside pressure, and that this is in no small part due to the influence of teachers unions that effectively circumvent any major reform efforts. For example, John E. Chubb and Terry M. Moe argue in *Politics, Markets, and America's Schools* that teachers unions "wage a war against principals—restricting their discretion, stripping them of managerial and policymaking power . . . purposely prevent[ing] [them] from staffing the organization and arranging incentives according to his best judgment."[4]

Despite the strength of the rhetorical debate about unions, from a theoretical perspective there is no definitive reason to believe that unions would either promote or hinder student achievement. We might expect unions to promote achievement by increasing the attractiveness of the teaching profession (e.g., by raising salaries), forcing major workplace issues to be addressed, or promoting the importance of education to the public at large. Conversely, unions might ultimately detract from achievement if they protect poor performers, cause educational resources to be misallocated, or lead to inefficient workplace rules or practices.

There is relatively little empirical work that directly links unionization and student achievement. Furthermore, the causal impacts of teachers unions on students are difficult to establish since unions do not arise randomly. Consequently, findings from research that directly links unionization to student outcomes are open to interpretation.

This chapter will explore the various ways in which teachers unions might affect students, review some of the existing empirical literature on this link, and ask what we still need to learn about the relationship between teachers unions and student achievement. First, however, a brief history of teachers unions is warranted.

HISTORY OF TEACHERS UNIONS

The National Education Association and the American Federation of Teachers are the two major U.S. teachers unions. Both grew out of other organizations and were formally founded in the early twentieth century: the NEA in 1907 and the AFT in 1916.[5] As schooling moved from a traditional one-room-schoolhouse structure that was locally controlled and community based to one of increased district centralization, superintendents were given greater authority to hire and fire school personnel, thus eroding individual teacher autonomy.[6] In large part, the demand for increased teacher professionalism came from the Progressive movement's call for reform. Progressives wanted U.S. youth to be Americanized through a standardized school curriculum set forth by cooperating teachers and schools. Teachers were also increasingly expected to be college educated, which led to many lower- and working-class women being pushed out of the profession because they could not afford to attend universities.

Along with the issues associated with professionalism, centralization made teachers' lives more complex. When districts in larger cities began to centralize, teachers were often transferred to schools across the city, which was especially challenging for female teachers. In the early 1900s many property owners would not rent apartments to single women, who therefore found it difficult to live on their own. The problems associated with teacher transfer became a key impetus for teachers to join a union. Although there are some differences between the two major unions (discussed briefly below), generally speaking, the teachers union movement began as a reaction to some of these changes occurring in K-12 schooling. The union foci of making the administration of schools more democratic and increasing teacher compensation (salary and benefits) are often referred to under the broad umbrella of efforts to "professionalize" teaching.[7]

The NEA began as a professional association that was affiliated with the American Legion. In the early stages the NEA focused on the importance of teachers demonstrating professionalism, culture, and competence. The NEA fought for both increased teacher salaries and increased teacher education requirements to help ensure the professional status of teachers. The AFT was founded in collaboration with the AFL-CIO and differentiated itself from the NEA by defining itself as the people's union rather than as a "professional" association. The AFT leadership did not believe that professionalism had benefited the majority of teachers.[8]

The number of unionized teachers grew steadily throughout the twentieth century, from roughly 2,000 (the total of both NEA and AFT membership) in 1900 to more than four million today. Union tactics, however, differed in some important ways. In particular, the AFT was initially much more willing than the NEA to use the power of collective bargaining—in which an organized body of teachers negotiates with the district on the conditions of employment—which became possible (though not employed) everywhere in 1962 when President Kennedy signed Executive Order 10988, allowing public employees to collectively bargain for salary and benefits.[9] Collective bargaining changed the relationship between teachers and administrators and dramatically increased AFT membership.[10] In fact, in the 1960s the NEA denounced the collective bargaining tactics of the AFT, fearing that they would decrease professionalism, and declared itself a white-collar union that was above such traditional labor union tactics. The NEA also denounced the AFT connection with the AFL-CIO, claiming that it would destroy teachers' independence.[11] However, when the AFT achieved successes through its use of collective bargaining, the NEA also decided to pursue collective bargaining tactics as a key part of their labor negotiations. While the collective bargaining tactics of the two teachers unions have been similar over the past 30 or so years, it was not until 2001 that the two unions formally agreed to begin to collaborate on issues of common interest. Currently the AFT is the smaller of the two unions with a little 1.3 million members, the NEA's membership of more than 2.7 million.[12]

Although the NEA calls itself a professional organization rather than a union, the two organizations play very similar functional roles. Both have been large, relatively strong labor unions for 30 years. Both have built their power around collective bargaining muscle, legislative brokering, and the sheer scale of their memberships. The AFT membership is more concentrated in large urban areas, whereas the NEA is more suburban and rural in nature; however, at the district level, bargaining approaches and contract demands are much more a product of the specific characteristics of the teachers represented than of the union affiliation of those teachers.[13] Both unions tend to oppose some types of school reform, such as vouchers that allow public monies to be used for private schooling,[14] but their positions do vary somewhat on the general issue of school choice (beyond vouchers) as well as on other educational reforms.

The organizations were actually close to a merger in 1998, drawn by the prospect of a union that would represent (at that time) 3.3 million members comprising 85 percent of public school teachers. NEA member delegates did not approve the terms of the merger, however. At this point there is no sign of the national organizations uniting, but numerous local affiliates and three state affiliates have merged.[15]

WHAT DO (TEACHERS) UNIONS DO, AND HOW MIGHT THEY AFFECT STUDENT ACHIEVEMENT?

A union is "an association of employees whose primary goal is to improve the well-being of its members. A union pursues its members' interests by acting as their exclusive agent in collective bargaining and via the political process. Union effects on wage and non-wage outcomes include both monopolistic and competitive aspects, or, more precisely, aspects that are both consistent and inconsistent with economic efficiency."[16] A significant body of both theoretical and empirical research investigates the role that unions play in labor markets.

Simple economic theory unambiguously predicts that unions should impact labor markets by restricting employment and raising compensation for union members. This theory is difficult to test for a variety of reasons, but chiefly because of the problem of isolating the "union effect" from other factors related to unionization. For example, unions might be more likely to form or be adopted by employees with particular attributes or in certain types of markets or industries. One would not want to misattribute the effect of employee or industry type to unionization.

Estimating the impact of unions is also challenging because their effects may spill over to nonunion employees. One study by Henry S. Farber and one by H. Gregg Lewis, for instance, identify two types of spillovers that unions have on nonunion wages. First, unionization has the potential to increase union wages and decrease union jobs, which in turn would increase the number of workers seeking jobs in nonunion firms or industries.[17] A second, less direct effect is that unions may change nonunion labor relations through a threat effect—that is, nonunion firms and employee relations may be impacted by the *potential* of unionization.

Theoretical and empirical research has illuminated some of the other ways that unions affect the labor market beyond the simple economic model, generating potentially positive and negative productivity effects. Unions may be effective at improving working conditions and reducing quits by allowing workers a "voice" as an alternative to leaving.[18] Employers left to their own devices may not become aware of employee dissatisfaction (perhaps because the costs to employers of learning this information are high). Unions, by voicing the issues leading to dissatisfaction, potentially serve the interests of employers by providing information to them that is used to create a more satisfying work environment, which leads to a reduction of costs associated with employee turnover. In short, unions provide a vehicle for employees to express their collective views, and this voice may forestall leaving.

Some research, by contrast, suggests unions negatively affect worker productivity by increasing absenteeism and diminishing the effectiveness of managerial practices designed to boost productivity.[19] There are, for instance, classic examples of negotiated "sick days" that end up being treated as vacation time, and labor agreements that require employers to use employees with specific credentials for even simple tasks that could be completed by any employee, both of which raise the cost of doing business.

Research on the net productivity impact of unions is mixed,[20] but there exists ample research focusing on the effects of unionization on working conditions and wages. The wage premium (i.e., the amount that unionized firms are estimated to pay in wages over that paid in nonunionized firms) associated with unionization is estimated to be in the 10 to 25 percent range.[21] Again, as discussed above, part of this premium may be because of the type of employee or industry rather than because of unions themselves. Research focused on disentangling the effects of unions on wages from other factors[22] suggests that the wage premium that can be *causally* attributed to unionization is in the neighborhood of 10 percent.[23]

Private-sector union membership has declined precipitously over the last three decades: roughly one in three workers belonged to a union in the late 1950s and early 1960s; as of 1998 fewer than one in ten workers are union members.[24] These numbers contrast sharply with public-sector unionization, which has been growing: in 1956, 12 percent of public-sector employees belonged to a union; by 1998 that number had grown to 39 percent. Much of this growth occurred in public schools.[25]

What impact might unions have in the context of education? Given what we know about the impacts of unions in general, we might hypothesize both direct and indirect as well as short- and long-term effects of teachers unions. Furthermore, one might imagine that the power of the union in a district is related to the extent to which the union's workforce is unionized (e.g., percentage of teachers that are unionized) and whether districts are covered by collective bargaining agreements.

The distinction between *unionization* and *collective bargaining* is conceptually important. On the one hand, if teachers exert influence on districts primarily as a consequence of demonstrated membership in a union, then state-level collective bargaining laws are potentially of little consequence. We might, for instance, expect to observe educational policies and practices that are similar in districts with similar union representation or strength (i.e., the percentage of teachers in a district belonging to, or active in, a teachers union). On the other hand, if teachers' influence comes primarily through the establishment of collective bargaining agreements, then state laws governing such agreements are likely to be far more important. In this case one might expect districts with very different union representation to have similar policies and practices if they fall into the same collective bargaining category: they have it or do not.

In practice it is difficult to isolate the effects of unionization from those of collective bargaining, and the two may in fact be interrelated; for example, states with strong teachers unions are likely to lobby for collective bargaining.

For this reason most literature does little to distinguish between these effects, and, unless otherwise noted, I will treat the discussion of the direction of the effects of unionization (i.e., whether they raise or lower student achievement) as consistent with the effects of collective bargaining.

One consequence of collective bargaining is that district-union contracts must be legally explicit and account for myriad potential differences between the two parties. Such a system may act to create wedges between management and employees;[26] change the mix of resources that are used in the school;[27] limit beneficial school reform strategies; cause districts to adopt less than ideal personnel policies;[28] or raise the cost of teacher dismissal, thus effectively protecting weaker teachers—any or all of which may result in inefficiencies in the delivery of education.

There is some evidence that unions lead to "backloading" of teacher pay—that is, increases in pay tend to go to more senior teachers at the expense of more junior teachers.[29] Unions also support teacher tenure, which greatly increases the cost of teacher dismissal. While not solely related to teacher tenure, the New York State School Board Association released estimates that in 1994 it cost an average of $177,000 and took approximately 455 days to fire a teacher; if the teacher appealed that decision, this cost increased to $317,000.[30] Finally, unions tend to be in favor of and lobby for seniority transfer policies, and such policies tend to have a strikingly negative impact on the quality of teachers serving in disadvantaged schools.[31]

A striking example of the domino effect that seniority transfer policies can have on a whole district comes from San Diego City Schools, which allows senior teachers within the district to apply for open positions through much of the summer prior to the start of a new school year. Such policies not only limit the ability of school system managers to assign the teachers they deem most appropriate for particular schools to those schools, but also they likely hurt the district's ability to recruit new teachers because the district cannot finalize assignments for newly hired teachers until the seniority transfer process has closed.[32] Consequently, teacher applicants wishing to work in San Diego may not know where to look for housing until immediately before they begin teaching.

While most of the anecdotal evidence about teachers unions focuses on their negative effects on personnel policies and teacher freedom, it is conceivable that the "exit-voice" role of unions discussed above also holds true for teachers unions. There is also some evidence that district-union bargaining and employment contracts have changed over time, and that some new district-union relationships have concentrated on "reform-style bargaining" that is more focused on issues related to student achievement.[33] Thus, the exit-voice argument and reform-style union model suggest that the existence of teachers unions might actually enhance educational productivity by providing teachers with a means of expressing discontent. This might lead school systems to alter policies, such that teacher discontent, absenteeism, and turnover are reduced and teacher productivity and student achievement are enhanced.[34] Julia Koppich argues that unions may enhance student achievement, pointing to cases where the unions bargain over issues other than just compensation. For instance, in Minneapolis, the union and district are working together to change the teacher tenure process, and in Montgomery County, Maryland, the two are working to develop a peer-review system for teachers. Some quantitative studies show that teachers unions affect the allocation of school resources, for instance by increasing the amount of paid preparation time and decreasing the student-teacher ratio.[35]

The above examples suggest that unions do lead to changes in school policies and practices; what is less clear, however, is whether these changes are actually productive or cost-effective ways of moving schools toward increased student achievement. It is also worth noting the implicit assumption of the exit-voice argument in the context of education: if these types of investments (and other changes in school district policies or practices) are in fact appropriate and productive in enhancing student achievement, then unions are in fact more in tune with what ultimately increases student achievement than are school districts (which have the option of establishing personnel policies in line with teacher desires with or without the existence of union pressure). Regardless, whether union influences on personnel policies are a net positive or negative on student achievement depends on the information and preferences of both teachers and district administrators, as well as the alignment of these preferences with student achievement. This means the short-term personnel- and pay-policy impacts of unions cannot be theoretically determined.

Unionization and collective bargaining may also have several longer-term, more indirect impacts on education. The most obvious potential long-term impact of teachers unions is that their existence helps to raise the salaries of the teaching profession above what they otherwise would be. As discussed above in the context of unions in general, this may occur directly through negotiations but also via indirect threat effects.

Higher (relative to salaries outside of the teaching profession) teacher salaries should increase interest in teaching, which one might guess would lead to an expansion of the labor pool from which school systems may select employees, and ultimately to higher-quality teachers. While this is a likely outcome, it is not a given, since the quality of the teacher selection process used by schools is suspect,[36] and the link between teacher compensation and teacher quality depends on the quality of this selection process—that is, if district human resource departments do not do a good job in selecting among job applicants, the quality of the applicant pool may not matter much.

Another potential upside of unionization for public education is the role that unions may play in promoting the importance of education to the public at large, which could lead to increases in educational spending.[37] On the one hand, the mobilization of the citizenry can be quite important in determining educational investments, particularly when voter turnout is low—as is often the case for school-related issues such as budget referenda.[38] Most of the evidence on this issue (discussed below) does show unionization to positively impact educational spending; however, the findings on the effects of this increased spending are mixed. On the other hand, it is entirely possible that on the whole (as opposed to just those districts with collective bargaining agreements), unions act to undermine the support of public education and spending. If teachers unions are thought to make public education less productive, the public may be less willing to provide tax support to increase K-12 expenditures.

Unions may have more direct long-term effects through their political power to influence school reform efforts. For instance, unions have tended to oppose reforms such as merit pay,[39] and recent research suggests that whether a district has collective bargaining is an important determining factor in the likelihood of that district employing a merit pay system.[40] Similarly, unions typically oppose school choice:[41] their position on vouchers that can be used to direct public monies into private schools is unequivocally negative, while their positions on other forms of school choice, such as inter- or intradistrict choice or charter schools, are more nuanced in the sense that they do not unequivocally oppose these types of choice policies.

To know whether the union influence on education reforms is helpful or harmful to student achievement, it is first necessary to know the effects of particular reforms on students. Research on matters such as the educational impact of school choice or pay reform policies on the educational system reaches mixed conclusions, so it is not clear whether the promotion of or opposition to such policies by teachers unions promotes or hinders the cause of furthering student achievement.

What should be clear at this point is that there is no definitive a priori expectation of the direction of the union effect on student achievement. Furthermore, the study of unionization's effects on students is quite complicated, given that there are potentially both short- and long-term effects of unions on school systems, and that the effects of union threats may influence nonunion (noncollective bargaining) school districts—perhaps causing them to have de facto policies and practices that are similar to districts where union influence is stronger.

The literature on unions' impacts on student achievement, described in the next section, only starts to answer the question posed at the beginning of this chapter: Are teachers unions good for students?

EMPIRICAL RESEARCH ON TEACHERS UNIONS' IMPACT ON STUDENT ACHIEVEMENT

The evidentiary base for drawing conclusions about the student achievement impacts of teachers unions is quite thin. However, a small body of qualitative, case study, research, and quantitative work does exist. I focus on the quantitative work here, which is quite varied in quality and yields mixed findings on union effects. The divergence of findings in the empirical literature may be explained by a variety of factors, including the time horizon the researchers focus on (since "snapshot looks" at union impacts may fail to fully account for their long-term effects); the interpretation of likely causal linkages between union impacts and student achievement, such as the impacts of increased teacher salaries on students; the comparison groups or characterization of unionization (e.g., collective bargaining versus non–collective bargaining districts or the percent of unionization) used by researchers; and the research methodologies and samples used by researchers. I describe these issues below in the context of reviewing the findings on the effects of teachers unions on student achievement.

The most positive findings for the effects of unionization tend to be based on state-level analyses. For example, a study by F. Howard Nelson and Michael Rosen focuses on the link between average student test scores and level of union impact as defined by either collective bargaining (where districts are bound to negotiate a contract with the union) or meet-and-confer (where districts are required to meet with union representatives but are not required to negotiate a final binding contract with them) agreements in each state.[42] They use statewide averages of both fourth grade National Assessment of Educational Progress (NAEP) reading scores and SAT scores to compare student performance between states that have (as determined by the authors) high levels of union impact, medium levels of union impact, and no union impact. States with "high" levels of union impact are those where 90 percent of the teachers are covered by collective bargaining or meet-and-confer agreements; states with "medium" levels of union impact are those where 50 to 90 percent of the teachers are covered by either collective bargaining or meet-and-confer agreements; and states where fewer than 50 percent of the teachers are covered by collective bargaining or meet-and-confer contracts are considered "nonunion" states.

The Nelson and Rosen research suggests that states with a high level of collective bargaining have significantly higher student achievement. For example, point estimates suggest that if you move from a nonbargaining state to a state with a high level of bargaining, average SAT scores will rise from 936 points to 979 points. While the results of this study are striking, it is important to note the possibility that the study suffers from "aggregation bias"—that is, the findings attributed to the effect of unionization are actually related to other state-level factors that are not included in the statistical model.[43]

The potential problem inherent with state-level analyses of the effects of unionization is that one must buy into the notion that the variables in the model adequately account for all the major factors that influence student achievement (aggregated to the state level). If the variables do not, then any unaccounted-for effects end up as part of the error term, and if these variables are correlated with the measures of unionization, then a key assumption of standard statistical models is violated and the estimates of the impact of unionization are incorrect.

The control variables included in the above study (e.g., state average per-pupil expenditure and student and population demographic factors) certainly account for much of the parental, community, and state policy influence on student achievement, but likely not all. And, as Eric A. Hanushek et al. point out, if an omitted factor is at the state level, such as state education policies, aggregation of variables to the state level will tend to bias the effects of schooling variables upward.[44]

Like Nelson and Rosen, Lala C. Steelman et al. examine the relationship between statewide unionization measures and averages of students' SAT and ACT performance. To indicate unionization levels in their regression models, the authors use a percentage that describes the number of teachers in each state who were represented by either collective bargaining or meet-and-confer agreements.[45] Also like Nelson and Rosen, the authors find (in most model specifications) that greater collective bargaining coverage increases student achievement.[46] To quote the study's authors, their findings "challenge the position that teacher unions depress student academic performance." They suggest that the link between unionization and achievement is a result of unions securing better pay and working conditions, which in turn attracts better teachers, and of unions pressing for smaller classes, lighter teaching loads, and increases in the standards for teacher licensing, all of which not only raise the "status of teachers but also the educational climate to which students are exposed."

Some anecdotal evidence suggests that the results reported in the two studies above are related to the aggregation of data to the state level, as a microlevel study by Michael Kurth that also focuses on SAT scores finds contrary results. The Kurth study examines the decline in SAT scores between 1972 and 1983, focusing on three possible explanations for the decline: a changing social environment (measured by the number of working women, urbanization, and divorce rate), a decrease in financial resources devoted to education (measured by local funding levels and consolidation), and the emergence of militant teachers unions (measured by the percentage of teachers covered by a collective bargaining agreement). In contrast to the state-level studies discussed above, Kurth finds that collective bargaining has a statistically significant negative impact on SAT scores, with average math and verbal SAT scores that are respectively 8.3 percent and 6.8 percent lower in states with collective bargaining than in states without collective bargaining.[47]

The main mechanism by which teachers unions are thought to aid student achievement is through increases in teacher quality that arise as a consequence of increases in teachers' salaries. Not surprisingly, quantitative research finds—consistent with the broader literature on unions—that unionization raises teachers' salaries.[48] Randall W. Eberts and Joe A. Stone, for instance, estimate that being a member of a teachers union raises salary anywhere from 7 to 21 percent. Furthermore, in some of their statistical models, they explicitly attempt to account for the possibility that union wages and membership are simultaneously determined—that is, the decision to join a union is contingent on the salary (perhaps due to a union/nonunion wage differential) and that salaries are, at least in part, dependent on the strength of unions. Failure to account for this possibility would likely overstate the impact of unions on salaries.[49]

It is not clear, however, that increases in salaries translate (at least directly) into increases in student achievement.[50] In fact, one might imagine that increases in educational resources are only one of three very important ways in which teachers unions (and collective bargaining) influence education, the others being their impact on policies and practices influencing the way in which resources are used, and on the educational process (the practices within schools) itself. For example, some evidence shows that much of the increases in teacher salaries in unionized districts goes to the back end (that is, they are awarded to more senior teachers) of the teacher salary schedule, but it is unclear whether these increases in salary have much impact on teacher effectiveness.[51]

A far more statistically sophisticated "black-box study"—meaning the research focuses on the relationship between unionization/collective bargaining and student achievement without assessing the reasons for the causal link between the two—by Caroline Hoxby finds significantly negative student achievement effects associated with teachers unions, despite increases in educational spending.[52] These findings are consistent with the notion that unions do serve to increase teachers' salaries but that these pay increases do not translate into increased teacher quality and student achievement.

Hoxby uses longitudinal U.S. census data from 1972, 1982, and 1992 to examine the relationship between school-level inputs and student dropout rates in unionized and nonunionized districts.[53] Unionized districts were defined as those where collective bargaining was reported, a contractual teacher agreement exists as a result of collective bargaining, and a teachers union exists with at least 50 percent of eligible teachers participating. A key aspect of this study is that Hoxby explicitly tries to account for the possibility that unionization is "endogenous"—that is, the level of unionization in a school district may be related to at least some key determinants of student achievement that are not accounted for in the statistical model.[54] The problem of endogeneity is similar to the issue of aggregation bias discussed above. In particular, the potential problem is that factors other than unionization are inappropriately attributed to unions.

Hoxby's study suggests that unionization leads to increased school spending (by about 12 percent), which is used to fund reductions in student-teacher ratios (by about one student per teacher) and increased teacher pay (by about 9 percent). But the increased spending does not seem to result in increased student performance, as unionized school districts have dropout rates that are 2.3 percent higher, all else equal, than nonunionized school districts. Hoxby draws the conclusion that the key difference between unionized and nonunionized districts is that increases in school resources do not matter in unionized districts because there is no "input efficacy." Unions appear to be primarily rent seeking: they raise school budgets and inputs while lowering student achievement. Hoxby's finding that unionization actually harms students, despite additional spending, suggests that unions are leading to changes in educational policies or practices that are counterproductive to student achievement. Unfortunately, it is not possible from a black-box study to determine how unionization changes the schooling process, or whether the effects might be different for different types of students.

Eberts and Stone use the New York State Department of Education data in a cross-sectional analysis to estimate the effects of unionization on state outcome variables.[55] This study is more nuanced than the Hoxby work in the sense that the authors use a multistep approach that allows them to estimate not only the direct effects of collective bargaining but also the effect that this process has on education through its impact on the inputs into the educational process. For example, they relate educational input and process variables—such as teacher education levels and the percentage of teacher time spent on instruction and class preparation—to student achievement and the impact of collective bargaining on these input and process variables. In doing so, they can trace out the pathways of effects by estimating how they change the input and process variables and then how these variables are predicted to impact student achievement. In addition, they estimate the impacts of bargaining on students of varying achievement levels. While the Eberts and Stone study provides a more nuanced look at the effects of unionization than the Hoxby study, it is less statistically sophisticated than Hoxby in addressing the potential of endogeneity.[56]

Eberts and Stone find the total (direct and indirect) effect of collective bargaining agreements is to raise student achievement by about 3 percent over that of districts without such agreements. However, this increase in achievement comes at a cost, as the operating expenses in districts with such agreements are about 15 percent higher per pupil than in comparably achieving districts without such agreements.

An interesting finding from this study is that the effects of bargaining are not the same for all students.[57] The overall 3 percent increase in student achievement is driven mainly by a large 7 percent increase in the achievement of students whose test performance is close to the mean. Students who are either well below or well above the mean level of achievement are marginally disadvantaged by the existence of collective bargaining agreements. The authors hypothesize that the divergent effects for students who fall at different points along the achievement distribution result from a standardization of teaching practices in collective bargaining districts such that students at the margins get less-specialized attention for their unique needs.

Eberts and Stone and the other studies reviewed in this section provide the beginnings of a multifaceted picture of the various impacts of unions on student achievement. But, as Table 1—which provides a summary of the above studies—suggests, the existing studies provide a mixed portrait of the role that unions play in influencing student achievement. Clearly, we are far from having the information that might be required to make well-informed policy decisions regarding unionization or collective bargaining. In the concluding section below, I describe the holes in the research and the data that would be necessary to begin filling them.

WHAT DO WE STILL NEED TO LEARN ABOUT THE EFFECTS OF UNIONS?

What do we still need to learn about the effects of unions? The answer is, quite a lot. The existing literature is hardly conclusive in regard to the net impact of unions on student achievement, and it provides little insight into the specific ways in which unions directly or indirectly influence schools in both the short and long terms. The one finding that the few existing teachers union studies seem to agree on is that unionization tends to lead to increases in school spending. Given the great deal of disagreement in the literature about whether or how

TABLE 1

Author(s)	Year	Aggregation Level	Attempt to Correct for Endogeneity	Findings
Nelson and Rosen	1996	State	No	• States with high level of collective bargaining have sig. higher student achievement. • If one moves from a nonbargaining state to a state with a high level of bargaining, avg. SAT scores will rise from 936 points to 979 points.
Hoxby	1996	District	Yes	• Per-pupil spending increases by 12.3% when teachers unionize, $p<.001$. • In unionized schools inputs do not matter, no "input efficacy." • In unionized schools dropout rates are 2.3% worse than in nonunionized schools.
Eberts and Stone	1984	Student	Not explicitly	• Students sig. below or above average perform better in nonunion districts. • Average students perform 7% better in union districts. • Overall, students in union districts perform 3% better on tests.
Steelman et al.	2000	State	No	• Greater collective bargaining coverage increases student achievement.
Kurth	1987	State	No	• Collective bargaining has a sig. negative impact on math and verbal SAT scores. • Average math and verbal SAT scores are 8.3% and 6.8% lower in states with collective bargaining.

increases in educational spending translate into student achievement gains, it is not surprising that these studies also disagree on this issue.[58]

It is also worth noting that, though they paint differing portraits of the effects of unionization, the studies cited in the previous section do not directly contradict one another, because they focus on different outcomes (varying different tests and dropout probabilities), use different data and data with different levels of aggregation, and define unionization in different ways.[59] The definition of unionization is certainly something that deserves greater scrutiny. The existing literature pays little attention to whether the effect of unionization differs depending on state labor laws, the extent of teachers union membership in districts, or the interaction of the two.

It is likely that in practice some of the questions about the impact of unionization on education cannot be answered in a convincing way. In particular, the potential systemic effects of unions on the public's willingness to support educational spending, on teachers' salaries and the consequent makeup of the teacher workforce, and on educational policies are all areas where unions conceivably play an important role, but there is no counterfactual to study where unions—and the threat effect they may have on nonunion districts—do not exist.[60] Nevertheless, much can be learned about precisely how unions change districts' educational policies and processes in the short term.

Despite the speculation, there is virtually no quantitative evidence about whether collectively bargained contracts in heavily unionized districts differ significantly from those where unions wield substantially less power. Collectively bargained contracts may explicitly extend seniority transfer rights for teachers, but are there any real systematic differences in the way teachers move from school to school in districts without collective bargaining? Contracts may place limits on class sizes or otherwise constrain the way districts allocate resources, but are there differences in practices that appear to be related to the level of unionization? Contracts generally specify the way teachers are evaluated and paid, but do we observe differences in these policies based on union strength in a district? We simply have no good answers for questions like these.

Finally, it is important to remember that virtually all of the research on the effects of unionization was conducted using schooling data set in an educational context very different from the one that exists today. Since the mid-1980s schools have increasingly operated under accountability pressure, and there is significantly greater school choice in the form of inter- and intradistrict choice, charter schools, and vouchers. These changes in educational context may well change the way unions function, and therefore their impacts on student achievement.

Unfortunately, the data necessary to do high-quality microlevel quantitative studies do not currently exist. Probably the best source of information on unionization as well as schooling policies and practices is the Schools and Staffing Survey (SASS). However, this survey does not include information on student achievement, nor does it have detail on the extent of union influence in particular school districts. On the one hand, state databases are a potentially rich source of information on the effects of unionization because states (under NCLB) are now required to test students annually in grades 3 through 8. On the other hand, state databases typically do not have any measures of union power or influence, nor do they have information about the policies and practices in particular districts. Thus, an ideal dataset would combine the achievement information available from state databases with elements of the SASS, and more detail on unionization. In the absence of this type of data, it is unlikely that we will see the type of high-quality research that will allow for well-informed policy judgments about unions or union-related policies (e.g., state policies governing collective bargaining). And until the time that we see this type of research, the weight of the rhetoric on either side of the "unions are good, unions are bad" debate will continue to rest on shaky empirical ground.

CHAPTER SEVEN

Teachers Unions and No Child Left Behind

PAUL MANNA

T his chapter examines the relationship between the No Child Left Behind Act of 2001 (NCLB) and teachers union interests. NCLB is the latest reauthorization of the Elementary and Secondary Education Act of 1965 (ESEA). Teachers unions enjoy opportunities to influence NCLB's implementation because the law relies on policy work in several venues across the country. The nation's thousands of school districts are particularly important. In those locales, union and district officials negotiate and then sign teacher contracts. Historically, these contracts have shaped school governance considerably,[1] and they still wield influence in the present environment.

Overall, I argue that NCLB's multifaceted content and its demanding implementation requirements present opportunities and potential threats to teachers unions as they attempt to advance their members' interests. The chapter develops this argument in four parts. The first part summarizes NCLB's major dimensions, including how the law addresses collective bargaining. The second part describes relationships between the policy venues responsible for carrying out NCLB and how those venues provide opportunities for teachers unions to influence the law. The third part analyzes NCLB's key dimensions through the lens of union preferences. The fourth section discusses how union reformers and federal education officials may affect the future relationship between NCLB and teachers unions.

THE NO CHILD LEFT BEHIND ACT

Using the text of NCLB (PL 107-110) and several sources,[2] this section outlines the components of the law particularly relevant to union interests and educational reform: teacher quality, annual testing, and adequate yearly progress (AYP). But before discussing these issues, I explain how NCLB's authors also addressed collective bargaining in the statute.

NCLB's coverage of teacher quality, testing, and AYP has received much attention since 2001. Among its many pages, the law also contains a short provision that addresses collective bargaining. That passage, which resides in the AYP portion of the law (section 1116d), reads, "Nothing in this section shall be construed to alter or otherwise affect the rights, remedies, and procedures afforded school or school district employees under Federal, State, or local laws (including applicable regulations or court orders) or under the terms of collective bargaining agreements, memoranda of understanding, or other agreements between such employees and their employers." Similar language appeared in the previous ESEA reauthorization, the Improving America's Schools Act of 1994 (IASA). To date, this provision has not provoked much popular press coverage or controversy. As NCLB implementation deadlines approach, however, and if state and federal officials vigorously enforce the law, this part of NCLB will likely become a hotter topic in bargaining discussions.

Also directly relevant to union members are NCLB's requirements that by 2005-06 schools must hire highly qualified teachers in core academic subjects.[3] What "highly qualified" means varies somewhat depending on whether a teacher is new or a veteran, and whether the teacher works in an elementary or a secondary school. The law also contains provisions governing qualifications of paraprofessionals, such as aides hired with funds from the ESEA's Title I.

Generally speaking, NCLB considers regular classroom teachers highly qualified if they hold at least a bachelor's degree, possess full state certification and are not teaching on a temporary license, and demonstrate competency in their subjects. Depending on the grade levels they teach and their experience, teachers can demonstrate subject matter competency by completing a college major in their subject, passing a state-designed test, or, for veteran teachers, by meeting a high objective uniform state standard of evaluation, known as HOUSSE. Because states can define certification requirements and HOUSSE procedures, what it means to be a highly qualified teacher can vary greatly from state to state. Title I paraprofessionals must also be highly qualified, which means they have completed at least two years of college and have demonstrated their skills through an examination or another mechanism proven to uphold rigorous quality standards.

NCLB's requirement for annual student testing is more prescriptive than the IASA of 1994, which included testing requirements but allowed more testing options. NCLB compels states to test all of their 3rd through 8th graders every year in reading and math starting in the 2005-06 school year. NCLB also requires states to conduct math and reading exams at least once during grades 10-12, and, starting in 2007-08, to implement science tests at least once annually for grades 3-5, 6-9, and 10-12. As in the 1994 reauthorization, NCLB lets states decide the material on these tests and the levels of proficiency students must attain.

Further, to guarantee that students of all backgrounds achieve at proficient levels or better, NCLB continues a requirement from the IASA that test scores be disaggregated by student subgroups. This provision prevents overall averages from suggesting all students are learning reading and math when key groups, typically more advantaged students, are driving the results. Thus, NCLB requires that states, school districts, and individual schools report test scores by racial group, gender, economic disadvantage, and disability, as well as for students learning English as a second language.

NCLB diverges from the IASA, however, in what can result from these disaggregated scores. These consequences emerge from NCLB's AYP provisions, which require states to define sufficient progress each year for each participating school and district. In practice, AYP usually refers to the state-defined percentage of a district's and school's students (including student subgroups) who must score at proficient levels on state assessments each year. Regardless of the definitions states have adopted, by the 2013-14 school year NCLB requires all students in all states to perform at proficient levels or better in key subjects, most notably reading and math. Schools must meet several requirements to remain on track for AYP, including that students in all subgroups demonstrate achievement consistent with the state's AYP goals. Put another way, if a school contains four student subgroups in fifth grade (e.g., low income, limited English, disabled, and African American), but only three achieve at expected levels, then the school will not have reached its AYP target. If a school receives Title I funds but fails to make AYP for two consecutive years, it is labeled "in need of improvement," which sets in motion several measures to lift the school's performance.

During the first year in improvement, schools become eligible for support to help develop improvement plans. Schools must also offer parents the option of transferring their children to another public school in the district. Schools that remain in improvement for a second year must allow parents to use part of their school's Title I money to obtain tutoring or related supplemental services from state-approved providers. Schools in improvement for three consecutive years must continue offering these parent options and must adopt corrective actions that could include significant changes in school personnel and organizational structures. Finally, schools in improvement for four consecutive years must undergo major organizational overhauls. This could include reconstituting the school (shutting it down and opening it from scratch), converting it to a public charter school, or having a private management company or the state run the school.

POLICY VENUES AND GROUP INTERESTS

This section develops a basic framework to understand how groups use venues to achieve their goals. In subsequent sections I relate this framework to NCLB and teachers union interests. To begin, consider the role that policy venues play in the American political system. Venues are institutions with the authority to act on behalf of all people in a specific political jurisdiction.[4] They are more than places where individuals debate issues and offer opinions. Rather, their inhabitants wield formal power, derived from public law, to pass legislation, craft rules, or adopt other orders that govern human and institutional behavior. Congressional committees, executive agencies, courts, state legislatures, and local special districts are all examples of policy venues.

The decentralized nature of American education means that several venues exercise authority over the nation's schools.[5] Key federal venues include Congress, the White House, the Department of Education, and the federal courts. Typically, states have parallel institutions and state boards of education. Regionally and locally, intermediate school districts, school boards, and individual schools round out the venue mix. This array of actors led authors of a recent volume to ask "Who's in charge here?" as they explored "the tangled web of school governance and policy."[6]

The web may be tangled, but it is analytically tractable. Venues are typically linked in two basic arrangements. The research literature on principal-agent theory describes one configuration as a delegation chain in which a principal, or boss, delegates authority to an agent, the boss's subordinate.[7] That agent then acts as a second principal because he or she delegates authority to yet another agent, thus creating a hierarchy. The hierarchy of a delegation chain implies that bosses can issue commands to control their subordinates. In reality, principals and agents in these chains constantly negotiate the terms of their agreements because they commonly possess different information and divergent goals. Most federal grant programs, including those in Title I of NCLB, illustrate that principals may possess formal authority over agents, but those subordinates are far from powerless.[8] In fact, classic works have shown that policymaking does not really end until agents implement laws at the street level.[9]

In addition to delegation chains, venues are also connected in policy networks. Networks contain more fluid and flexible relationships than the formal lines of authority in delegation chains.[10] Conceptually, one can consider individual venues in a network as nodes linked by informal bonds of common interest and lines of communication. In the broadest sense, networks may also contain embedded delegation chains. Research on the diffusion of policy innovation reveals the power of informal network ties. Ideas that prove successful or politically popular in one state venue, for example, can emerge relatively quickly in others as information spreads and experience accumulates.[11] Change occurs not because principals have sent orders down a delegation chain but because voluntary exchanges between officials across network nodes have fostered policy innovation.

Arrangements such as delegation chains and policy networks generate avenues for organized interests to enter the policy process. In general, I define organized interests or interest groups as membership and advocacy organizations that try to influence government policy.[12] Their concerns may be narrow or broad, and sometimes even benefit nonmembers. Organized interests have proliferated in the American political system since at least the 1960s.[13] Today it is hard to imagine a policy area that lacks even a small constellation of active groups. Education is no exception.[14]

Teachers unions are a powerful organized interest in the United States.[15] In representing educators, the National Education Association (NEA) and the American Federation of Teachers (AFT) wield significant power even though their opinions and strategies regarding NCLB and other reform matters sometimes diverge.[16] In part, unions possess power because their members reside in essentially all school districts, and thus all congressional districts, in the United States. That does not mean local union affiliates are equally adept or march in lockstep with their state and national organizations. Variation exists across unions as well. One author, for example, has suggested that the NEA has a top-down orientation while AFT locals operate with relatively more autonomy.[17]

Overall, literally thousands of union locals exist across the country. Their members are sometimes enthusiastic, lukewarm, or even hostile to the policy priorities of union leaders. A recent survey of teachers by the nonpartisan group Public Agenda found that more than 80 percent of teachers believed unions protected them against administrative abuses and prevented deterioration in their working conditions. Still, only 46 percent described their union as "absolutely essential," and 47 percent believed that unions sometimes prevented districts from firing incompetent teachers.[18] Thus, in using the term "union interests" I may sometimes overstate the degree of cohesion within unions themselves.

Despite diversity in their ranks, teachers unions are well positioned to advance their interests because they are highly organized and operate in local, state, and national policy venues. Union leaders work within and across these venues using different modes of coordinated action. That redundancy means that losses in one venue or with one tactic may not stifle union interests if members can achieve their goals in other ways. Pressing for legislative changes that filter through a delegation chain may enable unions to have broad systematic impacts on policy. When those efforts fail (and even when they succeed), unions can work laterally across networks to advance their members' interests, as when union locals press for similar priorities in collective bargaining discussions. Those impacts may be less systematic but still significant if successes aggregate across many network nodes.

AFT and NEA members have recognized that policy advocacy and local collective bargaining discussions can work together to achieve union goals. The unions' multivenue, multitactic approach illustrates how national and state venues are important for NCLB implementation. In short, all politics is not local after all. Still, history suggests that choices in the local venues where most union members work will powerfully influence whether NCLB advances or undercuts broader union interests.[19]

NCLB IMPLEMENTATION AND UNION INTERESTS

I rely on two types of evidence to study NCLB implementation and union interests. First are print sources, which include government and union documents, press accounts, and published reports. In particular, I considered a convenient sample of approximately 30 teacher contracts obtained via basic Internet searches. From that collection I identified a smaller subset based on geographic diversity, variation in school district characteristics, date of contract ratification, and whether state law guarantees collective bargaining rights to teachers. I focused on contracts ratified after 2001 to see if they explicitly addressed NCLB. Table 1 identifies this subset of contracts and relevant district characteristics.

Second, approximately 30 personal interviews inform my analysis. Most of these interviews occurred between May 2001 and June 2002. At that time those respondents worked in the policy community in Washington, D.C., and came from several governmental and nongovernmental organizations. The remaining interviews transpired during spring 2005 and involved a few similar respondents but focused primarily on teachers, district administrators, and union leaders in local venues. These respondents lived in New York, Michigan, Maryland, Florida, and Wisconsin.

TABLE 1. Summary of Teacher Contracts Consulted[a]

District	Contract period	Students[b]	Schools[b]
Albuquerque, NM	2002-04	88,120	144
Beech Grove City, IN	2003-07	2,445	5
Brevard County, FL	2004-05	72,601	110
Buckfield, ME	2003-06	660	2
Calvert County, MD	2001-04	17,153	25
Chicago, IL	2003-07	436,048	608
Davis, UT	2004-05	60,367	85
Denver, CO	2002-05	71,972	144
Minneapolis, MN	2003-05	46,037	144
Portland, OR	2003-05	51,654	104

Notes: (a) All contracts were downloaded from the Internet in January or February 2005. The full documents, quoted in subsequent pages, are available from the author. (b) Totals are based on the 2002-03 school year and come from the Common Core of Data District Locator, available at http://nces.ed.gov/ccd/districtsearch/.

As of mid-2005, my sources suggest that NCLB has not overwhelmingly influenced local collective bargaining discussions. Certainly the debates in national and state policy venues between union advocates and others have been noticeable and sometimes heated. In some local districts NCLB and bargaining have intersected. However, local conversations have been less salient in most school districts, in part because many of NCLB's deadlines are only recently coming to pass and guidance from the Department of Education has frequently been slow in coming or in flux.

People in national and local venues have told me that contract negotiations still tend to focus on bread and butter issues, such as the increasing costs of health care. Because contracts are often multiyear agreements, bargaining that concluded in the two years after NCLB became law would not have fully explored its ramifications. My interview respondents expect local bargaining will focus more on NCLB once key deadlines for testing and teacher quality arrive. Certainly some agreements have already tackled these issues, but it appears most have not. In general, across NCLB's key dimensions, which the rest of this section explores in detail, teachers unions have considered how policy advocacy and local bargaining can help align NCLB implementation with their members' interests.

Collective Bargaining Guarantees

Teachers unions have made protecting collective bargaining rights a top lobbying priority in federal venues. Union leaders believe that securing these rights will promote more consistent union influence over implementation as NCLB's requirements flow down the delegation chain to states and local school districts. Union advocacy in federal venues has also illustrated how NEA and AFT members recognize the synergies that can emerge when tactics across venues work in concert to promote union members' interests. Success in federal or state venues may facilitate union priorities in district bargaining over individual contracts.

The AFT called NCLB's bargaining provision "a key lobbying priority" because it "spells out a pivotal role for union-negotiated contracts and agreements in NCLB implementation. From public disclosure of teacher qualifications to use of school improvement funds for professional development under NCLB, the union-negotiated contract can hold great sway in keeping the process fair, constructive, and tuned to the law's worthy goals."[20] The NEA agreed with the need to protect bargaining rights and has reminded its members how it "pushed hard to keep the law from voiding protections that local affiliates have bargained into their contracts."[21] Underscoring these points, one Washington lobbyist centrally involved in NCLB advocacy, but not representing teachers unions, recalled to me that defending bargaining was a "make or break issue for NEA" during 2001.

The NEA and AFT's push for bargaining protections continued in regulatory venues as the Department of Education developed policies for NCLB's implementation. When a dear colleague letter from secretary of education Rod Paige appeared to suggest that proposed regulations would restrict collective bargaining rights for contracts adopted after January 8, 2002 (the day NCLB became law), union leaders and their supporters lobbied to preserve the rights they believed NCLB had guaranteed. The union position eventually prevailed when Secretary Paige withdrew the proposed regulations.[22] Antonia Cortese, of the New York State United Teachers, dubbed the victory "enormous—not only for protecting our members and their local unions—but for improving the overall effectiveness of this federal initiative."[23]

At first glance, NCLB's collective bargaining protections appear to align with a key union interest. The law and its supporting regulations recognize that bargaining occupies a legitimate role in NCLB implementation. Union advocates toiled to secure that protection and, thus, achieved a key objective. However, the law's bargaining protections may not pay dividends commensurate with the effort union lobbyists expended to win their approval. If so, the union drive to include broad bargaining protections in NCLB might have actually distracted union leaders from other substantive issues (such as teacher quality and testing) that are highly relevant to their members' interests.

One veteran Washington, D.C., education lobbyist told me that the AFT and NEA's vested interest in protecting bargaining rights made union leaders "side-tracked with a feint at the core of their powers." When early drafts of NCLB appeared to undercut bargaining rights, the national unions responded vigorously and, as this lobbyist conjectured, lost their focus and much potential influence on other more important elements of the law in 2001. Another ESEA expert disagreed, though, noting to me that the unions "are so well-funded and staffed, they can carry many issues at once without distraction or compromising their capacity to lobby full-force for any one of them." Citing as evidence the policy debates from 1994 and 2001, this person continued, "I was there for both IASA and NCLB; they [the teachers unions] had their lobbyists' eyes trained on all issues of importance to them."

It is unclear whether the AFT and NEA's effort to protect bargaining in NCLB will eventually pay off. As of mid-2005 high-profile showdowns over this part of the law have not occurred. However, conflicts may emerge if states or local school districts push policies that clash with the bargaining prerogatives of union members. Appearing to anticipate that possibility, NEA has advised its local affiliates to negotiate the following language into new teacher contracts: "Without the agreement of the Association, the Employer shall take no action to comply with ESEA, as amended, 20 USC 6301 et seq., that has an adverse impact on any bargaining member."[24] That language would protect union members against possible negative consequences of NCLB. In theory, at least, the law's bargaining protections could foster conditions where union members could persuasively argue their complaints through grievances and collective bargaining.

Recognizing the possible impact of the NEA's employee protection language, some districts have countered with language of their own. The Wisconsin Association of School Boards (WASB) warned its members that several union locals had "been making sweeping contract proposals" that copied NEA's language I just quoted. The WASB told its affiliates, "Do not agree to this language under any circumstances." Further, it suggested that local districts "focus on removing barriers to NCLB compliance from the teachers' collective bargaining agreement."[25] The Oregon School Boards Association (OSBA) went even further. It encouraged its members to push for contracts that included broad enabling language that could upset teachers but would give boards maximum flexibility to meet NCLB's demands. One "management rights article" that the OSBA suggested read as follows: "No provision in this Agreement shall be construed to prevent or prohibit the Board of Directors from taking required actions under the NCLBA of 2002 concerning school improvement, school corrective actions, or school restructuring."[26]

Responses to district questions from the Department of Education also suggest possible future conflicts. One guidance letter from a department official noted that NCLB's collective bargaining protections "must be implemented in concert with the purpose of Title I, which is quite clear: 'to ensure that all children have a fair, equal, and significant opportunity to obtain a high quality education and reach, at a minimum, proficiency on challenging State academic achievement standards and State academic assessments.'"[27] According to the letter, that means a school district using NCLB's Title I funds "must comply with all of the requirements of the act, notwithstanding any terms and conditions of its collective bargaining agreements." The letter emphasized that Congress intended new collective bargaining agreements to be consistent with NCLB's AYP requirements (section 1116). Based on the statute and congressional intent, the letter concluded, "It is our view that school officials, in renegotiating collective bargaining agreements or negotiating new agreements, should ensure that they preserve their authority to pursue a full range of options for implementing section 1116."

If school districts follow the approaches that the WASB, OSBA, and Department of Education suggest, then union efforts to preserve bargaining protections in NCLB may be mainly symbolic victories. Put another way, although NCLB affirms collective bargaining rights in local venues, union leaders in school districts still must work hard to make those protections meaningful. In some situations, as my Florida respondents suggested, aligning contracts with NCLB or getting union locals and districts to agree that existing contract language does not violate NCLB has not produced undue stresses at the moment. It is an open question, though, whether stresses will emerge in the future.

Teacher Quality

Three years into NCLB's implementation, how its teacher quality elements will unfold in practice remains uncertain. Because the law delegates to the states' discretion over certain aspects of teacher quality, union advocates have remained active in several policy venues to prevent regulatory and other actions from undermining their priorities. For example, as of early 2005 the Department of Education has not clarified what, if any, consequences will ensue if states or school districts do not employ highly qualified teachers in core subjects by 2005-06. Further, some states are still developing criteria for how teachers can demonstrate their highly qualified status. As key deadlines arrive and as state criteria emerge, union members and local school leaders will likely become more interested in these issues at district bargaining tables. Presently one can observe how NCLB's teacher quality dimension might support and clash with union interests.

In general, NCLB's emphasis on teacher quality affirms what union advocates push in their lobbying, public information campaigns, collective bargaining sessions, and messages to their members. Unions claim that students are much less likely to succeed academically without outstanding classroom teachers. Parents have recognized this for years. Today a growing research literature has produced systematic evidence that students who learn from talented teachers are more likely to excel.[28] This is especially true for children in disadvantaged schools and communities. Thus, NCLB's emphasis on the teacher's classroom role has helped advance the unions' core belief that education reform agendas will fail unless they recognize the key daily contributions of classroom teachers in local venues.

The need for highly qualified teachers also gives union members an entrée to argue for greater teacher pay and classroom support. Offering teachers higher salaries, which unions advocate in national, state, and local policy venues, is one way to attract more highly qualified individuals into the profession, they say. Promoting quality also suggests a parallel need for strong commitments to ongoing professional development for current teachers. For example, the NEA has advised its members that "the new law puts collective bargainers and local policy advocates squarely in the middle of efforts to improve professional development opportunities."[29] Former AFT president Sandra Feldman echoed this idea when she noted that NCLB provided an "opportunity . . . to replace meaningless requirements with high standards and sound practices for qualifying teachers," something that could produce better "professional development programs."[30]

Consistent with this advocacy from national union leaders, local teacher contracts routinely address district and teacher obligations for professional development. Sometimes these sections are relatively open ended. For example, the Buckfield, Maine, agreement addresses professional development in a single sentence. Other contracts describe professional development activities more elaborately, and some, in fact, have begun to explicitly earmark development funds to support NCLB implementation.

Consider Chicago's teacher contract, which contains a section titled "Educational Support Personnel and No Child Left Behind." That provision states the local district will provide up to $50,000 to help offset union expenses associated with helping "educational support personnel members of the bargaining unit to pass the test option required by No Child Left Behind." A memorandum of agreement accompanying the Portland, Oregon, teacher contract creates a joint labor-management committee to "manage those programs and funds . . . including but not limited to the career development fund and the inservice fund." The contract notes this committee's first priority is funding activities that "support the acquisition of knowledge and skills necessary for affected bargaining unit members to meet the qualification requirements for No

Child Left Behind." When teachers help make these development decisions, unions can influence the paths that NCLB-related training will take. Union involvement may also minimize uncertainty about possible consequences for teachers who do not meet the law's requirements.

Certainly NCLB's teacher quality provisions could potentially clash with union interests. AFT and NEA leaders have pressed these concerns in national policy venues. In 2004 Feldman addressed this topic in a letter to key congressional authors of NCLB. She noted that "many states have failed to develop the objective standard of evaluation required by law" to determine whether teachers are highly qualified, and that the Department of Education had not "addressed what would happen to paraprofessionals [e.g., Title I teacher aides] who are unable to demonstrate their qualifications by 2006 because states and districts have yet to develop the assessments required by the act."[31]

Feldman wanted Congress to clarify that teachers and paraprofessionals would not face punishments for delays in state venues. Such reassurances from Washington, through an amended NCLB or clearer regulations, would help local union affiliates address situations more consistently. For example, teachers may sometimes teach outside their content area due to staffing emergencies or unexpected contingencies. Technically these teachers might not be highly qualified in their assigned classrooms even though they are highly qualified in another field. Should responding to a pressing or unexpected local staffing need make otherwise highly qualified teachers vulnerable to sanctions? Union advocates have said no.

The NEA has anticipated that its members could face negative consequences if they fail to meet NCLB's highly qualified teacher requirements. The union recommended its members use collective bargaining to "play a meaningful role in establishing district responses if and when goals for higher qualified teachers are not met."[32] The OSBA has recognized this possible union response. Because NCLB does not specify what should happen to teachers not meeting the standard, the OSBA reasoned that "we may be seeing proposals at the bargaining table that forestall discipline or dismissal and insert additional training, remediation, assistance, and other efforts up to and including providing alternative work within the district."[33]

Federal deference to states on teacher certification issues may also cause NCLB's teacher provisions to clash with union interests. Recall that NCLB's definition of "highly qualified" primarily emphasizes subject matter expertise, while preserving state powers to determine teacher certification and licensing requirements. Section 200.56 of NCLB regulations issued December 2, 2002, supports state efforts to create routes to teaching via alternative certification and licensing.[34] Thus, individuals in alternative programs may count as highly qualified provided they are progressing satisfactorily (as their state defines) toward full certification. Unions have generally criticized alternative certification because they argue it will bring poorly trained people into the nation's classrooms.

NCLB's charter school elements reveal a further wrinkle in the certification issue. In Section 9101(23), the law exempts charter school teachers from the certification and licensing component of the highly qualified standard, as long as those teachers meet "the requirements set forth in the State's public charter school law." Thus, if a state does not require charter school teachers to have the same credentials as teachers in traditional public schools, then charter school teachers may be highly qualified without full certification. This flexibility clashes with union members who argue that charter teachers should meet the same requirements as teachers in regular public schools.

The distinction between charter and traditional teachers may have implications and produce local-level clashes in future bargaining sessions. Both sorts of teachers, defined as highly qualified by different criteria, could fall under the same contract. Laws in 16 states, for example, require traditional public schools that convert to charter status to remain bound to local collective bargaining agreements.[35] Those arrangements could become more common because one NCLB-defined route to improvement is for schools missing AYP to convert to charter status. If this path becomes popular, collective bargaining agreements will need to creatively address issues such as work rules, compensation, job security, and benefits for charter and noncharter teachers alike.[36] Addressing both kinds of teachers under the same districtwide contract will not be easy, especially if unions continue to resist broadly expanding charter schools.

Annual Testing

NCLB's requirements for annual testing in grades 3 through 8 have generated polarized opinions across the United States. Teachers unions have typically opposed the law's strong reliance on test results, arguing that focusing too much on testing can pull funds from other worthy initiatives, such as reducing class size, increasing teacher pay, and improving teacher working conditions. Union officials I spoke with from the NEA and AFT's national offices, and one union official in Florida, also criticized heavy reliance on student tests because results might be used to evaluate teachers without considering other measures of student success. They also worry that some tests might be used to evaluate teachers even though these tests might not have been designed for that purpose.

Despite these concerns, NCLB's testing could serve union interests in two ways. First, the data that tests generate may bolster union arguments that needy communities require additional funds for education. By focusing on student subgroups, NCLB will eventually generate mountains of data that document the performance of traditionally disadvantaged youngsters. Key architects of the law, including liberal members of Congress who are typically union allies, have argued that policymakers will be more likely to attend to less-fortunate students when testing data inform the debate. Several staff members I interviewed on Capitol Hill noted as much, and Democrat George Miller of California has voiced concerns when the Department of Education's regulatory choices have seemingly undercut the bite of NCLB's testing provisions.[37]

Some legal advocates are preparing to use NCLB's testing data in state and federal courts, two key policy venues, to highlight educational inequities.[38] If lawyers can link poor student performance to inadequate funding or large class sizes, then they may be able to persuade courts to remedy these situations through state finance reform or other means. Unlike the NEA's lawsuit, *Pontiac v. Spellings*, challenging NCLB implementation until additional federal dollars are forthcoming,[39] this legal strategy depends on the law moving forward and leverages its results to press for additional resources. Certainly that strategy is not without potential costs. However, it is perhaps ironic that the very mechanism that unions, particularly the NEA,[40] have often decried—annual testing—may help them increase school funding if the data prove persuasive in judicial and legislative venues.

NCLB's testing requirements have generated a second benefit for union advocates. Much like the school voucher issue often fosters strange political bedfellows, criticism of NCLB's approach has surged across the political spectrum since 2004. Leaders in typically Republican states, including Virginia, Utah, and Texas, have offered passionate arguments about testing that mirror common union criticisms.[41] This convergence likely does not foreshadow a new partnership between the GOP and the nation's largest teachers unions. However, if frustrations continue to build, the unions may be more able to change NCLB testing (and other matters) as Washington policymakers feel increasing pressure from local and state venues. Victories that the NEA and AFT failed to secure in national venues in 2001 may now be more attainable when networks of actors launch parallel criticisms or consciously coordinate.

Furthermore, if the law's testing requirements continue to draw fire, unions may have greater luck joining with local school districts to challenge NCLB.[42] The NEA's recent lawsuit, which involves districts in Michigan, Texas, and Vermont as plaintiffs, is an illustrative example of that possibility. Some local partnerships addressing NCLB have even appeared in collective bargaining agreements where unions and districts share frustrations. In Chicago, for example, the teacher contract creates a joint board-union commission to "study, discuss, formulate, and submit recommendations to the Chief Executive Officer and President of the Union regarding a joint legislative strategy to advance the shared interests of the Board and Union." One shared interest is to promote "passage of legislation" that will produce "modifications to No Child Left Behind." Similarly, a memorandum of agreement accompanying the Minneapolis teacher contract notes how "the new federal requirements of the Elementary Secondary Education Act or No Child Left Behind has compounded already onerous state testing and reporting requirements, which, in addition to District data collection and grant requirements, have compounded the blizzard of paperwork."

Although NCLB's testing requirements could enhance union interests, they may also undermine other union priorities. First, as noted earlier, test data that reveal achievement gaps may illuminate persistent student needs. However, policymakers could respond by expanding parental choice and encouraging more private-sector involvement in public schools, which the NEA and AFT have resisted, rather than increasing school funding. Choice supporters are pushing for this result. Reflecting on the 2001 legislative process, some congressional staff members I interviewed explained that the potential for greater school choice moved some reluctant congressional Republicans to support NCLB even though they worried about increasing Washington's role in the nation's schools.

Second, and perhaps more significantly, the flood of new testing data may increase pressure on unions to accept merit pay plans. As most educational observers know, nearly all teacher contracts use teacher experience and educational attainment to compute teacher salaries. Those variables produce a salary schedule, which identifies compensation levels for teachers who have served for a particular number of years (the row or "step" of the schedule) and who possess certain levels of educational training (the column or "lane" of the schedule). These salary schedules usually consider all regular classroom teachers the same.

The rigidity of the salary schedule creates challenges for districts and schools attempting to meet NCLB requirements. Deviating from standard schedules may be one way for districts to attract teachers in needed subjects. Similarly, districts may wish to pay more for teachers with exceptional skills whose service or degrees may understate their teaching potential. In a draft strategy document, the WASB noted how Wisconsin school districts should consider modifying "current pay systems to better retain and attract competent teachers," a change that could include "premium pay for teachers with difficult to find or multiple certifications."[43]

Offering bonuses or merit pay for teachers who help schools hit NCLB's accountability targets would also require districts to veer from the salary schedule model. Union affiliates have frequently challenged merit pay proposals linked to test score improvement. One union representative explained to me that tests are poor or incomplete indicators of teachers' good works, and that tests should not single out teachers because student success ultimately emerges from the long-term collective efforts of entire school staffs. The NEA has advised its locals to bargain against "the establishment of a two-tiered system that creates a super-salaried strata of elite teachers and educators," which merit or bonus pay plans could foster.[44]

Looking ahead, union resistance to expanding performance pay will likely be untenable in the long run. As a principal from New York State told me, when more NCLB data become available, citizens will hold teachers primarily responsible for student achievement and will eventually support rewarding teachers they believe produce superior results. He also noted that principal contracts increasingly incorporate pay-for-performance clauses, providing a foundation for extending such clauses to teacher contracts. Because in loosely coupled local networks "everyone looks at everyone else's contract," once test score performance finds a foothold in administrator contracts, "it will be easier to get it into others, too," he said. As evidence of this potential future trend, pay-for-performance arrangements have begun to appear in districts across the country. Policy choices in state venues often prompt or enable these local initiatives, which sometimes enjoy union support.

One example of how NCLB is influencing teacher pay comes from the Minneapolis teacher contract. In that district, teachers may earn additional "professional growth credits," which can reclassify teachers on the salary schedule "for each year of teaching in a designated Tier 1, Tier 2, *or 3rd year AYP school setting*" (emphasis added). Denver is another example. In the Mile High City, union members and the district created a pay-for-performance pilot from 1999 to 2003. Reflecting how policy choices in state venues can influence local districts, in a separate memorandum of agreement to the 2002-05 teacher contract, teachers and district officials also agreed on a framework to implement a state law offering incentive bonuses. The district plan focused on "improving the achievement of all students, closing the achievement gap and setting high standards." Among other things, the agreement made recruitment bonuses available to teachers who filled "a vacant position with all necessary qualifications (including the requirements of 'No Child Left Behind')."

Interestingly, unless altered, NCLB's testing requirements may create a barrier to vastly expanding merit pay. In the end, that would serve officially stated union interests. NCLB requires states to adopt tests that monitor achievement within grade levels but do not track particular students. In other words, the law is most concerned with comparing this year's fifth graders with next year's fifth graders. Conversely, a common version of the value-added model would use testing to track the progress of specific students and their cohorts in each grade. This model would involve assessing students at the beginning and end of the school year.

Advocates of the current NCLB framework have eschewed value-added testing because they believe it would leave children behind if students demonstrate progress but still do not achieve at grade level. However, using value-added scores may be the most effective way to implement merit pay for individual teachers. Value-added testing focuses on progress that can be related more directly, albeit still imperfectly, to a specific teacher's work. That would be better than the apples-to-oranges comparisons that can occur when student cohorts with diverse characteristics, which are unrelated to teacher performance, drive year-to-year score differences. Because NCLB does not allow states to use value-added accountability to meet AYP, it is debatable whether the law as presently written and enforced provides an adequate foundation to widely expand merit pay. Certainly that does not create an insurmountable barrier for advocates of the approach. NCLB does not prevent states or even local school districts from rewarding teachers based on value-added systems, so NCLB and these systems could exist simultaneously.

Adequate Yearly Progress and Schools in Need of Improvement

NCLB's choice provisions and corrective actions, which could involve privatizing management or closing schools that repeatedly miss AYP, appear to clash most directly with stated union interests. But some consequences could also bolster union positions. Remember that as of 2005, the complete menu of NCLB's AYP components has rarely played out because few schools have reached the latter stages of improvement status. Apparently large consequences, then, may yet unfold in unexpected ways. Still, it is worth considering some of the intersections between AYP and union interests where a minimal track record exists.

Union members may exercise new influence in local venues when schools reach improvement status. Consider two possibilities. First, recall that NCLB explicitly instructs schools failing to make AYP to establish improvement committees. NCLB does not clearly define specific tasks for how these committees must operate, so local collective bargaining agreements will sort out many of these details. Policies flowing from state venues also inform these choices. State laws in Florida, for example, govern aspects of the school improvement process.

By participating in improvement committees, union members could steer reform discussions toward their favored approaches. In one scenario, union advocacy and work on improvement committees, combined with community advocacy, could nudge local districts to support class size reductions in schools slated for major overhauls based on AYP. According to one national union official I spoke with, because NCLB provides much flexibility for local districts to select improvement strategies, unions would have important opportunities to argue for approaches they believe are supported by the evidence and that serve their members' interests.

The second school improvement issue that may serve union interests flows from NCLB's supplemental services requirements. As noted earlier, NCLB requires states to identify approved providers where parents can use their school's Title I money to buy additional help for their children. Controversy over local administration of supplemental services has emerged where district personnel and private providers both offer these services. In Chicago, for example, public school employees tutor 40,000 students and private providers instruct another 42,000. Local teachers unions in Rochester, New York, and Toledo, Ohio, are also supplemental service providers.[45] If parents respond favorably to supplemental instruction from unionized public school teachers, that could bolster union criticisms of private or nonprofit providers that are not required to employ instructors who meet NCLB's highly qualified definition. Parents who choose district-provided supplemental services will also minimize the number of Title I dollars flowing to nondistrict entities, thus serving another union interest.

The complicated logistics of implementing NCLB's supplemental services can affect union interests in other ways. The law requires districts and external providers to jointly formulate plans for increasing student achievement. Could contract protections or certification requirements in bargaining agreements also apply to supplemental providers who work outside the schools but coordinate closely with teachers and their students? The NEA has raised this question with its members, explaining that locals should negotiate for "codifying the definition and scope of the bargaining unit. For example, determining if outside agencies, such as community-based organizations that provide supplemental services required under ESEA are covered under collective bargaining agreements."[46] It is unclear how those clarifications might emerge in practice, but this potential illustrates how local choices at the end of NCLB's delegation chain can influence how this AYP provision plays out. Thinking more speculatively, if supplemental service providers become de facto school employees who work closely with regular schoolteachers, creative union locals may try to recruit these providers into their ranks.

NCLB provisions that govern school improvement may also threaten union interests. Perhaps most significant, principals and district administrators will certainly seek more aggressive control of teacher assignment to help schools make AYP. It is hard to overstate the importance of this issue. The NEA has resisted involuntary transfers based solely on a district-defined need to meet AYP; it has advised its members to bargain for contract language that specifies, "No bargaining unit member shall be involuntarily transferred in order to implement a school improvement plan developed pursuant to ESEA."[47] But being able to shuffle personnel is particularly important when districts wish to move especially skilled or veteran teachers to schools serving the neediest students.[48] This is a challenging argument for unions (or anyone else) to rebut given that union advocates and researchers see strong links between quality teachers and student performance.

Contracts often contain elaborate procedures to govern teacher assignment. Two features are especially common. First, contracts usually guarantee teachers due process procedures for within-school assignments, voluntary and involuntary transfers between schools, and layoffs. For instance, Minneapolis teachers subject to internal reassignment are afforded a four-step process that allows them to question the reassignment decision. The contract in Utah's Davis School District contains parallel, but simpler, procedures for involuntary transfers or reassignments. Davis's procedures give teachers due process while also affording principals and district officials some discretion.

Second, seniority typically weighs heavily in assignment decisions. In Albuquerque, New Mexico, a certified teacher with three or more consecutive years of service "shall not be laid off if there is an available teaching position in the District for which the instructor is certified and qualified." If involuntary transfers or reductions become necessary in the Davis School District and no volunteer steps forward, "the teacher in the grade level or subject area where the position is being eliminated who has the least overall seniority in the District will be identified as the one for transfer." However, while general regard for seniority is important, it does not imply absolute deference. The New Mexico contract also notes that changes in assignment "shall be based on verifiable instructional program environments." When laying off teachers in Portland, Oregon, the district is supposed to account for seniority but also consider "special qualifications, areas of experience, program, minority employment, and levels of training."

In today's environment where concerns over test-based accountability and AYP are paramount, district administrators and local boards have pressed and will continue to press for greater control over teacher assignments. Tensions over this issue vividly emerged during recent contract negotiations in Boston and Philadelphia. The Boston superintendent Thomas W. Payzant and the

Philadelphia schools' chief executive officer Paul G. Vallas proposed to give district administrators more power to assign teachers in schools not making AYP. In March 2004, Payzant and the Boston Teachers Union compromised by giving the superintendent some additional, but relatively limited, flexibility that still protected seniority rights. Specifically, the Boston agreement allowed the superintendent to identify five low-performing district schools and to freeze half their teaching vacancies. He could then fill those slots with teachers regardless of seniority or other transfer rights. Payzant could repeat the process the following year if a school did not improve student scores.[49]

In Philadelphia, Vallas had craved similar powers over staff assignments. After lengthy negotiations, the final teacher contract met with Vallas's approval, even though some groups thought it deferred too much to seniority. Among other things, the agreement gave principals at current schools, in consultation with school Staff Selection Committees (made up of parents and teachers), control over half of their building vacancies. The selection committee would recommend candidates, but the principal would make the final hiring decision. Principals in new schools would have even more power over staff selection.[50]

CHALLENGES, OPPORTUNITIES, AND UNCERTAINTIES AHEAD

In the interest of space, this chapter has set aside examining whether union priorities on NCLB might serve student interests. Other chapters in this volume shed light on that subject, directly and indirectly. Despite the present hoopla surrounding NCLB, the law is still in its infancy when measured against the trajectory of its long-term objectives. Ultimately NCLB embraces a hugely ambitious goal: to guarantee that the nation's students will be proficient in reading and math by 2013-14. As that deadline approaches it will be interesting to watch how two broad issues affect the future relationship between NCLB and teachers union interests.

The first issue is the potential growth of "reform unionism."[51] This movement focuses on tempering the adversarial debates that often ensue when union advocates and their critics engage in national and state venues or in local collective bargaining discussions. In the words of the Teacher Union Reform Network (TURN), this shift could protect teachers but simultaneously "restructure the nation's teachers' unions to promote reforms that will ultimately lead to better learning and higher achievement for America's children," a goal consistent with NCLB's spirit.[52]

It is debatable whether reform unionism will generate the progress its advocates have promised.[53] Evidence from Chicago, where the union and district have collaborated to turn around failing schools,[54] and in Florida, where my respondents described local district successes emerging from collaborative interest-based bargaining, suggests that unions do not always approach reforms with the skepticism that their adversaries sometimes claim. The recent NEA lawsuit challenging NCLB as an unfunded mandate, however, may have undermined some of the union's credibility with borderline critics. Advocates of reform unionism will need to do much heavy lifting to transform their vision into a national movement. Skeptics doubt this transformation is even possible. If the movement succeeds, though, it may help improve NCLB's long-term impact.

A second issue influencing NCLB's future relationship to teachers unions and collective bargaining is how strictly policymakers in federal venues enforce the law. Since 2002 the Department of Education has struggled to send clear signals and consistent guidance down the NCLB delegation chain.[55] Many potential benefits or threats to union interests will emerge only if the federal government holds actors in state and local venues accountable for faithful implementation of NCLB. Today, even though federal officials have promised to hold states and localities to NCLB's provisions, the law's success will continue to depend as much on politics and federal persuasion as it will on tough enforcement. Parents dissatisfied with NCLB could give union advocates important political support as unions coordinate allies in national, state, and local venues to change the law. Alternatively, if parents react more favorably and NCLB supporters beat back critics, unions will have to work more creatively to sustain their interests. Unions and their adversaries will certainly study where federal officials bend or hold firm as Washington fields future waiver requests or responds to complaints.

Perhaps the biggest challenge facing union advocates and their critics is how to translate broad agreement on key principles into specific actions that benefit the nation's students. Even amid the advocacy swirling about NCLB, all serious educational observers recognize a few basic facts. Most schools and students are not performing as well as they could. Achievement gaps among youngsters foster inequities that can snowball during adolescence and adulthood. The nation's classrooms need more great teachers, especially in areas with high concentrations of disadvantaged students.

Serious observers also recognize that teachers unions and NCLB will likely remain fixtures of the nation's educational landscape for many years to come. Realistically, union advocates and their critics will never see all their wishes completely fulfilled. Perhaps the best scenario for NCLB success, then, would be for advocates and critics to reach for pragmatic, perhaps even second-best but still useful, solutions to address the country's persistent educational challenges.

CHAPTER EIGHT

The Educational Value of Democratic Voice
A Defense of Collective Bargaining in American Education

LEO CASEY

t is an old axiom, too often neglected and forgotten, that unions are organized expressions of solidarity. They exist for the purpose of furthering the interests their members hold in common, and they use the power of concerted action and collective organization to realize those interests. Historically, particular manifestations of unified action and organization, especially strikes and collective bargaining, have come to be associated with unions. But it is worth recalling at the outset of an examination of collective bargaining in education that these different forms of union organization are not the ends of unionism, but means for fulfilling its raison d'être, solidarity in service of the common good of union members.

The common good of educators that teachers unions pursue is largely congruent, I argue in this essay, with the educational interests of the students whom they teach. The working conditions of teachers are, in significant measure, the learning conditions of students, and so improvements in the work lives of teachers generally translate into improvements in the education of students. To the extent that the common good of teachers is realized, therefore, it directly (such as in the case of lower class size) or indirectly (such as in salary and pension policies that promote the retention of accomplished teachers) improves the quality of education for students. Moreover, the contemporary focus of teachers and their unions on the quality of teaching, captured in the notion of teacher professionalism, is indispensable to efforts to enhance the quality of education that students receive. As an early collective bargaining slogan of New York City's United Federation of Teachers (UFT) put it, "teachers want what students need."

In order to sustain these propositions, I will address, in turn, the major arguments that are most often made against them. First, in answer to misunderstandings of collective bargaining in education as limited to matters of narrow economic self-interest, I shall develop an analytical model of teacher unionism as "democratic voice" and show how collective bargaining is one of its three primary strategies. I will then take up the mistaken substitution of a particular historical form of teacher unionism, based on the precepts of industrial unionism and limited to questions of salaries, working conditions, and due process, for teacher unionism generally. Here I will demonstrate how, over time, postindustrial forms of teacher unionism, with a focus on teacher professionalism and the quality of teaching, have emerged. Finally, I will address contentions concerning particular features of collective bargaining agreements and their purported ill effects on education. Since New York City has been a bellwether of teacher unionism since it adopted the first significant educational collective bargaining agreement in the early 1960s, I shall pay particularly close attention to developments there, using them as exemplars of wider trends.

TEACHERS UNIONS AND DEMOCRATIC VOICE

A proper understanding of the ways in which teachers unions promote the common good of their members demonstrates that they do far more than look after the narrow economic self-interest of their members, as their critics charge.[1] When unions function as instruments of solidarity, they provide what one might call "democratic voice" for their members. I use the term "voice" here in the sense developed by the economist Albert Hirschman in his classic text *Exit, Voice, and Loyalty*. Hirschman argues that whenever faced with difficult and undesirable conditions, human actors have a choice between leaving for another, hopefully better situation, the "exit" option, or staying and working to change those conditions, the "voice" option:

> Voice is here defined as any attempt at all to change, rather than to escape from, an objectionable state of affairs, whether through individual or collective petition to the management directly in charge, through appeal to a higher authority with the intention of forcing change in management, or through various types of actions and protests, including those that are meant to mobilize public opinion.[2]

While "exit" is a classically economic, market reaction to untenable conditions, "voice" is the political response, rooted in democratic notions of participatory decisionmaking. At the center of voice is the civic principle that the human actor has the right and obligation to join with others of a similar interest and mind and make changes for the better in those conditions. When unions function as the democratic voice of their members, they extend the principles of democratic governance to the work lives of working people: this is why the broader vision of unionism has often been described as an "economic democracy."

Seen in this context, collective bargaining is simply one set of *means* for unions to exercise democratic voice on behalf of their members. It involves, without question, efforts to win a decent and fair standard of living and economic security for those members and to secure basic rights and due process in the workplace. But it also has much broader horizons, extending to the conditions of labor in the fullest sense. For teachers unions, the purview of collective bargaining includes teaching as a profession and a vocation, and the quality of schools and education, precisely because these matters involve teachers' democratic voice.

THE THREE PRIMARY STRATEGIES OF DEMOCRATIC VOICE

Just as important, collective bargaining is only *one* set of means for unions to exercise democratic voice on behalf of their members. It is useful, I contend, to think of democratic voice in teachers unions through the image of a three-legged stool, with three distinct, but interrelated and interdependent, strategies being employed: collective bargaining, political action, and professional development. This tripartite typology is not meant to be exhaustive; teachers unions employ other strategies that fall outside of it, such as public relations work, media outreach, and legal action. Yet these other efforts are largely ancillary to the three main strategies and dependent on their success.

The usefulness of this tripartite schema might be best seen through an illustration. Violence in schools is an issue of great concern for teachers and other staff, and a growing focus of work by teachers unions. It is an especially pivotal issue within education, since a safe and orderly environment in a school is a threshold question: a disorderly and chaotic school with a high rate of violent incidents and crimes quickly becomes a school in educational trouble. Violence is also an issue where, contrary to the ideological frame of teachers union critics, the interests of teachers, students, and the community at large closely mesh. A school where teachers are assaulted is a school where no one is safe and education suffers grievously; conversely, a school that is safe and orderly is a place where teachers want to work, where families want to send their children, and where real teaching and learning can occur.

In New York City the UFT has employed all three strategies of democratic voice to address the issue of school violence. Clauses have been negotiated into the collective bargaining agreement that require each school to establish a school safety committee with a membership of supervisors and pedagogical staff, and to have this committee develop a school safety plan for ensuring the safe and orderly functioning of the school. The contract created an expedited procedure for filing complaints when the safety plan is not followed, and it mandated reporting of assaults against staff. Procedures are laid out for the removal of violent students, who may be a threat to themselves and others, and for the referral of disruptive students, who may impede education for an entire class.[3]

Through political action and lobbying, the UFT and its state affiliate, NYSUT, secured the passage of Safe Schools against Violence in Education (SAVE) legislation, which made assaults of teachers a felony and required school districts to develop school safety plans, establish programs for violence prevention such as peer mediation and conflict resolution, and create SAVE rooms in every school, to which disruptive and violent students can be sent on the authority of a teacher or principal.[4] The UFT was also pivotal in obtaining the public funds that established violence prevention programs for students in most of the city's schools.[5]

Through its own School Safety Department, the UFT runs a number of workshops and courses that prepare its own members to handle and manage violence-prone students in ways that de-escalate confrontations and avoid physical conflicts. The UFT works with victims of school violence, providing them psychological counseling and legal representation, and has its own database of school safety incidents to provide a check and balance on the Department of Education's self-reporting. It does safety audits of schools, providing them with a full accounting of where the school safety plan is well designed and functional and where it needs to be revamped and better implemented. Union access to victims of school violence and to schools for the purpose of performing the last two functions is guaranteed by the collective bargaining agreement.

It is also worthy of note that many educational policies supported by teachers unions, from initiatives that break down the anonymity of large schools by establishing smaller learning communities and smaller classes in which teachers and students get to know each other well to the insistence that schools be staffed with the full complement of professional counseling services (guidance counselors, social workers, and school psychologists), have a demonstrably positive effect on school safety and tone.[6]

One could examine issue after issue that is paramount to teachers unions today, and demonstrate how they are promoted, in different ways, through all three strategic approaches that comprise the exercise of teachers' democratic voice. Efforts to achieve the educational benefits of lower class size, for example, are addressed through contractual limits on class size, through legislation and referenda that target lower class sizes, and through professional development, which provides teachers with the pedagogical tools to use smaller class size to maximum benefit.

What becomes clear through these illustrations is that an analysis of teachers union work that extracts the collective bargaining approach from the other two strategic areas of teachers union work, political action and professional development, would fail to capture the full breadth and scope of what is, in fact, an interlocking effort of democratic voice. A singular focus on collective bargaining in examining the school violence issue, for example, would completely miss the unions' vital work in violence prevention. It is the combination of the three strategies, the three different avenues of democratic voice, that gives teachers unions their efficacy and power: the whole is much more than the sum of its parts.

THE LIMITS OF COLLECTIVE BARGAINING AS DEMOCRATIC VOICE

The tripartite approach to teacher democratic voice is necessitated in part because in each of these strategic arenas, the union faces different limits and obstacles to achieving its goals. Consequently, the union sets out to accomplish different goals through the three different avenues. In collective bargaining, the obvious limit and obstacle lies in the fact that such bargaining is conducted with another party, the management of the schools, which has a different set of interests and goals. Every particular collective bargaining situation has its own balance of forces, depending on the relative power of the two parties, but even unions entering into collective bargaining from a position of considerable strength have to engage in a process of give and take to reach an agreement. More progressive-minded school district leadership and unions work to move negotiations beyond a stridently adversarial process, yet collaborations and partnerships start at best with overlapping, and not identical, interests and goals. It follows, therefore, that collective bargaining agreements involve numerous compromises and are not an unqualified expression of the democratic voice of union members. At the same time that a contract guarantees union members a certain level of remuneration, a certain quality of working conditions, enumerated rights, and due process, it also imposes on those same members certain obligations. Virtually every collective bargaining agreement, to cite just the most obvious example, includes a "no strike" clause for its duration.

The point is worth making here because its significance extends far beyond the fallacious arguments that are often levied against teachers unions, holding them responsible for parts of collective bargaining agreements that clearly reflect the demands and interests of management. If one is going to argue that education would be better off without collective bargaining, then, as a matter of intellectual honesty, one is compelled not only to make a case that restricting the democratic voice of teachers and creating a more unfettered school management will result in a better-quality education, but also to show how the actual policies and practices of the current school management would result in that end, were that management "freed" from having to reach and implement collective bargaining agreements with their employees. Given the recent proliferation of school district leaders lacking any meaningful educational background and training, and the very short tenure of many of them, that is a rather steep mountain to climb. In districts like New York City, it is now the teachers union, not the district management, that is the center of educational expertise. The union holds the historical memory of what has and has not worked in the schools, and it has the educational wherewithal, lacking on the management side, to understand what led to success and to failure.

Among the union ranks are some who have lost sight of the fact that collective bargaining entails compromises between the interests of management and the interests of labor, and thus, of the limits of collective bargaining as an expression of democratic voice. They have adopted what might be called a "pure and simple industrial unionism," in which the collective bargaining agreement acquires the status of sacred scriptures, and unionism consists of being completely faithful to the letter of the contractual law.[7] In a paradigmatic way, a set of means of unionism is mistaken for its ends: fidelity to the contract becomes the end of unionism, and the limits and compromises required by that particular means become obscured and even forgotten.

In a context where collective bargaining itself is under attack, it is absolutely necessary for unionists to defend vigilantly the progress that has been made and the rights that have been established through that process. But a dogmatic and blind adherence to the letter of the contractual status quo actually disarms that struggle and constricts the union's ability to function as the democratic voice of teachers. Specifically, "pure and simple industrial unionism" prevents unionists from seeing contracts in a historical context. If they are to be a truly effective democratic voice of their members today, it is necessary for teachers unions to have this historical vision and to understand the historical transformation of collective bargaining in education in which we are now engaged.

COLLECTIVE BARGAINING IN HISTORICAL PERSPECTIVE

When the UFT negotiated the first major educational collective bargaining agreement in 1962, it took as its template the contracts of the progressive industrial unions of the era, such as Walter Reuther's United Auto Workers. In 1962 there was a reasonably good fit between those contracts and the world of New

York City public education, because city schools, like the rest of American public education, were largely organized along industrial principles of mass production.[8] Over the course of the first half of the twentieth century, a major campaign had been waged to bring the standardization wrought by Frederick Taylor's "scientific management" and Henry Ford's mass production assembly line to public education. There were limits to the reach of this effort: one need only read the speeches of the first president of the American Federation of Teachers (AFT), Margaret Haley, to see the signs of teachers defending their craft from the "deskilling" that came with Taylorism and Fordism.[9] Yet in matters of the formal structure of the schooling, such as the organization of the school day and the development of the school curriculum, standardization made dramatic inroads. The school day everywhere was divided up into instructional periods of equal length, and the core curriculum and classes taught in those periods were increasingly homogenized from one school to the next.

Industrial-style collective bargaining agreements codified this standardization of school life, adopting industry's framework as its terms of reference. The workday and duties of teachers were defined through universal standards that applied to all: every teacher would teach a set number of periods and classes a day, for example, with the other periods in the school day reserved for lunch, preparation for classes, and other school duties. From the union point of view, these universal standards reined in supervisory arbitrariness, thus introducing a measure of fairness into the system, and placed limits on the extension and intensification of work. From the management point of view, universal standards confirmed a minimum level of acceptable work and performance against which teachers could be measured. And since the standards applied to all schools in a district, teachers became as interchangeable as assembly line workers.

To be fair, it must be noted that teachers unions made a valiant effort, from the very start, to break new collective bargaining ground. The men and women of the democratic left, which led the UFT in its first collective bargaining negotiations, knew their labor history, and they were motivated by syndicalist visions of worker self-management and by older traditions of craft unionism, in which skilled workers retained essential control over the knowledge and practice of their craft, as much as they modeled themselves after progressive industrial unions. One finds many remarkable educational demands among the list the UFT submitted for its first contract, demands that extended far beyond limits on class size and relief from nonprofessional, nonteaching chores.[10]

Consider these examples. Drawing on craft union traditions, and reflecting the large numbers of teachers who came into the system without the proper preparation, the UFT proposed an apprenticeship for all future New York City public school teachers, the Teacher Internship Program. Under this proposal a new teacher would be apprenticed with an experienced, accomplished teacher for a period of two to three years, during which time she would master the fundamentals of teaching in a practical setting. During this apprenticeship period the teacher intern would have a reduced class load, which would gradually be increased to full size as the apprenticeship progressed and the teacher's skills improved. The UFT also put forward a proposal for a comprehensive program that would attract experienced, qualified teachers to what were called, in the euphemism of the day, "hard to staff" schools. The proposal argued for many of the supports, such as lower class sizes, proven curricular programs, and literacy specialists, that New York City finally but all too briefly provided 40 years later, in partnership with the UFT, in the Chancellor's District.[11]

But in those first contract negotiations, the UFT found what teacher unionists throughout the United States later discovered in subsequent years, that school districts fiercely resisted giving the union and its members a meaningful say in educational policy. This was an area of "management rights," the districts insisted. In this stance, the districts had on their side the national collective bargaining norms established by the Wagner Act when it created the National Labor Relations Board (NLRB), even though they did not directly apply to public employees. The NLRB had brought into being an adversarial regime of labor relations in which a wall of separation was established between management and labor, with obligatory topics of collective bargaining being restricted to issues of wages, working conditions, and due process. And initially, school districts were able to use this weight of precedent to thwart teachers union contractual initiatives on matters of educational policy.

EDUCATION IN A CHANGING GLOBAL KNOWLEDGE ECONOMY

From the viewpoint of a "pure and simple industrial unionist," the historic victory of school district management at the onset of collective bargaining for teachers settled the question of teacher voice in the formation of educational policy. The contractual status quo followed the industrial union model, and that model had to be protected from change in every respect. And to read many teachers union critics, one would think that the "pure and simple industrial unionism" reflected the contemporary reality of teacher unionism.[12] But the visionaries among teachers union leaders, men and women like Al Shanker and Sandy Feldman, never lost sight of the fact that there is a world of difference between the mass production of automobiles and the education of youth. Under their leadership, teachers unions seized every available opportunity to breach the industrial-style collective bargaining wall of separation between management and labor that had placed educational issues outside of their purview. As a result of their efforts, a new postindustrial paradigm of teacher unionism and collective bargaining is now emerging.

One dramatic turning point arose in 1983, with the appearance of *A Nation at Risk*. In retrospect, one can see that this report signaled the start of a long period of dramatic changes in American education, as the nation began to struggle with how the emergence of a global knowledge economy, and the new demands on schools that came with it, would change American institutions of teaching and learning. But this was far from obvious at that time, as it was easy to lose the actual import of the document in its extravagant and hyperbolic rhetoric, and in the fact that it was generated by a national administration that was no friend of public education. Al Shanker showed foresight in refusing to join the "circle the wagons" forces that were prepared to defend the educational status quo at all costs, and demonstrated remarkable leadership in successfully convincing the ranks of the AFT that the challenge of *A Nation at Risk* had to be faced head on.

What was at stake? The old industrial economy had produced a substantial number of manual labor jobs in basic manufacturing sectors such as steel and automobiles, jobs that required only a minimal education, and yet, when unionized, still provided an income that could support a middle-class standard of living. These jobs were rapidly disappearing, and the only middle-class jobs that replaced them required a much more substantial level of skill in areas such as literacy and numeracy, as well as problem-solving expertise. High school graduation and some measure of postsecondary education were becoming preconditions of decent employment, and primary and secondary education would have to raise their standards to meet this new reality. Out of this understanding the "standards movement" in American education was born, with the AFT playing a prominent role. In the wake of this development, teachers unions around the nation began to negotiate educational policy questions in their collective bargaining agreements.

A UNION OF "PROFESSIONALS"

Participation in the standards movement led American teachers unions to a new emphasis on the quality of teaching, centered on a renewed notion of teacher "professionalism." Professionalism is what one might call, in the language of political science, an "essentially contested concept." Like the idea of "democracy," the very meaning of the term is the subject of constant political contention. In the early days of organizing, school districts would deploy it against unions, on the premise that "professionals" did not belong to a union or strike. But the idea of professionalism taken up by teachers unions in the late 1980s had a rather different meaning, one that focused on the notion that a profession ensures the quality of the service it provides to the public by educating and policing itself. To perform that function, it must have regulative control over the body of knowledge and the set of skills that its members master and use in their work.

Perhaps no project better embodied this idea of professionalism than the National Board for Professional Teaching Standards (NBPTS), a Shanker-inspired project that was launched in the late 1980s with the strong support of both national teachers unions. Based on the model of the medical profession, in which board certification in an area of specialty indicates that a doctor or surgeon has met an exacting standard of excellence in the field, NBPTS developed an intensive process for certifying an analogous level of excellence in teaching, focused on five core propositions of what accomplished teachers know and are able to do. Teachers union efforts around the NBPTS employed all three avenues of democratic voice: pay differentials for NBPTS certified teachers were negotiated into collective bargaining agreements; political action led state governments to provide supports for the NBPTS certification process and pay incentives for NBPTS certified teachers; and locals developed programs of professional development designed to support members in the exhaustive certification process.

The important role of union professional development in the promotion of NBPTS was a sign that it was maturing into a central component of teachers union work. The demands of the knowledge economy and the standards movement for graduates with higher-order thinking and problem-solving skills required, in turn, more powerful and more sophisticated pedagogy. The five core propositions of NBPTS put forward a vision of that pedagogy in its insistence that teachers actively engaged students in their learning, drawing connections among the subjects being taught and connections between what is being learned and "real life" problems and questions.[13] In order to realize this vision, teachers had to become "self-reflective practitioners," thinking systematically about their teaching and learning from their experiences.[14] Professional development was indispensable in that process.[15] In New York City the UFT developed its network of Teachers' Centers, which now has sites and outreach centers with professional development staff in more than 250 schools.

In focusing on the promotion of teacher professionalism, teachers unions found themselves calling on the rich history of the American labor movement, just as the founders of the UFT had four decades prior. Craft union traditions, such as apprenticeships and master craftspeople, provided a fecund source of models for ensuring the quality and integrity of teaching. In this vein, locals began to negotiate peer evaluation/review and peer intervention programs, mentoring programs for new teachers, and career ladders that included positions of lead or master teacher.[16] Where such programs were started, accomplished teachers assumed a pivotal role in inducting new teachers into the profession and schools, in evaluating the performance of teachers, in providing professional development for other teachers, and in working with senior teachers who were having difficulties in the classroom to help them improve—and when improvement was not possible, to counsel them out of teaching and into new employment.

These programs were not without their critics. For "pure and simple industrial unionists," peer evaluation and peer review destroy worker solidarity by having teachers play a role in what management alone should do, the evaluation of other teachers.[17] Using the same logic, any differentiation among teachers, such as having the more accomplished identified as lead teachers and given more leadership responsibilities, also undermines teacher solidarity. Bereft of a historical understanding of collective bargaining, such unionists see a "deskilled" and homogenized teacher workforce as the basis of union solidarity. An identical conclusion has been reached on different grounds by the fiercest critics of teachers unions, who were intent on maintaining unfettered management rights at all costs.[18] While maintaining that teachers unions are completely uninterested in the quality of education, they oppose vigorously union programs designed to address precisely that question.

In New York City the UFT negotiated several contractual clauses designed to define and promote teacher professionalism. A process known as "professional conciliation" was developed to resolve conflicts between teachers and supervisors over matters of pedagogy and teaching approaches, and an alternative system of evaluation to the standard observation, designed to promote professional development and self-reflection, was created. Specific attention was given to defining the rights and responsibilities of teachers with regard to lesson planning, and teachers were relieved from nonprofessional "building assignments" to perform professional tasks such as curriculum development, parent outreach, and working on performance-based assessment activities.[19]

THE INSTITUTIONS OF SCHOOLING UNDERGO CHANGE

The changes to American education that have come in the wake of the knowledge economy have made the industrial factory paradigm for organizing schools increasingly problematic. In the knowledge-based economy, the management hierarchies of the industrial order are flattening, the autonomy of work units is increasing, and a premium is placed on worker participation. The elaborate division of labor and specialization that defined the industrial economy is being replaced by flexible, multiskilled, broad tasks performed by work teams. Learning and work, thinking and doing are becoming more and more integrated.[20] All of these trends run against the organizational grain of the factory model school.

By the end of the twentieth century, schools were emerging that embodied more the logic of the new knowledge economy than the old industrial order. Reflecting the diversification of the economy, the schools were much more diverse in size, in curricular focus and design, in pedagogical approach, and in governance. One particular manifestation of this development is the "small schools" movement, which embodies so many knowledge economy features, such as the insistence on autonomy, the flattening of hierarchy, and the focus on teamwork and teacher participation in important school decisions.[21] There is real potential in these new schools, just as there is in the knowledge economy generally, for teacher (and worker) empowerment and the improvement of education.

But these new schools also posed a problem for teachers unions, as the sheer variety of their organizational forms did not easily fit within the terms of collective bargaining agreements built on an industrial union template, with its codes of standardization. In New York City the UFT took the initiative well over a decade ago in negotiating a School Based Option (SBO) into the collective bargaining agreement to address this problem. SBOs allow a school to change contractual rules and Department of Education regulations governing matters such as class size, rotation of assignments/classes, and teacher schedules and day by agreement of the school union, with a 55 percent vote of the members in the school, and the school administration.[22] In the current contract negotiations, the UFT has proposed an experiment that would dramatically broaden this approach. In 50 schools where the administration and teaching faculty have a history of working together collaboratively and democratically, they would be empowered to negotiate their own school-based contract on how to run the school, with only a few districtwide essentials predetermined—base salary and benefits, due process, safety, and the need for an instructional program that meets state standards.[23]

In a parallel development, the UFT negotiated a School Based Transfer and Staffing Plan, which allowed schools to develop their own qualifications for staff in their schools, based on the specific character and needs of their academic program, and to select all of their staff through their own school-based personnel committee, the majority of whom must be teachers.[24] The plan is now in use in more than 600 schools in New York City.

At the heart of the proposal for a school-based contract, and of the already established school-based option and school-based transfer and staffing plan, is the notion that what is important is that the union and collective bargaining enable democratic voice for teachers, not that they be faithful to all of the details of the industrial union paradigm that shaped its first contracts. When a single model for organizing a school is codified through detailed universal standards of the industrial union sort, teachers in schools that seek to organize themselves differently become, in effect, disenfranchised. What the proposal for a school-based contract does is increase democratic voice for teachers by according them the power to fashion agreements over the educational design of their schools in ways that best serve the needs of their students and school. The new model trades contractual clauses that place narrowly circumscribed limits on what management can and cannot do for the capacity of teachers to actually shape, in fundamental ways, the way their school is organized and functions. In this aspect, a school-based contract is a giant step toward teacher professionalism. Indeed, as the important decisions on the design of the educational program are delegated to the union chapters and members to negotiate with the school leadership, new opportunities for creating a more participatory and vibrant union culture at the school level begin to unfold.

These new postindustrial modalities of collective bargaining draw the usual critics, united by a common inability to understand the functioning of democratic voice. Among the "pure and simple industrial unionists," the proposal for school-based contracts is condemned as "preemptive concessions," just as the school-based options and school-based transfer and staffing plans had been excoriated in the past, because any deviation from the industrial union template is a surrender to management.[25] Among critics of teachers unions, these initiatives are generally greeted with no more enthusiasm. Despite the talk of the problems of centralized, bureaucratic authority and the need for school autonomy, the bottom line, as one Manhattan Institute study reported, is that in devolving power to the school, the school-based transfer and staffing plan developed by the UFT "actually diminishes the principal's authority over hiring."[26] Even though the plan gives the school personnel committee control of all hiring for the school, the principal has to share that power with teachers, who comprise a majority of the committee, and this does not sit well with those whose substantive agenda is unfettered management power.

TEACHERS UNIONS AND EDUCATIONAL POLICY

The changes in American education that began with A Nation at Risk are far from complete. Given the powerful forces that are contending over the character of those changes, it would be foolhardy to venture predictions on the ultimate form of American education that will emerge from this period, or what that form will mean for teachers unions and collective bargaining. As much as some on the right prophesy an American education under the reign of laissez-faire markets, it is no less plausible to imagine a vibrant and healthy postindustrial American public education, with teachers unions and collective bargaining playing a major role. Indeed, one could make a very persuasive case that for-profit educational corporations have intrinsically centralizing and homogenizing effects on schooling, given their quick resort to economies of scale to build and maintain a profit margin. Centralizing and homogenizing tendencies run counter, of course, to an educational design that fits the knowledge-based economy. A system of postindustrial public education would be much better suited to supporting a diversity of schools operating with a great deal of autonomy in their educational programs.

Yet even in the midst of these historical changes, some conclusions can be drawn from the historical perspective on collective bargaining in education I have sketched here. The broad claim that teachers unions are concerned only with "bread and butter" issues and do not care about education and teacher professionalism is clearly unfounded. While not every teachers union will pursue educational objectives with pioneering initiatives the way New York City and the other union locals affiliated with the national Teacher Union Reform Network have done, many locals will follow a well-blazed trail. Just witness the numbers of states in which teachers unions have worked to add educational issues to mandatory topics of collective bargaining. The critical problem today, more often than not, is the lack of a partner willing and able to pursue new and meaningful educational reforms that respect democratic voice for teachers on the school district side of the table. That is certainly what holds back educational progress in New York City today.

An intellectually honest and frank discussion must start with the acknowledgment, therefore, that the real issue of teachers union critics is *how* unions approach educational issues, not that teachers unions fail to do so. Once one gets to the core of the question, the claim is that teachers unions generally and collective bargaining in particular diminish the quality of American public education as a consequence of the limits democratic voice for teachers imposes on the discretion and authority of management.

A small body of literature has examined the relationship between teacher unionism and the quality of education.[27] While the weight of that literature clearly falls on the side of a positive relationship between teacher unionism and the quality of schooling, it is far from definitive. The great bulk of the literature on both sides of the question takes the form of statistical analyses, using SAT and ACT scores or dropout rates as proxies for the quality of education, followed by an examination of the correlation between those indices and teachers union density and collective bargaining. The use of such analytically thin and relatively impoverished measures of the quality of education, and the speculative ways in which the correlations are subsequently explained, means that the conclusions are of extraordinarily limited value.

But it is possible nonetheless to have a meaningful conversation about the relationship between teacher unionism and collective bargaining, on the one hand, and the quality of education, on the other hand, if we are willing to discuss the specific ways in which collective bargaining impacts the quality of education. A valuable starting point would be a consideration of the findings of Richard Freeman and James Medoff's *What Do Unions Do?*[28] Looking at private-sector unions in the United States, Freeman and Medoff found that unionized establishments experienced a much lower rate of turnover in their workforce than otherwise comparable nonunionized enterprises. This lower turnover resulted, in large part, from the fact that unionized workers were able to use the union and collective bargaining to improve the conditions of the workplace and to have a say in its operations. In other words, since unions gave workers voice, they were less likely to use exit. The reduced costs of on-the-job training and recruitment and the higher level of skill in the workforce in the unionized establishments led to a higher rate of productivity, especially when combined with positive managerial responses to unionism that stressed more rational personnel policies.

TEACHER QUALITY AND DEMOCRATIC VOICE

These findings are particularly relevant for education. Teaching is an extraordinarily demanding and difficult craft, requiring a thorough knowledge of subject material, a solid grasp of pedagogy, an understanding of child or adolescent psychology, and strong skills of classroom management. Under ideal conditions of a solid preparation, good mentoring, and appropriate professional development, it takes years of active classroom teaching for a teacher to master all of the fundamental tools of the profession.[29] Just as in the case of other highly skilled workers, an exceptional investment is made in novice teachers at the start of their professional careers in expectation of returns on that investment in the future. Unfortunately, many American teachers begin their professional careers under considerably less than ideal conditions and take much longer to achieve full competency, or leave the profession altogether in defeat.

In a reflection of the challenging nature of teaching, and of the extraordinary practical education and professional development required to become skilled in it, education research confirms that the classroom teacher is the most critical factor in the education of a student.[30] A qualified, experienced teacher has more of a positive effect on a student's learning than any other educational variable, including class size, design of the academic program and curriculum, and school mission and size. By the same token, unprepared and inexperienced teachers lacking the fundamental tools of teaching have a negative effect on a student's learning, and a student rarely recovers from having several such teachers in a row. Accomplished teachers are particularly important in the education of struggling students and in bridging the achievement gap.[31]

To the extent that teachers exercise exit in large numbers and there is a high turnover rate in a school or district, there is a loss of the investment in their human capital. But even more important, the quality of education suffers, as teachers who have had opportunities to master the fundamental skills of teaching are replaced by novice teachers who have not had those opportunities. This is why one of the primary indicators of an academically failing school is a high rate of staff turnover.[32] While high staff turnover is heaviest in schools serving communities of poor people, it is a wide national crisis. Nearly one out of every two new American teachers leaves education by their fifth year.[33]

The complaints of teachers joining in this exodus read like a litany of pleas for voice.[34] Exiting teachers feel that their work as teaching professionals is neither respected nor supported. They complain of being underpaid, especially given the difficulty of their work, and of being unprepared for the pedagogical and social challenges they faced. They feel that their views and insights were ignored and disregarded by their administrators and school district. The poor conditions in their schools, with student disrespect, unruliness, and violence being the major complaints, are also mentioned.

To what extent do teachers unions have an impact, along the lines that Freeman and Medoff found among private-sector unions, that reduces the rate of teacher turnover in American education, and thus improves the quality of instruction? One cannot reach a definitive conclusion here, as this question has not been examined in any depth in the literature. Yet some evidence clearly supports the presence of a link. We know that there are much higher rates of turnover in charter schools, in most private schools, and in Catholic schools, where the numbers of unorganized, nonunion schools are also much higher than in traditional, largely unionized public schools.[35] We also know that one of the most significant factors in reducing the rate of turnover, by more than half, is a strong mentoring program, which teachers unions have consistently advocated and supported.[36] One can tentatively conclude that there is a link, although much more analysis needs to be done before we are able to measure the extent of the link and definitively settle the question. The sheer scope of the retention crisis also means that there are considerable opportunities for teachers unions to have a much greater impact in this area through a more concentrated effort on educational issues.

This question also casts some light on an issue that often draws the criticism of teachers union critics, the role of seniority in collective bargaining agreements.

Teachers union critics argue that having seniority play a role in determining salary schedules or establishing priority in assignment prevents administrators from rewarding individual performance, and thus from maximizing educational resources.[37] But the effect of eliminating seniority considerations altogether, Freeman and Medoff show, is to skew incentives in favor of those prepared to use the exit option, the younger, less-experienced and less-skilled employees, and against older, more-experienced and more-skilled employees who want a voice option and a long professional career.[38] In making lifelong career decisions, as opposed to short-term financial gain choices, an individual will be concerned with issues of job security and incremental improvements in salary over time, as he or she anticipates midlife matters such as mortgage payments and the cost of college tuition for children. Teachers unions' insistence on a role for seniority in pay scales and assignments thus plays a positive role in retaining experienced, skilled teachers. The key issue is how to balance the good achieved by a system of seniority with other goods, such as the need to create schools with distinct educational programs and pedagogical approaches or the need to compensate appropriately teachers who take on exceptional duties. The school-based staffing and transfer plan negotiated by the UFT addresses the first of these issues by allowing for the development of school-specific job qualifications, and for the consideration of factors in addition to seniority in the selection of staff. Changes in compensation, which I shall address below, would address the second of the issues.

THE RETENTION CRISIS AND TEACHER QUALITY

Examining the underlying causes of the "retention crisis," Richard Ingersoll argues that school districts historically adopted a labor relations strategy that depended heavily on recruitment rather than retention, for the specific purpose of minimizing the costs of educational labor.[39] Just as turn-of-the-19th-century industrialists recruited low-wage immigrants from eastern and southern Europe to undermine worker solidarity and unions, thus maintaining a high profit margin by hindering efforts to improve working conditions, school districts kept the costs of public education low by maintaining teaching as a "lower status, easy-in/easy-out, high turnover occupation."[40] Poor preservice preparation, with low standards and requirements; relatively unselective entry criteria; and front-loaded salaries that pay newcomers relatively well compared to veterans: all of these policies favor recruitment over retention, Ingersoll notes. But there is a price to keeping down the cost of educational labor through high turnover: the quality of teaching suffers.

Ingersoll concludes that contemporary school districts continue to favor the same policies, with the same consequences. But today the demands of a global knowledge economy on American public education are such that American schooling must dramatically improve its quality, and to do so, it must improve the quality of its teaching. Moreover, today teachers unions are actors in the political equation, and they constitute a countervailing force against the continuation of a high-turnover, low-cost, and thus lower-quality educational workforce.

Nonetheless, the move toward a more professional, high-quality teaching workforce is by no means assured. At the close of the 20th century, another option emerged, taking its cue from the "rush to the bottom" that has accompanied the spread of the global economy, rather than from the demand for a highly educated workforce the global economy has produced. The advocates of this strategy believe that they can deliver a highly marketable, if not necessarily top quality, education by having "deskilled" teachers employ "teacher-proof" curricula and programs, and by compensating for the lack of teacher skill with the intensification of teachers' (and students') work—a much longer school day, week, and year.[41] Such intensification necessarily leads to teacher burnout and a high rate of turnover, and so reproduces itself with cycle upon cycle of low-skill teaching.

TEACHER QUALITY IN A COLLECTIVE BARGAINING CONTEXT

It is in this context—the drive to intensify teacher work as a substitute for teacher quality—that one should understand the current complaints about how "few hours" teachers work, and how "well paid" they are for it.[42] In the realm of the actual world, cross-occupational comparisons of salaries continue to show that teachers earn much less than other professions that require a similar level of education and preparation.[43] While there is a mixed body of evidence about the short-term effects of teacher pay, there is more convincing, if nonetheless still preliminary, evidence of a long-term positive relationship between teachers' salaries and student achievement outcomes.[44] Since one of the few points on which different economists agree is the existence of a teachers union wage premium of somewhere between 5 and 20 percent, it would seem that teachers union improvements in teachers' salaries have the effect of making the job more attractive to a wider pool of prospective teachers, including those with more intellectual ability, from which the actual teaching force is selected. While an increase in the intellectual aptitude of prospective teachers addresses only a small part of what needs to be done to improve the quality of teaching—and is not a substitute for the rest of the agenda—it does make a contribution.

This having been said, it remains true that a narrowly conceived industrial-style salary schedule, with salary increases related solely to the length of service and the number of educational credits a person has accrued, is an unnecessarily restrictive method for promoting teaching quality. Such a schedule should be supplemented with pay differentials that reward teachers for exceptional knowledge and skills they acquire, such as NBPTS certification, and for taking on extraordinary tasks, such as working as a lead teacher, providing mentoring and professional development for colleagues, and working in a high-poverty school in need of educational improvement. Incentives, both financial and professional, could be provided to teachers who volunteer to teach in low-performing schools. In this way teachers can be rewarded for what they know and what they do when those skills and that work go above and beyond the ordinary call of teaching duty.[45]

Where such proposals differ from merit pay schemes is that they are universal in scope, open in principle to all teachers who want to participate, and based on objective standards. As long as union principles of equity—which are not the same as an absolute, homogenized equality—are met, teachers unions should have no problems with such differentiation among teachers, especially in the context of improving the quality of schooling. By contrast, merit pay schemes promoted by teachers union critics invariably involve a system of winners and losers, no matter how well every individual teacher performs, and usually give complete discretion to the supervisor to determine who qualifies as a "superior" teacher.

A similar attempt to create unfettered management rights bedevils efforts to reform dismissal and disciplinary procedures. Contrary to the image promoted by their critics, teachers unions are among the more forceful advocates for the reform of due process and dismissal procedures under collective bargaining agreements. Teachers themselves demand nothing less, since competent teachers pay part of the price for colleagues who cannot or will not perform when they receive students who were in those teachers' classes. Moreover, "justice delayed is justice denied" for the teachers wrongfully disciplined or dismissed. There is little question that most disciplinary and dismissal processes could and should be expedited, with the elimination of largely redundant steps, and that much shorter time lines for hearings and decisions could and should be established. What teachers unions cannot and will not agree to is the wholesale elimination of due process, with the establishment of the "at will" standard of employment that is used in the nonunionized, private sector. Under such a standard, a teacher could be disciplined or dismissed, without appeal, for any reason whatsoever, provided that the action does not violate legal prohibitions of discrimination against protected classes of individuals. That is, once again, simply unfettered management power.

Much of the same needs to be said about the often-heard claims that inflexible "work rules" in the collective bargaining agreements prevent administrators from providing a quality education. The lack of specificity in this charge is revealing. Exactly which work rules are hindering the quality of education?[46] The ones that place a cap on the size of classes? The ones that limit the total number of classes and the number of classes in a row without a break a teacher can be assigned? The ones that require school and district administrators to provide textbooks, educational technology, and other basic instructional materials for education? The ones that require school administrators to remove disruptive students from a class? The ones that require the school district to keep school buildings in sufficient repair as to be safe and healthy? The ones that relieve teachers from nonprofessional assignments so they can perform professional educational work? The ones that call for a reduction in bureaucratic paperwork? Inquiring educators need to know.

CONCLUSION

Almost a half century after collective bargaining first took root in American education, we are still debating the most fundamental issues concerning its meaning and purpose. These are questions about the exercise of power and the role of democracy in the organization of American schooling. For opponents of collective bargaining, its greatest fault is not in its particulars on this or that issue, but in the fact that it limits and restricts management power. Theirs is a vision of unfettered management authority, founded on the theory that management will simply "do the right thing" when allowed to function as "benevolent despots," with nothing but the discipline of the "invisible hand" of the marketplace to weed out the incompetent and the abusive. So-called "union power" is a problem because it limits the exercise of management power.

Yet there are reasons why democrats believe in the need to limit and check the exercise of power. An understanding of the nature of power lies behind the insistence that there is no legitimate governmental authority that does not ultimately rest with the consent and the participation of the governed. The logic of that understanding of power is played out in, among other places, the American Constitution, in the checks and balances we have placed on the use of power in government, and in the requirements for broad agreement on fundamental governmental decisions.

This democratic understanding of power would appear to be no less applicable to the use of power in education supported by the public and established to serve public purposes than in any other public institution. Perhaps this explains why the attacks on teacher unionism and collective bargaining in public education issue forth from the same quarters that would undo the public character of American education and hand it over to private powers unaccountable to the public. Their vision of governance in education is in the autocratic tradition of Hobbes, with management functioning as an absolutist sovereign, rather than in the democratic tradition of Jefferson.

Is it not telling in this regard that collective bargaining for teachers flourishes only in free and democratic societies, and that it has been denied and repressed under dictatorships and totalitarian regimes of both the far left (communism) and far right (fascism), from apartheid South Africa and Pinochet's Chile to Mao's China and Castro's Cuba? Or that the great bulk of the misnamed "right to work" states in the United States that prohibit collective bargaining for teachers today lie in the Deep South, where America's democratic traditions have been most violated and challenged?

At stake here, when all is said and done, is whether or not we believe that democratic voice for educators, the women and men whose daily labor is the education of our young people, is a positive force and an essential component of the success of students and schools. One need not even agree with the larger democratic ethos of voice to see its practical necessity here, for it seems almost axiomatic that no reform, no effort to improve the quality of education, will work without the willing participation of the teachers on its front lines. But for those of us who remain faithful to that broader vision of democracy, of a people determining their own destiny through an education of, by, and for the American public, democratic voice for teachers is a core value and principle.

I would like to thank Tom Dickson of the UFT Archives and Dan Golodner of the AFT Archives at the Walter Reuther Library of Wayne State University for their assistance in locating documents from the first collective bargaining negotiations in New York City, and Abe Levine, Andy Rotherham, and Richard Rothstein for their comments on earlier drafts of this essay. The opinions expressed in this essay, and the responsibility for them, are entirely my own.

CHAPTER NINE

The As-Yet-Unfulfilled Promise of Reform Bargaining
Forging a Better Match between the Labor Relations System We Have and the Education System We Want

JULIA E. KOPPICH

When the National Commission on Excellence in Education released *A Nation at Risk* in 1983, declaring that a "rising tide of mediocrity" had engulfed American education, it triggered a firestorm of activity. *Risk*, and its companion reports that followed, launched the contemporary education reform movement. Calling for fundamental changes in the American way of education, reform advocates took schools to task for contributing to the nation's flagging economic competitiveness. The Industrial Age, they said, had become the Information Age right under the noses of American captains of industry, who had barely seemed to take notice. The road to economic recovery, said reform proponents, began at the classroom door.

Criticisms focused on schools' lack of academic rigor, on the "dumbing down" of textbooks and the watering down of coursework, on lax teacher preparation curricula, low teacher salaries, and inadequate teacher professional decisionmaking authority. Reform advocates lamented the persistence of educational structures and instructional strategies that might have served students well in the early to mid-20th century but would not equip them to be successful (and thereby assist the United States to regain the economic advantage) in the then-rapidly-approaching 21st century.[1]

Through the ebbs and flows of 20 years of economic and political cycles, this reform movement has had enormous sticking power. Yet one significant area of education has remained virtually untouched by reform recommendations. Reading any of the myriad reports that have shaped contemporary education reform, one is hard pressed to find more than a glancing reference to unions or collective bargaining. Despite labor-management relations' power to influence much of the shape and substance of education policy and practice, the written documents that have driven the reform agenda have treated labor relations as a mere incidental sidelight, an addendum to the more critical aspects of education. None has seriously entertained the notion of fundamentally reforming labor-management relations or collective bargaining.

The critics who have complained of the slow pace of reform have not, however, been so silent. Their rhetoric has often laid at the feet of the teachers unions much of the blame for the grindingly slow and often frustratingly difficult work of trying to bring change to American schooling. Unions, they say, are too mired in the traditional and unwilling to embrace anything that resembles reform. The collective bargaining process, they say, renders relationships between teachers and administrators needlessly fractious. The contracts that result from the bargaining process, they say, so constrain teachers' and administrators' degrees of professional freedom that the slightest effort at change is stymied. In short, say the critics, promising education reforms have been blunted by an archaic system of labor relations. Remove that obstacle—eliminate collective bargaining—and education reform will flower.

There are, of course, many on the opposite side of this argument. Union traditionalists argue that it is precisely *because of* collective bargaining that schools and districts have developed and maintained procedural rules and regulations that bring order to what would otherwise be a hopeless jumble of inconsistently applied edicts and dicta.

Critics on both ends of this argument have some truth on their side. Unions have often been reluctant to embrace reform. Too-rigid employment contracts can serve to limit even the best-intended education improvement approaches. Labor-management relations can be brutally antagonistic. At the same time, unions and bargaining developed as they did to counter real-world situations. In so doing, collective bargaining has served a useful and important purpose. It has rationalized what remains an exquisitely bureaucratic system, creating agreed-on rules of the game and procedures. Eliminating it hardly seems the answer. But reshaping it might be.

This chapter takes up the issue of what has been called "reform bargaining" or "professional unionism."[2] It takes as a point of departure the small group of reforming unions that, perhaps in ways never intended or anticipated by the authors of the early reform reports, have used education reform as the bridge to a new form of teacher unionism. These unions are bringing about change by reassessing what it means to be a teachers union; by examining anew their role, purpose, and the source of their legitimacy; and by rethinking to whom they are responsible and for what. These unions are, in short, paying a refreshing visit to long-unexamined beliefs and, in the process, shaping new answers to old questions.

Yet simply recounting the story of reforming unions does not paint a complete picture. After two decades of education ferment, only a handful of these organizations remain. Those who wished for a halo effect—that reform unionism would take hold and spread as a natural phenomenon—have been forced to face disappointment. Likewise, those who assumed (or hoped) that reform unionism would be crushed under the weight of the pressure to change too much too quickly have not been given reason to celebrate.

If reform unionism is to fulfill its promise and bring about a new era of labor-management relations, more suited to contemporary times and the demands of 21st-century education, it may well need a catalyst. That catalyst, as this chapter will suggest, could come in the form of a reshaped collective bargaining law that reframes the purpose of labor-management relations to recast the outcome of negotiated agreements.

The chapter begins by briefly tracing the history of collective bargaining in education as a way to provide background and context. It then takes up the much more recent, and still evolving, experience of reform unionism—the promises and pitfalls—and concludes with a brief discussion about the prospect of reshaping labor law.

THE PRECURSORS TO REFORM UNIONISM

Reform unionism was preceded by two earlier stages, what Charles Taylor Kerchner and Douglas E. Mitchell called "generations" of labor relations.[3] The first was a period called "meet and confer" and the second the era of "industrial unionism."

When Meet and Confer Was the Order of the Day

Not very long ago, teachers held little sway over the conditions of their employment. Until at least the mid-1960s in most states, and well into the 1970s in many, salaries, benefits, and the circumstances under which teachers worked were determined by a process called "meet and confer," a kind of quasi-negotiation.

On the management side of the bargaining table sat the administration and school board. Representing the consolidated interests of the school district, management spoke with a single voice. On the employee side of the table sat representatives of various groups of teachers—high school science teachers, third grade teachers, middle school English teachers, and so on. Each group approached bargaining intent on securing what it could for its own constituents. But these teachers felt no obligation to act on behalf of the collective whole. As a result, management often quite successfully played one group against another. Moreover, management was under no legal obligation to discuss specific topics or even to reach any sort of agreement with its employees. Teachers, thus, only half-jestingly dubbed the process "meet and defer." At times the parties did agree to commit their discussions to writing. This most often took the form of memoranda of understanding that spelled out mutual commitments, but they carried no legal weight. The district (or the union, for that matter) could abrogate any or all parts of these agreements without reason or warning.

Meet and confer was not an irrational process, nor was it a particularly conscious effort to hold teachers powerless. The meet and confer approach assumed that teachers achieved their influence because their interests were coincidental with school district goals. In other words, teachers were (already) powerful because they wanted what the school district wanted.[4] In this sometimes functional but often clumsy system, classic paternalism prevailed. Teachers were spoken for; they did not speak for themselves.

The bonds of meet and confer began to fray with the social activism of the 1960s. Increasingly, teachers came to see their interests as different from administrators', their views as sometimes divergent, and they began to look in other directions for alternative means by which to deal with their school district employers.

Industrial Unionism Comes to Education

On April 11, 1962, New York City's 5,000-member United Federation of Teachers, an affiliate of the American Federation of Teachers (AFT), called a strike. This action was not greeted warmly by the city's powerbrokers. Newspapers called the strike leaders (including a young Albert Shanker) "hotheads." The secretary of the Central Labor Council announced that the strike "serves no social or economic purpose." New York law made striking punishable by firing, and the president of the New York City Board of Education declared, "Teachers themselves have terminated their employment."

The New York teachers' strike ended in 24 hours. No one was fired. The *New York Times* editorialized for higher teacher salaries. Governor Nelson Rockefeller came to the city's aid with additional money for schools. And teachers had a contract. This was a defining moment in public school labor relations, a watershed event that marked a permanent change in the relationship between teachers and their public school employers.[5] For the next decade and a half, one state after another would adopt legislation authorizing collective bargaining for education employees.

The Shape of Industrial Unionism

Industrial unionism was shaped by the National Labor Relations Act (NLRA), the centerpiece of American labor law. Enacted during heightened public support for organized labor in the period of the New Deal, the NLRA gave employees in the private sector the right to "form, join, or assist labor organizations, to bargain collectively through representatives of their own choosing, and to engage in concerted activities for the purpose of collective bargaining or other mutual aid and protection."

Collective bargaining is the process by which a group of employees selects a single organization to negotiate on its behalf a legally binding contract covering, in the usual language of the law, "wages, hours, and other terms and conditions of employment."[6] Teacher collective bargaining took its cues from the unionism of America's industries. When collective bargaining came to education, unions of educators used patterns of bargaining transported nearly wholesale from the nation's factories. Thus, state teacher collective bargaining laws closely resemble the federal private-sector statute.

The events of 1962 in New York City were not the beginning of teachers' efforts to organize in unions and engage in collective action. But until New York, most of these efforts were highly localized and often frustrated by the courts. In 1917, one year after Margaret Haley, an elementary school teacher, founded the AFT in Chicago, that city's Board of Education prohibited teachers from joining unions. The board's decision was affirmed by the Illinois Supreme Court. Until 1930 public-sector analogues to "yellow dog contracts," which prohibited individuals from joining unions as a condition of employment, regularly were upheld by the courts. In 1959 Wisconsin became the first, and for a time the only, state to recognize the right of teachers to join unions and bargain collectively with their employer. But the New York City action was the first to gain national attention and served as a springboard for legislative response across the country.

As collective bargaining laws evolved, they took on similar colorations. The laws all describe a process for identifying a bargaining unit—in other words, the individuals to be covered by a contract (usually determined to be a "community of interest"). They outline the legal scope of the agreement—the subjects that must be negotiated, may be negotiated, and are prohibited from being negotiated. They specify the duty of both union and management to bargain in good faith to reach an agreement and outline quasi-legal procedures (mediation and fact finding) to resolve labor-management impasses.

When teacher unionism adopted industrial unionism, it quickly came to be defined by industrial unionism's guiding principles: (1) separation of labor and management; (2) adversarial labor-management relations; and (3) protection of individual interests. Separation of labor and management signifies hierarchy. Jobs are categorized, classified, and separated. Teachers perform tasks different from those of administrators. That strict line of demarcation allows management to retain its sphere of authority and the unions to retain theirs. The notion that there might be reasonable crossover, that teachers' and administrators' responsibilities might intersect in the usual performance of their duties, is anathema to this system.

The NLRA discourages union-management cooperation as a means of warding off the development of company unions. Teacher collective bargaining laws contain no such admonition, but adversarial labor-management relations come as a borrowed consequence of industrial-style unionism.[7] Union and management become jousters on an ever-shifting battleground in which the object of the contest is to distribute the available spoils of bargaining (dollars, people, time, etc.).[8]

The third characteristic of industrial unionism is a focus on individual rights and interests. Traditional teachers' contracts establish terms and conditions of employment by detailing the accrued rights of those individuals whose professional lives are governed by it.[9]

Defending the Status Quo

On the one hand, industrial-style collective bargaining gave teachers voice and influence when they had none. It became legitimate for teachers to represent their own interests—decent salaries and benefits, professionally acceptable working conditions—and bargain these with management.[10] Unions grew and became more powerful as they organized their activity around traditional functions: negotiating ever more elaborate work rules and processing grievances when alleged violations of those rules occurred.

On the other hand, industrial unionism circumscribed teaching and created a kind of professional chasm between teachers and administrators. The uniformity of contract rules failed to recognize teachers' expertise as professionals, their need and desire to exercise professional judgment in the performance of their duties, and the interests they legitimately shared with management. Moreover, industrial unionism relegated unions to a backseat role in terms of shaping the educational policy that so intimately impacted their members' work lives.[11]

Simply put, industrial-style collective bargaining put both union and management in the position of defending the status quo. Both came to accept (or at least tolerate) the existing balance of powers whether or not this distribution contributed to a more effective education system. By the mid- to late 1980s, as education reform progressed, a handful of union leaders and superintendents began to recognize that a status quo labor relations system was an imperfect match with the reformed education system they increasingly saw as necessary.

FROM INDUSTRIAL UNIONISM TO REFORM BARGAINING

When *A Nation at Risk* made national headlines in 1983, a betting person would have put money on both the AFT and the National Education Association (NEA) railing against the report as just another instance of blame the schools, another exercise in unwarranted "teacher bashing." Such a person would have lost half the bet.

The AFT and Education Reform

The AFT, under the leadership of its president, Albert Shanker (the "hothead" of the 1962 New York strike), took an unexpected tack. Speaking to the AFT convention in Los Angeles in the summer of 1983, Shanker told the delegates: "In a period of great turmoil and sweeping changes, those organizations and individuals who are mired in what seems to the public to be petty interests are going to be swept away in the larger movement. Those . . . who are willing and able to participate, to compromise, and to talk will not be swept away. On the contrary, they will shape the direction of all the reforms and changes that are about to be made."[12] Shanker was positioning the AFT to be a player in education reform.

Soon thereafter the organization openly acknowledged problems with the education system, said the system needed to change, and asserted that teachers (and their union) needed to be part of the solution. While many skeptics among the AFT's longtime members wondered if perhaps something in the water in Washington, D.C., had affected their organization's president, Shanker held his ground, telling teachers that whatever the accomplishments of collective bargaining, the process had fallen short. "We have not been able to achieve all that we had hoped for through the bargaining process," he said, "and it is now time to go beyond it to something additional and quite different."[13]

The AFT aggressively embraced the standards and accountability movement. It launched its "Making Standards Matter" series, an unsentimental, analytical look at each state's student achievement standards, including their academic rigor and the extent to which they were linked to state accountability systems.

The organization supported consequences for teachers whose professional performance was substandard, endorsed the testing of teachers new to the profession, and sanctioned some forms of alternative compensation, including higher pay for teachers in hard-to-staff schools and subjects. At the same time, the AFT increased the size and relative importance of its Educational Issues Department and launched its biennial professional issues conference, Quality Educational Standards in Teaching, or QuEST.[14]

The AFT's expanded direction caught on with many of the union's powerful, and visible, local leaders. In places such as Cincinnati, Minneapolis, and Rochester (New York), the teachers union championed previously off-limits issues such as developing and implementing more effective teacher evaluation systems, reforming tenure, and designing less restrictive, more flexible contracts.

The NEA's Stance

The NEA initially took the route the pundits had predicted. The organization eschewed nearly all reform and warned its members away from it. That began to change, however, when Bob Chase was elected president. In a February 1997 speech to the National Press Club in Washington, D.C., titled "It's Not Your Mother's NEA," Chase called for re-creating the NEA as a "champion of quality teaching and quality education." He named his approach New Unionism.

In a burst of frankness, Chase acknowledged the NEA as a traditional, narrowly focused union that spent its time "butting heads" with management over "bread and butter" issues of salaries, benefits, and working conditions. He declared this focus utterly inadequate to the needs of contemporary education and called for higher academic standards, less bureaucracy, schools better connected to parents and communities, and a collective bargaining system focused on school and teacher quality.[15]

At the NEA convention in the summer of 1997, at Chase's urging, the NEA abandoned its long-standing opposition to peer review.[16] This action broke an organizational logjam, making it safe to talk in the NEA about formerly "undiscussable" topics and giving a tacit green light to NEA locals who were on the cusp of negotiating reform-oriented contracts.

THE SHAPE OF REFORM CONTRACTS

Reform contracts, whether negotiated by AFT or NEA locals, have several similar features that distinguish them from industrial contracts. They (1) blur the lines of distinction between union and management; (2) are negotiated using a process of labor-management cooperation; and (3) expand the scope of negotiations to include issues of educational policy.

Blurring the Lines of Distinction

In reform contracts, the separateness of labor and management is replaced by a sense of the collective aspect of work. Organizational hierarchies become flatter as lines of demarcation between what is strictly management work and what is teaching work are blurred. In so doing, the lines between what is solely the district's responsibility and what is the union's are also blurred. Reform unions assume joint custody for reform with management as they consider what makes educational sense for the school system and its students.[17]

One of the clearest demonstrations of valuing the collective nature of the work is seen in the reform union's emphasis on protecting the quality of teaching. Reform unions view this as an essential element of their responsibility. Typically, ensuring the quality of teaching by, for example, socializing new teachers into the profession and periodically appraising the performance of all teachers, is solely within the purview of the administration. Administrators manage new teacher induction programs and evaluate new and experienced teachers alike.

But reform unions that have entered into a partnership with their school district management assume a significant share of responsibility for ensuring both that new teachers start off on the right professional foot and that more experienced teachers practice at a high level or are removed from the classroom. Unions such as those in Cincinnati, Columbus (Ohio), Minneapolis, and Montgomery County (Maryland) have worked with their respective districts to design and implement well-structured teacher induction and evaluation programs. These rigorous peer assistance and review programs are based on standards of good teaching and result in both new teachers and underperforming experienced teachers either being helped to improve or helped out of the profession. This activity is a fundamental departure from industrial unionism, in which, in the name of colleague solidarity, no teacher would ever presume to appraise the professional performance of another. In reform unions that have adopted peer review, one of the union's premier organizational obligations is to be the guardian of professional standards.

In another effort to enhance teacher quality, the Denver Classroom Teachers Association and the Denver Public Schools have jointly created a new teacher compensation system that breaks ranks with the traditional way of paying teachers based on longevity and college credits. Denver substitutes a system in which teachers advance in pay based on demonstrated knowledge and skills and increased student achievement. In effect, better teachers earn more money.

The Minneapolis Federation of Teachers and the Minneapolis Public Schools, at the urging of the union, replaced the pro forma, largely ineffective means of determining teachers' eligibility for tenure with a rigorous three-year process of professional development and peer and administrator evaluation. Tenure is earned in Minneapolis, not simply offered as a reward for time served.

Reform unions, then, assume joint responsibility with management for areas that traditionally are left to management alone. In so doing, these unions send the message that it is as much their obligation as the administration's to ensure that those in the classroom are well equipped to do their jobs effectively. Assuming joint custody for reform requires the union and district to alter the way in which they do business with each other. They must find common ground and a more conciliatory way of working together.

Finding Common Ground with Management

In industrial bargaining, labor relations are permanently contentious as union and management vie for the upper hand in negotiations. Any crack in the bargaining armor of either side is taken as a sign by that side's constituents that it has "sold out" or "gone soft." Lost in adversarial negotiations are opportunities for teachers and administrators to explore mutual professional values, goals, and expectations, or even to acknowledge that such mutuality might exist.

Reforming unions (and their school districts) use bargaining processes that allow union and management to find common ground. Traveling under the umbrella of "win-win," interest-based, or collaborative bargaining, negotiations aim to reach mutually desired goals. "Hard on the problem, not hard on each other" is collaborative bargaining's functional slogan. Negotiators learn to separate people from problems, focus on interests rather than positions, and generate a variety of possibilities before deciding on the terms of an agreement.[18]

Cooperative labor relations necessitate a shift in mindset, a reexamination of what Peter M. Senge calls "mental models."[19] They require that both union and management develop an improved ability to view the world from the other's perspective, and a new understanding of the labor relationship as a partnership rather than a contest. The union, for example, must come to understand district finances and true budget conditions and must be able to acknowledge tight money times when the facts so indicate. The district must be able to appreciate the union's position in advocating for a moratorium on involuntary teacher transfers when management thinks it is just exercising administrative flexibility by moving teachers around.

Collaboration also requires that union and management develop an ongoing relationship that spans the time between contract negotiations, that enables the parties to meet periodically to solve problems as they crop up rather than letting them fester. Thus, reform contracts often contain a provision for monthly (or quarterly) meetings between the superintendent and union president to engage in such problem-solving sessions. These are meetings between decision-makers, not messengers, where real work can get done and issues can be ironed out before they reach the formal grievance stage.

A collaborative union-management relationship implies trust. Each side must believe that the other is acting, at least in part, with both sides' interests at heart. While personal trust between individuals may be ideal, trust in the process can suffice. A working relationship can flourish in an atmosphere in which both union and management behave in accord with their words. But trust, once achieved, is fragile and can be fleeting. Predicated on the computation of risks,[20] it can quickly unravel if one side springs something on the other or backtracks on a commitment.

Finally, effective union-management partners understand that collaborative bargaining is not an end in itself. The reason to change the labor-management relationship is not solely to alter the tenor of discourse. Cooperative labor-management relations do not represent a return to the era of meet and confer, when the interests of teachers and the district were assumed to be perfectly meshed. Even in the most collaborative of partnerships, union and management will continue to find areas of disagreement. But they will disagree about different kinds of issues. The result of the most productive labor-management collaborations is education improvement as the parties expand their discussions beyond the traditional triumvirate of wages, hours, and working conditions to include issues that lie at the heart of teaching and learning.

Expanding the Envelope

In traditional bargaining, unions operate within a relatively narrow frame of negotiable items. This frame is designed to reinforce the maxim that labor represents employees' economic and day-to-day work concerns and management makes policy and operational decisions. Thus, teacher transfer policy may be negotiable, but curriculum typically is not. Class size may be negotiable, but textbook selection usually is not.

Industrial contracts serve relatively limited purposes. They codify the terms and conditions that shape teachers' work lives. They protect teachers from arbitrary and capricious actions of the employer through uniform, standardized work rules. A traditional contract serves as a statement of the accrued rights of individual teachers in which nearly any teacher complaint on wages, hours, and conditions is subject to adjudication via the grievance procedure.

But the scope of the agreement—what is included in the contract—also circumscribes the parameters of the labor-management relationship. To the extent that the union is excluded from discussions of education policy—curriculum, instructional materials, the content of professional development, and the like—teachers are left out of that decisionmaking loop. This situation seems to defy logic. While teachers do not have a monopoly on educational wisdom, their first-hand perspective gives them a unique and critical vantage point from which to assess the efficacy of educational policy decisions.[21] Omitting them from this arena seems an approach destined to create more problems than it solves.

Interestingly, scope is the one area of collective bargaining law that has been subject to some reform in recent years. Each of these state efforts—in Wisconsin, Illinois, and Pennsylvania, for example—has been aimed at limiting the sweep of negotiable issues. The operating theory has been that by reducing the union's influence in matters that sit at the core of the school district's operations, reform would proceed more smoothly and at a quicker pace. There is scant evidence that this theory has played out in practice.

Reform contracts move in exactly the opposite direction where scope is concerned. They break the boundaries of traditional scope and cover a range of issues that venture well into the territory of educational policy. The district's agenda becomes part and parcel of the union's agenda. For example, the Montgomery County Education Association and the Montgomery County Public Schools entered a labor-management partnership that resulted in the union's involvement in building the district's budget as union and district together developed and implemented MCPS' major reform effort aimed at improving teacher quality: the Professional Growth System (PGS). The PGS includes a peer assistance and review program for teachers new to the profession and for underperforming experienced teachers, an administrator-driven standards-based evaluation system for tenured teachers not deemed to be in professional jeopardy, and an extensive school-based professional development program tied to increasing student achievement.

The recently negotiated contract between the Rochester Teachers Association and the Rochester City Schools includes a new provision for "contract schools" whose expressed purpose is "to improve school performance and focus on student achievement."[22] Beginning as a pilot in the 2005-06 school year, faculties of participating schools will be given the authority to negotiate with the principal new contract agreements tailored to the school's student learning needs. These agreements will supplant parallel provisions of the master contract. School-based agreements can cover areas such as work year (the distribution of days), teacher assignments, teaching conditions, class size, and the structure of the student day. The principal and union faculty representative will be authorized to sign off on the contract changes.

Reform unions view collectively bargained contracts as both a means to establish the boundaries of work rules and a device to engage their members in conscious thought about the ways in which their professional actions impact on their public obligations.[23] Reform contracts, thus, speak both to teachers' individual interests and to the profession's public duties. They recognize the intersection of personal interests and collective professional obligations. They attempt to answer the question, "If teachers' primary responsibility is to students, how can they most effectively carry out their work?" That question is answered not from the perspective of what makes life easier and more pleasant for the adults, but what conditions will enhance student learning prospects.

Expanded scope is an acknowledgment, by both union and management, that if schools are to be improved, teachers must be active participants in the effort.[24] To the extent that unions and management are willing and able to extend the traditional contract boundaries to encompass crucial issues of improving the quality of teaching and levels of student learning, education reform has a fighting chance. Where unions or management put roadblocks in the way of opening discussions to matters of educational policy, reform is likely to be stymied.

Reform unions, then, understand that change is not an option. They accept that defending the status quo is no longer a tolerable proposition. They work to develop cooperative relationships with their school district counterparts. They believe in an expanded education policy role for teachers and their union.[25] And reform unions recognize that embracing educational change, and assuming a significantly expanded role for the union, requires enhancing organizational capacity.

THE INTERNAL WORK OF REFORMING UNIONS: BUILDING ORGANIZATIONAL CAPACITY

Unions, like all organizations, tend to cling to the familiar, performing the functions they traditionally have, acting in ways to which they have long been accustomed. The conventional union liturgy of negotiating narrowly defined contracts and being confrontational with management is what many of these organizations know best.

Perhaps it is not surprising, then, that many union locals continue to glory in the battles of the early days of collective bargaining, when teachers unions were first being recognized as powerful and influential entities. These union locals prefer to fight, or refight, the old wars, even if the reasons for those wars no longer exist, the battles might be more successfully joined using different approaches, or the members' interests have changed. The merged AFT-NEA San

Francisco teachers union, for example, in 2005 embarked on a nostalgia tour of a strike a quarter of a century earlier, a time that at least half the teachers now working in the district do not recall and in which they have little interest. While this may have been a sincere effort to remind younger members of their organizational roots, it also highlights the disjuncture between a traditional union and a reform union.

Reform unions face numerous challenges. They must persuade longtime members that a new way of doing business does not mean abandoning traditional union values or issues. They must remain mindful that the fact that unions today are able to focus energy and attention on an expanded range of educational issues owes in no small measure to the hard work and accomplishments of those who went before. At the same time, they must convince newer members, or potential members, that the union is an important vehicle for educational improvement. This is not an easy sell, even in the places where it is most consistent with reality.

Teachers hired at the height of the civil rights movement and shortly thereafter are truly a different generation. They value job security and autonomy, are wary of competition, and oppose differential treatment. Newer teachers, by contrast, bring to their jobs a penchant for variety, teamwork, risk taking, and entrepreneurial opportunities. The former set of values is a good fit with the type of collective bargaining that built the power of teachers unions; the latter is not.[26] Reform unions attempt to strike a balance between the two sets of values: they understand the importance of history but do not long to return to the past. They recognize that they must continue to advocate on behalf of traditional union concerns—professional salaries, decent benefits, and respectable working conditions—but also acknowledge that many union members want something more and different from their organization.

Employees no longer see a clear distinction between "bread and butter" issues and professional issues.[27] As internal NEA and AFT polls indicate, teachers want their union to pay attention to both. They are interested in an organization that cares as much about how they do their jobs—and helps them to gain skills as accomplished professionals—as what they are paid or what their health plan is like. In short, teachers who are the immediate future of the unions want those unions to be, as Thomas Kochan says, occupational community-building entities.[28] Expanding the union's organizational repertoire, assuming responsibility for the profession as well as for the professionals, requires that reform unions rethink their organizational structures and processes.

What kinds of internal organizational issues do reform unions confront? Between 1999 and 2002, six teachers union locals—three AFT and three NEA—set about to find out.[29] Part of a U.S. Department of Education–funded project, these six reform-oriented unions began the work of assessing their existing organizational capacity and then developing plans to more effectively align programs, human and fiscal resources, and communications so as to position the unions to occupy a more prominent place as leaders in education improvement.

The first phase of the project involved an organizational self-study in which each of the project locals, often using the services of an outside consultant, conducted an internal review, examining the union's governance structure, staff roles and responsibilities, school site representation system, community and school district partnerships, and communication with members. Five findings from the self-studies cut across all participating locals and are likely more widely applicable to other unions that are positioning themselves for reform.

First, securing ongoing union leadership is a continuing dilemma. Participating union leaders acknowledge that they give little thought to leadership succession, to who will replace them once their terms of office expire or they choose to retire. This is a dilemma particularly in NEA locals, most of which have term limits for president of two four-year terms. Finding someone to carry on the reform legacy is a nagging worry.

Second, the school site representation system, the union's face at the work site, is often less effective than it needs to be. This issue plays itself out in one of two ways. Either too many of the school representatives are simply mailbox stuffers, delivering the union's periodic printed matter but taking no more active role in the organization, or the union has a dual representation system. Some reform unions that have moved into the professional issues arena find themselves with two school representatives, one who handles traditional union contract issues and another who deals with teachers' professional concerns. The dilemma is that these two roles are seen nearly as mutually exclusive, giving the union a kind of split personality that teachers are often hard pressed to reconcile.

Third, union staffs' jobs have changed little, even in changing unions, creating a troubling mismatch between staff roles and the union agenda. Many longtime union staffers are more comfortable with the work of industrial bargaining and do not wholeheartedly embrace the union's expanded focus. Reform unions are thus faced with the prospect of retraining existing staff to accept and assume new roles, or replacing them.

Fourth, union budgets tend to be based on long-existing categories rather than on contemporary or emerging program needs. Reform unions must develop strategies either to generate additional revenue or, more often, to reallocate existing resources to new union efforts. Allocating resources to shifting organizational priorities often collides with the interests of longstanding union constituencies who are reluctant to see their organization change.

Fifth, the union's communication with members does not always hit the mark. Especially in districts with large numbers of younger teachers, the so-called Generation-Xers, both the union's methods of communication (which may tend to focus on the written rather than the electronic) and the message (much on traditional union issues, little on teachers' professional concerns) fail to resonate with those teachers on whom the union's future depends.[30]

The results of the union capacity project illustrate the enormous task that reforming unions face as they work to position the union to be the organization that speaks for teaching as well as for teachers. This is work that requires a particular kind of leader.

Leadership for Reform Unionism

Organizational change requires leaders who think differently. Reform union leaders must be able to help teachers to assume the obligation to be active partners in the development and implementation of educational policy, to tackle thorny issues of colleague competence and resource allocation, to come to terms with the definition of good teaching and issues of educational quality, and to assume their share of responsibility for student learning outcomes. At the same time, leaders of reform unions must tread the line between advocating grand strategies of reform and continuing to care about and work on members' day-to-day work problems. They must not lose sight of the union's traditional obligations while simultaneously expanding members' horizons. They must challenge union orthodoxy while remaining true to union principles.

Leaders of reform unions must develop thick skins. When these unions take bold and risky steps, they often are castigated—by management and their own members—for overstepping their bounds, venturing into territory that is not properly theirs. Such was the case in 1981 when the Toledo Federation of Teachers became the first in the nation to advocate peer review, or, more recently, in New York City when the United Federation of Teachers developed a curriculum to accompany the district's new language arts standards. Criticism did not revolve around the quality of the UFT's work. Critics simply asserted that it was not the union's place to undertake the task.

Leaders of reform unions must also be able to say "no." Not everything labeled a "reform" is good or worthwhile or educationally sound. Sometimes the union is right to reject a reform proposal. But leaders of reform unions must be able to view a proposal from all sides and then make a decision on the basis of the idea's educational efficacy, even if recommending it seems to complicate the work lives of the organization's members.

Effective leaders of traditional unions motivate followers by appealing to their self-interest and immediate concerns. They respond to what members say they want but make little effort to encourage members to reach beyond their obvious concerns. By contrast, effective leaders of reform unions are what the political scientist James McGregor Burns called "transformational leaders."[31] They influence major changes in attitudes and assumptions of organization members. They build the commitment for the organization's expanded mission, objectives, and strategies. And they accomplish all of this while continuing to grow the organization.

THE PROSPECTS FOR REFORM UNIONISM

The discussion of reform unionism raises at least two fundamental questions: (1) Can unions really be simultaneously concerned with traditional working-condition issues and professional issues? and (2) Why has reform unionism not spread more broadly? The experience of reform unions suggests that the first question can be answered in the affirmative. Reform unions have bridged what conventional wisdom would have us believe is the unnatural divide between classic wages, hours, and conditions of employment and issues central to building a quality profession. The answer to the second question is more complicated but is likely found in the actions and dispositions of organizations and institutions to which reform unions, or union locals that are seeking direction, might turn for help.

Seeking Support for Reform Unionism

Reform unions, and their leaders, sometimes go it alone. When the Denver Classroom Teachers Association, an affiliate of the NEA, decided to embark with its school district on the development of a new teacher compensation system, the union did so over the objections of its parent organization. So it is possible for reform unions to frame a different agenda even in the absence of support from their usual allies. But the journey is certainly more comfortable, if not easier, if a local union believes it is not working alone, that there are like-minded compatriots with the same goals facing the same challenges.

So where can reform-minded unions turn for guidance, direction, and even permission for an expanded agenda?

The AFT and NEA

At this juncture, neither the AFT nor the NEA is at the forefront of promoting a reform union agenda. A combination of leadership turnover and shifting political realities has resulted in alterations in these national organizations' priorities.

At the AFT, Al Shanker, on his death in 1997, was succeeded as president by Sandra Feldman. She was the longtime leader of the New York City AFT, the

United Federation of Teachers, the union's largest local and Shanker's original home base. For the five years of her tenure, Feldman maintained a less visible, albeit still proreform, stance. She did not attempt to move the organization away from its teaching and learning agenda, and even urged the union in one new direction, as an advocate of universal early childhood education. But Feldman was a much less vocal advocate for education reform than Shanker had been, and the organization's public presence assumed a lower profile under her leadership.

Feldman chose not to seek a second term due to ill health in 2004. The AFT presidency was then assumed by Edward McElroy, who had served as the union's second-in-command since 1992 and ran for the position unopposed. A former president of the Rhode Island Federation of Teachers, McElroy, at least early in his tenure, seems to be more focused on traditional trade union issues (e.g., current discussions about restructuring the AFL-CIO) and less concerned with enhancing the union reform agenda. McElroy is rarely seen publicly speaking out on education reform issues, nor does he write prominently about the kinds of education improvement strategies the AFT has, in recent history, championed.

To be sure, a central issue occupying the AFT leadership's time and attention is the federal No Child Left Behind Act (NCLB). The AFT early on urged its members to be cautious in being too harsh on the law, saying that whatever its shortfalls, NCLB remained the largest federal commitment to the education of children in poverty and contained provisions the union had long supported, including requiring a highly qualified teacher in every classroom and disaggregating standardized test scores by race. But as the reality of NCLB implementation has hit states and districts, the AFT has been under increasing pressure from its state and local leaders to take a more forceful, less conciliatory stance.

It would not be fair to assert that the AFT has completely abandoned leadership for reform. The spring 2005 issue of its flagship magazine, *American Educator*, for example, is devoted to a fresh examination of standards-based reform and accountability. Including articles written by notable academics in the field, the message of the magazine is that, while there may be a need for midcourse corrections, standards-based education, and the accountability for results that accompanies it, is right for America. And the AFT's professional issues conference in the summer of 2005 included sessions on a range of reform issues, standards and accountability among them, but also teaching literacy in high schools, improving mathematics instruction, closing the achievement gap, and using data to drive instruction.

The NEA story is a little different. In 2002 delegates to the NEA convention elected a new president. Due to the NEA's term limit requirement, Bob Chase could not run again. Delegates chose Reg Weaver, a former president of the Illinois Education Association who had served as NEA vice president for six years under Chase, to be the organization's new president. Weaver defeated Denise Rockwell, a vice president of the merged (AFT and NEA) United Teachers of Los Angeles (UTLA), for the office. Though their campaign platforms seemed quite similar on the surface, most reform NEA unions supported Rockwell's candidacy.

Weaver's first term of office has been marked by the NEA's frontal assault on NCLB, culminating in the organization's April 2005 suit against federal officials, challenging the law as an unfunded mandate. In addition to the union's anti-NCLB actions, Weaver has brought the organization back to many pre–Chase era positions, adopting a generally antireform stance. New Unionism has all but disappeared from the NEA agenda.

But perhaps it would be a mistake to read the elections of McElroy and Weaver as members' rejection of their unions' reform agendas. Particularly in the NEA, presidents historically are selected through a kind of "moving through the chairs" sequence. It was Reg Weaver's turn, and hard for the organization to buck that tradition. In the NEA the voices of reform were not loud enough, or perhaps not yet loud enough, to overcome the voices of the status quo.

The AFT has been shaken by two unexpected leadership turnovers in just a few years. Even those who might have preferred a more aggressive union reformer in the top spot of that organization were understandably reluctant to subject it to more internal turmoil.

Finally, it should be emphasized that both union presidents are faced with different, and in some ways more difficult, political situations than their immediate predecessors. The AFT and NEA are attempting to negotiate a terrain studded with policy landmines—the continuing, and frustrating, plight of urban schools; increasing public enchantment with charters despite these schools' rather mixed records; and the growing, albeit loosely coupled, coalition of minorities and the political right, which supports at least experiments with privatization efforts such as vouchers. Wrapped around all of this is an administration in Washington that is not always friendly to public schools and is downright hostile to teachers unions.[32]

Whatever the reasons—and whether they portend a permanent return to more traditional unionism or simply a temporary detour on the way to making reform unionism a more fixed entity—at this moment (summer 2005), neither the AFT nor the NEA is positioning itself to pursue much of a union reform agenda.

The Teacher Union Reform Network

The Teacher Union Reform Network (TURN) is a collaboration of more than 20 NEA and AFT locals, most reform minded. TURN was born in 1996 when Adam Urbanski, president of the Rochester (New York) Teachers Association, an AFT affiliate, and Helen Bernstein, then-president of UTLA, called together reform-minded union leaders.

TURN participants now meet quarterly to exchange ideas, share war stories, and gain fresh perspective from like-minded colleagues. TURN locals have adopted a mission statement that includes as goals for their unions "improving the quality of teaching" and "seeking to expand the scope of collective bargaining to include instructional and professional issues." Clearly these are in line with a reform union agenda. However, TURN has experienced some internal tensions of its own.

Since TURN locals have made clear that they have no ambition to become a third (national) union, they also have determined to take no collective positions on issues of substance. Neither do they push TURN members whose reform agendas have become lax to expand their horizons. Thus, consideration of the hot topics of the day, be they standardized testing, teacher tenure, or the structure of the compensation system, tends to be confined to internal debates with neither resolution nor action attached.

Moreover, within TURN there has long been an almost unspoken, but nonetheless evident, tension about whether the core mission of the network is to reform education or to reform unions, or both. The result is that discussions of union reform are often subsumed under more global discussions of education reform, which renders them both safer and more distant.

The Institute for Teacher Union Leadership

An effort in its infancy, the Institute for Teacher Union Leadership (ITUL) aims to train the next generation of progressive union leaders. ITUL grew out of the conviction of a small group of TURN members (both AFT and NEA) that reform unionism can be sustained only if the succeeding group of union leaders comes to office with a reform union agenda.

ITUL plans to offer an 18-month training program to teams of leaders and potential leaders from a select group of union locals. Training will include a weeklong summer institute and mentoring by experienced reform union leaders for a period of about a year following the summer training. ITUL's first full year of operation began in the summer of 2005. Its success, or failure, is yet to be written.

FORECASTING THE FUTURE

What, then, is the future of reform unionism? As Richard Kahlenberg points out in his chapter in this volume, reform union presidents in a number of union locals—Chicago and San Francisco, among them—have suffered recent electoral defeats to challengers who are more traditional unionists.[33] Do these results sound the death knell for reform unionism? Perhaps this is just stubborn optimism, but it seems that pronouncing the reformist era over is somewhat premature. Local elections are often just that, the product of individual local circumstances, not necessarily the harbinger of a larger pattern. For every San Francisco there is a Montgomery County, where the previous progressive union leader (who could not run again because of term limits) was succeeded by an equally progressive union leader. And hope glimmers in places such as Milwaukee, long the bastion of stubbornly traditional union leadership, where teachers have elected a consciously progressive union president.

On the one hand, it is far too early to write reform unionism's obituary. Too many reform union adherents remain in leadership positions to assume that this union direction will simply whither away. On the other hand, reform unionism is much less visible than it was a few years ago. Despite the best efforts of the most energetic TURN locals and whatever the potential of ITUL, it seems likely that sustaining reform unionism, and encouraging its spread, will require a different kind of action.

REFRAMING COLLECTIVE BARGAINING TO RESHAPE EXPECTATIONS

Collective bargaining policies enacted in the 1960s and 1970s shelter industrial-style unionism, offering support to traditional union leaders but providing neither reform unions nor management much encouragement. To be sure, union locals that have made progress in reform bargaining have done so without changing collective bargaining policies. They have developed cooperative labor-management relationships and expanded the range of negotiated issues to include improving teaching and learning. But the spread of reform unionism seems to have hit a brick wall. As education reform has become increasingly bound up in concerns about test score accountability, teachers have come to feel under siege and unions have hunkered down. The result is that current policies, unchanged in decades, frame a particular vision of collective bargaining, a vision increasingly out of step with the contemporary obligations of education.

It is time to consider a new policy approach to bargaining. It is time to reframe the purpose of collective bargaining to reshape expectations for the outcomes of the process. In particular, newly framed collective bargaining policy should (1) legitimize labor-management cooperation and (2) expand the scope of bargaining to encompass education policy.

Labor-Management Cooperation to Improve Student Achievement

Among the lessons to be drawn from reform bargaining are the following:

1. Union and management can form productive partnerships that recognize the parties' mutual dependencies and their common membership in a professional community.

2. The ultimate goal to which effective reform-minded unions and management are committed is improving student achievement.

A new collective bargaining law could formally recognize labor-management interdependency and the primacy of improving student achievement by obliging union and management to negotiate consensually arrived-at student achievement goals. These goals—measurable indicators of what students should know and be able to do—would then form the foundation for the negotiated contract. Contract provisions—the agreements about teacher working conditions—would be shaped by the exigencies of student learning conditions. Class size, teacher assignment, school resource distribution, and the like all would be a function of students' instructional needs. These would vary from school to school, necessitating a procedure for tailoring agreements to school circumstances, the details of which could be left to the union-management partners.

The result of this new approach—requiring union and management to develop a partnership that enables them to reach agreement on student achievement goals—would have the effect of reshaping the expectations of the bargaining process by reframing the purpose of the agreement. The central thrust would be to devise strategies, jointly endorsed by teachers and the administration, that contribute to improving student learning. Within these strategies for student improvement would be the professional employment conditions that enable teachers to be effective practitioners.

This system would not be possible within a narrowly restrictive scope of bargaining. Thus, revised bargaining policy requires expanding scope to encompass matters that currently fall into the educational policy arena.

Expanding Scope

Serious discussion about improving student achievement involves serious consideration of issues such as curriculum, assessment, resource allocation and deployment, standards for hiring and continued employment, incentives for improved performance, and consequences for failure to improve. A scope of negotiations that does not include those issues central to the educational enterprise places all-but-insurmountable roadblocks in the way of education improvement.

Confronting *Yeshiva*

Any statutory expansion of scope will need to confront the *Yeshiva* dilemma.

In 1974 the unaffiliated faculty at Yeshiva University in New York petitioned the National Labor Relations Board for the right to represent full-time faculty at 10 of the university's 13 schools. University management claimed that faculty were not employees. The administration's case was based on its assertion that, since faculty recommendations on matters such as hiring and tenure were often accepted, faculty were actually managers and supervisors, making them ineligible to engage in collective bargaining.

The NLRB sided with the faculty, who then voted to have the Yeshiva University Faculty Association represent them in contract negotiations. The university appealed the NLRB's decision to the U.S. Supreme Court. In a five-to-four decision, the Court ruled in favor of the university. It denied the faculty collective bargaining rights on the grounds that they "exercise authority which in any other context unquestionably would be managerial."[34]

Although this case is not entirely analogous to the situation of public school teachers, the *Yeshiva* decision has had a chilling effect on subsequent considerations of expanding scope to include traditionally managerial (or quasi-managerial) responsibilities. Any revision to collective bargaining law will need to deal expressly with the issues raised by *Yeshiva*. At least two states have made modest efforts in this direction. In both instances the statutory changes related specifically, and exclusively, to establishing new systems of teacher evaluation.

Collective bargaining laws typically specify that members of the same bargaining unit are prohibited from evaluating other members of the unit. Thus, under the law, teachers are precluded from participating in systems of peer review in which experienced teachers, jointly selected by a union-management committee, evaluate the professional practice of colleagues. But peer review became an accepted, and successful, practice in Toledo and spread to other cities in Ohio, including Cincinnati and Columbus. That state then changed the relevant state statutes to render peer review legal.

California proceeded down a similar track. In 2001 the state determined to require peer review in all districts. But California's collective bargaining law contained the prohibition against intrabargaining unit member evaluation. Rather than opening up the bargaining statute, the state instead enacted a new law, specifically about peer review, which held that a member of a bargaining unit who evaluated another member of that same unit remained a unit member and could not be declared a supervisor.

A new conception of collective bargaining, then, would center negotiated agreements on improving student achievement, sanction collaborative labor-management relations, and expand the scope of bargaining to include matters of education policy. Of course, the question arises, "Is this an opportune time to venture into the public policy arena?" The answer is, perhaps not surprisingly, both a forceful "yes" and "no."

The best of times, the worst of times

In significant ways a window of opportunity has been created to reshape collective bargaining policy. The changing nature of work and workers has been recognized for some time. In 1985 the AFL-CIO Committee on the Evolution of Work wrote in *The Changing Situation of Workers and Their Unions*, "Workers, particularly better educated workers, [seek] increasing discretion at the workplace as the role of work [begins] to morph from a straight economic transaction . . . to the opportunity for personal growth and professional enrichment."[35]

Teachers, like other educated workers, view their jobs as opportunities for self-expression and self-development. They want to feel their voices are heard and count with their employers.[36] They want to be able to exercise professional judgment without being unnecessarily constrained by rules and regulations. A survey of 700 teachers in charter schools, for example, showed that what these teachers value most about their work situation is freedom from district strictures.[37]

At the same time, teachers continue to believe they need a framework of safeguards. They say that they work in highly politicized environments in which they are still vulnerable to the actions of school administrators, school board members, and parents. And they credit their unions with protecting them from the vagaries of school politics.[38] But clearly teachers—particularly those hired in the 1980s and later—want their union also to be their professional organization. They look to the union to be as concerned with the professional tools and experiences teachers need to do their jobs effectively as it is with the financial and other "bread and butter" aspects of their jobs.

That teachers want unions, but somewhat different kinds of unions, or at least unions with expanded functions, bodes well for revised collective bargaining policy focused on labor-management cooperation and an expanded scope of bargaining. The contemporary political climate may not be hospitable, however.

As Lorraine McDonnell and Anthony Pascal observed nearly two decades ago, "The collective bargaining process and the resulting contract can serve either as an efficient vehicle for shaping and implementing new approaches to teacher professionalism . . . or as a major hindrance to reform."[39] So why not give more unions a legislative jolt in the direction of reform? Perhaps the simplest answer lies in the meanness of contemporary political times and the unpredictability of the policymaking process.

This is a precarious time for teachers unions. Those who would like to see unions disappear altogether, who are quick to brand unions as the sole force applying the brakes to education reform, are well organized and well funded and wield considerable political clout. The former secretary of education Rod Paige garnered much publicity, not all of it negative, when he labeled the National Education Association a "terrorist organization" as a result of the NEA's vocal opposition to many of the provisions of the Bush administration's No Child Left Behind Act. And, as previously noted, the forces that seek to privatize education, effectively eliminating public schools and their unions, have gained substantial influence in policy circles.

In addition, the policymaking process itself is problematic. What may begin as a well-intentioned policy reform enters the maelstrom of the decisionmaking process and can emerge as something bearing little resemblance to, or even having the opposite effect of, the original.

Where does that leave us? As in life, in policy, timing is everything. It seems certain that those who hope to see reform unionism flower will need to devise a broader strategy to bring more adherents into this tent. Ultimately, in order to institutionalize reform unionism, it is likely that bargaining policy will need to be revamped. This should not be taken as a repudiation of historical union principles. New labor policy is in order not because history was wrong but because history is just that.[40]

Reframed collective bargaining public policy can be a tool to shape a new, and more productive, future of labor-management relations. It is for others more adept at reading the political tea leaves to determine when the time is right for such policy action.

CHAPTER TEN

Union Power and the Education of Children

TERRY M. MOE

etween the 1960s and the early 1980s, the American system of public
education was transformed by a dramatic shift in its balance of power.
In earlier times the system's key power holders were the administrative
professionals charged with running it. Teachers had little power, and they were
unorganized aside from their widespread membership in the National Education
Association (NEA), which was controlled by administrators. But in the 1960s
states began to adopt laws that, for the first time, promoted collective bargaining for public employees. And when the American Federation of Teachers (AFT)
launched an aggressive campaign to organize teachers, the NEA turned itself into
a labor union to compete, and the battle was on in thousands of school districts.
By the time the dust settled in the early 1980s, virtually all districts of any size
(outside the South) were successfully organized, collective bargaining was the
norm, and the teachers unions—with millions of members and loads of money—
were by far the most powerful force in American education.[1]

This new system, defined and protected by union power, has been in equilib-
rium now for more than 20 years. On the surface it looks very much like the
system of school boards, superintendents, and local democracy bequeathed us
by Progressive reformers nearly a century ago.[2] But the Progressives did not
bequeath us a system of union power. This is a modern development, one with
profound consequences that make the modern system qualitatively different
from the one it replaced.[3]

The unions now shape the public schools from the bottom up through collective bargaining agreements that affect virtually every aspect of school organization and operation. They also shape the schools from the top down by influ-

encing the education policies of government and blocking reforms they find threatening to their interests. It is difficult to overstate how extensive a role they play in making today's schools what they are, and in preventing them from being something different.[4]

With few exceptions, education scholars take this pervasive union influence as one of the great givens of public education. They don't challenge or question it. They don't even study it. This is a serious mistake with far-reaching consequences, and not simply because the unions are too important to overlook. For there are persuasive reasons to think that the power of the teachers unions is in many ways quite bad for public education and ultimately works to the disadvantage of children.

I will be arguing that the problems associated with union power are inherent to the unions as organizations, are very much to be expected, and cannot be eliminated by some sort of "reform unionism" that relies on the unions themselves to adopt a more enlightened, public-spirited approach. It follows that, if public education is to escape the stultifying drag of the unions' grip on the system—and if the system, therefore, is to evolve into a new form that is better suited to providing a quality education to children—it will happen only through reforms that weaken or eliminate union power over the schools.

INTERESTS AND ORGANIZATION

The teachers unions are often misunderstood. Their friends think about them in much the same way they think about teachers: as caring deeply about kids, promoting quality education, and fighting for important social principles. Their enemies see them as nothing short of malevolent: as oligarchic organizations that force unwilling teachers to join and are unconcerned about the best interests of kids. Neither is an adequate characterization. To understand the teachers unions, we have to get beyond stereotypes and think about them as social scientists might think about any organization.

Consider business firms, for example. Economists have done an excellent job of understanding these organizations by recognizing that profit is the fundamental interest that drives their behavior. Thus, economists fully expect firms to pollute the water and air when polluting is less costly than not polluting, and they are right. This is why we have laws against pollution. The problem is not that firms are malevolent and out to destroy the environment. The problem is that their interests are different from the public's interest in a clean environment.

Teachers unions can be understood in much the same way, except they are not driven by profits. Their survival and well-being depend on their ability to attract members and resources, and these define their fundamental interests. It follows that the unions have an interest in pushing for stronger collective bargaining laws, because these enhance their success in gaining members and resources. Similarly, they have an interest in protecting member jobs. They have an interest in fighting for higher salaries, more valuable health and retirement benefits, better working conditions, and other job-related things that their members want. They have an interest in pressing for reduced class sizes, and in other ways increasing the demand for teachers. They have an interest in fighting for higher education budgets and higher taxes. And so on.[5]

None of this has anything to do, at least directly, with what is best for children. It is possible, of course, that some union objectives—higher spending and smaller classes, for example—are actually good for kids. Yet there is no strong evidence that this is so;[6] and even if there were, any benefits for children would be accidental by-products of what the unions do in their own self-interest. It is quite clear, on the other hand, that self-interest often leads them to do things that are *not* good for kids, such as protecting the jobs of incompetent teachers. Just as business firms knowingly pollute if it is in their self-interest to do so, so the teachers unions knowingly pursue objectives that are bad for kids. They don't do it because they are malevolent. They do it because they are normal organizations guided by their own interests.

The unions' critics sometimes argue, in addition, that the unions pursue their own interests at the expense of *teachers* too. Indeed, it is commonly claimed—even by observers much more mainstream in their views—that to the extent the unions are problems for public education, the problems are due to the unions themselves and not the teachers. Teachers are viewed more sympathetically, and sometimes as victims who are simply being used.[7]

It is reasonable to wonder whether the unions actually do represent their members. After all, in order to overcome the collective action problem that has plagued the union movement from the beginning—namely, that employees have incentives to free-ride rather than contribute to the collective effort—the unions' solution has essentially been coercive. They have fought for collective bargaining laws that, in effect, force employees to join a union (or to pay agency fees, which are considered their "fair share" of the group effort) if a majority votes the union in.[8] For some teachers, therefore, membership in the union is not voluntary and not an indication that they support the union in collective bargaining or politics. Regardless of why they join, moreover, teachers are generally unable to drop out of the union (or stop paying their "fair share") if the union pursues objectives they disagree with. The union has them trapped, along with their money, and this is true whether the union represents them or not. So why should it represent them?[9]

This situation is less problematic than it seems, however. Teachers may differ from one another in many respects, but they are all employees of the school system, and as employees they have certain interests in common. They have an interest in job security. They have an interest in better salaries, health plans, and retirement packages. They have an interest in taking time off. They have an interest in smaller classes. They have an interest in gaining rights in the workplace. When teachers join unions, *these* are the interests they want represented—job-related interests. The teachers who are forced to join have basically the same job-related interests as the teachers who join voluntarily.

Two properties of union organization have a lot to do with how member interests find expression in union behavior. One is that union leaders are elected, and thus can be thrown out of office if they fail to represent members. The second is that the unions are more likely to be effective, whether in collective bargaining or politics, if members are cohesive and support the unions' efforts. Both these properties—the mechanisms of democracy and the requirements of effectiveness—are imperfect. But they do give leaders incentives to respond to what their members want.

If we focus on local unions and their core function of collective bargaining, there is good evidence that teachers do indeed feel represented. In a national survey of 3,328 teachers that I carried out in 2003, 94 percent of teachers in districts with collective bargaining said that, if membership were purely voluntary, they would still choose to join and pay dues to their local union. When asked how well their union represents their interests in collective bargaining, 83 percent indicated that they are satisfied.[10] A study by Public Agenda of a national sample of 1,345 teachers points to similarly positive conclusions of a more general nature: 84 percent believe that it is "absolutely essential" or "important" for teachers to have unions, 81 percent agree that "without collective bargaining, the working conditions and salaries of teachers would be much worse," and 81 percent agree that "without unions, teachers would be vulnerable to school politics or administrators who abuse their power."[11]

These findings reflect favorably on the unions. But they also tell us something very basic about union power: that when the unions wield power in their own self-interest, they wind up promoting the job-related interests of teachers, who support them for it. Moreover, just as union interests are not the same as the interests of children, so teacher interests are not the same as the interests of children. Teachers expect their unions to press for more benefits, to get them more time off, to protect them from administrators, to impose restrictive work rules, and in a host of other ways to promote their job-related interests—and none of this is premised on what is best for children.

When the unions engage in behavior that is contrary to the best interests of children, then, teachers are complicit in what they are doing. It is a mistake to think that the unions are the source of these problems, and that teachers are somehow not responsible and are even victims themselves. Exceptions aside, teachers *are* responsible and they are *not* victims. As things now stand, the unions do the teachers' bidding in a powerful way. But if the unions did not exist, teacher interests would continue to be the same employee interests that they are now, and they would still come into conflict with the interests of children. In the final analysis, the real problem here is not union power per se, but *employee power* exercised on behalf of *employee interests.*

COLLECTIVE BARGAINING AND LOCAL POLITICS

Collective bargaining is the core function of the teachers unions and the bedrock of their well-being, because it is through collective bargaining that they attract members, get resources, and wrest benefits from "management." But there is also a symbiotic relationship between collective bargaining and politics. The members and money they gain from collective bargaining can be, and routinely are, converted into political resources—campaign contributions, campaign workers, full-time lobbyists—that generate political power. And by exercising that power in the political process, they are able to strengthen labor laws, boost their membership (e.g., by lobbying for smaller classes), win new job rules and teacher benefits, and in other ways promote their organizational interests. Success in collective bargaining boosts success in politics. Success in politics boosts success in collective bargaining. This being so, the teachers unions—indeed, all public-sector unions—have strong incentives to be more than just bargaining organizations, and to invest resources in gaining and exercising political power.

Collective Bargaining and School Board Politics

At the local level, where collective bargaining actually takes place, this symbiotic connection to politics is readily apparent. The teachers unions are blessed with a situation that private-sector unions can only dream of: the "management" team (the school board) is elected by the public.[12] So by taking part in electoral campaigns, the unions can help select the very people they will be bargaining with. These same people, moreover, will make official decisions on issues ranging from budgets to curriculum.[13]

Union clout in local elections is likely to be substantial, especially when elections are held at off times with few citizens voting, as is often the case. In many districts the teachers unions may be the only organized force in electoral campaigns. They have money to make contributions to candidates, generate publicity, and the like. And they can field activists to make phone calls, ring door bells, and otherwise help ensure that friends are elected and enemies defeated.

Even in large districts with many organized groups, the teachers unions are likely to be the only real players who focus single-mindedly on education—in contrast to business and community groups, for example, which have many different policy concerns.[14] Parents, meantime, tend to be wholly unorganized outside (perhaps) the PTA—which is a parent-teacher organization, not simply a parent organization, and almost always an ally of the unions.[15]

There is almost no empirical research on the role of teachers unions in school board elections. But three recent studies of my own, all of California school districts, shed useful light on the subject. The first investigates one of many possible mechanisms of union influence: teacher voting.[16] It shows that teachers who live in the districts where they work (and thus are eligible to vote there) vote at much higher rates—anywhere from two to seven times higher—than ordinary citizens. Because the average turnout in these off-year elections is a mere 9 percent, the turnout differential alone is often enough to shift outcomes in the unions' favor. And this is quite apart from all the *other* resources that unions are able to mobilize on their candidates' behalf.

This same study also provides important evidence on teachers' political motivation. It does so by showing that teachers who live and work in a given district, and thus have an occupational stake in its electoral outcomes, consistently vote at much higher rates than teachers who live in the same district but don't work there and thus do *not* have an occupational stake in the outcome. The latter, in fact, vote at low rates not much higher than those of average citizens. The upshot is that teacher participation in politics appears to be highly self-interested.

The second study cuts to the chase, investigating union impact on the outcomes of school board elections.[17] It shows that, for candidates who are not incumbents, union support increases the probability of winning by .56—an astounding level of impact. For incumbents, who are already likely to win (and cannot have their probability boosted a lot higher), union support increases the probability of victory by .20. Clearly, unions are quite successful at putting "their" people on local school boards, and this ensures that they will often be bargaining with friends—elected officials who are supposed to be representing the public (and children) but in fact are beholden to the unions.

The third study, based on a survey of school board candidates, looks at the dynamics of school board elections in greater detail.[18] It finds, among other things:

- The unions are typically the most powerful participants in school board elections.
- The unions are about equally powerful in districts of all sizes. Union power is not just a phenomenon of large, urban districts.

- The unions are quite successful at seeing to it that the winning candidates are those with the more sympathetic attitudes toward collective bargaining.
- The unions are the major players in these elections, but they are constrained and do not always get everything they want. First, they sometimes face opposition from other organized groups, especially in large districts. Second, because incumbents are more difficult to defeat, the unions sometimes support incumbents who are not as prounion as they would like in order not to alienate an eventual winner. Third, because voting patterns are shaped by the political culture of a district, unions in conservative districts sometimes find themselves supporting candidates who are less prounion than they would like in order not to lose. Fourth, when people are elected to the school board, the experience of being on the board—and part of "management"—seems to make them less prounion over time; as a result, the unions cannot count on gaining complete control of school boards even when they are continually successful in elections.

It would be extreme, then, to say that unions totally dominate their school boards—but there is still a serious problem here. School board elections are supposed to be the democratic means by which ordinary citizens govern their own schools. The board is supposed to represent "the people." But in many districts it really doesn't. For with unions so powerful, employee interests are given far more weight in personnel and policy decisions than warranted, and school boards are partially captured by their own employees. Democracy threatens to be little more than a charade, serving not as a mechanism of popular control but as means by which employees promote their own special interests.

The problem of employee power would be less consequential if school districts operated in a competitive environment. For then, were the unions to push their own interests at the expense of school performance, parents could easily take their kids elsewhere—and the unions would find that fewer people wanted to attend their schools, teacher employment would drop, and membership rolls and financial resources would suffer. Faced with competition, unions would have to moderate their demands to protect their own interests.

But school districts do not operate in a competitive environment. And this gives unions another advantage in pursuing their own interests: they can impose costs and work rules that their members want, without regard for the impacts on school performance. Because parents and students have nowhere to go, the unions suffer no penalties. Indeed, the unions come out ahead: making their members happy, demonstrating their potency, and maintaining their membership and finances.

The problem of employee power would also be less serious if districts, schools, and teachers were held accountable for their performance. In a true accountability system, there would be consequences for poor performance: unproductive employees would lose their jobs, pay and resources would be affected, the public would be informed about who is and is not doing the job, and so on. The unions would then have to think twice about imposing costs and work rules without regard for their effects on performance. They would have to moderate their demands.

Yet districts, schools, and teachers have never really been held accountable for their behavior. Recent reforms are trying to change this. But the tradition is that performance is not systematically measured or put to use for evaluative purposes, and there are no consequences when student learning is inadequate. No one loses a job. Schools do not close. Resources and pay are not used as incentives. The unions therefore have no reason to worry about the connection between their self-interested demands and the performance of the schools. If their exercises of power make the schools worse, they suffer no negative consequences.[19]

All things considered, then, the teachers unions are free to approach collective bargaining with a singular concern for their own special interests. And that is what we should expect of them. To say as much is not to launch an ideological attack on the unions, but simply to recognize the reality of the situation—as people directly involved in collective bargaining do. Here is an account from a basic practitioner-oriented (and entirely nonideological) text on the subject:

> The bargaining agent representing teachers exists solely to articulate and try to achieve the goals determined to be in the self-interest of its members. The welfare of the school as an institution may, in fact, be advanced by teacher organizations seeking to achieve the interests of teachers. But that is a by-product. The bargaining agent represents teachers and their interests. The collective bargaining process is predicated upon the union or association being an advocate of a special-interest group—the members of the bargaining unit.20

Contracts and Work Rules

It is too bad all Americans cannot just sit down and read a few collective bargaining contracts that school districts have to live by. Most people, I hazard to guess, would be absolutely shocked. When my Stanford students—who are quite educated, and mostly liberal Democrats—first take a look at some of these contracts, they can't believe what they are seeing. These documents tend to include:

- Rules that require that teachers be paid on a salary schedule, based only on their years of experience and education, not on their performance.

- Rules that make it virtually impossible to dismiss teachers for poor performance.
- Rules that limit the discretion of principals in assigning teachers to classes, with limits based on teacher seniority.
- Rules that allow teachers to make voluntary transfers to other schools, and to resist being transferred away from their existing schools, based on seniority.
- Rules that require principals to give advance notice to teachers before visiting their classrooms to evaluate their performance.
- Rules that prohibit the use of standardized student tests for evaluating teacher performance.
- Rules that give teachers guaranteed preparation times of a specified number of minutes per day.
- Rules that limit the number of faculty meetings and their duration.
- Rules that limit the number of parent conferences and other forums in which teachers meet with parents.
- Rules that limit how many minutes teachers can be required to be on campus before and after school.
- Rules that limit class size.
- Rules that limit the number of courses, periods, or students a teacher must teach.
- Rules that limit the nonteaching duties that teachers can be asked to perform, such as yard duty, hall duty, or lunch duty.
- Rules that allow teachers to take paid sabbaticals.
- Rules that give teachers liberal options for time off with pay (such as "personal" leave days).
- Rules that put important decisions—about school policy, assignments, transfers, noninstructional duties—in the hands of committees on which teachers participate and may have a majority.
- Rules that allow teachers to accumulate unused sick leave for years, and eventually to convert it into cash windfalls.
- Rules that provide for complicated, time-consuming grievance procedures.
- Rules that give teachers who are union officials time off (which means their classes must be taught by substitutes) for performing union duties.
- Rules that give the union access to school mailboxes, bulletin boards, classrooms, and other facilities to use for its own purposes.xxi

For every contract rule, the unions are quick to give reasons why it is good not only for teachers but also for children. Their theme, invariably, is that there is no conflict between the interests of teachers and the interests of children. Teacher transfer rights are good, for example, because they limit the unfairness of managerial discretion, and they allow teachers to seek out (or remain in) the jobs for which they are best suited, all of which benefits kids. Limits on faculty meetings, parent conferences, and noninstructional duties are good because scarce teacher time can be devoted instead to the education of kids. And so on.[21]

The unions also make a more general claim to justify their proliferation of rules. They say that they are dedicated to professionalizing the occupation of teaching, and that the point of collective bargaining and all its rules is to ensure that teachers are treated like professionals. The more professional teachers are, the higher their overall quality and the better off kids are.[22]

On the surface these arguments seem plausible. There is some truth to them, and because collective bargaining is so rarely studied there is usually no research to contradict them with hard evidence. Closer scrutiny, however, suggests that there is a substantial downside to these collective bargaining rules—and even to professionalization—that the unions simply do not talk about.

Consider seniority-based transfer rules. These rules are fundamental to any assessment of collective bargaining, and reformers are increasingly objecting to them. When Philadelphia's abysmally performing school system was recently taken over by the state, for example, the state-appointed administrator wanted to eliminate union transfer rights, arguing that they made it impossible for him to assign good teachers to needy schools. The union fiercely resisted any change, and its spokesman used (among other things) the prevailing lack of evidence to justify its position. "There's not a single study," he said, "to show that seniority [rights] are detrimental to education."[23]

This claim about the research literature was true at the time. But hard evidence or no, there are compelling reasons for thinking that transfer rights should have profoundly negative effects on the schools. The simplest reason is the one given by the Philadelphia administrator: these rules make it impossible for the district to allocate teachers to their most productive uses—which could hardly be more basic to effective organization. We can also take the logic further by looking at it from the standpoint of teacher choice: transfer rights give senior teachers much more latitude in choosing where to teach, and they can be expected to use it to leave the schools they find undesirable—schools filled with disadvantaged kids—in favor of schools they find more desirable.[24] In districts with transfer rules, then, disadvantaged schools should find themselves burdened with even more inexperienced teachers than they otherwise would. And because research has shown that inexperienced teachers tend to be lower in quality than experienced teachers, this means that transfer rules should have the unintended effect of undermining the quality of education for the neediest children.[25]

This line of reasoning is clear, coherent, and leads to simple expectations. In a recent study, I subjected it to an empirical test using evidence from a sample of California districts and schools.[26] The statistical model in this analysis is designed to explain the within-district distribution of teachers across schools, and the estimation shows that transfer rules do in fact have a considerable impact. In particular, it shows that a school's level of disadvantage, as measured by the minority composition of its student body, has far more impact than any other factor in determining the school's percentage of inexperienced teachers—and that the magnitude of this impact increases substantially as transfer rights increase in strength. The stronger the transfer rights in a district, the more latitude its senior teachers have in choosing where to teach, and the more serious the problems that disadvantaged schools are burdened with.

Because the empirical literature is so limited, we usually cannot evaluate collective bargaining with such direct evidence. Even so, there are compelling reasons for expecting certain outcomes. Any objective observer should expect transfer rules to create quality problems for disadvantaged schools, simply by virtue of the way these rules expand the choices of senior teachers. Similar arguments can be made—and expectations derived—for other contract rules too. Here, briefly, are a few of the general arguments that need to be made.

(1) Most generally, any notion that contract rules simultaneously promote the interests of both teachers and children, and that there is no conflict between the two, is simply false. This is not to say that contract rules never have consequences that are positive for children. It is to say that they clearly have some consequences that are negative.

(2) These negative consequences happen to be profoundly important for the operation of schools. Because of restrictive work rules, the most consequential of all educational inputs—teachers—cannot be allocated to their most productive uses, administrators are denied the discretion to manage their schools, costs are higher than they should be, and schools are buried in excessive bureaucracy. These problems are fundamental, and they can only be expected to undermine the effectiveness of school organization.

(3) The positive consequences are not in the same league. Consider four areas of impact that the unions trumpet as profoundly positive: professionalism, teacher compensation, teacher involvement in decisionmaking, and limitations on class size. Enhancing teacher professionalism sounds good, but in practice it typically boils down to an emphasis on certification, master's degrees, and staff development, none of which has been shown to be important for student learning.[28] Increasing teacher compensation also sounds good, but unions demand across-the-board raises for all teachers, regardless of their competence or productivity, which is a grossly inefficient way to spend scarce resources.[29]

Increasing teacher involvement in decisionmaking sounds good too, but it means that employee interests are given even more weight in the policies and practices of schools, and these interests are often in conflict with what is best for kids.[30] And finally, limitations on class size sound good and may sometimes be good, but they involve enormous costs, and evidence suggests that the benefits for student learning are very small by comparison.[31]

(4) There should be no mystery why the negatives far outweigh the positives. The negative effects are to be expected, because the unions use their power in collective bargaining to pursue teacher (and union) interests that are not the same as the interests of children. The positive effects come about accidentally, only when these interests happen to coincide.

(5) Moreover, the negative effects are genuinely due to collective bargaining: they are forced on the districts by the unions and thus are usually practices the districts would *not* follow if they did not have to. The same is typically not true of positive effects: if the districts seek to promote quality education, they need not be forced into adopting rules or expenditures that help them do that. To the extent there are positives associated with union-imposed requirements, therefore, they are positives that the districts would tend to pursue *on their own*. It follows that, in calculating the net impact of unionization, we surely need to count the negatives, but the same is not true of the positives, many and perhaps all of which would be adopted by districts in the absence of collective bargaining.

(6) As monopolies run by elected politicians, the districts may not be as strongly motivated by quality education as we would like, and there may indeed be occasions on which they must be forced to take actions that are good for kids. But the solution to this problem is not collective bargaining, which generates profoundly negative consequences along with any good ones, and which empowers actors who are less concerned with quality education than the districts are. The solution is to push for reforms that give the districts the right incentives, and to make sure they can act on them without the self-interested constraints imposed by unions.

Given these expectations, well-designed empirical research ought to show that collective bargaining is—on the whole—detrimental to quality education. As I said, this line of research is very limited. But a small literature does exist that, beginning in the 1980s, has attempted to determine whether collective bargaining per se has an impact on how much students learn—and this, in the end, is the question that needs to be answered.

Unfortunately, it is difficult to extract solid evidence from these studies.[32] Most of them base their analysis on comparisons between jurisdictions that have collective bargaining and those that do not, and this is problematic. When states are being compared, the states without collective bargaining are almost all southern and border states, which are different from the collective bargaining states in many ways—culturally, ethnically, politically, economically—that doubtless affect their schools. When comparisons are across districts, the same sorts of biases arise. There are other problems as well. Studies at the state level, for example, require such a gross level of data aggregation—with a single test score representing student achievement for the whole state, and so on—that there is little hope of discovering causes and effects at the lower (district) levels; these studies, moreover, sometimes measure student performance by means of SAT and ACT scores, which are taken by select students and are not good measures of learning among students generally.

Not surprisingly, this literature yields mixed findings on the impact of collective bargaining. Some studies say it leads to better performance, some say it leads to worse performance, but we cannot be confident that they are telling us anything valid. It is perhaps worth noting that these studies agree on the nonacademic effects of collective bargaining: that it increases pay and fringe benefits, the teacher-student ratio, and the overall costs of education. We have to be cautious about these results, given the underlying problems; but their uniformity is heartening, and the findings are what ought to be expected.

One study stands apart from all the others. This is an analysis by Caroline M. Hoxby that assesses the impact of collective bargaining by looking at districts before and after the unions gain bargaining rights—a unique design that only she has employed.[33] What she shows, through a highly sophisticated statistical analysis, is that the agreed-on conclusions of the rest of the literature are borne out: collective bargaining increases district spending, teacher salaries, and teacher-student ratios. But she also shows that, even though collective bargaining increases school inputs, it actually *decreases their productivity,* and the unions' overall impact on school performance is *negative* (as measured by the dropout rate). Her bottom line is that collective bargaining is bad for schools.

I think it is no accident that Hoxby's innovative analysis, published in one of the most prestigious peer-reviewed journals in economics, arrives at negative conclusions about the impact of collective bargaining. It is unfortunate that we don't have more good studies and a bigger, more sophisticated literature for bringing evidence to bear. But we just don't. We can only hope that more scholars pursue this kind of research and begin to fill the evidence gap.

UNION POLITICS AND EDUCATION REFORM

Through collective bargaining, the teachers unions shape the organization and performance of the public schools from the bottom up. Yet the unions also influence the schools from the top down by taking political action to influence public policy.

Given their core interests, the unions are compelled to seek political power. Their members are government employees whose salaries, fringe benefits, and retirement packages are all funded through government budgets and taxes. New and expanded education programs mean more money and more jobs. Stronger collective bargaining laws translate into easier organizing. Virtually every kind of workplace rule can be imposed through new legislation. And so can reforms that threaten the unions' interests—and need to be stopped.

The teachers unions have responded to these incentives by developing formidable political organizations. The NEA and AFT together have more than four million members nationwide, massive financial resources, and networks designed for coordinated political action. In elections they spend huge sums on campaign contributions, almost always in support of Democrats, and in many states they are routinely among the top few contributors; they also put troops on the ground in virtually every political district in the country—again, in support of Democrats—and these troops can prove far more potent than money. Between elections, they exercise power through active, well-financed lobbying organizations. And they are active as well in administrative arenas and the courts.[34] Throughout American society, few other interest groups can claim such political clout. Indeed, a long-running study of state-level politics found the teachers unions to be the single most powerful interest group *in the entire country* throughout the 1990s, and in 2002 ranked them a close second behind general business organizations.[35]

The unions' remarkable power does not mean they can simply have what they want from state and national governments. Part of the reason is that, at these levels, the unions have more opponents than they do locally. But the larger reason is that, in a separation of powers system, the policymaking process is filled with veto points that any proposal must overcome to achieve passage. Getting a major proposal enacted is very difficult, and the unions will often fail or be forced into compromises—although their batting average is likely to be higher than that of other groups. The flip side is that blocking legislation is very easy by comparison—for success at just one veto point is all that is needed—and this means that the unions can use their power to great effect when all they want to do is block.

Given the ground we have covered, here is what we should expect from the teachers unions in the politics of education:

(1) They will use their political power to pursue their core interests—in attracting members and resources and promoting the job-related interests of

teachers—regardless of what is best for children or the broader public.

(2) Because they are uniquely powerful within their sector, the unions will be the de facto leaders of public education in the political process, and their interests will heavily influence how the interests of public education are defined and pursued.

(3) They will be quite successful at blocking or watering down education proposals they do not like, particularly those involving major reforms that—however beneficial to children—seriously threaten their core interests.

(4) They will be less successful at getting favorable legislation or funding.

(5) In an era of constant demands for reform, therefore, the main impact of the teachers unions will be to block or weaken promising reforms, and thus to protect the status quo.

These expectations are a virtual playbook of how the politics of education has actually unfolded in recent decades. To get a sense of this, let's look at three realms of education policy. The first consists of mainstream efforts to improve the schools through incremental change. The second and third have to do with reform efforts that involve major changes in the system—accountability and school choice.

Mainstream Politics

Just as the teachers unions were completing their rise to power in the early 1980s, they were confronted with one of the signature events of modern American education: the publication of *A Nation at Risk*, which highlighted the urgent need for reform and generated a national movement for change that has continued to the present day.[36] The unions have been threatened by some aspects of this movement. But with powerful groups and politicians eager to improve the public schools, it has also given them attractive opportunities to push for the things they would otherwise want.

The unions' actions have been entirely predictable. Year in and year out, they pressure tirelessly for more money (and higher taxes) regardless of the problem being addressed. If the focus is on low-performing inner-city schools, their solution is more money—arguing that these schools do not have the resources needed to do a good job. If the focus is on teacher quality, their solution is to raise salaries dramatically for all existing teachers, and to spend additional money on training and professional development. If children with special needs are lagging, the solution is to create huge, big-budget programs that funnel money to the schools and teachers of those kids.[37]

The unions are also intensely concerned with increasing the number of teaching jobs (and union members), which only fuels their push for more money.

When money is pumped into low-performing schools, or when it is pumped into special-education programs, more jobs are created for teachers. The same is true for the most popular mainstream reform of our day, class size reduction. The unions are enthusiastic supporters of smaller classes, arguing that they allow for more effective teaching and are thus beneficial for children.[38] It is not coincidental, however, that class size reduction can be achieved only by hiring new teachers and is among the most expensive approaches to reform the states could possibly adopt. The unions have also begun pushing for all-day kindergarten and for publicly provided preschool—which, they say, are necessary if kids (especially poor kids) are to be prepared for elementary schools, but which would also require huge numbers of new teachers, vastly expand the ranks of union membership, and cost untold billions of dollars.[39]

Another strand of union "reform" has to do with workplace rules—which, through political action, the unions can win for all teachers in an entire state, rather than relying on the usual district-by-district approach. Any examination of state education codes reveals all sorts of laws that look like they came right out of collective bargaining contracts. They might require, for example, that every teacher get a 30-minute lunch break, that layoffs and rehirings be based on seniority, that standardized tests not be used for teacher evaluations, or that teachers can accumulate sick leave up to specified amounts. Indeed, education codes are often just as eye opening as collective bargaining contracts for their detail, restrictiveness, and promotion of teacher self-interest.

The unions also argue for "reforms" under the rubric of professionalization. They use this language when they press for higher pay and restrictive work rules. But it is also central to their justifications for other objectives—for example, stronger certification criteria, more time (and compensation) for professional development, and extra compensation for teachers with advanced degrees and certificates. They also argue that, as professionals, teachers should be self-regulating; and they have pushed for regulatory mechanisms that are controlled by teachers—and thus by the unions themselves. For example, they want teachers to have the option of getting national certification (and to be paid more for it), and this certification process is controlled by the National Board for Professional Teaching Standards, which in turn is colonized by the unions. They also argue that teachers should be trained at education schools accredited by the National Council for Accreditation of Teacher Education, in which the unions have heavy influence.[40]

The unions have been fairly successful at shaping education policy and weaving their interests into the fabric of the system. They have been less successful at getting the funding and teacher pay that they want, but this is not surprising.

K-12 education is already soaking up nearly half of state education budgets, and many other groups are fighting over the same money in what are essentially zero-sum battles. Without significantly higher taxes, which voters resist, the states literally cannot afford to spend a great deal more on the schools or across-the-board pay increases for teachers.

The more telling question is whether the unions' objectives in mainstream politics are ultimately good for kids. The answer is essentially the same as for collective bargaining. The unions pursue their own interests in politics, and policies good for the unions are often bad for kids. This is surely true for many restrictive work rules that find their way into state education codes, because these are simply special-interest provisions that make schools more difficult to manage and more costly to operate. They were never intended to be good for kids. It might seem that a better case can be made for the unions' larger political goals—more spending (and taxes), higher pay, smaller classes—but these are problematic as well. Consider the following:

(1) Research suggests that increases in spending do not have much impact on student performance. While money is necessary to operate schools, and while more money could in principle be put to good use, it is not put to good use now. Extra funds are used unproductively and do little to improve the schools.[41] It is worth remembering that Washington, D.C., which has among the worst schools in the nation, spends about 70 percent more than the national average on each of its students.[42]

(2) In teaching, as in any occupation, increases in pay should attract higher-quality people. But across-the-board pay raises for all teachers are an enormously costly and unproductive way to do this.[43] Kids are the losers if unproductive teachers are paid more than they are worth, and kids are the losers if productive teachers are paid less than they are worth. Kids are better off, and the system is better able to attract good teachers and shed bad ones, if pay is linked to productivity—which, of course, it isn't.

(3) Research indicates that lowering class size by the amounts normally considered—say, from 30 to 25 or from 22 to 20—does not have much impact on student learning.[44] Because it is so expensive to carry out, we get very little bang for our buck with this approach to reform. There should be other, far more productive ways of getting kids to learn more.

These reforms are not in themselves bad for kids. Children are not worse off because a state spends more money on the schools or pays teachers more or lowers its class size. Even so, children *are* worse off when the opportunity costs of these reforms are taken into account. For when reforms are pursued that are unproductive, there are other ways the resources could be allocated that would be more beneficial to kids, and kids are worse off in the sense that better alternatives are forgone in favor of inferior ones. This is the right way to think about the issue.

Many alternatives to the usual mainstream reforms are never seriously considered, even though they require no major restructuring of the system. One reason is that alternatives that threaten union interests have no chance of passing, so they do not make it onto the agenda—or even into people's minds when they entertain possibilities. Consider the following thought experiment. Suppose the unions really were concerned first and foremost about the best interests of kids and were not driven by their own self-interest. All sorts of reforms would suddenly become possible. Most obviously, the unions (and their Democratic allies) would take aggressive action to ensure that mediocre and incompetent teachers are identified and removed from the classroom. They would favor requiring veteran teachers to pass rigorous tests of substantive competence. They would favor making the removal process quick and easy. They would take all steps necessary to ensure that children are not trapped in classrooms with teachers who cannot teach—for what could be worse?

But this whole line of reform, so obvious it is embarrassing, is off the table. Far from taking aggressive action to weed out low-performing teachers, the unions *protect* them and do everything they can to ensure that no member ever loses a job. They also make it clear to politicians that they will block any reforms that threaten teacher jobs, and that they will punish anyone supporting such efforts. The explanation is simple: the unions act in their own self-interest, not in the interests of kids.

The Politics of Accountability

Accountability is not a mainstream reform. In a true accountability system, clear standards indicate what children are expected to know, tests reliably measure whether children are learning the material, and consequences attach to whether the standards are being met. The point is to measure what is going on, but also to give everyone involved—students, teachers, administrators—incentives to perform.[45]

The idea of accountability is new to public education. Traditionally, teachers have had substantial autonomy in the workplace, they have had total job security, and they have been paid without regard for how productive they are. This is what most of today's teachers expect and want, and it is the deal they thought they were accepting when they became teachers in the first place. The accountability movement threatens to take that deal away from them. It threatens to erode their autonomy, to shake up their comfortable arrangements for jobs and pay, and to demand that they work differently, work harder, and produce more. These changes are not welcome.[46]

Although the teachers unions will not say it outright, they are opposed to true accountability. This position squares with member opinion, but there are other reasons for it as well. The unions know that, if performance is routinely measured, the data can lead to threatening consequences. Publicity that the schools are underperforming, for instance, is likely to put teachers in a bad light and generate pressures for change. Performance data also provide objective grounds for having unproductive teachers fired, which is the last thing the unions want, and for creating a system in which teacher pay is linked to productivity, which threatens to create competition among members, undermine solidarity, and give administrators more discretion.

Politically, the unions have their hands full on this issue. Accountability is common sense, and it is broadly popular with the general public—which means that most politicians, including the unions' Democratic allies, find it difficult to oppose. It has focused the reformist energies of business leaders, who strongly believe that accountability is necessary for effective performance. And it has been embraced by governors and presidents—who, unlike legislators, are held directly responsible for improving the schools and have broad constituencies that make them less susceptible to special-interest groups (including unions). Every governor now wants to be the education governor, every president the education president.

The accountability movement emerged in the late 1980s as it became clear that mainstream reforms were not doing much good. And it picked up steam during the 1990s, gaining ground in virtually all 50 states—especially, and not coincidentally, in some of the right-to-work states, such as Texas and North Carolina. In 2001 it marked its greatest victory with congressional passage of the No Child Left Behind Act (NCLB), which for the first time imposed a uniform set of accountability requirements on all of the nation's schools.[47]

Throughout this period, the unions could have followed an outright blocking strategy. But this would have been difficult due to the impressive power arrayed on the other side. And it would have been damaging to the unions' public image (and ultimately to their political clout) had they positioned themselves as unyielding opponents of a broadly popular reform. So they settled on a more sophisticated strategy: of "supporting" accountability, participating in the design of the new accountability systems, and using their power to promote designs that don't hold teachers accountable in any meaningful way.[48]

The key elements of any accountability system are standards, testing, and consequences. Standards alone need not be threatening to union interests, so over the past decade the unions have been enthusiastic proponents of standards-based reform and have played up this aspect of accountability—as though standards are what accountability is all about. Yet they do not favor true academic rigor or high passing bars, because student failure reflects badly on teachers. Unions favor standards that are relatively easy to meet, and they react to poor test results by claiming that the standards and passing bars are themselves poorly conceived and need to be changed (by weakening them).[49]

Tests can be more problematic than standards, in the unions' eyes, but they can also be quite acceptable under the right conditions. Until recently they were rarely a threat because their results were essentially secret. They were used internally by the school system and passed along to parents, but they were not made public or used to judge school or teacher performance. Accountability changed all that. Today it is common for the states to publicize test scores, and these scores provide an objective basis on which schools and teachers can—in principle—be held accountable for their performance.

The unions cannot flat-out oppose testing, because testing is too popular and too obviously necessary for accountability. So they pursue their opposition in more subtle ways. They argue, for example, that the tests currently in use (whatever they might be) are deeply flawed, need revision, and cannot provide valid measures of student or teacher performance; that testing and test preparation eat into valuable teaching time; and that teachers wind up teaching to the test rather than teaching a balanced curriculum.[50] What they support, as alternatives to tests, are methods that involve the teachers' own subjective judgments: course grades, assessments of student portfolios, assessments of student effort. Because these assessments of student performance are ultimately the basis for evaluating the teachers themselves, such a system essentially allows the teachers to write their own performance evaluations. Needless to say, this is hardly a reliable means of determining how much students are really learning or how well teachers are really teaching them. It is simply a method of supporting a nonthreatening version of accountability—while opposing the real thing.[51]

Standards and testing create problems for the unions, but they are even more concerned about having consequences attached to performance. Most important, no member should ever lose a job, and there should be no weeding-out process by which the schools rid themselves of low-performing teachers. Other kinds of sanctions—pay cuts, reductions in funding—are verboten as well. So are commonsense policies that might lead to such sanctions: for example, the testing of veteran teachers to ensure competence in the classroom. And so are pay-for-performance plans that would link teacher compensation to how much their students learn.[52]

If consequences are to be adopted, the unions insist that they take the form of rewards: bonuses for high-performing teachers or, far preferable, bonuses for high-performing schools (with the unions deciding how rewards are distributed among teachers). A union-preferred accountability system, then, would exercise accountability—if at all—entirely through a system of positive inducements. There would only be winners. No losers.

None of this is motivated by what is best for kids. Virtually anyone who studies organizations—or for that matter, almost anyone who is responsible for running an organization—would agree that some form of accountability system is essential if organizations are to do their jobs effectively.[53] And since children are the beneficiaries of school effectiveness, this is another way of saying that a serious, well-functioning accountability system for the public schools is good for children. What the unions are doing in opposing true accountability, and in distorting the way standards, tests, and consequences are designed within the policymaking process, is *not* good for children.

The Politics of School Choice

Public education has always been a top-down system in which public officials and bureaucrats (including teachers) directly provide educational services to children. This system has taken almost no advantage of markets—which is unfortunate, for perhaps the best-confirmed canon of social science is that markets are powerful means of promoting efficiency and making people better off. To note as much is not to argue for a "free market" in education. It is to say that, just as our economy is highly productive because it is a mixed system of government and markets, and just as many spheres of social policy—from Medicare to food stamps to public housing—have benefited from reliance on both, so the education system would benefit by moving away from its extreme top-down model toward a mixed system that takes greater advantage of choice and competition. The task is to settle on the right structures—the right designs—for creating a productive balance. But there is no reason that well-intentioned people who care only about children could not do that.[54]

A greater role for markets would do two basic things. First, it would allow children and parents to choose their own schools and thus, most important, to leave low-performing schools for better ones—an option especially valuable for children who are poor or minority, as they are disproportionately stuck in bad schools. Second, precisely because families are empowered to leave bad schools, all schools and teachers are put on notice that, if they don't do their jobs well, they are likely to lose children, money, and jobs—and this gives them incentives to perform and innovate. Thus, choice is immediately beneficial to the children exercising it. But it also changes incentives at the very heart of the system and in this way radiates improvement throughout public education.

It should be obvious why choice is threatening to the unions. Because of choice, some schools lose children, money, and jobs, and the teachers in those schools are faced with cutbacks and pressures to change. More generally, when children move to charter schools or use vouchers to attend private schools, the regular public schools as a whole have smaller enrollments, less money (in the aggregate), and fewer jobs, and the unions stand to lose members and resources. In the process, because choice puts competitive pressure on the public schools to adopt performance-enhancing reforms, the inefficiencies imposed through collective bargaining become vulnerable to scrutiny and criticism, as does union power generally. Little wonder, then, that since the choice movement first gained momentum during the 1980s, the teachers unions have been fierce opponents.[55]

That self-interest is driving their opposition is nowhere more apparent than in their relentless fight against vouchers. Consider what happened in inner-city Milwaukee when, in 1990, local parents and advocates for the poor rose up to demand vouchers so that disadvantaged children could escape failing public schools. What the children needed, and were obviously being denied, was a good education. And they needed it right away, not in 10 or 20 years, when public school reform might possibly (but probably would not) turn the schools around, and when these children would be permanently behind. What did the unions do? Did they work with parents and advocates to get these kids into good schools right away, even if the schools happened to be private? No way. The unions *went to war against them* and unleashed all their political weapons to ensure that not one child or one dollar found its way out of the public system. In the end, the poor—aided by Republican and conservative allies (because abandoned by their usual allies)—won a small pilot program. But the unions had shown their true stripes, and they had done what they could (with much success) to hobble a program for disadvantaged kids.[56]

In the years since, the unions have not changed their position on vouchers by even an inch. The voucher movement has focused its energies on seeking vouchers for disadvantaged kids, and the unions have used all their power to prevent change and keep these kids right where they are. In a few cases, the voucher side has won limited programs—in Cleveland, Florida, Colorado, Washington, D.C., Pennsylvania, Arizona. But for every victory there have been many more defeats, and countless battles were never even fought because union opposition made them hopeless. For each of the voucher victories, moreover, the unions have continued the fight in the courts, and have had a good deal of success at plumbing state constitutions to find provisions—including blatantly anti-

Catholic Blaine amendments written 100 years ago—on which judges can declare the voucher programs unconstitutional.[57]

Throughout this period researchers have tried to study the impact of vouchers. The results have been mixed, although the best of these studies show that vouchers have had positive effects for African American children.[58] The unions have acted aggressively to play up any negative findings, to debunk positive ones, and to use these arguments in political battles to convince the public and politicians that vouchers do not benefit children.[59] But the evidence itself, pro or con, has nothing to do with the unions' opposition. They were opposed to vouchers before there were any studies. The studies are simply additional weapons in the war.

Charter schools are also threatening to the unions, but not as much as vouchers are. At least charters are within the public sector, they are somewhat under the control of districts, and there are political means of keeping them at bay. The problem is that they allow children, money, and jobs to flow out of the regular public schools—where union members work—and into charter schools, where teachers usually need not be unionized or covered by collective bargaining contracts. Charters also put pressure on the regular schools to be more effective and to change, which in turn leads to pressure on collective bargaining. So the proliferation of charters only generates a proliferation of problems for teachers unions.[60]

There is a big demand among urban constituents for alternatives to the regular schools, so Democrats have good reasons to be tolerant toward charters—and indeed, to use charters as a fallback means of fighting vouchers.[61] This has been their strategy, and it explains why there are now approximately 3,400 charter schools nationwide, attended by roughly 1 million children. The unions are realists, and they publicly claim to support charter schools too.[62] But they privately oppose them, and they use their power to push for highly restrictive designs—demanding, for example, that there be low ceilings on the number of allowable charters, that the districts (which have incentives to limit competition) have sole chartering authority, that charters have less funding than the regular schools, that they have no access to public school buildings, and that charter teachers must be union members and covered by the contract.[63] Unions also do what they can to publicize any research that reflects negatively on charters, and they have even done their own "research"—which showed up recently on the front page of the *New York Times*—to show that charters are outperformed by the regular public schools.[64]

The unions' role in the politics of choice is a graphic demonstration of their single-minded pursuit of self-interest. Surely many children can benefit by leaving bad schools for better ones, whether the schools are public or private. Surely the incentives that choice generates in schools and teachers—incentives to perform, to innovate, to be responsive—can be put to good, healthy use in improving the schools generally, to the benefit of all kids. This is not rocket science. All it requires is a serious effort to take advantage of what markets can contribute to the education of children—which is not everything, but something—and the good intentions to find specific forms of choice that, when embedded in a well-designed governmental structure, can give positive results. But the unions are not even remotely serious about putting choice to good use, and they are not well intentioned in seeking what is best for kids. To them, choice is simply a threat to be defeated.

LOOKING TO THE FUTURE

The teachers unions think of themselves as progressive, but in fact they are the most conservative force in American education. They use their power to protect the status quo and to prevent the adoption of changes that, if wisely designed, could improve the schools and benefit children. Portraying the unions this way is not a matter of ideology or union bashing. It is a simple matter of realism and honesty. For people whose first loyalty is to children, there is no avoiding the conclusion that the unions are an enormous problem for public education.

What can be done? The best-known strategy goes under the label "reform unionism," which has attracted quite an audience within the education community. The idea is that teachers unions have long been following the industrial model of blue-collar unionism, with its focus on material benefits and contract rules, while the requirements of a modern, fast-changing "knowledge society"—for highly educated workers, for truly effective schools—call for a more flexible, professional approach to teaching and a different model of unionism.[65] Adherents believe that, once union leaders are enlightened about all this, they will be persuaded to embrace the new model, under which a dramatically reformed version of teacher unionism will:

- Actively promote what is best for children and quality education, not just the material interests of teachers.
- Move away from the formal rules and rigidities of collective bargaining contracts.
- Promote teacher professionalism and pursue the kind of influence compatible with it—namely, collaborative partnerships between teachers and administrators, with teachers playing an integral role in school governance and policymaking.

"Reform unionism" is an exercise in wishful thinking. It assumes that unions can be persuaded to forgo their fundamental interests—and they are never going to do that. Their fundamental interests are not choices but are deeply rooted in the determinants of organizational survival and well-being, and they necessarily take precedence over everything else. It would be nice to believe that enlightened, reform-minded leaders can turn the unions around; and indeed, some self-proclaimed union reformers have formed an organization of their own—the Teachers Union Reform Network (TURN)—based on just those principles. But this group will never have much impact. Reform leaders cannot help but find themselves heavily constrained by the requirements of their own organizations—that they represent the job-related interests of their members and protect their membership rolls and resources—and if they don't toe the line in these respects, they won't last long. Union reformers usually talk a good game, and they may well believe what they say. But when push comes to shove, they *behave* in ways that promote the fundamental interests of their unions.

Without intending to be, "reform unionism" is also dangerous. It is dangerous because it is fanciful, making claims that are unfounded and encouraging expectations that will never be borne out. It is also dangerous for a more substantive reason: it argues that the way to improve education is to forgo industrial-style work rules and involve teachers as true professionals in the governance of their schools. This is an out-of-the-frying-pan-into-the-fire kind of proposal. The underlying presumption is that teachers can be motivated by what is best for kids and that there is no conflict between the teachers' own interests and those of children. But this simply isn't true. And because it isn't, involving teachers in school governance ensures that the interests of children will be given even *less* priority than they are now, and teacher interests more. In the end, the school-governance aspirations of "reform unionism" can lead only to greater union power over schools, which is exactly the opposite of what needs to happen.

How, then, can the power of the unions be reduced? Two approaches offer the greatest promise. They fit together nicely and can be employed at the same time. But given the unions' political clout, progress is likely to be slow and episodic.

The first approach involves the expansion of accountability and choice. By insisting that performance be measured and made public, accountability inevitably brings pressure on the unions to stop protecting low-performing teachers, imposing unproductive work rules, increasing costs, and making the schools bureaucratic. Such pressure may convince the unions to moderate their demands somewhat, simply as a matter of strategy. But it can also convince voters and public officials, including some of the unions' own allies, that something needs to be done to curb their power. The recent, much-publicized hearings on collective bargaining in New York City, a bastion of liberal Democratic power, are just one indication of how other elites can turn on the unions when performance becomes a critical issue.[66]

School choice is more subversive still. By allowing kids and resources to leave the regular public schools, and by forcing these schools to compete with nonunion schools, the expansion of choice ensures that the unions will lose members and resources and thus become smaller and less politically powerful. It also forces them to behave more moderately, because to the extent they resist reforms that would make public schools more productive, they will be slitting their own throats.

So far, the choice and accountability movements have not gone far enough to make a real dent in union power. And using that power, the unions have seen to it that both reforms are but pale versions of what they ought to be. But these movements continue to make incremental progress. As they do, the unions will be faced with mounting challenges, and their power is likely to ebb.

The second and more direct approach is simply to press for legislation designed to undermine union power. Progress will not come easily, as the unions will unleash every last weapon in their arsenal to prevent such bills from passing. But if they are somewhat weakened in the future, or if there are windows of opportunity in states where they are relatively weak right now, these legislative changes can actually succeed.

The most drastic measure would be to prohibit collective bargaining in public education. This would be difficult to accomplish, but I think it is the right thing to do if one is solely concerned about children and schools. Short of this home-run measure, here are some other proposals that make good sense:

- Prohibit unions from spending a member's dues on politics unless that member has given explicit prior consent in writing.
- Make teacher strikes illegal, backed by swift and heavy penalties, and require that they be strictly enforced.
- Limit the scope of bargaining to issues of compensation and working conditions, narrowly construed, so that most aspects of schooling are not subject to union negotiations.
- Do away with seniority rights in assignments and transfers, and give administrators the authority to allocate teachers to their most productive uses.
- Make it quick and easy, based on evidence of low performance, to get rid of teachers who are not doing their jobs well.
- Do away with the traditional salary schedule, require that teacher pay be linked to performance, and allow districts to respond to market considerations (e.g., by raising the pay of math and science teachers).

Most people in the education community, and most scholars and researchers who study public education, are sympathetic to the teachers unions, and they are sure to be outraged at suggestions for undermining union power and collective bargaining. But this kind of sympathy is misplaced.

The purpose of the public education system is to educate children. Teachers are employees of the system, hired to carry out this purpose—and when things are done right, this is the only reason they are hired. Teachers and their unions may want total job security. They may want lots of time off. They may want the right to transfer out of disadvantaged schools. They may want protective work rules. They may want power over education policy. And more. But important as teachers are to the provision of quality education—and they are clearly the most important single ingredient—the interests of children are the main criterion by which all inputs, including human inputs, should be judged. Whether teachers should have any job security at all, and exactly what types of job security they should have, is properly determined by what is best for children. The same calculation applies for work rules, transfer nights, and all other issues that bear on the role of teachers in public education—including the power of their unions. The education system is not a jobs program. It does not exist for the benefit of the adults who run it. It exists to educate children.

Conclusion

JANE HANNAWAY
ANDREW J. ROTHERHAM

Collective bargaining by teachers is the biggest impediment to improving American public schools. Collective bargaining by teachers is essential to any school improvement effort. These two stark and absolutist views have for too long framed the limited discussion about the impact of collective bargaining by teachers on public education. This is unfortunate because, as the chapters in this book show, collective bargaining by teachers is one of the most important areas of education policy, bearing directly and indirectly on students, teachers, schools, and school districts. Nevertheless, because of the largely ideological back and forth about teachers unions and collective bargaining, it has gone largely unexamined by scholars and analysts and received surprisingly scant attention in the media.

The preceding chapters represent a variety of viewpoints and analytic perspectives. They are not the final word or beyond debate and criticism, but they do serve as a baseline for an essential discussion that is long overdue in education policy. They also make two things abundantly clear. First, polarizing positions in this debate overstate the case on both sides. Second, genuine issues and real problems demand the attention of policymakers.

Yet it is difficult to sort out the various issues because the stridency and politicization of the debate have discouraged most scholars and analysts (with some noteworthy exceptions such as Charles Kerchner, Julia E. Koppich, Tom Loveless, and Terry M. Moe) from examining collective bargaining by teachers. Put plainly, examining this issue is a risky proposition for a young scholar at most schools of education today. In fact, even as we were seeking support for this project and recruiting authors, more than one person wished us well and told us that this was an important avenue for inquiry but just too hot for them to touch. This is an unfortunate state of affairs and counterproductive to the serious inquiry this topic demands.

And it does demand attention. While some argue that the increased attention to the role of teachers unions and collective bargaining now is merely indicative of the rightward drift of American politics over the last generation and another example of conservative efforts to weaken sources of liberal political power rather than a genuine policy issue, we disagree. Attention to this and other "third rail" issues is a natural consequence of the evolution of education policymaking during the past few decades. During that time a rough consensus about the broad contours of national school improvement efforts has been reached, and policymakers and policy analysts are now turning their attention to the thornier issues.

This change is occurring in no small part because the past 15 years have seen an unprecedented focus on school improvement as three successive presidents, Republicans and Democrats, have made school reform a prominent part of their domestic policy agenda and with striking similarities in their approaches. The first President Bush convened the nation's governors (with the help of then-Arkansas governor Bill Clinton) for the first national education summit and set the nation on the path to standards-based education reform. President Clinton subsequently codified this agenda in national policy through his landmark reauthorization of the Elementary and Secondary Education Act (ESEA) and championed greater public-sector choice in education through charter schools and public school choice. President George W. Bush furthered the agenda by attaching real consequences for achieving standards in his revision of ESEA, commonly referred to as No Child Left Behind. In other words, despite plenty of noise, the broad parameters of the educational debate are relatively settled for today and the immediate future.

Collective bargaining agreements are a prime example of the more difficult subsurface issues that are now attracting the interest of policymakers. These agreements and the process by which they are reached are politically contentious and exert a great deal of leverage over school and school district operations. That it is not just political or educational conservatives paying attention to collective bargaining by teachers but also traditionally left-leaning groups like the Citizens' Commission on Civil Rights and the Education Trust speaks to the broad saliency of the issue among serious policy actors.

What can we conclude at this early stage? First, the too often unstated obvious: there are many excellent public schools where collective bargaining does not exist and many where it does, and likewise many awful public schools where teachers either do or do not bargain collectively. In short, collective bargaining by teachers is not an absolute determinant of school quality one way or the other at the school level. Critics too often minimize the reality that if collective bargaining by teachers were curtailed or eliminated tomorrow, serious structural and institutional obstacles to school improvement—such as inequitable state school finance schemes, inadequate state department of education capacity, and a dearth of human capital in key areas—would remain. Conversely, if collective bargaining were no longer in force, many avenues that allow teachers to have voice in the operations and activities of their schools would still exist. Outstanding schools with a collaborative and collegial culture exist in the absence of collective bargaining.

Despite the claims of many advocates, collective bargaining by teachers is not completely benign. Common provisions of collective bargaining agreements, as well as the accompanying politics, complicate school improvement efforts in significant ways. One need not be an enthusiastic proponent of school choice to see that individual schools (and the teachers in them) too often enjoy insufficient autonomy as a result of bargaining agreements. Nor need one be hostile toward organized labor to conclude that the process described by Frederick M. Hess and Andrew P. Kelly consumes energy and talent (on both sides of the bargaining table) that could be better spent on other educational endeavors. Similarly, as Paul T. Hill shows in this volume, common provisions in collective bargaining agreements have an adverse effect on intradistrict school finance and efforts to improve equity for poor and minority students, and Paul Manna illustrates the collision course between some of No Child Left Behind's provisions intended to do the same and some National Education Association policy positions.

These issues are not easy to discuss publicly. For one thing, the enormous political power of the teachers unions has served to stifle discussion and debate. No one wants to offend the powerful. In addition, too often questioning collective bargaining is equated with attacking teachers. This is simply untrue. Teachers are rightly among the most respected members of our society. When asked by pollsters about occupations they respect or trust, Americans consistently rank teachers at the top. This is understandable; with more than three million public school teachers nationwide, many people have teachers in their immediate families. And it is not just Jaime Escalante capturing the public imagination. Many people know, or have experienced firsthand, an exceptional teacher who goes the extra mile or perseveres in the face of adversity or challenges.

Yet teachers unions are more than the sum of their individual members. They are large, established, institutional players in education policymaking. Thus, their impact on policy must be analyzed through the lens of their aggregate effects, codified most notably in bargaining agreements, not merely through emotionally compelling anecdotes, personal experience, or the fact that for many they are more sympathetic than many other national interest groups.

The various analyses in this volume lead us to draw seven broad conclusions. First, collective bargaining was the right intervention at the right time for teachers. Prior to the introduction of collective bargaining in education, teachers were too often treated arbitrarily and capriciously, underpaid, and denied a voice in educational decisions and their workplace. As Richard D. Kahlenberg's chapter shows, bold action by Albert Shanker set in motion positive changes to these issues. This was all well and good. But the environment has changed, as have the demands being put on public schools. The emphasis of today's educational policies is on results, while, as Hess and Kelly show, the emphasis of most collective bargaining agreements remains on process and inputs.

Likewise, teachers were treated poorly in part because they were largely a captive labor pool. Women and minorities had few professional opportunities beyond teaching for much of the last century. Today's labor market is different. Schools and school districts must compete vigorously for talent. Money is not the only dimension of this competition, but it is one tool. Many of the provisions of collective bargaining agreements, however, particularly restrictions on earnings for high performers and a lack of salary differentiation to compensate for scarce skills or especially challenging assignments, handcuff schools and school districts in the competition for excellent employees.

In addition, while nominally tools of teacher empowerment, too often collective bargaining agreements restrict what teachers can do professionally. It is a sad irony that while many critics of today's approaches to education governance decry a "corporate" model of education governance, they nonetheless steadfastly defend an industrial approach to bargaining that treats teachers as interchangeable parts governed by prescriptive rules rather than as professionals.

Second, the lack of empirical evidence on the effects of collective bargaining by teachers on educational practice, finance, and operations is striking. Dan Goldhaber's chapter in this volume shows both how little evidence exists and also how much of what has been put forward as evidence is substantially flawed in one way or another. Granted, this is to some extent cause by larger problems in terms of data about various educational issues. However, relative to its importance in public education, collective bargaining by teachers remains substantially underexamined.

Third, as Henry S. Farber discusses in his chapter analyzing distinctions between public- and private-sector unions, vitally important distinctions exist between collective bargaining in the private sector and collective bargaining by teachers. Facile comparisons between bargaining by, for instance, autoworkers or steelworkers and bargaining by teachers fall apart under scrutiny. The distinctions carry enormous import for formulating educational policy and understanding education politics. Most important, there is little external competition in public education, reducing extrinsic incentives for management-labor cooperation. Likewise, the public schools cannot go out of business or relocate elsewhere to do business, eliminating a key check on labor demands that exists in much of the private sector.

In addition, in the private sector when management and labor sit down to negotiate a contract, both sides are free to represent their interests and a healthy tension exists. By contrast, because local teachers unions play such a significant role in school board politics and elections, and in shaping legislation through substantial lobbying efforts, the interests of management are often compromised in negotiations. In essence, the governance arrangements for public schools allow the teachers unions to often exercise leverage on both sides of the bargaining table because they play a large role in choosing who the management is in the first place and many of the rules of the game.

Conversely, unlike private industries such as the automobile industry, teachers are more fungible than some other workers. In most industrial fields, specialized skills mean specialized jobs are not interchangeable. A highly skilled plumber still cannot, without retraining, install transmissions on automobiles. In the private sector this specialization gives labor additional leverage because it constrains the available labor pool and assignment of workers. However, although "out of field" teaching is frowned on, in education management can, and regularly does, assign teachers to subjects outside their specialties. The ability to do this can to some extent weaken labor's leverage in education.

Fourth, many bargaining agreements have serious problems. As several chapters in this volume show, what is good for teachers is not axiomatically good for students. For example, veteran teachers have an interest in seniority provisions that give them more control over choosing their school and teaching assignment. Yet such provisions restrict the ability of school leaders (whether principals or teams of teachers themselves) to control who works in their school and build a cohesive team. More troubling, these provisions exacerbate, if not in part cause, the maldistribution of teaching talent that leaves the neediest students the most ill served. Education is one of the few, if not only, industries in which the least-qualified and experienced personnel disproportionately hold the most challenging jobs.

Unfortunately, debate about how to address this problem has too often been framed as a series of false choices and stark delineations between the status quo and mandatory assignment of teachers to schools regardless of their preference. In fact, various incentive schemes and other reforms offer a fertile middle ground for policymakers and are not at odds with the overall goals of collective bargaining. Seniority has long served as a proxy for quality in the absence of better indicators. However, new approaches to measuring teacher effectiveness, and the abundance of data in the wake of No Child Left Behind will lead to more nuanced determinations of effectiveness and more solid bases for developing productive interventions. Unfortunately, overall, collective bargaining agreements currently fail to incorporate or anticipate these reforms.

Fifth, it is unfair to lay all the blame for the current state of affairs at the feet of the teachers unions. There is much truth to the cliché that both management *and* labor sign any bargaining agreement. As Hess and Kelly show, some of the problems with today's contracts result from poor negotiating by school administrators and an unwillingness or inability to fully exploit favorable language in bargaining agreements. Moreover, the similarity in behavior across various kinds of school districts with various (or no) collective bargaining arrangements speaks to ingrained institutional norms among administrators. In addition, too often community groups and other stakeholders are not as involved in, or aware of, the collective bargaining process as they should be. They, and the media that too frequently gives the bargaining process and the particulars of the agreements perfunctory treatment, also share responsibility.

Sixth, asking teachers unions to look after the interests of their members and the children they serve is asking them to shoulder a responsibility exceptional in organized labor. Unions were, and are, formed to look after the interests of workers. To be sure, this does not mean, as some critics contend, that the actions of teachers unions are overall or even predominantly antagonistic to the interests of children. On the contrary, numerous positions generally supported by teachers unions benefit both teachers and students. For instance, assuming a sufficient supply of talented teachers, efforts to lower class sizes in the early grades both improve the quality of instruction and ease the workload of teachers. Likewise, efforts to increase public support and public resources for education also benefit students as well as teachers.

Yet while a "dual bottom line" often benefits teachers and students, it is naive to think that the interests of teachers, as articulated through their union and codified in collective bargaining agreements, do not at times conflict with the best interests of students. For instance, it is hard to reconcile the practices that Paul T. Hill describes, common to many bargaining agreements, with the best interests of low-income youngsters. The "single salary schedules" in most bargaining agreements preclude using financial incentives as one strategy to attract teachers to hard-to-staff schools. It is difficult to see how this restriction benefits students but easy to see how, despite its historical roots in education, it fits into an industrial model of labor-management relations.

Finally, too often other political concerns cloud analysis and discussion of these issues. In the middle of the 20th century, about one in three workers was in a union. Now, at the dawn of the 21st, barely more than one in ten is. And today it is public-sector workers, not private-sector, who comprise much of labor's muscle. As the fortunes of private-sector labor have waned, public-sector unions—and in particular the teachers unions, which now form the backbone of public-sector unionization—have assumed an increasingly prominent position in Democratic politics and progressive causes. Yet how collective bargaining impacts public education policy and practice is a vitally important issue that must be analyzed on its own merits, costs, and benefits divorced from whatever downstream political effects various changes may have. When other considerations subtly or directly bear on this conversation, it does not serve the interests of an objective analysis about what is best for children of any public education system.

RECOMMENDATIONS

Reforming teacher collective bargaining suggests the same riddle Madison wrestled with in Federalist 10. Essentially, many proposed remedies are as troublesome as the problems they would seek to address.

Legal issues notwithstanding, even many of those with concerns about the adverse impact of common provisions of collective bargaining agreements are reticent to support any reform that would curtail bargaining rights or political activity by teachers unions because of the broader precedents this action would set for organized labor more generally. Moreover, banning teachers from bargaining collectively or curtailing certain aspects of contracts through statutes would merely exacerbate today's antagonistic environment rather than build consensus around reforms. In other words, shifting the focus of the debate to whether or not teachers unions should be able to enshrine certain things in contracts would move the focus of the debate even further from the interests of children than it is now.

Consequently, we submit that these issues are best addressed through the local, state, and national political process and that the solutions are largely political ones. The problem is not that the teachers unions enjoy too much power or leverage, it is that other constituencies exercise too little. Obviously, this analysis speaks to broader questions in education policymaking and politics, but it is through those processes that collective bargaining agreements, such as they are today, are manifested.

We make three recommendations based on the analyses in this volume. The first recommendation focuses on information issues; the second and third focus on structural issues. The three are related in the sense that together they are likely to lead to better-informed and less-polarized discussions about teacher collective bargaining policies, and greater opportunities for involvement in policymaking about these issues.

First, what should come through strongly in this volume is that issues associated with collective bargaining in education require much more research and analysis than they have thus far received in order to promote effective and equitable policymaking. Today, in the absence of empirical evidence, defenders of traditional collective bargaining by teachers assert that it is essential, while many critics build a circumstantial case that it is harmful. To develop good policy, it is imperative that there be more discussion, analysis, and research about collective bargaining by teachers and its effects.

More transparency is an essential part of that process and this conversation. One basic step toward this end is for newspapers to publish and disseminate bargaining agreements so that the community and various stakeholders can easily access them. Public documents with broad import are routinely published, and in a local community few documents have the impact on local civic life that these contracts do. To their credit, some teachers unions publish these agreements on their websites to facilitate accessibility, but such openness is not the norm. Where newspapers fail to inform the public about these agreements, local philanthropists and community groups should arrange for bargaining agreements to be printed and widely disseminated, including as supplements in local newspapers. There is a clear public interest in access to these documents, because they help determine how large amounts of public educational resources are allocated.

At the national level, the federal government should collect more information about teachers union membership, the number and dispersion of bargaining units, and other objective data that researchers, analysts, and policymakers can use. Easily accessible, comparable, and transparent data will better help analysts and researchers study this issue and provide a common base of evidence from which the conversation can move.

The philanthropic community could also play a role. Philanthropy has a natural and understandable tendency to support projects where strategies are clearly observable and outcomes are quantifiable. These efforts are no doubt meritorious, but it is vital that foundations also support research and policy analysis about complicated issues of management and governance, including collective bargaining by teachers. Such issues fly below most radar screens yet establish the hard-to-see scaffolding for school reform efforts. Foundations can also help by sponsoring efforts to increase awareness about these issues among the public and local stakeholder groups. In addition, foundations that seek to help other interests in this debate—for instance, low-income and minority students—can fund training to give local activists and officials the necessary preparation and tools to engage in this process.

Our second recommendation is for broad involvement in school board elections and politics, which is essential to ensure the public interest is well served. Too often school board elections or primaries are held at times different from other local, state, and national elections. Although the research evidence about the impact of such scheduling is mixed, it is plausible that in at least some cases it limits turnout and increases the clout of organized groups, most notably the local teachers unions. Because scheduling school board elections concurrently with other elections for local, state, and national office has no adverse effect on the public interest, doing otherwise is difficult to justify. Both increasing information about collective bargaining agreements and holding school board elections at times when the public is already engaged are likely to have important beneficial effects on the range and level of involvement of the general public and local civic and business groups in school board elections. This awareness and involvement will help ensure a vigorous debate so that strong unions and strong countervailing pressures can complement one another.

Third, while better information about collective bargaining agreements and more awareness of school board politics will no doubt activate new stakeholder groups, we also recommend that local communities seek to expand the stakeholders represented in the bargaining process and to incorporate performance benchmarks in contracts. In this book Julia E. Koppich proposes incorporating student achievement goals into contracts. Making contracts more performance based would force discussion of the trade-offs associated with various provisions in terms of what is best for students. In addition, local communities should initiate processes to ensure that, within reason, other stakeholders are able to observe and participate in the bargaining process. Obviously, only two parties will sign the bargaining agreement, but greater public access to the process and greater stakeholder input would have clear benefits.

Today the debate is about expanding or restricting the scope of bargaining. Instead, it needs to be about new approaches to bargaining, because the education environment is changing. Overall, in states where teachers can elect whether or not to join unions, the membership of teachers unions is generally declining, and the membership of alternative teachers associations is rising in some states as well. This is not just a political shift away from organized labor. Younger teachers increasingly do not see the relevance of teachers unions to their work or professional interests and have many other opportunities to participate in the political process. Moreover, as Susan Moore Johnson and Morgaen L. Donaldson point out, younger teachers are more likely to favor the sort of salary innovations that teachers unions generally oppose and restrict in collective bargaining agreements, and are more likely to be adversely affected by current practices common to these agreements. Similarly, teachers in fast-growing parts of the education sector, in particular charter schools, tend to eschew teachers unions. These dynamics present a challenge but also a vital opportunity for progressive leaders in the teachers unions. An atomized teaching force without a strong collective voice at the state and national level on major issues is not in the best interest of teachers.

But the highest stakes are not the welfare of teachers unions; they are the welfare of students. The collective intent of state and federal policies is to increase the performance orientation of public schools. Greater emphasis on results and greater choice in delivery of educational services are trends that will define education policy for the foreseeable future and have potentially powerful benefits for children. Yet the bargaining contracts that our schools work under generally represent outmoded norms and institutions and are out of step with these changes. Reorienting these contracts toward today's imperatives—equity, performance, and student learning—is essential for teachers unions, public schools, and, most important, students.

Notes

CHAPTER ONE   The History of Collective Bargaining among Teachers (Kahlenberg)

1. Charles Taylor Kerchner, Julia E. Koppich, and Joseph G. Weeres, *United Mind Workers: Unions and Teaching in the Knowledge Society* (San Francisco: Jossey-Bass, 1997), p. 13; Dale Ballou and Michael Podgursky, "Gaining Control of Professional Licensing and Advancement," in *Conflicting Missions? Teachers Unions and Educational Reform*, ed. Tom Loveless (Washington, DC: Brookings Institution Press, 2000), p. 86; Myron Lieberman, *The Teacher Unions: How the NEA and AFT Sabotage Reform and Hold Students, Parents, Teachers, and Taxpayers Hostage to Bureaucracy* (New York: Free Press, 1997), p. 4; Peter Brimelow, *The Worm in the Apple: How the Teacher Unions Are Destroying American Education* (New York: HarperCollins, 2003), p. 171; Thomas Toch, "Why Teachers Don't Teach," *US News & World Report*, February 26, 1996, pp. 62ff.; Terry Moe, "No Teacher Left Behind," *Wall Street Journal*, January 13, 2005, p. A12.

2. U.S. Department of Labor, Bureau of Labor Statistics, *Union Members in 2004* (Washington, DC, U.S. Government Printing Office, 2005), p. 1. For 1950s figures, see Steven Greenhouse, "Worried about Labor's Waning Strength, Union Presidents Form Advisory Committee," *New York Times*, March 9, 2003, p. 21.

3. In 1960 the NEA had 700,000 members and the AFT had 50,000 members. Diane Ravitch, *The Troubled Crusade: American Education, 1945-1980* (New York: Basic Books, 1983), pp. 313-314. See also Lieberman, *Teacher Unions*, p. 1; Terry M. Moe, "A Union by Any Other Name," *Education Next* 1, no. 3 (Fall 2001): 40-41. Today the AFT claims 1.3 million members and the NEA 2.7 million members, according to the groups' websites. See http://www.nea.org/aboutnea/index.html and http://www.aft.org/about/index.htm. The 4-million-member figure includes some nonteachers—nurses, paraprofessionals, and the like. Moe, "A Union by Any Other Name," p. 41 (about half of AFT members are teachers, as are about four-fifths of NEA members).

4. Toch, "Why Teachers Don't Teach." See also Brimelow, *Worm in the Apple*, p. 140.

5. Brimelow, *Worm in the Apple*, p. 52. See also Thomas Toch, "Tensions of the Shanker Era: A Speech That Shook the Field," *Education Week*, March 26, 1997, available online at www.edweek.org/ew/articles/1997/03/26/26toch.h16/html.

6. Originally called the National Teachers Association, it became the NEA in 1870. Wayne J. Urban, *Why Teachers Organized* (Detroit: Wayne State University Press, 1982), pp. 111-112; Kerchner et al., *United Mind Workers*, pp. 6-7; Maris A. Vinovskis, "Teachers Unions and Educational Research and Development," in *Conflicting Missions? Teachers Unions and Educational Reform*, ed. Tom Loveless (Washington, DC: Brookings Institution Press, 2000), p. 213; Ravitch, *Troubled Crusade*, pp. 47-48; Don Cameron, *The Inside Story of the Teacher Revolution in America* (Lanham, MD: Scarecrow Education, 2005), p. 66.

7. Urban, *Why Teachers Organized*, p. 138.

8. A. H. Raskin, "He Leads His Teachers Up the Down Staircase," *New York Times Magazine*, September 3, 1967, p. 4.

9. Marjorie Murphy, *Blackboard Unions: The AFT and the NEA, 1900-1980* (Ithaca, NY: Cornell University Press, 1990), p. 72.

10. Urban, *Why Teachers Organized*, pp. 66-86.

11. Murphy, *Blackboard Unions*, pp. 83-84; Urban, *Why Teachers Organized*, p. 9.

12. Robert J. Braun, *Teachers and Power: The Story of the American Federation of Teachers* (New York: Simon & Schuster, 1972), p. 48.

13. Braun, *Teachers and Power*, p. 136.

14. Murphy, *Blackboard Unions*, p. 211.

15. Urban, *Why Teachers Organized*, p. 99.

16. Murphy, *Blackboard Unions*, p. 102.

17. Joseph C. Goulden, *Jerry Wurf: Labor's Last Angry Man* (New York: Atheneum, 1982), p. 26.

18. Murphy, *Blackboard Unions*, p. 162.

19. Lee Anderson, "All Should Be Free to Choose," *Chattanooga Times Free Press*, June 1, 1999, p. B7; Murphy, *Blackboard Unions*, p. 148.

20. Max Green, *Epitaph for American Labor: How Union Leaders Lost Touch with America* (Washington, DC: AEI Press, 1996), p. 162.

21. Murphy, *Blackboard Unions*, pp. 210-211. See also Urban, *Why Teachers Organized*, p. 138.

22. Murphy, *Blackboard Unions*, p. 99; Urban, *Why Teachers Organized*, p. 85 (Chicago); and Braun, *Teachers and Power*, pp. 29-33 (Cleveland and Chicago). See also Philip Taft, *United They Teach: The Story of the United Federation of Teachers* (Los Angeles: Nash Publishing, 1974), p. 8 (Seattle).

23. Albert Shanker, "Reflections on Forty Years in the Profession," in *Reflections: Personal Essays by 33 Distinguished Educators*, ed. Derek L. Burleson (Bloomington, IN: Phi Delta Kappa Educational Foundation, 1991), p. 326.

24. Murphy, *Blackboard Unions*, pp. 87-88.

25. Urban, *Why Teachers Organized*, p. 15.

26. Shanker, "Reflections," p. 327.

27. Murphy, *Blackboard Unions*, p. 277.

28. Richard B. Freeman and James L. Medoff, *What Do Unions Do?* (New York: Basic Books, 1984), pp. 46-48.

29. Murphy, *Blackboard Unions*, p. 210. See also Urban, *Why Teachers Organized*, p. 140.

30. U.S. Department of Education, National Center for Education Statistics, *Digest of Education Statistics, 2003*, Table 69, p. 89 (14.6% of public school teachers lacked a bachelor's degree in 1961 and just 0.9% by 1970) (Washington, DC: U.S. Government Printing Office, 2004).

31. Murphy, *Blackboard Unions*, p. 212; Albert Shanker, "Where We Stand," *New York Times*, September 8, 1996; David Hill, "Shanker Stands the Test of Time," *Education Week*, February 21, 1996, available online at www.edweek.org/ew/articles/1996/02/21/22shank.h15.html; Susan Moore Johnson and Susan M. Kardos, "Reform Bargaining and Its Promise for School Improvement," in *Conflicting Missions? Teachers Unions and Educational Reform*, ed. Tom Loveless (Washington, DC: Brookings Institution Press, 2000), p. 16; Sol Stern, *Breaking Free: Public School Lessons and the Imperative of School Choice* (San Francisco: Encounter Books, 2003), p. 104; Author interview with George Altomare, September 6, 2003, New York, NY.

32. Butte, Montana, appears to be the first site of a teacher collective bargaining agreement, forged in 1936. In an unusual twist, the school board, dominated by unionized miners, suggested to teachers that they bargain collectively with the board. Pawtucket, Rhode Island, and East St. Louis, Illinois, also saw early collective bargaining agreements. St. Paul, Minnesota, was the site of the first teacher strike in 1946. American Federation of Teachers, *Building on the Past for a Better Future* (Washington, DC: Author, 1990), film.

33. Hill, "Shanker Stands"; Leonard Buder, "Cogen Seeks Post in National Union," *New York Times*, April 26, 1964, p. 75; Raskin, "He Leads His Teachers," p. 30.

34. Albert Shanker, "Teacher Unions: Past, Present and Future Influence," *American Educator* 21, nos. 1, 2 (Spring/Summer 1997): 14; Raskin, "He Leads His Teachers," p. 30; Lieberman, *Teacher Unions*, p. 15.

35. Lieberman, *Teacher Unions*, p. 18.

36. Murphy, *Blackboard Unions*, p. 214. Teachers did not use the Wisconsin law until 1964. Howard L. Fuller, George A. Mitchell, and Michael E. Hartmann, "Collective Bargaining in Milwaukee Public Schools," in *Conflicting Missions? Teachers Unions and Educational Reform*, ed. Tom Loveless (Washington, DC: Brookings Institution Press, 2000), p. 121.

37. Hill, "Shanker Stands."
38. Braun, *Teachers and Power*, pp. 60-61; David Selden, *The Teacher Rebellion* (Washington, DC: Howard University Press, 1985), p. 62; Taft, *United They Teach*, p. 121; Daniel H. Perlstein, *Justice, Justice: School Politics and the Eclipse of Liberalism* (New York: Peter Lang, 2004), p. 21.
39. Taft, *United They Teach*, p. 80; "Collective Bargaining: Laying the Foundation," *American Teacher*, April 1997, p. 8; Murphy, *Blackboard Unions*, p. 212; Selden, *Teacher Rebellion*, p. 34; Interview with Altomare.
40. Hill, "Shanker Stands."
41. Raskin, "He Leads His Teachers," p. 30.
42. Murphy, *Blackboard Unions*, p. 215.
43. Interview with Altomare.
44. Hill, "Shanker Stands"; Raskin, "He Leads His Teachers," pp. 29-30; Murphy, *Blackboard Unions*, p. 213.
45. Braun, *Teachers and Power*, p. 62.
46. Raskin, "He Leads His Teachers," p. 30.
47. Hill, "Shanker Stands."
48. Lieberman, *Teacher Unions*, p. 13; Braun, *Teachers and Power*, p. 62; Murphy, *Blackboard Unions*, p. 215.
49. F. Howard Nelson, "Collective Bargaining," American Federation of Teachers, October 1990, available at http://www.aft.org/research/reports/collbarg/shankers.htm.
50. *Business Week*, December 30, 1961, quoted in Perlstein, *Justice, Justice*, p. 21.
51. Murphy, *Blackboard Unions*, p. 214.
52. Murphy, *Blackboard Unions*, p. 216; Taft, *United They Teach*, p. 127.
53. Murphy, *Blackboard Unions*, p. 222.
54. Braun, *Teachers and Power*, p. 138; Selden, *Teacher Rebellion*, p. 76.
55. Shanker, "Reflections," p. 328; Stern, *Breaking Free*, p. 112; Taft, *United They Teach*, p. 121.
56. Charles Cogen and Albert Shanker, "Unions Say Class Conditions as Well as Pay Must Improve," *New York Times*, July 22, 1963, p. 22; Taft, *United They Teach*, p. 141.
57. Shanker, "Reflections." See also Charles Taylor Kerchner and Julia E. Koppich, "Organizing around Quality: The Frontiers of Teacher Unionism," in *Conflicting Missions? Teachers Unions and Educational Reform*, ed. Tom Loveless (Washington, DC: Brookings Institution Press, 2000), p. 299.
58. Lieberman, *Teacher Unions*, p. ix; Brimelow, *Worm in the Apple*, p. 56. Lieberman also takes the extreme position that even negotiating teacher wages and hours is antidemocratic (p. 64).
59. Lieberman, *Teacher Unions*, p. 15.
60. Kerchner et al., *United Mind Workers*, pp. 7, 186.
61. Raskin, "He Leads His Teachers," p. 29.
62. Kerchner and Koppich, "Organizing around Quality," p. 308; Kerchner et al., *United Mind Workers*, p. 186.
63. Bayard Rustin, acceptance speech for the 1968 John Dewey Award, United Federation of Teachers (referencing the 1966 speech) (New York: United Federation of Teachers Archives, New York University, Tamiment Institute), p. 10.
64. Taft, *United They Teach*, pp. 149-151; Braun, *Teachers and Power*, p. 161; Raskin, "He Leads His Teachers," p. 29.
65. Murphy, *Blackboard Unions*, pp. 1, 214.
66. Selden, *Teacher Rebellion*, p. 115.
67. Murphy, *Blackboard Unions*, p. 224.
68. Murphy, *Blackboard Unions*, p. 1; Cameron, *Inside Story*, pp. 60, 74.
69. Lieberman, *Teacher Unions*, p. 16.
70. Cameron, *Inside Story*, pp. 75-77; Linda Chavez and Daniel Gray, *Betrayal: How Union Bosses Shake Down Their Members and Corrupt American Politics* (New York: Crown Forum, 2004), p. 114.
71. Cameron, *Inside Story*, p. 77.

72. Lieberman, *Teacher Unions*, p. 21. Some districts have gone back and forth between the NEA and AFT, but incumbency has its advantages.

73. Murphy, *Blackboard Unions*, p. 214.

74. Lieberman, *Teacher Unions*, p. 48. An additional seven states allow local districts to bargain, and nine prohibit bargaining.

75. Lieberman, *Teacher Unions*, pp. 61-62; Bruce S. Cooper, "An International Perspective on Teachers Unions," in *Conflicting Missions? Teachers Unions and Educational Reform*, ed. Tom Loveless (Washington, DC: Brookings Institution Press, 2000), pp. 262-263 (also noting that most European countries provide for the right of public employees to strike).

76. Raskin, "He Leads His Teachers," p. 30.

77. Murphy, *Blackboard Unions*, p. 220.

78. "Why the Surge in Teachers' Strikes," *US News & World Report*, September 18, 1978, p. 79.

79. See, for example, Michael H. Cimini, "1982-1997 State and Local Work Stoppages," *Compensation and Working Conditions* (Fall 1998): 39, available online at www.bls.gov/opub/cwc/archive/fall1998brief3.pdf. Annually, there were fewer than ten strikes involving more than 1,000 public school teachers between 1982 and 1997.

80. Lieberman, *Teacher Unions*, p. 1; Moe, "A Union by Any Other Name," pp. 40-41; AFT and NEA websites.

81. Lieberman, *Teacher Unions*, p. 21 (for 1971); Murphy, *Blackboard Unions*, p. 209 (for the late 1970s). See also Cooper, "International Perspective," p. 249; Brimelow, *Worm in the Apple*, pp. 17, 235; U.S. Department of Education, National Center for Education Statistics, *Schools and Staffing Survey, 1993-94* (Washington, DC: U.S. Government Printing Office, 1996).

82. Toch, "Why Teachers Don't Teach"; Brimelow, *Worm in the Apple*, pp. 81-82.

83. Lieberman, *Teacher Unions*, p. 4. See also Brimelow, *Worm in the Apple*, p. xiii; Douglas McCray, "Working with the Enemy," *New York Times Education Life*, January 16, 2005, p. 29. When state and local affiliates are included, the estimated revenue tops $2 billion. Stern, *Breaking Free*, p. 118.

84. Lieberman, *Teacher Unions*, pp. 84, 87.

85. Chavez and Gray, *Betrayal*, p. 119, citing Charles Lewis.

86. Lieberman, *Teacher Unions*, p. 2.

87. Joe A. Stone, "Collective Bargaining and Public Schools," in *Conflicting Missions? Teachers Unions and Educational Reform*, ed. Tom Loveless (Washington, DC: Brookings Institution Press, 2000), pp. 49-51. This research is consistent with studies finding a significant wage and benefits premium for union members as a whole. Freeman and Medoff, *What Do Unions Do?* pp. 46-48.

88. U.S. Department of Education, National Center for Education Statistics, *Digest of Education Statistics, 2003*, Table 69, p. 89 (Washington, DC: U.S. Government Printing Office, 2004).

89. Freeman and Medoff, *What Do Unions Do?* pp. 7-8, 20-21, 95.

90. Donald Boyd, Hamilton Lankford, Susanna Loeb, and James Wyckoff, "The Preparation and Recruitment of Teachers," in *A Qualified Teacher in Every Classroom? Appraising Old Answers and New Ideas*, ed. Frederick M. Hess, Andrew J. Rotherham, and Kate Walsh (Cambridge, MA: Harvard Education Press, 2004), pp. 152-153.

91. Johnson and Kardos, "Reform Bargaining," p. 13.

92. U.S. Department of Education, National Center for Education Statistics, *Digest of Education Statistics, 2002*, Table 65, p. 77 (Washington, DC: U.S. Government Printing Office, 2003).

93. Stone, "Collective Bargaining," p. 51.

94. See, for example, Lawrence Mishel and Richard Rothstein, eds., *The Class Size Debate* (Washington, DC: Economic Policy Institute, 2002) (with contributions by Alan B. Krueger, Eric A. Hanushek, and Jennifer King Rice).

95. Johnson and Kardos, "Reform Bargaining," p. 13.

96. Stone, "Collective Bargaining," p. 51.

97. Kerchner and Koppich, "Organizing around Quality," pp. 295-296 (describing staff development contractual provisions in Dade County, Minneapolis, and New York).

98. Richard Elmore and Deanna Burney, "Investing in Teacher Learning: Staff Development and Instructional Improvement in Community School District #2, New York City" (New York: National Commission on Teaching and America's Future, August 1997).

99. Paul E. Barton "Unequal Learning Environments: Discipline That Works," in *A Notion at Risk: Preserving Public Education as an Engine for Social Mobility*, ed. Richard D. Kahlenberg (New York: Century Foundation Press, 2000), pp. 235-236 (Texas and West Virginia), 246 (Minneapolis), and 229-234 (relationship between discipline and achievement). For reference to New York's early contract provisions on discipline, see Fred M. Hechinger, "School and Teacher–Repercussions of the Strike," *New York Times*, October 1, 1967, Section IV, p. 9.

100. Interview with Albert Shanker, 1988, American Jewish Committee Oral History Collection, Dorot Jewish Division, New York Public Library, p. 9.

101. Myron Lieberman, "The Ruminations of a Right-Wing Extremist," *Phi Delta Kappan*, November 1998, pp. 229-232. See also author interview with Phil Kugler, August 4, 2004, Washington, DC. (Shanker, speaking at Oberlin College in 1968, was asked, "What about the children?" and responded, "I don't represent the children. I represent the teachers.")

102. Joseph Berger, "Albert Shanker, 68, Combative Leader of Teachers, Dies," *New York Times*, February 23, 1997, p. 1.

103. Fuller et al., "Milwaukee Schools," p. 128; Stern, *Breaking Free*, p. 24.

104. Brimelow, *Worm in the Apple*, p. 41.

105. Toch, "Why Teachers Don't Teach."

106. Toch, "Why Teachers Don't Teach"; Caroline Hoxby and Andrew Leigh, *Pulled Away or Pushed Out? Explaining the Decline of Teacher Aptitude in the United States*, available at http://post.economics.harvard.edu/faculty/hoxbyleigh_pulledaway.pdf. Note that some argue the single salary schedule is not necessarily attributable to collective bargaining. The single salary schedule exists in nonbargaining states as well. Kerchner and Koppich, "Organizing around Quality," p. 293. See also Lieberman, *Teacher Unions*, 214. The practice has been around for 100 years, long before the advent of collective bargaining for teachers. Lewis C. Solomon, "Recognizing Differences: Let's Reward Good Teachers," *Education Next 5*, no. 1 (Winter 2005): 16.

107. Lieberman, *Teacher Unions*, p. 221.

108. "Bob Dole's Acceptance Speech," August 15, 1996, NewsHour Convention Speeches, available online at www.pbs.org/newshour/convention96/floor_speeches/bob_dole.html.

109. "Always Setting the Standard," *American Teacher*, April 1997, p. 4.

110. The three speeches included a January 1985 speech at the National Press Club, an April 1985 speech to New York State United Teachers in Niagara Falls, and a July 1985 speech to the AFT's QuEST conference.

111. Albert Shanker, "The Making of a Profession," reprinted in *Journal of Negro Education 5*, no. 1 (Summer 1986): 421, 405. See also Gene I. Maeroff, "Shanker Urging Shift in Strategy to Aid Teachers," *New York Times*, April 28, 1985, p. 1.

112. Shanker, "The Making of a Profession," p. 412.

113. Johnson and Kardos, "Reform Bargaining," p. 8.

114. "Always Setting the Standard," pp. 4-5; William Lowe Boyd, David N. Plank, and Gary Sykes, "Teachers Unions in Hard Times," in *Conflicting Missions? Teachers Unions and Educational Reform,* ed. Tom Loveless (Washington, DC: Brookings Institution Press, 2000), p. 196.

115. Kerchner et al., *United Mind*, p. 187; and Kerchner and Koppich, "Organizing around Quality," p. 309. See also Kerchner and Koppich, "Organizing around Quality," p. 304, referencing the Yeshiva case (1980; about the problem of divided loyalties when workers act like management).

116. Kerchner et al., *United Mind Workers*, p. 90; Kerchner and Koppich, "Organizing around Quality," p. 290; Johnson and Kardos, "Reform Bargaining," p. 29.

117. Kerchner and Koppich, "Organizing around Quality," pp. 288 (Cincinnati), 291 (Rochester).

118. Gene I. Maeroff, "Shanker Backs Teacher Merit Pay Based on Standard National Test," *New York Times*, July 12, 1985, p. A1.

119. Jay Mathews, "For Elite U.S. Teachers, Cachet and More Cash," *Washington Post*, February 9, 2005, p. A10. See also Kerchner and Koppich, "Organizing around Quality," p. 289 (Los Angeles and New York districts provide premiums to teachers with national board certification).

120. "Always Setting the Standard," p. 5.

121. James G. Cibulka, "The NEA and School Choice," in *Conflicting Missions? Teachers Unions and Educational Reform,* ed. Tom Loveless (Washington, DC: Brookings Institution Press, 2000), p. 161; Cindy Currence, "AFT Head Backs Voucher Proposal for Public Schools," *Education Week*, May 8, 1985, available online at http://www.edweek.org/ew/articles/1985/05/08/05220004.no4.html; Shanker, "The Making of a Profession," p. 414.

122. Sara Mosle, "The Answer Is National Standards," *New York Times Magazine*, October 27, 1996, p. 45.

123. Kerchner and Koppich, "Organizing around Quality," pp. 286-288; Johnson and Kardos, "Reform Bargaining," p. 26.

124. "Always Setting the Standard," p. 6.

125. Ann Bradley, "The End of an Era," *Education Week*, March 5, 1997, available online at http://www.edweek.org/ew/articles/1997/03/05/23aft.n16.html; Adam Urbanski, "Reform or Be Reformed," *Education Next* 1, no. 3 (Fall 2001): 54.

126. Sandra Feldman, "Thank you, Al—I miss you terribly," *New York Teacher*, March 10, 1997, pp. 10S-11S.

127. Finn quoted in Edward B. Fiske, "Profile: Albert Shanker—Where He Stands," *New York Times*, November 5, 1989, p. 34.

128. Mosle, "The Answer Is National Standards."

129. Lieberman, *Teacher Unions*, p. 199.

130. Kerchner et al., *United Mind Workers*, pp. 4, 87.

131. Thomas Toch, "America's 'Most Militant Teacher' Calls for Reform," *US News & World Report*, February 26, 1996, p. 70.

132. Johnson and Kardos, "Reform Bargaining," p. 16, citing *Steele v. Louisville and Nashville Railroad Company*, 323 U.S. 192 (1944).

133. Cameron, *Inside Story*, p. 106 (risk, standardized testing, charter schools, and National Board for Professional Teaching Standards); Kerchner et al., *United Mind Workers*, p. 88 (peer review); statement of Mary Hatwood Futrell in Carnegie Forum on Education and the Economy, *A Nation Prepared: Teachers for the 21st Century* (New York: Carnegie Corporation of New York, May 1986), p. 117 (reservations about National Board for Professional Teaching Standards); Cibulka, "The NEA and School Choice," pp. 155-156 (public school choice and charter schools).

134. Fiske, "Profile," p. 34.

135. Bob Chase, "The New NEA: Reinventing the Teacher Unions for a New Era," *Vital Speeches of the Day*, April 1, 1997, pp. 372-375.

136. Toch, "Tensions of the Shanker Era."

137. Cibulka, "The NEA and School Choice," p. 169.

138. Charles Taylor Kerchner, "Deindustrialization," *Education Next* 1, no. 3 (Fall 2001): 47; Kerchner and Koppich, "Organizing around Quality," p. 282 (Columbus). See also Johnson and Kardos, "Reform Bargaining," p. 32 (discussing three districts).

139. Kerchner, "Deindustrialization," p. 48. See also Kerchner and Koppich, "Organizing around Quality," p. 290.

140. Matthew Miller, *The Two Percent Solution: Fixing America's Problems in Ways Liberals and Conservatives Can Love* (New York: Public Affairs, 2003), p. 121.

141. David Herszenhorn, "Failing Teachers Face a Faster Ax," *New York Times*, January 15, 2004, p. A1.

142. McCray, "Working with the Enemy," pp. 28-36. See also Brad Jupp, "The Uniform Salary Schedule: A Progressive Leader Proposes Differential Pay," *Education Next* 5, no. 1 (Winter 2005): 10-12.

143. Julia E. Koppich, "The As-Yet-Unfulfilled Promise of Reform Bargaining: Forging a Better Match between the Labor Relations System We Have and the Education System We Want," in this volume.

144. McCray, "Working with the Enemy," p. 31.

145. McCray, "Working with the Enemy," p. 31.

146. NEA Resolutions, 2001-02, p. 403, cited in Chavez and Gray, *Betrayal*, p. 112.

147. NEA Resolutions 2001-02, p. 305, cited in Chavez and Gray, *Betrayal*, p. 134.

148. Sam Dillon, "Teachers' Union and Districts Sue over Bush Law," *New York Times*, April 21, 2005, p. 1.

149. McCray, "Working with the Enemy," p. 28; Brimelow, *Worm in the Apple*, p. 185.

150. Bess Keller, "Elections Give No Easy Fix on Union Course: Union Leaders, Watchers Mull Whether the 'New Unionism' Is Retreating," *Education Week*, March 16, 2005, pp. 3, 15.

151. Author interview with Adam Urbanski, July 16, 2004, Washington, DC.

152. Julia E. Koppich, comments at Urban Institute PPI Conference on Teacher Collective Bargaining, Washington, DC, May 17, 2005.

CHAPTER TWO   Union Membership in the United States (Farber)

1. Prepared for the "Teacher Collective Bargaining Conference," sponsored by the Urban Institute and the Progressive Policy Institute, Washington, DC, May 16-17, 2005. The author may be contacted at Industrial Relations Section, Firestone Library, Princeton University, Princeton, NJ 08544-2098. E-mail: farber@princeton.edu.

2. These data are derived from the May CPS from 1973 to 1981 and from the merged outgoing rotation group files of the CPS from 1983 to 2004. There are no data on union membership in the CPS for 1982.

3. Due to the relatively small numbers of police and firefighters in the CPS, these employment levels are computed as three-year moving averages to reduce sampling variation.

4. The CPS asks a worker if he or she is a member of a labor union on the current job. If the worker responds in the negative, the worker is asked if he or she is covered by a collective bargaining agreement on the current job. I classify a worker as covered if he or she reports being a member or being covered if not a member. I make no adjustment for workers who are covered by union agreements but are not union members.

5. These figures are based on my tabulations of the merged outgoing rotation group files of the CPS and do not include self-employed workers.

6. Richard B. Freeman, "Contraction and Expansion: The Divergence of Private Sector and Public Sector Unionism in the United States," *Journal of Economic Perspectives* 2, no. 2 (1988): 63-88; Paul C. Weiler, "Promises to Keep: Securing Workers' Rights under the NLRA," *Harvard Law Review* 96 (1983): 1769-1827.

7. Paul Alan Levy, "The Unidimensional Perspective of the Reagan Labor Board," *Rutgers Law Journal* 16 (1985): 269-390.

8. Henry S. Farber and Bruce Western, "Accounting for the Decline of Unions in the Private Sector, 1973-1998," *Journal of Labor Research* (2001).

9. This framework is similar to those presented by William T. Dickens and Jonathan S. Leonard, "Accounting for the Decline in Union Membership, 1950-1980," *Industrial and Labor Relations Review* 38, no. 3 (1985): 323-334, and by Freeman, "Contraction and Expansion."

10. The union membership rate in 1982 is calculated as the average of the 1981 and 1983 values.

11. The question changed from asking about membership in a labor union to asking about membership in a labor union or employee association like a labor union. This is of real consequence for many public-sector workers such as teachers, police, and firefighters, who often belong to professional associations, and it is consistent with the dramatic increase in the public-sector union membership rate from 25.9 percent in May 1976 to 33.5 percent in May 1977.

12. The states with RTW laws are (in census code order) Iowa, North Dakota, South Dakota, Nebraska, Kansas, Virginia, North Carolina, South Carolina, Georgia, Florida, Tennessee, Alabama, Mississippi, Arkansas, Louisiana, Oklahoma, Texas, Idaho, Wyoming, Arizona, Utah, and Nevada.

13. Henry S. Farber, "Right-to-Work Laws and the Extent of Unionizaton," *Journal of Labor Economics* (July 1984): 319-352.

14. David T. Ellwood and Glenn Fine, "The Impact of Right-to-Work Laws on Union Organizing," *Journal of Political Economy* 95, no. 2 (1987): 250-73. There is a sharp contrast between the federal sector and the state and local sectors. Unions in the federal sector generally cannot bargain over compensation issues, and this severely limits their role. Additionally, there are no interstate differences in the relevant legal environment. For these reasons I omit federal government employees in the remainder of my analyses.

15. Richard B. Freeman and Robert G. Valletta, "The NBER Public Sector Collective Bargaining Law Data Set," in *When Public Sector Employees Unionize*, ed. Richard B. Freeman and Casey Ichniowski (Chicago: University of Chicago Press, 1988), pp. 399-419; Henry S. Farber, "The Evolution of Public Sector Bargaining Laws," in Freeman and Ichniowski, *When Public Sector Employees Unionize*, 129-166.

16. Freeman presents an analysis of the growth of labor unions in the public sector and its relationship to the change in the legislative environment. Richard B. Freeman, "Unionism Comes to the Public Sector," *Journal of Economic Literature* 24, no. 1 (1986): 41-86.

17. Freeman and Valletta, "The NBER Pubic Sector Collective Bargaining Law Data Set."

18. Kim Reuben of the Urban Institute graciously made these data available to me.

19. Richard B. Freeman and Robert G. Valletta, "The Effects of Public Sector Labor Laws on Labor Market Institutions and Outcomes," in Freeman and Ichniowski, *When Public Sector Employees Unionize*, pp. 81-106.

20. Freeman and Valletta, "The Effects of Public Sector Labor Laws."

21. Farber presents an analysis of threat effects of unions in the private sector, and he finds some evidence that wages of nonunion workers are positively affected by the threat of union organization. Henry S. Farber, "Nonunion Wage Rates and the Threat of Unionization," *Industrial and Labor Relations Review* 58, no. 3 (2005): 335-352.

CHAPTER THREE   Scapegoat, Albatross, or What? (Hess and Kelly)

1. William Ouchi, *Making Schools Work: A Revolutionary Plan to Get Your Children the Education They Need* (New York: Simon & Schuster, 2003); Peter Brimelow, *The Worm in the Apple: How Teachers Unions Are Destroying American Education* (New York: HarperCollins, 2003); Myron Lieberman, *The Teacher Unions: How the NEA and AFT Sabotage Reform and Hold Students, Parents, Teachers, and Taxpayers Hostage to Bureaucracy* (New York: Free Press, 1997); John E. Chubb and Terry M. Moe, *Politics, Markets, and America's Schools* (Washington, DC: Brookings Institution Press, 1990).

2. The Education Partnership, "Teacher Contracts: Restoring the Balance" (Providence, RI: Author, March 2005), pp. 4, 7.

3. Ronald D. Henderson, Wayne Urban, and Paul Wolman, *Teachers Unions and Education Policy: Retrenchment or Reform?* (Greenwich, CT: JAI Press, 2004); David L. Smith and Lynn Coffin, *Q&A—I Am the NEA: The Most Provocative Questions Asked of Education Professionals Today and How to Answer Them* (Washington, DC: National Education Association, 2004).

4. Susan Moore Johnson, *Teachers at Work: Achieving Excellence in Our Schools* (New York: Basic Books, 1990); Charles T. Kerchner, *A Union of Professionals: Labor Relations and Education Reform* (New York: Teachers College Press, 1993); Charles T. Kerchner, Julia E. Koppich, and Joseph G. Weeres, *United Mind Workers: Unions and Teaching in the Knowledge Society* (San Francisco: Jossey-Bass, 1997); Albert Shanker, *The Making of a Profession* (Washington, DC: American Federation of Teachers, 1985). See also chapter 9 by Julia E. Koppich in this volume.

5. Howard Nelson, personal communication, June 14, 2005.

6. Bess Keller, "Phila. Activists Cite Lost Opportunity on Teachers' Pact," *Education Week*, November 17, 2004, p. 9.

7. In September 2004, the former U.S. deputy secretary of education, Eugene Hickok, asserted in *Education Week* that districts must "uphold the spirit and content of the law," and "if a contract binds administrators from being able to assign the best teachers to the neediest areas, that would be tough." As quoted in Catherine Gewertz, "Collective Bargaining Law Bumping Up against No Child Left Behind Law," *Education Week*, September 8, 2004, pp. 1, 20.

8. Carl Krueger, "State Collective Bargaining Policies for Teachers" (Denver: Education Commission of the States, 2002), retrieved October 12, 2004, from http://www.ecs.org/clearinghouse/37/48/3748.htm; Malcolm M. Duplantis, Timothy D. Chandler, and Terry G. Geske, "The Growth and Impact of Teachers' Unions in States without Collective Bargaining Legislation," *Economics of Education Review* 14, no. 2 (1995): 167.

9. These 2001-02 data are from the National Center for Education Statistics, supplemented by calls to state education agencies.

10. Duplantis et al., "The Growth and Impact of Teachers' Unions," p. 167.

11. While the First Amendment explicitly constrains only the U.S. Congress, the Supreme Court has applied the protections pertaining to freedom of association to the states through the Fourteenth Amendment's "due process" clause. A 1968 appeals court decision codified this right for teachers, noting, "Teachers have the right of free association, and unjustified interference with teachers' associational freedom violates the due process clause of the 14th amendment." *McLaughlin v. Tilendis* (1968), 398 F.2d 287. As quoted in Louis Fischer, *Teachers and the Law*, 5th ed. (New York: Addison Wesley Longman, 2003), p. 60.

12. Fischer, *Teachers and the Law*, pp. 48, 57.

13. Fischer, *Teachers and the Law*, p. 12.

14. David L. Angus and Jeffrey Mirel, *Professionalism and the Public Good: A Brief History of Teacher Certification* (Washington, DC: Thomas B. Fordham Foundation, 2001), p. 32.

15. Joel Spring, *The American School: 1642-2000*, 5th ed. (New York: McGraw Hill, 2000).

16. Myron Lieberman, *Understanding the Teacher Union Contract: A Citizen's Handbook* (New Brunswick, NJ: Transaction, 2000), p. 19.

17. The teachers union and the administration are required by law to negotiate in "good faith." This does not mean they must come to an agreement, only that they must both go into the negotiations willing to give and take. The teachers union additionally has a "duty to fair representation" in administering the contract, requiring that it not favor any one teacher over another and that it pursue the interest of all teachers equally.

18. Ron Wilson, *Negotiator's Notebook: The Life Cycle of Labor and Management Relations* (Portland: Oregon School Boards Association, December 2000).

19. Kerchner et al., *United Mind Workers*; Susan Moore Johnson and Susan M. Kardos, "Reform Bargaining and Its Promise for School Improvement," in *Conflicting Missions? Teachers Unions and Educational Reform*, ed. Tom Loveless (Washington, DC: Brookings Institution Press, 2000), pp. 7-46.

20. Interview with national AFT official C, June 1, 2005.

21. Telephone interview with national NEA official, February 18, 2005.

22. For more about California's Public Employee Relations Board, visit http://www.perb.ca.gov/.

23. Penny Howell, *Collective Bargaining: Explaining California's System* (Palo Alto, CA: EdSource, 1999), p. 7.

24. Districts are usually required to bear the costs of printing and distribution, but the union may occasionally take up some of this responsibility. Though it may seem trivial given the other, more consequential elements of the contract, the dynamics of this clause are illuminating. As Myron Lieberman notes, the union may agree to pay for only part of printing and distribution if it is granted the right to include commentary or extraneous information in the printed contract. The printing and distribution clause illustrates how minutely restrictive these agreements can get. See Lieberman, *Understanding the Teacher Union Contract*, pp. 48-50.

25. Interview with national AFT official A, June 1, 2005.

26. Lorraine M. McDonnell and Anthony H. Pascal, *Organized Teachers in American Schools* (Document No. R-2407-NIE) (Santa Monica, CA: RAND, February 1979), pp. 56-57.

27. McDonnell and Pascal, *Organized Teachers in American Schools*, p. 58.

28. Lorraine M. McDonnell and Anthony H. Pascal, *Teacher Unions and Education Reform* (Document No. JRE-02) (Santa Monica, CA: RAND, April 1988).

29. Pamela Riley, with Rosemarie Fusano, La Rae Munk, and Ruben Peterson, *Contract for Failure: The Impact of Teacher Union Contracts on the Quality of California Schools* (San Francisco: Pacific Research Institute, 2002).

30. Howard Nelson, personal communication, June 14, 2005.

31. For a review of the 1980s literature, see Duplantis et al., "The Growth and Impact of Teachers' Unions," p. 169.

32. William H. Baugh and Joe A. Stone, "Teachers, Unions, and Wages in the 1970s: Unionism Now Pays," *Industrial and Labor Relations Review* 35, no. 3 (1982): 368-376.

33. Caroline M. Hoxby, "How Teachers' Unions Affect Education Production," *Quarterly Journal of Economics* 111, no. 3 (August 1996): 671-718.

34. Joe A. Stone, "Collective Bargaining and Public Schools," in *Conflicting Missions? Teachers Unions and Educational Reform,* ed. Tom Loveless (Washington, DC: Brookings Institution Press, 2000), pp. 47-68.

35. Howard Fuller, George Mitchell, and Michael Hartmann, "Collective Bargaining in Milwaukee Public Schools," in *Conflicting Missions? Teachers Unions and Educational Reform,* ed. Tom Loveless (Washington, DC: Brookings Institution Press, 2000), pp. 110-149.

36. Contracts usually include only teachers, but some may also cover counselors, school psychologists, librarians, and so on.

37. Interview with national AFT official B, June 1, 2005.

38. Interview with national AFT official A, June 1, 2005.

39. Sally Klingel, "Interest-Based Bargaining in Education" (Washington, DC: National Education Association, 2004).

40. Wilson, *Negotiator's Notebook*, p. 6.

41. L. Descarpentrie and C. A. Sloan, "Factors Affecting the Collective Bargaining Process in Public Schools," *Journal of Collective Negotiations in the Public Sector* 20, no. 3 (1991): 193-207.

42. Klingel, "Interest-Based Bargaining in Education" p. 51.

43. Brad Jupp, "The Uniform Salary Schedule," *Education Next* 5, no. 1 (Winter 2005): 10-12.

44. Nancy Mitchell, "DPS Won't Ask for Pay Hikes; Voters Will Decide on Bond Issue, Taxes on November Ballot," *Rocky Mountain News*, August 22, 2003, p. 6A; Nancy Mitchell, "Teachers OK Plan for Fewer Work Days and No Pay Raise," *Rocky Mountain News*, August 30, 2003, p. 23A.

45. Allison Sherry, "DPS to Study Pay in Other Districts: Denver Schools, Union Seek Data to Compare Compensation," *Denver Post*, August 26, 2004, p. B02.

46. Julie Poppen, "Denver Teachers Clear Path for Strike; Union Files Notice with State Officials," *Rocky Mountain News*, March 16, 2005, p. 4A.

47. Klingel, "Interest-Based Bargaining in Education," p. 17.

48. Wilson, *Negotiator's Notebook*.

49. Klingel, "Interest-Based Bargaining in Education."

50. Telephone conversation with North American Association of Education Negotiators official, February 9, 2005.

51. Howard Nelson, personal communication, June 14, 2005.

52. Interview with national AFT official D, June 1, 2005.

53. NEA Today, *A Vast Cadre of Human Resources* (Washington, DC: NEA, January 2001).

54. Telephone conversation with national NEA official, February 18, 2005.

55. Frederick M. Hess, *School Boards at the Dawn of the 21st Century: Conditions and Challenges of District Governance* (Alexandria, VA: National School Boards Association, 2002).

56. Telephone conversation with New York BOCES negotiator, March 9, 2005.

57. Ana Beatriz Cholo, "Teachers Union Offer Rejected; Feud over Local Leadership Continues," *Chicago Tribune*, July 7, 2004.

58. Conversation with national union official, April 20, 2005.

59. Hess, *School Boards at the Dawn of the 21st Century.*

60. Lieberman, *The Teachers Unions*, p. 75.

61. Terry M. Moe, "Teachers Unions and School Board Elections," in *Besieged: School Boards and the Future of Education Politics*, ed. William Howell (Washington, DC: Brookings Institution Press, 2005), pp. 254-287.

62. Telephone conversation with former Milwaukee superintendent Howard Fuller, March 15, 2005.

63. Conversation with New York BOCES negotiator, March 9, 2005.

64. Telephone conversation with national union official, April 20, 2005.

65. McDonnell and Pascal, *Organized Teachers in American Schools*, p. vii.

66. McDonnell and Pascal, *Teacher Unions and Education Reform*, p. 52.

67. Phone conversation with national union critic, May 18, 2005.

68. William Lowe Boyd, David N. Plank, and Gary Sykes, "Teachers Unions in Hard Times," in *Conflicting Missions? Teachers Unions and Educational Reform*, ed. Tom Loveless (Washington, DC: Brookings Institution Press, 2000), pp. 174-210.

69. Telephone conversation with national NEA official, February 18, 2005.

70. Interview with national AFT official C, June 1, 2005.

71. Telephone conversation with New York BOCES negotiator, March 9, 2005.

72. E-mail correspondence with NEA official, March 30, 2005.

73. Telephone conversation with NEA official, February 9, 2005.

74. Cynthia Smith, Cathy Cowan, Art Sensenig, and Aaron Catlin, "Trends: Health Spending Growth Slows in 2003," *Health Affairs* 24, no. 1 (January/February 2005): 185-194.

75. Linda Jacobson, "Teacher Salary Gains Tempered by Health-Benefit Costs, Says AFT," *Education Week* 23, no. 42 (2004).

76. Mary Armstrong, "Teachers Union Questions Facts Offered by School Board," *St. Louis Post-Dispatch*, August 25, 2003, p. B7.

77. Telephone conversation with national NEA official, February 18, 2005.

78. McDonnell and Pascal, *Organized Teachers in American Schools*, p. 26.

79. Ann Boyko, "School Employee Strikes Fell in 2003-2004 School Year," *School Leader News*, July 23, 2004 (published by the Pennsylvania School Boards Association, Cumberland).

80. Bess Keller, "Few Teachers' Strikes Mark U.S. Landscape," *Education Week* 24, no. 6 (2004): 3.

81. Personal communication with AFT official, June 15, 2005.

82. Boyd et al., "Teachers Unions in Hard Times."

83. Boyko, "School Employee Strikes Fell."

84. "Teachers Strike in Philadelphia, Parents Make Daycare Plans," retrieved October 28, 2000, available online at http://www.cnnstudentnews.cnn.com/2000/US/10/28/philly.teachers.

85. Phone conversation with NEA official, April 12, 2005.

86. Personal communication with NEA official, February 17, 2005.

87. Bess Keller, "Bad Blood," *Education Week* 24, no. 5 (2004): 25-28.

88. Keller, "Bad Blood."

89. Chris Kenning, "3,000 at Louisville Rally Make It One of Largest," *Courier-Journal* [Louisville, KY], September 28, 2004, p. 1A.

90. Kenning, "3,000 at Louisville Rally."

91. When students joined the rallying teachers, another Oklahoma City official commented, "It's great to see that we have students who take their education and relationship with their teachers so seriously." Both quotations are from Michael Bratcher, "Teachers to Protest School Board Meeting," *Daily Oklahoman* [Oklahoma City], April 16, 2003, p. 5.

92. Michael Casey, "Paterson Teachers Demonstrate: 500 Demand Raises, Contract Settlement," *The Record* [Paterson, NJ], January 17, 2001, p. L1.

93. Personal communication with AFT official, June 15, 2005.

94. Phone conversation with Henry Krokowsky, president of the Appleton Education Association, February 17, 2005.

95. Phone conversation with Peter Tirri, Paterson Education Association, January 20, 2005.

96. Personal communication with AFT official, June 15, 2005.

97. Phone conversation with Richard Colvin, June 16, 2005.

98. Susan Barnes-Gelt, "Teachers Need Refresher Course in Fairness," *Denver Post*, October 8, 2003, p. B7.

99. Matthew Marx, "Columbus Teachers OK Contract; Economy Being Blamed for Lowest Raises in 20 Years," *Columbus Dispatch*, May 30, 2003, p. 2B.

100. LaRae Munk, *Collective Bargaining: Bringing Education to the Table* (Midland, MI: Makinac Center for Public Policy, 1998).

101. Karen Helland and Corrie White, *Collective Bargaining and the Public Schools: Turning the Focus to Students* (Olympia, WA: Evergreen Freedom Foundation, 2000).

102. Riley et al., *Contract for Failure.*

103. Education Partnership, "Teacher Contracts."

104. Dale Ballou, *Teacher Contracts in Massachusetts* (Boston: Pioneer Institute, 2000).

105. McDonnell and Pascal, *Teacher Unions and Education Reform*, p. 66.

106. Personal communication with AFT official, June 15, 2005.

107. Ballou, *Teacher Contracts in Massachusetts*, p. ix.

108. "Contract Agreement between the Paterson (N.J.) School District and the Paterson Education Association," 2000-01–2001-04, pp. 23-24.

109. *Professional Handbook* (Parkway, MO: Parkway School District, July 2002), p. 30.

110. "Contract Agreement and Partnership between School District No. 1 in the City and County of Denver, State of Colorado, and Denver Classroom Teachers Association," September 1, 2002–August 31, 2005, clauses 8-2-1 and 8-2-2.

111. "The Agreement and the Memorandum of Understanding between the Appleton Area School District and the Appleton Education Association," July 1, 2001–June 30, 2003, pp. 52-53.

112. "Agreement Between Board of Directors Little Rock School District and the Little Rock Classroom Teachers Association, 2000-2003," p. 41.

113. Springfield, Massachusetts, contract, 27.

114. St. Louis Board of Education Policy Statement with the St. Louis Teachers Union Local 420, available online at www.sps.org/humanresources, pp. 11-13.

115. "Collective Bargaining Agreement 2004-05 between the Board of Education of Independent School District Number 89 of Oklahoma County, Oklahoma, and the Oklahoma City AFT Local 2309, of the American Federation of Teachers AFL-CIO of Oklahoma City, Oklahoma," pp. 18-19.

116. "Employee Handbook for Teachers, Counselors, and Librarians" (Kansas City, MO: Kansas City School District, 2000-03), p. 6.

117. Interview with sitting urban superintendent, March 20, 2005.

118. Myron Lieberman, personal communication, May 16, 2005.

119. Interview with Leo Casey, June 7, 2005.

120. "Agreement between the Columbus [Ohio] Board of Education and the Columbus Education Association 2003-04," available online at 222.ceaohio.org/contract/2003-2004contract.htm, p. 3.

121. McDonnell and Pascal, *Organized Teachers in American Schools*, p. 31.

CHAPTER FOUR   The Costs of Collective Bargaining Agreements (Hill)

1. On how local school boards have made concessions on work rules and other issues in lieu of salary increases, see Lorraine McDonnell and Anthony Pascal, *Organized Teachers in American Schools* (Santa Monica: RAND, 1979). See also Lorraine M. McDonnell and Anthony H. Pascal, *Teacher Unions and Educational Reform* (Santa Monica: RAND, 1988).

2. Another possible reason is that some school boards are captured by teachers unions, as evidenced by the recent firing of San Diego superintendent Alan Bersin by a newly elected board majority of avowed union sympathizers. For the same point made more generally, see Terry M. Moe, "Teachers Unions and the Public Schools," in *A Primer on America's Schools*, ed. Terry M. Moe (Stanford, CA: Hoover Press, 2001).

3. See Terry M. Moe, "A Union by Any Other Name," *Education Next* 1, no. 3 (Fall 2001): 40-45.

4. An unpublished paper by Terry Moe, provisionally titled "Bottom-Up Structure: Collective Bargaining, Transfer Rights, and the Education of Disadvantaged Children," will provide strong quantitative evidence on how transfer rules affect the distribution of teachers within districts and also districts' overall access to quality teachers.

5. For a comprehensive overview of costs imposed by teacher collective bargaining agreements in one state, see Lisa Blais and Valerie Forti, *Teacher Contracts: Restoring the Balance* (Providence, RI: The Education Partnership, 2005).

6. Michael Podgursky, "Fringe Benefits," *Education Next* 3, no. 3 (Summer 2003): 71-78.

7. Source: Chicago public school budgets provided the author in the course of an analysis of possible responses to district financial crises.

8. Source: http://www.cps.k12.il.us/AtAGlance.html.

9. Current Chicago Collective Bargaining Agreement, Article 6, High School, pp. 35-36.

10. Iowa: http://www.iccsd.k12.ia.us/personnel/TeachCon2.htm.

11. Personal communication, New York Archdiocesan school superintendent Catherine Hickey, March 6, 2005.

12. On Baltimore and Oakland, see Stephen Kiehl, "In a Quandary over Schools," *Baltimore Sun*, March 3, 2004, p. A1.

13. For big-city district population changes between the 1990 and 2000 censuses, see http://www.cgcs.org/reports/gainslossesenroll.html.

14. For a detailed account of how these processes work out in one major school district, see Ruth Curran Neild, Elizabeth Useem, and Elizabeth Farley, *The Quest for Quality: Recruiting and Retaining Teachers in Philadelphia* (Philadelphia: Research for Action, 2005).

15. See, for example, Alan Borsuk, "Some Officials Aim to Loosen Teachers' Job Security," *Milwaukee Journal*, March 2000, available online at http://www.jsonline.com/news/metro/mar00/firing 04030300a.asp.

16. For fresh evidence about the effects of urban districts' recruitment timetables, see Jessica Levin and Meredith Quinn, *Missed Opportunities: How We Keep High-Quality Teachers Out of Urban Classrooms* (Washington: New Teacher Project, 2005).

17. John K. DiPaolo, *Towards an Open Teacher Hiring Process: How the Boston Public Schools and the Boston Teachers Union Can Empower Schools to Hire and Keep the Best Teams* (Boston: Boston Plan for Excellence in the Public Schools, March 2000).

18. William J. Baumol, "Macroeconomics of Unbalanced Growth," *American Economic Review* 62 (1967): 415-26.

19. Kati Haycock, "No More Settling for Less," *Thinking K-16* 4, no. 1 (Spring 2000).

20. Neild et al., *The Quest for Quality*, p. 6.

21. Julian R. Betts, Kim S. Rueben, and Anne Danenberg, *Equal Resources, Equal Outcomes? The Distribution of School Resources and Student Achievement in California* (San Francisco: Public Policy Institute of California, 2000).

22. Education Trust West, *California's Hidden Teacher Spending Gap: How State and District Budgeting Practices Shortchange Poor and Minority Students and Their Schools* (Oakland: Author, 2005).

23. One possible measure of the difference in teachers hired by inner cities and other districts is the rate at which teachers fail state qualification exams. Compared to teachers in the rest of New York State, New York City teachers were six times as likely to fail the liberal arts and science exam, twice as likely to fail math, and seven times as likely to fail the elementary teaching exam. Haycock, "No More Settling for Less."

24. Neild et al., *The Quest for Quality*, p. 12.

25. Levin and Quinn, *Missed Opportunities*, pp. 15-19.

26. Former AFT president Sandra Feldman has argued that teachers do not avoid disadvantaged students but instead shun the conditions that districts have created in poverty neighborhood schools. See Sandra Feldman, "It's Not the Kids, It's the Conditions," *Thinking K-16* 4, no. 1 (Spring 2000).

27. Available online at http://www.uft.org/member/rights/working/faq_olr/sbo/.

28. Personal communications, New York City chancellors' office officials.

29. Neild et al., *The Quest for Quality*, p. 32.

30. Neild et al., *The Quest for Quality*, p. 22.

31. Marguerite Roza, "Rethinking Data Capacity," in *Making School Reform Work*, ed. Paul T. Hill and James Harvey (Washington, DC: Brookings Institution Press, 2004).

32. Neild et al., *The Quest for Quality*, p. 16.

33. Kacey Guin, "Chronic Teacher Turnover in Urban Elementary Schools," *Education Policy Analysis Archives* 12, no. 42 (August 2004).

34. Chicago ACORN, *Where Have All the Teachers Gone? The Costs of Teacher Turnover in Acorn Neighborhood Schools in Chicago* (Chicago: Association of Community Organizations for Reform Now, 2003).

35. Marguerite Roza and Paul T. Hill, "How Within-District Spending Inequities Help Some Schools to Fail," in *Brookings Papers on Education Policy 2004*, ed. Diane Ravitch (Washington, DC: Brookings Institution Press, 2004).

36. Marguerite Roza, Lawrence Miller, and Claudine Swartz, *Peeling Back the Layers of Spending: An Examination of District Expenditures in Denver Public Schools* (Seattle: Center on Reinventing Public Education, forthcoming 2005).

37. The freshest evidence comes from the study of Philadelphia by Neild et al. They show that poverty neighborhood schools are 1.7 times as likely as high-income schools to employ teachers in their first year. See Neild et al., *The Quest for Quality*, p. 18.

38. Karen Hawley Miles and Marguerite Roza, *Assessing Inequities in School Funding within Districts: A Tool to Prepare for Student-Based Budgeting* (Providence, RI: Annenberg Institute for School Reform, 2002), available online at http://www.schoolcommunities.org/portfolio/sbb_tool.html.

39. Dick Lilly, "Payroll Cause of Schools' Budget Wars," *Seattle Post-Intelligencer*, January 25, 2005.

40. From an article in *School Clips*, a monthly e-mail newsletter sent to subscribers by the Boston Plan for Excellence in 2000, titled "New Coalition Makes Contract Reform a More Public Issue." More than 30 organizations have already signed on to the newly formed Boston United for Children, which is pushing for specific reforms in this teacher contract: allowing a school team—principal-headmaster, teachers, parents—to fill all teacher vacancies based on an applicant's qualifications, not seniority; scheduling more time for professional development; requiring only a majority vote of the faculty (it is now two-thirds) to make changes in school operation; and continuing to lower class size in the early grades. The following organizations, among others, have signed on to Boston United: Black Ministerial Alliance, Boston Municipal Research Bureau, Citywide Parents Council, Cooperative Metropolitan Ministries, Critical Friends, Freedom House, Greater Boston Chamber of Commerce, Hispanic Office of Planning and Evaluation (HOPE), Massachusetts Advocacy Center, NAACP-Boston, Parents United for Child Care, Ten-Point Coalition, and Urban League of Eastern Massachusetts.

41. The intellectual underpinnings of this effort came from a white paper issued by the Boston Plan for Excellence. See DiPaolo, *Towards an Open Teacher Hiring Process*.

42. Marguerite Roza and Karen Hawley Miles have created an online tool that would permit any major district to calculate real dollar spending levels for all schools and identify salary and other factors that

drive internal inequities. Available online at http://www.schoolcommunities.org/resources/APRD/welcome.php.

43. Personal communication, Susan Sclafani.

44. Mary Beth Celio and James Harvey, *Buried Treasure: Developing a Management Guide from Mountains of School Data* (Seattle: Center on Reinventing Public Education, 2005).

45. Marguerite Roza and various collaborators have discovered that per-pupil funding within school districts is much more variable than between districts in a given state. They have just started to report on these findings publicly. See Marguerite Roza and Kacey Guin, "Inequities in Texas Education Funding: A Longitudinal Examination of Differences at the Inter- and Intra-District Level," paper presented at the annual meeting of the American Education Finance Association, 2005.

46. *Hobson v. Hansen*, 269 F. Supp. 401 (DDC 1967).

CHAPTER FIVE   The Effects of Collective Bargaining (Johnson and Donaldson)

1. Daniel F. McCaffrey, J. R. Lockwood, Daniel M. Koretz, and Laura S. Hamilton, *Evaluating Value-Added Models for Teacher Accountability* (Santa Monica, CA: RAND, 2003); William Sanders and June Rivers, *Cumulative and Residual Effects of Teachers on Future Student Academic Achievement* (research progress report), University of Tennessee Value-Added Research and Assessment Center, Knoxville, 1996.

2. Linda Darling-Hammond, Deborah J. Holtzman, Su Jin Gatlin, and Julian Vasquez Heilig, *Does Teacher Preparation Matter? Evidence about Teacher Certification, Teach For America, and Teacher Effectiveness,* paper presented at the annual meeting of the American Educational Research Association, Montreal, 2005.

3. Robert L. Reid, ed., *Battleground: The Autobiography of Margaret A. Haley* (Urbana: University of Illinois Press, 1982), p. 280.

4. Julie Blair, "Gen-Xers Apathetic about Union Label," *Education Week* 21, no. 20 (2002): 16-18.

5. Susan Moore Johnson and Susan M. Kardos, "Reform Bargaining and Its Promise for School Improvement," in *Conflicting Missions? Teachers Unions and Educational Reform*, ed. Tom Loveless (Washington, DC: Brookings Institution Press, 2000), p. 36.

6. Johnson and Kardos, "Reform Bargaining," p. 37.

7. Samuel Johnson, "Review of Dr Lucas's Essay on Waters," *Literary Magazine* 2 (1756), p. 39.

8. See, for example, Richard J. Murnane, Judy Singer, John B. Willett, James J. Kemple, and Randall J. Olsen, *Who Will Teach? Policies That Matter* (Cambridge, MA: Harvard University Press, 1991).

9. David Lipsky and John Drotning, "The Influence of Collective Bargaining on Teachers' Salaries in New York State," *Industrial and Labor Relations Review* 27 (1973): 35.

10. William H. Baugh and Joe A. Stone, "Mobility and Wage Equilibration in the Educator Labor Market," *Economics of Education Review* 2, no. 3 (1982): 253-274.

11. Caroline M. Hoxby, "How Teachers' Unions Affect Education Production," *Quarterly Journal of Economics* 111, no. 3 (1996): 671-718.

12. In "How Teachers' Unions Affect Education Production," Hoxby arrived at this estimate using differences-in-differences and instrumental variables strategies, both of which attempt to reduce the bias caused by omitted variables. These strategies enabled Hoxby to conclude that unionization was driving the salary differential rather than other observed or unobserved differences between unionized and nonunionized districts. As Hoxby states, these results rest on "the essential restriction . . . that timing of passage of a relevant law is uncorrelated with the timing of an acceleration in other statewide variables that directly affect students or schools" (p. 684). This assumption is somewhat weak since one could imagine factors, such as particularly poor working conditions statewide, that might stimulate state unionization laws *and* affect students and schools through other mechanisms, such as increased direct pressure to increase teachers' salaries statewide.

13. Steve Farkas, Jean Johnson, Tony Foleno, Ann Duffett, and Patrick Foley, *A Sense of Calling: Who Teaches and Why* (New York: Public Agenda, 2000).

14. Sylvia Allegretto, Sean Corcoran, and Lawrence Mishel, *How Does Teacher Pay Compare? Methodological Challenges and Answers* (Washington, DC: Economic Policy Institute, 2004).

15. Richard Vedder, "Comparable Worth," *Education Next* 3 (Summer 2003): 14-19.

16. Allegretto, Corcoran, and Mishel, *How Does Teacher Pay Compare?*

17. Lynn Olson, "Finding and Keeping Competent Teachers," *Education Week/Quality Counts 2000*, January 13, 2000, pp. 12-18.

18. Jennifer Park, "ERS Releases Nationally Representative K-12 Salary Data," *Education Week*, April 13, 2005, pp. 14-17.

19. Sean Corcoran, William Evans, and Robert Schwab, "Changing Labor-Market Opportunities for Women and the Quality of Teachers, 1957-2000," *American Economic Review* 94, no. 2 (2004): 230-235; Murnane et al., *Who Will Teach?*

20. Murnane et al., *Who Will Teach?*

21. Susan Moore Johnson, *Teachers at Work: Achieving Success in Our Schools* (New York: Basic Books, 1990).

22. Susanna Loeb and Marianne Page, "Examining the Link between Teacher Wages and Student Outcomes: The Importance of Alternative Labor Market Opportunities and Non-Pecuniary Variation," *Review of Economics and Statistics* 82, no. 3 (2000): 393-408.

23. Dale Ballou and Michael Podgursky, *Teacher Pay and Teacher Quality* (Kalamazoo, MI: W. E. Upjohn Institute for Employment Research, 1997).

24. Allegretto, Corcoran, and Mishel, *How Does Teacher Pay Compare?*

25. Ballou and Podgursky, *Teacher Pay and Teacher Quality.*

26. Dale Ballou, "Do Public Schools Hire the Best Applicants?" *Quarterly Journal of Economics* 111, no. 1 (1996): 97-133.

27. Loeb and Page, "Examining the Link."

28. Dominic J. Brewer, "Career Paths and Quit Decisions: Evidence from Teaching," *Journal of Labor Economics* 14, no. 2 (1996): 313-339.

29. David Figlio, "Can Public Schools Buy Better-Qualified Teachers?" *Industrial and Labor Relations Review* 55, no. 4 (2002): 686-699.

30. See Loeb and Page, "Examining the Link."

31. Johnson, *Teachers at Work*; Susan Moore Johnson and the Project on the Next Generation of Teachers, *Finders and Keepers: Helping New Teachers Survive and Thrive in Our Schools* (San Francisco: Jossey-Bass, 2004); Richard M. Ingersoll, "Teacher Turnover and Teacher Shortages: An Organizational Analysis," *American Educational Research Journal* 38, no. 3 (2001): 499-534.

32. Alan Odden, "Rewarding Expertise," *Education Next* 1, no. 1 (2001): 16-24.

33. Caroline M. Hoxby and Andrew Leigh, "Pulled Away or Pushed Out? Explaining the Decline of Teacher Aptitude in the United States," *American Economic Review* 94, no. 2 (2004): 236-240.

34. Hoxby and Leigh's "Pulled Away or Pushed Out?" relies on assumptions similar to the ones on which Hoxby's 1996 study rests. It is limited by the fact that it does not verify that the instrumental variable, unionization law passage, is not directly correlated with the outcome, the share of high-aptitude women in teaching. Moreover, Hoxby and Leigh's outcome measure—the average SAT score of the college an individual attended—is a very rough measure of individual aptitude. The highest scoring female graduates from average institutions may be entering teaching. Despite its limitations, Hoxby and Leigh's study represents a large methodological step toward understanding how unionization and pay may influence the composition of the teaching force.

35. Johnson et al., *Finders and Keepers*, p. 22.

36. Sheila N. Kirby, Mark Berends, and Scott Naftel, "Supply and Demand of Minority Teachers in Texas: Problems and Prospects," *Educational Evaluation and Policy Analysis* 21, no. 1 (1999): 47-66; Murnane et al., *Who Will Teach?*

37. Erling E. Boe, Sharon A. Bobbitt, Lynne H. Cook, Summer D. Whitener, and Anita L. Weber, "Why Didst Thou Go? Predictors of Retention, Transfer, and Attrition of Special and General Education Teachers from a National Perspective," *Journal of Special Education* 30, no. 4 (1997): 390-411; Ingersoll, "Teacher Turnover and Teacher Shortages."

38. Murnane et al., *Who Will Teach?*

39. Boe et al., "Why Didst Thou Go?"; Daniel Mont and Daniel I. Rees, "The Influence of Classroom Characteristics in High School Teacher Turnover," *Economic Inquiry* 34 (1996): 152-167.

40. Susan Moore Johnson, "Incentives for Teachers: What Motivates, What Matters," *Educational Administration Quarterly* 22, no. 3 (1986): 54-79; Richard J. Murnane and David K. Cohen, "Merit Pay and the Evaluation Problem: Why Some Merit Pay Plans Fail and a Few Survive," *Harvard Educational Review* 56, no. 1 (1986): 1-17.

41. Johnson, "Incentives for Teachers"; Murnane and Cohen, "Merit Pay and the Evaluation Problem."

42. Johnson et al., *Finders and Keepers.*

43. Brad Jupp, "The Uniform Salary Schedule," *Education Next* 5, no. 1 (Winter 2005): 10-12.

44. Alan Odden and Carolyn Kelley, *Paying Teachers for What They Know and Do: New and Smarter Compensation Strategies to Improve Schools* (Thousand Oaks, CA: Corwin Press, 2002); Lewis Solmon, "Recognizing Differences," *Education Next* 5, no. 1 (Winter 2005): 16-20.

45. Odden and Kelley, *Paying Teachers for What They Know and Do.*

46. Jupp, "The Uniform Salary Schedule." Notably, a performance-based pay plan that had been successfully bargained in Cincinnati in 2000 was abandoned in 2002 before it was fully implemented, after the union president was unseated by an opponent who challenged the quality of the evaluation process on which the plan was based.

47. Johnson et al., *Finders and Keepers*; Edward Liu, Susan Moore Johnson, and Heather G. Peske, "New Teachers and the Massachusetts Signing Bonus: The Limits of Inducements," *Educational Evaluation & Policy Analysis* 26, no. 3 (2004): 217-236.

48. Ingersoll, "Teacher Turnover and Teacher Shortages"; Susan Moore Johnson and Sarah E. Birkeland, "Pursuing a 'Sense of Success': New Teachers Explain Their Career Decisions," *American Educational Research Journal* 40, no. 3 (2003): 581-617; Johnson et al., *Finders and Keepers.*

49. Milbrey W. McLaughlin and Joan Talbert, "Teacher Professionalism in Local School Contexts," in *Teachers' Professional Lives*, ed. Igor F. Goodson and Andrew Hargreaves (Washington, DC: Falmer Press, 1996); Susan J. Rosenholtz, *Teachers' Workplace: The Social Organization of Schools* (New York: Longman, 1989).

50. Michael Luekens, Deanna Lyter, Erin E. Fox, and Kathryn Chandler, *Teacher Attrition and Mobility: Results from the Teacher Follow-Up Survey, 2000-01* (Washington, DC: National Center for Education Statistics, 2004).

51. General Accounting Office, *School Facilities: America's Schools Not Designed or Equipped for 21st Century* (No. HEHS-95-95) (Washington, DC: Author, 1995).

52. National Education Association, *Status of the American Public School Teacher, 2000-2001* (Washington, DC: Author, 2003).

53. Quality Education Data, *QED's School Market Trends: Teacher Buying Behavior & Attitudes, 2001-2002* (Denver: Quality Education Data, 2002).

54. Public Education Network, *The Voice of the New Teacher* (Washington, DC: Author, 2004).

55. Jack Buckley, Mark Schneider, and Yi Shang, *The Effects of School Facility Quality on Teacher Retention in Urban School Districts* (Chestnut Hill, MA: National Clearinghouse for Educational Facilities, 2004), p. 9.

56. Johnson, *Teachers at Work.*

57. Lorraine M. McDonnell and Anthony H. Pascal, *Organized Teachers in American Schools* (Santa Monica, CA: RAND, 1979).

58. Kirby et al., "Supply and Demand of Minority Teachers in Texas"; Mont and Rees, "The Influence of Classroom Characteristics on High School Teacher Turnover."

59. STAR (Student/Teacher Achievement Ratio), a controlled experiment conducted in Tennessee between 1985 and 1989, now offers convincing evidence that small class size in the early grades has long-lasting, positive effects for students. American Educational Research Association, "Class Size: Counting Students Can Count," *Research Points: Essential Information for Education Policy* 1, no. 2 (2003): 1-4. Conducted in kindergarten through third grade, this experiment showed that limiting classes to 13 to 17 students had a positive impact on students' performance in reading and mathematics when compared with classes of 22 to 25 students. Subsequent research in Wisconsin found similar results, with a higher level of positive impact for "children living in poverty" (p. 3). "While small classes benefit all kinds of students, much research has shown that the benefits may be greatest for minority students or students attending inner-city schools" (p. 3). Notably, the positive benefits of being in small classes for three or four years in the early grades continue after students return to larger classes in the upper grades.

60. Charles R. Perry, "Teacher Bargaining: The Experience in Nine Systems," *Industrial and Labor Relations Review* 33 (1979): 13-14.

61. Randall Eberts and Joe A. Stone, *Unions and Public Schools: The Effects of Collective Bargaining on American Education* (Lexington, MA: Lexington Books, 1984); Hoxby, "How Teachers' Unions Affect Education Production."

62. Farkas et al., *A Sense of Calling*, p. 20.

63. Eberts and Stone, *Unions and Public Schools*; Hoxby, "How Teachers' Unions Affect Education Production."

64. W. Allgood and Jennifer King Rice, "The Adequacy of Urban Education: Focusing on Teacher Quality," in *Fiscal Policy Issues in Urban Education*, ed. C. F. Roellke and Jennifer King Rice (Greenwich, CT: Information Age, 2002).

65. Richard J. Murnane and Barbara Phillips, "Learning by Doing, Vintage and Selection: Three Pieces of the Puzzle Relating Teaching Experience and Teaching Performance," *Economics of Education Review* 1, no. 4 (1981): 83-100; Jonah Rockoff, *The Impact of Individual Teachers on Student Achievement: Evidence from Panel Data* (Cambridge, MA: National Bureau of Economic Research, 2003).

66. Eric Hanushek, John F. Kain, and Steven G. Rivkin, "Why Public Schools Lose Teachers," *Journal of Human Resources* 39, no. 2 (2004); Elizabeth Useem, "The Retention and Qualifications of New Teachers in Philadelphia's High-Poverty Middle Schools: A Three-Year Cohort Study," paper presented at the annual conference of the Eastern Sociological Society, Philadelphia, 2003.

67. Jessica Levin and Meredith Quinn, *Missed Opportunities: How We Keep High Quality Teachers Out of Urban Classrooms* (Washington, DC: New Teacher Project, 2003); Edward Liu and Susan Moore Johnson, "New Teachers' Experiences of Hiring: Late, Rushed, and Information-Poor," *Educational Administration Quarterly*, forthcoming, 2006.

68. Elizabeth Useem and Elizabeth Farley, *Philadelphia's Teacher Hiring and School Assignment Practices: Comparisons with Other Districts* (research brief) (Philadelphia: Research for Action, 2004).

69. AFT and NEA, "Peer Assistance and Review: An AFT/NEA Handbook," paper presented at "Shaping the Profession That Shapes the Future: An AFT/NEA Conference on Teacher Quality," Washington, DC, 1998, p. E5.

70. Paul Toner, 2003 memo regarding evaluation process to Cambridge Teachers Association Faculty (CTAF) representatives.

71. Luz Cázares and Alex Harris, "Professionalism through Collaboration: A Social Cost-Benefit Analysis of the Toledo Plan," unpublished manuscript, Harvard University, 2002.

72. Daniel C. Lortie, *Schoolteacher: A Sociological Study* (Chicago: University of Chicago Press, 1975).

73. Johnson et al., *Finders and Keepers*.

74. Morgaen L. Donaldson, "On Barren Ground: How Urban High Schools Fail to Support and Retain Newly Tenured Teachers," paper presented at the annual meeting of the American Educational Research Association, Montreal, 2005.

75. Laurie Lewis, Basmat Parsad, Nancy Carey, Nicole Bartfai, Elizabeth Farris, and Becky Smerdon, *Teacher Quality: A Report on the Preparation and Qualifications of Public School Teachers* (Washington, DC: National Center for Education Statistics, U.S. Department of Education, Office of Educational Research and Improvement, 1999).

76. Richard Elmore and Deanna Burney, *Staff Development and Instructional Improvement in Community District 2, New York City* (New York: National Commission on Teaching and America's Future and Consortium for Policy Research, 1997); Michael Garet, Andrew Porter, Laura Desimone, Beatrice Birman, and Kwang Suk Yoon, "What Makes Professional Development Effective? Results from a National Sample of Teachers," *American Educational Research Journal* 38 (Winter 2001): 915-945.

77. Patrick Shields, Camille Esch, Daniel Humphrey, Marjorie Wechsler, Christopher Chang-Ross, Alix Gallagher et al., *The Status of the Teaching Profession 2003: Research Findings and Policy Recommendations* (Santa Cruz, CA: Center for the Future of Teaching and Learning, 2003).

78. Judith Warren Little, "Norms of Collegiality and Experimentation: Workplace Conditions of School Success," *American Educational Research Journal* 19, no. 3 (1982): 325-340.

79. Sharon Feiman-Nemser, "From Preparation to Practice: Designing a Continuum to Strengthen and Sustain Teaching," *Teachers College Record* 103, no. 6 (2001): 1013-1055.

80. Thomas Smith and Richard Ingersoll, "Reducing Teacher Turnover: What Are the Components of Effective Induction?" *American Educational Research Journal* 41, no. 2 (2004): 681-714.

81. Ann Weaver Hart and Michael J. Murphy, "New Teachers React to Redesigned Teacher Work," *American Journal of Education* 98 (1990): 224-250.

82. Robin Henke, Xianglei Chen, and Sonya Geis, *Progress through the Teacher Pipeline: 1992-93 College Graduates and Elementary/Secondary School Teaching as of 1997* (Washington, DC: U.S. Department of Education, National Center for Education Statistics, 2000).

83. Farkas et al., *A Sense of Calling*, p. 14.

84. "The Future of Work: Career Evolution," *The Economist*, January 2, 2000.

85. Heather G. Peske, Edward Liu, Susan Moore Johnson, David Kauffman, and Susan M. Kardos, "The Next Generation of Teachers: Changing Conceptions of a Career in Teaching," *Phi Delta Kappan* 83, no. 4 (2001): 304-311.

86. Daniel Goldhaber and Emily Anthony, *Can Teacher Quality Be Effectively Assessed?* (Washington, DC: University of Washington, Evans School of Public Affairs, Center for Reinventing Public Education, 2004).

87. Jill Harrison Berg, "Board Certification during Teaching's Second Stage: Redefining the Profession through Roles," paper presented at the annual meeting of the American Educational Research Association, Montreal, 2005.

88. Charles T. Kerchner and Julia E. Koppich, *A Union of Professionals: Labor Relations and Educational Reform* (New York: Teachers College Press, 1993).

89. Theodore R. Sizer, *Horace's Compromise: The Dilemma of the American High School* (Boston: Houghton-Mifflin, 1984).

90. Roger Fisher and William Ury, *Getting to Yes: Reaching Agreement without Giving In* (Boston: Houghton-Mifflin, 1981).

91. Blair, "Gen-Xers Apathetic About Union Label"; Johnson et al., *Finders and Keepers*.

CHAPTER SIX   Are Teachers Unions Good for Students? (Goldhaber)

1. National Education Association (NEA), retrieved September 15, 2004, from http://www.nea.org/aboutnea; American Federation of Teachers (AFT), retrieved September 15, 2004, from http://www.aft.org. The full NEA mission statement is: "To fulfill the promise of a democratic society, the National Education Association shall promote the cause of quality public education and advance the profession of education; expand the rights and further the interest of educational employees; and advocate human, civil, and economic rights for all." The full AFT mission statement is: "The

mission of the American Federation of Teachers, AFL-CIO, is to improve the lives of our members and their families, to give voice to their legitimate professional, economic and social aspirations, to strengthen the institutions in which we work, to improve the quality of the services we provide, to bring together all members to assist and support one another and to promote democracy, human rights and freedom in our union, in our nation and throughout the world."

2. Wisconsin Education Association, retrieved February 16, 2005, from http://www.weac.org/BARGAIN/2004-05/dec04/rankings.htm.

3. John King, "Paige Calls NEA 'Terrorist Organization,'" CNN *Washington Bureau*, February 23, 2004.

4. John E. Chubb and Terry M. Moe, *Politics, Markets, and America's Schools* (Washington, DC: Brookings Institution Press, 1990).

5. Charlene Haar, Myron Lieberman, and Leo Troy, "The NEA and AFT Teacher Unions in Power and Politics" (Washington, DC: Education Policy Institute, 1994), retrieved January 24, 2005, from http://www.educationpolicy.org/files/neaftbk/httoc.htm; AFT website, retrieved September 15, 2004 (see note 1).

6. Marjorie Murphy, *Blackboard Unions: The AFT and the NEA, 1900-1980* (Ithaca, NY: Cornell University Press, 1990).

7. William A. Streshly and Todd A. DeMitchell, *Teacher Unions and TQE: Building Quality Labor Relations* (Thousand Oaks, CA: Corwin Press, 1994).

8. Murphy, *Blackboard Unions*.

9. Streshly and DeMitchell, *Teacher Unions and TQE*. Wisconsin became the first state to pass a collective bargaining law for public employees in 1959.

10. Collective bargaining consists of negotiations between an employer and a group of employees, often represented by a union or other labor organization, that determine the conditions of employment. Collective bargaining for public school teachers is currently allowed in 33 states. Where it is allowed, collective bargaining always occurs at the school district level, within specific limits set by state policy. Though some states allow teachers to bargain over issues such as curriculum or classroom management, most limit the scope of bargaining to wages, hours, and other conditions of employment such as health benefits, vacation time, or pension plans. Twenty-four states prohibit strikes and nine states permit them.

11. Murphy, *Blackboard Unions*.

12. AFT website, retrieved September 15, 2004; NEA website, retrieved September 15, 2004 (see note 1).

13. Haar et al., "The NEA and AFT Teacher Unions in Power and Politics"; Ann Bastian, "What Happened to the Merger?" *Rethinking Schools Online* 13, no. 1 (Fall 1998), available online at http://www.rethinkingschools.org/archive/13_01/unions.shtml.

14. James G. Cibulka, "The NEA and School Choice," in *Conflicting Missions? Teachers Unions and Educational Reform*, ed. Tom Loveless (Washington, DC: Brookings Institution, 2000), pp. 150-173.

15. *US Newswire*, July 15, 2002, retrieved June 13, 2005, from http://releases.usnewswire.com/GetRelease.asp?id=6181.

16. Barry T. Hirsch and John T. Addison, *The Economic Analysis of Unions: New Approaches and Evidence* (Boston: Allen & Unwin, 1986), p. 9.

17. Henry S. Farber, "Nonunion Wage Rates and the Threat of Unionization," *NBER Working Paper Series*, Working Paper No. 9705, 2003; H. Gregg Lewis, *Unionism and Relative Wages in the United States* (Chicago: University of Chicago Press, 1963). Analyzing the systemic effects of this is complex, since union and nonunion workers may be substitutes for each other in production such that increased union wages lead to an increase in demand, and consequently earnings, for nonunion workers.

18. Richard B. Freeman, "Individual Mobility and Union Voice in the Labor Market," *American Economic Review* 66, no. 2 (1976): 361-368; Richard B. Freeman and James L. Medoff, *What Do Unions Do?* (New York: Basic Books, 1984).

19. Steven G. Allen, "Trade Unions, Absenteeism, and Exit-Voice," *Industrial and Labor Relations*

Review (April 1984): 331-345. Brian Bemmels, "How Unions Affect Productivity in Manufacturing Plants," *Industrial and Labor Relations Review* (January 1987): 241-253.

20. Steven G. Allen, "How Much Does Absenteeism Cost?" *Journal of Human Resources* (Summer 1983): 379-393; Bemmels, "How Unions Affect Productivity"; Charles Brown and James L. Medoff, "Trade Unions in the Production Process," *Journal of Political Economy* 86, no. 3 (1978): 355-378; Robert Mefford, "The Effect of Unions on Productivity in a Multinational Manufacturing Firm," *Industrial and Labor Relations Review* (October 1986): 105-114.

21. Farber, "Nonunion Wage Rates."

22. Lawrence M. Kahn "Unionism and Relative Wages: Direct and Indirect Effects," *Industrial and Labor Relations Review* 32 (1979): 520-532; David Neumark and Michael L. Wachter, "Union Effects on Nonunion Wages: Evidence from Panel Data on Industries and Cities," *Industrial and Labor Relations Review* 49 (1995): 20-38; Gauthier Lanot and Ian Walker, "The Union/Nonunion Wage Differential: An Application of Semiparametric Methods," *Journal of Econometrics* 84 (1998): 327-249; Farber, "Nonunion Wage Rates."

23. David G. Blanchflower, "Changes over Time in Union Relative Wage Effects in Great Britain and the United States," in *The History and Practice of Economics: Essays in Honour of Bernard Corry and Maurice Peston*, vol. 2, ed. Sami Daniel, Philip Arestis, and John Grahl (Lyme, NH: Edward Elgar, 1999), pp. 3-32. Some research, like Blanchflower's, suggests the premium has been decreasing in recent years. Sherwin Rosen, "Trade Union Power, Threat Effects, and the Extent of Organization," *Review of Economic Studies* 36 (1969): 185-196; Orley Ashenfelter, George E. Johnson, and John H. Pencavel, "Trade Unions and the Rate of Change of Money Wages in the United States Manufacturing Industry," *Review of Economic Studies* 39 (1972): 27-54; Edward P. Lazear, "A Competitive Theory of Monopoly Unionism," *American Economic Review* 74 (1983): 631-643; Farber, "Nonunion Wage Rates." Research on the indirect impact of unionization on nonunion firms has examined two effects—the increase in nonunion labor supply and the increased threat of unionization for nonunion firms—that work in opposite directions. The relative sizes of these effects remain an empirical question.

24. Henry S. Farber and Bruce Western, "Accounting for the Decline of Unions in the Private Sector, 1973-1998," *Journal of Labor Research* 22 (2001): 459-485. Farber and Western attribute much of this decline to changes in the relative numbers of jobs in the union and nonunion sectors, and found little evidence that the decline was due to changes in union organizing efforts.

25. Farber and Western, "Accounting for the Decline of Unions."

26. Anthony M. Cresswell and Michael J. Murphy, *Teachers, Unions, and Collective Bargaining in Public Education* (Berkeley, CA: McCutchan, 1980).

27. Darius Lakdawalla, "The Declining Quality of Teachers," *NBER Working Paper Series* (Working Paper No. W8263), April 2001, available online at http://ssrn.com/abstract=268344.

28. Victoria Van Cleef, "Half Empty or Half Full? Challenges and Progress in Hiring Reform," in *Urban School Reform: Lessons from San Diego*, ed. Frederick M. Hess (Cambridge, MA: Harvard Education Press, 2005), pp. 177-198.

29. Hamilton Lankford and James Wyckoff, "The Changing Structure of Teacher Compensation, 1970-94," *Economics of Education Review* 16 (1997): 371-384.

30. D. Morgan McVicar, "Firing Teachers Is Costly, Arduous—and Rare," *Providence Journal*, May 4, 1998.

31. Terry M. Moe, "Bottom-Up Structure: Collective Bargaining, Transfer Rights, and the Education of Disadvantaged Children," Working Paper, Stanford University, 2005.

32. Van Cleef, "Half Empty or Half Full?"

33. Susan Moore Johnson and Susan Kardos, "Reform Bargaining and Its Promise for School Improvement," in *Conflicting Missions? Teachers Unions and Educational Reform*, ed. Tom Loveless (Washington, DC: Brookings Institute, 2000), pp. 7-46.

34. One might imagine that the exit-voice argument for unions is particularly applicable to teaching, as teachers may know and care about their students more than average workers know or care about the "product" they are engaged in producing.

35. Julia E. Koppich, "Addressing Teacher Quality through Induction, Professional Compensation, and Evaluation: The Effects of Labor-Management Relations," *Educational Policy* 19, no. 1 (2005): 90-111; Randall W. Eberts and Joe A. Stone, *Unions and Public Schools: The Effect of Collective Bargaining on American Education* (Lexington, MA: Lexington Books, 1984); Morris M. Kleiner and Daniel L. Petree, "Unionism and Licensing of Public School Teachers: Impact on Wages and Educational Output," in *When Public Sector Workers Unionize,* ed. Richard B. Freeman and Casey Ichniowski (Chicago: University of Chicago Press, 1988), pp. 305-319; Caroline M. Hoxby, "How Teachers' Unions Affect Education Production," *Quarterly Journal of Economics* 111, no. 3 (1996): 671-718.

36. Dale Ballou, "Do Public Schools Hire the Best Applicants?" *Quarterly Journal of Economics* 111, no. 1 (1996): 97-133.

37. Rob Greenwald, Larry V. Hedges, and Richard D. Laine, "The Effect of School Resources on Student Achievement," *Review of Educational Research* 66, no. 3 (1996): 361-396; Eric A. Hanushek, "The Impact of Differential Expenditures on School Performance," *Educational Researcher* 18 (1986): 45-51. It is, however, important to acknowledge that there is a vigorous academic debate as to whether increases in educational spending generally result in better academic outcomes for students.

38. Allan J. Brokaw, James R. Gale, and Thomas E. Metz, "Explaining Voter Behavior Towards Local School Expenditures: The Impact of Public Attitudes," *Economics of Education Review* 9 (1990): 67-72.

39. AFT website, retrieved September 15, 2004; NEA website, retrieved September 15, 2004 (see note 1).

40. Dan D. Goldhaber, Hyung-Jai Choi, Michael DeArmond, and Daniel W. Player, "Why Do So Few Public School Districts Use Merit Pay?" Working Paper, University of Washington, 2005.

41. Cibulka, "The NEA and School Choice."

42. F. Howard Nelson and Michael Rosen, *Are Teachers' Unions Hurting American Education?* (Milwaukee: Institute for Wisconsin's Future, 1996).

43. Only two other variables in their regression were found to be statistically significant: the number of test takers and the test takers squared. However, the models included the following controls (aggregated at the state level): percent urban, number of private high school grads, spending per pupil, income per capita, percent minority, meet-and-confer only, and a dummy variable for states from the South.

44. Eric A. Hanushek, Steven G. Rivkin, and Lori L. Taylor, "Aggregation and the Estimated Effects of School Resources," *Review of Economics and Statistics* 78, no. 4 (1996): 611-627.

45. Lala C. Steelman, Brian Powell, and Robert M. Carini, "Do Teacher Unions Hinder Educational Performance?" *Harvard Educational Review* 70, no. 4 (2000): 437-466. Their data come from the 1993-94 Schools and Staffing Survey. School district officials were asked if their teachers were represented by collective bargaining and/or meet-and-confer agreements.

46. They used the following controls: percentage of student age population taking the SAT, square root of percentage taking the SAT, parental education, African American percentage, Latino percentage, Asian American percentage, sex composition, and median income.

47. Michael Kurth, "Teachers' Unions and Excellence in Education: An Analysis of the Decline in SAT Scores," *Journal of Labor Research* 8, no. 4 (1987): 351-367.

48. Harris L. Zwerling and Terry Thomason, "Collective Bargaining and the Determinants of Teachers' Salaries," *Journal of Labor Research* 16 (1995): 467-484; Eberts and Stone, *Unions and Public Schools;* Alexander B. Holmes, "Union Activity and Teacher Salary Structure," *Industrial Relations* 18 (1979): 79-85.

49. Eberts and Stone, *Unions and Public Schools.* In those models that explicitly attempt to account for this possibility, they find union wage premiums that are similar to those found using simpler statistical models.

50. Hanushek, "The Impact of Differential Expenditures."

51. Lankford and Wyckoff, "The Changing Structure of Teacher Compensation"; Dale Ballou and Michael Podgursky, *Teacher Pay and Teacher Quality* (Kalamazoo, MI: W. E. Upjohn Institute for Employment Research, 1997).

52. Hoxby, "How Teachers' Unions Affect Education Production."

53. Hoxby, "How Teachers' Unions Affect Education Production."

54. Hoxby, "How Teachers' Unions Affect Education Production." Hoxby utilizes an instrumental variables technique where the identifying instruments are variables indicating differences in timing and passage of state laws that facilitate unionization.

55. Eberts and Stone, *Unions and Public Schools*.

56. That said, the Eberts and Stone study is still far more compelling than the majority of research on this topic.

57. Eberts and Stone, *Unions and Public Schools*. Also interesting (though somewhat paradoxical and contrary to the "exit-voice" argument for unionization discussed in the previous section) is that, when surveyed, teachers covered by collective bargaining agreements appear to be significantly less satisfied with a variety of aspects of their jobs.

58. Hanushek, "The Impact of Differential Expenditures"; Greenwald et al., "The Effect of School Resources on Student Achievement."

59. It is certainly conceivable that differences in findings are driven by the empirical strategies employed, since the cited studies range considerably in methodological sophistication.

60. Caroline M. Hoxby and Andrew Leigh, "Pulled Away or Pushed Out? Explaining the Decline of Teacher Aptitude in the United States," *American Economic Review* 94, no. 2 (2004): 236-240. To some extent there are ways to assess these issues even in the absence of the above counterfactual. For example, Hoxby and Leigh examine the decline in public teacher aptitude since 1960 and conclude that much of the decline can be attributed to pay compression due to unionization. But, in practice it is quite difficult to assess precisely what the longer-term impacts of unions are because of the difficulty of measuring the "threat impact" unions have on nonunionized districts.

CHAPTER SEVEN   Teachers Unions and No Child Left Behind (Manna)

1. Frederick M. Wirt and Michael W. Kirst, *The Political Dynamics of American Education* (Berkeley, CA: McCutchan, 1997); Tom Loveless, ed., *Conflicting Missions? Teachers Unions and Educational Reform* (Washington, DC: Brookings Institution Press, 2000); David T. Conley, *Who Governs Our Schools? Changing Roles and Responsibilities* (New York: Teachers College Press, 2003).

2. Center on Education Policy, "A New Federal Role in Education" (Washington, DC: Author, 2002); Center on Education Policy, "From the Capital to the Classroom: State and Federal Efforts to Implement the No Child Left Behind Act" (Washington, DC: Author, 2003); House Committee on Education and the Workforce, "House-Senate Panel Approves H.R. 1 Education Reform Bill" press release, December 11, 2001; Wayne Riddle, "Education for the Disadvantaged: ESEA Title I Reauthorization Issues" (Washington, DC: Congressional Research Service, 2002); Wayne Riddle, "K-12 Education: Highlights of the No Child Left Behind Act of 2001 (P.L. 107-110)" (Washington, DC: Congressional Research Service, 2002).

3. Core academic subjects are English, reading or language arts, mathematics, science, foreign languages, civics and government, economics, arts, history, and geography.

4. Frank R. Baumgartner and Bryan D. Jones, *Agendas and Instability in American Politics* (Chicago: University of Chicago Press, 1993).

5. Conley, *Who Governs Our Schools?*

6. Noel Epstein, ed., *Who's in Charge Here? The Tangled Web of School Governance and Policy* (Denver and Washington, DC: Education Commission of the States and Brookings Institution Press, 2004).

7. Gary J. Miller, *Managerial Dilemmas: The Political Economy of Hierarchy* (New York: Cambridge University Press, 1992); Jonathan Bendor, Amihai Glazer, and Thomas Hammond, "Theories of Delegation," *Annual Reviews of Political Science* 4 (2001): 235-269.

8. Bendor et al., "Theories of Delegation"; Terry M. Moe, "Politics, Control, and the Future of School Accountability," in *No Child Left Behind?* ed. Paul E. Peterson and Martin R. West (Washington, DC: Brookings Institution Press, 2003).

9. Michael Lipsky, *Street-Level Bureaucracy: Dilemmas of the Individual in Public Services* (New York: Russell Sage Foundation, 1980); James Q. Wilson, *Bureaucracy: What Government Agencies Do and Why They Do It* (New York: Basic Books, 1989).

10. H. Brinton Milward and Keith G. Provan, "How Networks Are Governed," in *Governance and Performance: New Perspectives*, ed. Carolyn J. Heinrich and Laurence E. Lynn Jr. (Washington, DC: Georgetown University Press, 2000).

11. Virginia Gray, "Innovation in the States: A Diffusion Study," *American Political Science Review* 67, no. 4 (1973): 1174-1185; Michael Mintrom and Sandra Vergari, "Policy Networks and Innovation Diffusion: The Case of State Education Reforms," *Journal of Politics* 60, no. 1 (1998): 126-148.

12. Frank R. Baumgartner and Beth L. Leech, *Basic Interests: The Importance of Groups in Politics and in Political Science* (Princeton, NJ: Princeton University Press, 1998); Jeffrey M. Berry, *The Interest Group Society*, 3rd ed. (New York: Longman, 1997).

13. Robert H. Salisbury, "The Paradox of Interest Groups in Washington—More Groups, Less Clout," in *The New American Political System*, ed. Anthony King (Washington, DC: American Enterprise Institute, 1990).

14. Diane Ravitch, *The Language Police: How Pressure Groups Restrict What Students Learn* (New York: Alfred A. Knopf, 2003); Wirt and Kirst, *The Political Dynamics of American Education*.

15. Michael W. Kirst, "A History of American School Governance," in *Who's in Charge Here?* ed. Noel Epstein (Denver and Washington, DC: Education Commission of the States and Brookings Institution Press, 2004).

16. The NEA's complaints have been more comprehensively critical of NCLB, while the AFT has more consistently expressed general support for the law's principles and even some of its strategies. The AFT's critiques have tended to focus on specific aspects of the law, such as how AYP is calculated. See Julia E. Koppich, "A Tale of Two Approaches—The AFT, the NEA, and NCLB," *Peabody Journal of Education* 80, no. 2 (2005): 137-155.

17. Koppich, "A Tale of Two Approaches."

18. Steve Farkas, Jean Johnson, and Ann Duffett, "Stand by Me: What Teachers Really Think about Unions, Merit Pay, and Other Professional Matters" (New York: Public Agenda, 2003).

19. David Tyack and Larry Cuban, *Tinkering toward Utopia: A Century of Public School Reform* (Cambridge, MA: Harvard University Press, 1995).

20. AFT, "NCLB Watch," November 2003, retrieved March 1, 2005, from http://www.aft.org/pubs-reports/american_teacher/nov03/nclb.html.

21. NEA, "No Child Left Behind?" May 2003, retrieved March 8, 2005, from http://www.nea.org/neatoday/0305/cover.html.

22. Rod Paige, "Dear Colleague Letter to Education Officials Regarding Implementation of No Child Left Behind," June 14, 2002, retrieved September 21, 2004, from http://www.ed.gov/print/policy/elsec/guid/secletter/020614.html. For the proposed regulations, see the *Federal Register*, August 6, 2002, pp. 50994 and 51018. The *Federal Register* of December 2, 2002 (p. 71763) describes the withdrawal of these proposed regulations. The register is online at http://www.gpoaccess.gov/fr/index.html.

23. New York State United Teachers, "Regs Leave Contract Protections in Place," January 15, 2003, retrieved January 15, 2005, from http://www.nysut.org/newyorkteacher/2002-2003/030115nochildleftbehind.html.

24. NEA, "ESEA Action Guides: Collective Bargaining/Policy-Making" (Washington, DC: Author, 2002).

25. Wisconsin Association of School Boards (WASB), "Bargaining over PI34 and No Child Left Behind," 2004, retrieved March 1, 2005, from http://www.wasb.org/employee/2004_PI34NCLB.pdf.

26. Oregon School Boards Association (OSBA), "Human Resource and Collective Bargaining Impacts of the No Child Left Behind Act of 2002," May 6, 2003, retrieved January 15, 2005, from http://www.osba.org/hotopics/funding/nclb/nclbimpa.pdf.

27. Many thanks to Michael Petrilli at the Department of Education for sharing this letter with me.

28. Kati Haycock, "The Elephant in the Living Room," in *Brookings Papers on Education Policy*, ed. Diane Ravitch (Washington, DC: Brookings Institution Press, 2004); Jennifer King Rice,

Understanding the Effectiveness of Teacher Attributes (Washington, DC: Economic Policy Institute, 2003); Charles Clotfelter, Helen F. Ladd, and Jacob Vigdor, "Teacher Quality and Minority Achievement Gaps," paper presented at the annual research conference of the Association for Public Policy Analysis and Management, Atlanta, October 2004.

29. NEA, "ESEA Action Guides."

30. Sandra Feldman, "QuEST Conference Keynote Address," July 10, 2003, retrieved November 9, 2004, from http://www.aft.org/presscenter/speeches-columns/speeches/feldman071003.htm.

31. Sandra Feldman, "Letter to Congress—NCLB Implementation," February 2, 2004, retrieved March 8, 2005, from http://www.aft.org/topics/nclb/downloads/ImplementationLetter.pdf.

32. NEA, "ESEA Action Guides."

33. OSBA, "Human Resource and Collective Bargaining Impacts."

34. NCLB regulations are available at the U.S. Department of Education's website at http://www.ed.gov/policy/elsec/reg/edpicks.jhtml?src=ln.

35. Alex Medler, Bryan Hassel, and Todd Ziebarth, *Collective Bargaining and Teachers Unions in a Charter District* (Denver: Education Commission of the States, 2003), p. 1.

36. Medler et al., *Collective Bargaining*, p. 1.

37. Lynn Olson, "Testing Rules Would Grant States Leeway," *Education Week*, March 6, 2002, p. 1.

38. Siobhan Gorman, "Can't Beat 'Em? Sue 'Em!" December 2001, retrieved December 18, 2001, from http://www.washingtonmonthly.com.

39. The NEA filed the suit in April 2005 and posted the complaint and other information on its website at http://www.nea.org/lawsuit/index.html. The U.S. Department of Education has posted a brief response at http://www.ed.gov/news/pressreleases/2005/04/04202005.html. Retrieved from both sites on April 26, 2005.

40. The AFT has generally been more enthusiastic about student testing and standards than the NEA. See Koppich, "A Tale of Two Approaches."

41. Jo Becker and Rosalind S. Helderman, "VA Seeks to Leave Bush Law Behind," *Washington Post*, January 24, 2004; Justin Gest, "Texas Fined for No Child Defiance," *Houston Chronicle*, April 25, 2005; Sam Dillon, "Utah Vote Rejects Part of Education Law," *New York Times*, April 20, 2005.

42. See the chapters by Frederick M. Hess and Andrew P. Kelly, and Terry M. Moe in this volume.

43. WASB, "2005-07 Proposed School Board Teacher Bargaining Goals," n.d., retrieved March 4, 2005, from http://www.wasb.org/employee/0507teacher_goals_d2.pdf.

44. NEA, "ESEA Action Guides."

45. Catherine Gewertz, "Chicago, Ed. Dept. Settle Tutoring Dispute," *Education Week*, February 9, 2005, p. 3; Koppich, "A Tale of Two Approaches," p. 140.

46. NEA, "ESEA Action Guides."

47. NEA, "ESEA Action Guides."

48. Jeff Archer, "Districts Targeting Teacher Seniority in Union Contracts," *Education Week*, April 12, 2000, p. 5.

49. Bess Keller, "Boston Teachers Reach Contract Settlement," *Education Week*, March 31, 2004, p. 5.

50. Bess Keller, "Phila. Activists Cite Lost Opportunity on Teachers' Pact," *Education Week*, November 17, 2004, p. 9; Bess Keller, "Phila. Principals Gain Say in Hiring under New Pact," *Education Week*, October 20, 2004, p. 4.

51. Susan Moore Johnson and Susan M. Kardos, "Reform Bargaining and Its Promise for School Improvement," in *Conflicting Missions? Teachers Unions and Educational Reform*, ed. Tom Loveless (Washington, DC: Brookings Institution Press, 2000); Adam Urbanski, "Improving Student Achievement through Labor-Management Collaboration in Urban School Districts," *Educational Policy* 17, no. 4 (2003): 503-518; Charles Taylor Kerchner and Julia E. Koppich, *A Union of Professionals: Labor Relations and Educational Reform* (New York: Teachers College Press, 1993).

52. Cited from the TURN website; retrieved March 8, 2005, from http://www.gseis.ucla.edu/hosted/turn/turn.html.

53. Terry M. Moe, "No Teacher Left Behind," *Wall Street Journal*, January 13, 2005; Justin Torres, "Don't Believe the 'New Union' Hype," February 10, 2005, retrieved March 8, 2005, from http://

www.edexcellence.net/foundation/gadfly/archive.cfm; Andrew Rotherham, "Fordham Unsheathed!" February 14, 2005, retrieved March 8, 2005, from http://www.eduwonk.com; Charles Taylor Kerchner, "Deindustrialization," *Education Next* 1, no. 3 (2001): 46-50.

54. Ana Beatriz Cholo, "Union Seeks to Save 8 Schools," April 26, 2005, retrieved April 27, 2005, from http://www.chicagotribune.com.

55. Ellen Forte Fast and William J. Erpenbach, "Revisiting Statewide Educational Accountability under NCLB" (Washington, DC: Council of Chief State School Officers, 2004).

CHAPTER EIGHT   The Educational Value of Democratic Voice (Casey)

1. See, for example, Terry M. Moe, "No Teacher Left Behind: Unions Don't Have Children's Best Interests at Heart," *Wall Street Journal*, January 22, 2005.

2. Albert O. Hirschman, *Exit, Voice, and Loyalty: Responses to Decline in Firms, Organizations, and States* (Cambridge, MA: Harvard University Press, 1970), p. 30.

3. Articles 9 and 10B, and Appendix B, of the 2000-03 Collective Bargaining Agreement between the New York City Department of Education and the United Federation of Teachers. The full collective bargaining agreement for teachers is available online at http://www.uft.org/member/rights/contracts/current_teachers_contract/. As this book went to press, the UFT and the DOE negotiated a new contract that altered some of the clauses discussed in this chapter. This chapter is based on the contract in effect prior to November 2005.

4. A description of the main features of the SAVE legislation is available online at http://www.mhric.org/scss/save.html.

5. As a result of UFT lobbying, a portion of the "Safe City, Safe Streets" special tax levy during the 1990s went to support these programs in the schools.

6. Large schools and overcrowded schools have a significantly higher rate of school safety incidents. J. F. DeVoe, Katharin Peter, Phillip Kaufman, Amanda Miller, Margaret Noonan, Thomas Snyder, and Katrina Baum, *Indicators of School Crime and Safety: 2004* (NCES 2005–002/NCJ 205290) (Washington, DC: U.S. Government Printing Office, 2005), p. 68, available online at http://nces.ed.gov/pubs2005/2005002.pdf.

7. The phrase "pure and simple trade unionism" was first adopted by cigar makers' union president Adolph Strasser as a renunciation of trade union goals broader than wages, working conditions, and due process. Howard M. Gitelman, "Adolph Strasser and the Origins of 'Pure and Simple' Trade Unionism," in *The Labor History Reader*, ed. Daniel Loeb (Urbana: University of Illinois Press, 1985).

8. Raymond Callahan, *Education and the Cult of Efficiency: A Study of the Social Forces That Have Shaped the Administration of Public Schools* (Chicago: University of Chicago Press, 1962); Kate Rousmaniere, *City Teachers: Teaching and School Reform in Historical Perspective* (New York: Teachers College Press, 1997).

9. The classic account of the deskilling of labor under industrial production is Harry Braverman's *Labor and Monopoly Capital: The Degradation of Work in the Twentieth Century* (New York: Monthly Review Press, 1974). Braverman's analysis has been criticized for failing to capture the ongoing struggles over the labor process and control of knowledge and skill. Richard Edwards, *Contested Terrain: The Transformation of the Workplace in the Twentieth Century* (New York: Basic Books, 1979). The school was even more of a "contested terrain" than the factory. Richard Altenbaugh, "Teachers and the Workplace," in *The Teachers' Voice*, ed. Richard Altenbaugh (London: Falmer Press, 1992).

10. The demands discussed here are drawn from primary documents in the UFT Archives, 52 Broadway, New York, NY 10010.

11. Deinya Phenix, Dorothy Siegel, Ariel Zaltsman, and Norm Fruchter, *Virtual District, Real Improvement: A Retrospective Evaluation of the Chancellor's District, 1996-2003* (New York: Institute for Education and Social Policy of New York University, June 2004), available online at http://www.nyu.edu/iesp/publications/ChanDistRpt.pdf.

12. For numerous examples in this vein, see Sol Stern, *Breaking Free: Public School Lessons and the Imperative of School Choice* (San Francisco: Encounter Books, 2003).

13. The five core NBPTS propositions are available online at http://www.nbpts.org/about/coreprops.cfm.

14. Donald Schön, *The Reflective Practitioner: How Professionals Think in Action* (New York: Basic Books, 1983); and *Educating the Reflective Practitioner* (San Francisco: Jossey-Bass, 1987).

15. See Charles Taylor Kerchner and Julia E. Koppich, eds., *A Union of Professionals: Labor Relations and Educational Reform* (New York: Teachers College, 1993); Nina Bascia, *Unions in Teachers' Professional Lives: Some Social, Intellectual and Practical Concerns* (New York: Teachers College Press, 1994); Nina Bascia, "Triage or Tapestry? Teacher Unions' Work toward Improving Teacher Quality in an Era of Systemic Reform" (Seattle: University of Washington, Center for the Study of Teaching and Policy, 2003), available online at http://www.ctpweb.org/.

16. American Federation of Teachers (AFT) and National Education Association, *Peer Assistance and Peer Review: An AFT/NEA Handbook*, available online at http://www.aft.org/pubs-reports/down loads/teachers/parhndbk.pdf.

17. Joel Jordan, "Peer Review and New Teacher Unionism: Mutual Support or Policing?" *Against the Current* 14, no. 4 (September/October 1999), available online at http://www.solidarity-us.org/atc/82Jordan.html.

18. Myron Lieberman, *Teachers Evaluating Teachers: Peer Review and the New Unionism* (New Brunswick, NJ: Transaction, 1998).

19. 2000-03 New York City Collective Bargaining Agreement, Articles 8E and 7B8. The implementation of Article 8E was laid out in Chancellor's Special Circular no. 28, 1990-91.

20. AFL-CIO Committee on the Evolution of the Workplace, "The New American Workplace: A Labor Perspective," in *Unions and Workplace Reorganization*, ed. Bruce Nissen (Detroit: Wayne State University Press, 1997).

21. Deborah Meier, *The Power of Their Ideas: Lessons for America from a Small School in East Harlem* (Boston: Beacon Press, 2002); Michelle Fine, ed., *Chartering Urban School Reform: Reflections on Public High Schools in the Midst of Change* (New York: Teachers College Press, 1994).

22. 2000-03 New York City Collective Bargaining Agreement, Article 8B.

23. This proposal develops the idea for school-based compacts put forward by Charles Taylor Kerchner, Julia E. Koppich, and Joseph G. Weeres, *United Mind Workers: Unions and Teaching in the Knowledge Society* (San Francisco: Jossey-Bass, 1997). See the opening statement of UFT president Randi Weingarten at the contract negotiations, available online at http://www.uft.org/news/speeches/negotiations/index.html.

24. 2000-03 New York City Collective Bargaining Agreement, Article 18F.

25. William Johnson, "New York Teachers Fear for Working Conditions as Union Leader Offers Preemptive Concessions," *Labor Notes* no. 300 (March 2004), available online at http://www.labor notes.org/archives/2004/03/articles/c.html.

26. Dale Ballou, "The New York City Teachers' Union Contract: Shackling Principals' Leadership" (Civic Report No. 6) (New York: Manhattan Institute, June 1999), p. 6, available online at http://www.manhattan-institute.org/html/cr_6.htm. Without the school-based plan, the principal controls all of the new hires and half of the transfers, while the other half of transfers are filled on a seniority basis; under the school-based plan, all hires and transfers go through the committee, where teachers are a majority.

27. For a review of the body of literature, see Robert Carini, "Teachers Unions and Student Achievement," in *School Reform Proposals: The Research Evidence*, ed. Alex Molnar (Greenwich, CT: Information Age, 2002), available online at http://www.asu.edu/educ/epsl/EPRU/documents/EPRU%202002-101/Chapter%2010-Carini-Final.pdf.

28. Richard B. Freeman and James L. Medoff, *What Do Unions Do?* (New York: Basic Books, 1984).

29. This is why actual teaching experience is one of the key attributes of teaching quality. Jennifer King Rice, *Teacher Quality: Understanding the Effectiveness of Teacher Attributes* (Washington, DC: Economic Policy Institute, 2003).

30. Education Trust, "The Real Value of Teachers: If Good Teachers Matter, Why Don't We Act Like It?" in *Thinking K-16* 8, no. 1 (Spring 2004): 3-32, available online at http://www2.edtrust.org/NR/rdonlyres/5704CBA6-CE12-46D0-A852-D2E2B4638885/0/Spring04.pdf; Education Trust, "Good Teaching Matters: How Well Qualified Teachers Can Close the Gap," in *Thinking K-16* 3, no. 2 (Summer 1998): 1-7, available online at http://www2.edtrust.org/NR/rdonlyres/0279CB4F-B729-4260-AB6E-359FD3C374A7/0/k16_summer98.pdf.

31. The pioneering statistical work in this area has been done by William Sanders. William Sanders and Sandra Horn, "The Tennessee Value-Added Assessment System (TVAAS): Mixed-Model Methodology in Educational Assessment," available online at http://www.sas.com/govedu/edu/mixed_model.pdf; William Sanders and Sandra Horn, "Research Findings from the Tennessee Value-Added Assessment System (TVAAS) Database: Implications for Educational Evaluation and Research," available online at http://www.sas.com/govedu/edu/ed_eval.pdf.

32. Kacey Guin, "Chronic Teacher Turnover in Urban Elementary Schools," *Education Policy Analysis Archives* 12, no. 42 (August 2004), available online at http://epaa.asu.edu/epaa/v12n42/.

33. These often-cited figures are derived from the annual Schools and Staffing Survey and Teacher Follow-Up Survey of the National Center for Education Statistics. For the latest report, see Michael T. Luekens, Deanna M. Lyter, Erin E. Fox, and Kathryn Chandler, *Teacher Attrition and Mobility* (Washington, DC: National Center for Education Statistics, August 2004), available online at http://nces.ed.gov/pubs2004/2004301.pdf.

34. Susan Moore Johnson and the Project on the Next Generation of Teachers, *Finders and Keepers: Helping New Teachers Survive and Thrive in Our Schools* (San Francisco: Jossey-Bass, 2004).

35. On the turnover rate in Catholic and private schools, see Richard Ingersoll, "Is There Really a Teacher Shortage?" (Seattle: Center for the Study of Teaching and Policy, September 2003), pp. 15ff., available online at http://www.ctpweb.org. For the turnover rate in charter schools, see AFT, "Do Charter Schools Measure Up? The Charter School Experiment after 10 Years" (Washington, DC: AFT, 2002), p. 28, available online at http://www.aft.org/pubs-reports/downloads/teachers/charterreport02.pdf.

36. AFT, "Do Charter Schools Measure Up?" p. 20.

37. See, for example, Terry M. Moe, "Teacher Unions," in *A Primer on America's Schools*, ed. Terry M. Moe (Stanford, CA: Hoover Institution Press, 2001).

38. Freeman and Medoff, *What Do Unions Do?* chapter 8.

39. Ingersoll, "Is There Really a Teacher Shortage?" pp. 17-18.

40. Ingersoll, "Is There Really a Teacher Shortage?" pp. 17-18.

41. See Richard Ingersoll, *Who Controls Teachers' Work? Power and Accountability in America's Schools* (Cambridge, MA: Harvard University Press, 2003); Andy Hargreaves, *Changing Teachers, Changing Times: Teachers' Work and Culture in a Post-Modern Age* (New York: Teachers College Press, 1994).

42. Michael Podgursky, "Fringe Benefits," in *Education Next* 3, no. 3 (Summer 2003): 71-76; available online at http://www.educationnext.org/20033/pdf/71.pdf. It approaches the surreal to pretend that a teacher's workday limited to the amount of time spent in direct classroom instruction, as Podgursky does, just as it would be to describe a lawyer's workday solely in terms of the time spent in court or a surgeon's workday solely in terms of the time spent in the operating room.

43. According to *Education Week*'s 2000 *Quality Counts* report, teachers at the start of their career with bachelor's degrees earn $7,894 less than similarly aged college graduates; at the height of their career, the gap has grown to $23,655. The differentials are even greater for teachers with master's degrees: at the height of their career, they earn $32,511 less than other similarly aged master's degree holders outside of teaching.

44. Sylvia Allegretto, Sean Corcoran, and Lawrence Mishel, *How Does Teacher Pay Compare? Methodological Challenges and Answers* (Washington, DC: Economic Policy Institute, 2004).

45. Allen Odden and Carolyn Kelley, *Paying Teachers for What They Know and Do: New and Smarter Compensation Strategies to Improve Schools* (Thousand Oaks, CA: Corwin Press, 1997).

46. These examples are all from the 2000-03 New York City Collective Bargaining Agreement, Articles 7 through 10.

CHAPTER NINE   The As-Yet-Unfulfilled Promise of Reform Bargaining (Koppich)

1. National Commission on Excellence in Education, *A Nation at Risk* (Washington, DC: U.S. Department of Education, 1983).
2. Charles Taylor Kerchner and Julia E. Koppich, *A Union of Professionals: Labor Relations and Educational Reform* (New York: Teachers College Press, 1993).
3. Charles Taylor Kerchner and Douglas E. Mitchell, *The Changing Idea of a Teachers' Union* (New York: Falmer Press, 1988).
4. Kerchner and Mitchell, *The Changing Idea of a Teachers' Union*.
5. Kerchner and Mitchell, *The Changing Idea of a Teachers' Union*.
6. All collective bargaining laws for public employees are state laws.
7. Julia E. Koppich, "A Tale of Two Approaches—The AFT, the NEA, and NCLB," *Peabody Journal of Education* 80, no. 2 (2005): 137-155.
8. Richard E. Walton and Robert B. McKersie, *A Behavioral Theory of Labor Negotiations* (New York: McGraw-Hill, 1965).
9. Charles Taylor Kerchner, Julia E. Koppich, and Joseph T. Weeres, *United Mind Workers: Unions and Teaching in the Knowledge Society* (San Francisco: Jossey-Bass, 1997).
10. Kerchner and Mitchell, *The Changing Idea of a Teachers' Union*.
11. Kerchner et al., *United Mind Workers*; Susan Moore Johnson and Susan M. Kardos, "Reform Bargaining and Its Promise for School Improvement," in *Conflicting Missions? Teachers Unions and Educational Reform*, ed. Tom Loveless (Washington, DC: Brookings Institution Press, 2000).
12. Albert Shanker, "A Nation at Risk," American Federation of Teachers convention proceedings, reprinted in *The Power of His Ideas: Al in His Own Words* (Washington, DC: American Federation of Teachers, 1996).
13. Albert Shanker, *The Making of a Profession* (Washington, DC: American Federation of Teachers, 1985).
14. Koppich, "A Tale of Two Approaches."
15. Robert Chase, "It's Not Your Mother's NEA," speech before the National Press Club in Washington, DC, February 5, 1997.
16. Peer review is a system in which teachers evaluate the professional performance of other teachers. Initially begun by the AFT local in Toledo, Ohio, in 1981, peer review, when done well, is extremely effective, often resulting in teachers making the recommendation to dismiss colleagues for poor performance.
17. Kerchner and Koppich, *A Union of Professionals*; Jonathan Brock and David Lipsky, *Going Public: The Role of Labor-Management Relations in Delivering Quality Government Services* (Champaign, IL: Industrial Relations Association, 2003).
18. Roger Fisher and William Ury, *Getting to Yes: Negotiating Agreement without Giving In* (New York: Penguin Books, 1984).
19. Peter M. Senge, *The Fifth Discipline: The Art and Practice of the Learning Organization* (New York: Doubleday, 1990).
20. Roderick M. Kramer and Tom R. Tyler, "Whither Trust?" in *Trust in Organizations: Frontiers of Theory and Research*, ed. Roderick Kramer and Tom Tyler (Thousand Oaks, CA: Sage, 1996).
21. David Tyack and Larry Cuban, *Tinkering toward Utopia: A Century of Public School Reform* (Cambridge, MA: Harvard University Press, 1995).
22. Contract between the Rochester City School District and the Rochester Teachers Association, Rochester, New York, July 1, 2004.
23. Kerchner and Koppich, *A Union of Professionals*.
24. William Lowe Boyd, David N. Plank, and Gary Sykes, "Teacher Unions in Hard Times," in *Conflicting Missions? Teachers Unions and Educational Reform,* ed. Tom Loveless (Washington, DC: Brookings Institution Press, 2000); Tyack and Cuban, *Tinkering toward Utopia*.
25. Kerchner and Koppich, *A Union of Professionals*.

26. Susan Moore Johnson, "Teaching's Next Generation: Who Are They? What Will Keep Them in the Classroom?" *Education Week*, June 7, 2000; Julia E. Koppich, "Addressing Teacher Quality through Induction, Professional Compensation, and Evaluation: The Effects on Labor-Management Relations," in *Educational Policy* 19, no. 1 (January/March 2005): 90-111.

27. David Kusnet, *Finding Their Voices: Professionals and Workplace Representation* (Washington, DC: Albert Shanker Institute, 2000).

28. Thomas Kochan, "Building a New Social Contract at Work" (presidential address delivered at the 52nd annual meeting of the Industrial Relations Research Association, n.d.).

29. The six participating locals were Albuquerque, Denver, Minneapolis, Montgomery County (MD), Seattle, and Syracuse. The project operated under the auspices of TURN, the Teacher Union Reform Network, and was directed by Julia Koppich.

30. Julia E. Koppich, *Union Capacity Building: The TURN OERI Project*, report for the U.S. Department of Education, May 2003.

31. James McGregor Burns, *Leadership* (New York: Harper & Row, 1978).

32. Koppich, "A Tale of Two Approaches."

33. Richard D. Kahlenberg, "The History of Collective Bargaining among Teachers," this volume.

34. 33416 US267,94 S. Ct.

35. *The Changing Situation of Workers and Their Unions* (Washington, DC: AFL-CIO, 1985), p. 12.

36. Kusnet, *Finding Their Voices*.

37. Julia E. Koppich, Margaret R. Plecki, and Patricia Holmes, *New Rules? New Roles? The Professional Work Lives of Charter School Teachers* (Washington, DC: National Education Association, 1998).

38. Steve Farkas, Jean Johnson, and Ann Duffett, *Stand by Me: What Teachers Really Think about Unions, Merit Pay, and Other Professional Matters* (New York: Public Agenda, 2003).

39. Lorraine M. McDonnell and Anthony H. Pascal, *Organized Teachers in American Schools* (Santa Monica, CA: RAND, 1988).

40. Julia E. Koppich and Charles Taylor Kerchner, "Negotiating What Matters Most: Rethinking Teacher Collective Bargaining," *Education Week*, February 12, 2003, pp. 56, 41.

CHAPTER TEN   Union Power and the Education of Children (Moe)

1. Myron Lieberman, *The Teacher Unions* (New York: Free Press, 1997); Marjorie Murphy, *Blackboard Unions* (Ithaca, NY: Cornell University Press, 1990); Maurice Berube, *Teacher Politics* (New York: Greenwood Press, 1988).

2. David Tyack, *The One Best System* (Cambridge, MA: Harvard University Press, 1974).

3. For a prescient early statement about this transformation of the system, see William J. Grimshaw, *Union Rule in the Schools* (Lexington, MA: Lexington Books, 1979).

4. Terry M. Moe, "Teachers Unions and the Public Schools," in *A Primer on America's Schools*, ed. Terry M. Moe (Stanford, CA: Hoover Press, 2001).

5. Lieberman, *The Teacher Unions*; Moe, "Teachers Unions and the Public Schools."

6. Eric A. Hanushek, "The Economics of Schooling: Production and Efficiency in Public Schools," *Journal of Economic Literature* 24, no. 3 (September 1986): 1141-1177; Eric A. Hanushek, "Assessing the Effects of School Resources on Student Performance: An Update," *Educational Evaluation and Policy Analysis* 19, no. 2 (Summer 1997): 141-164; and Eric A. Hanushek, "The Evidence on Class Size," in *Earning and Learning: How Schools Matter*, ed. Susan B. Mayer and Paul E. Peterson (Washington, DC: Brookings Institution Press, 1999).

7. Lieberman, *The Teacher Unions*; Peter Brimelow, *The Worm in the Apple* (New York: HarperCollins, 2003).

8. Mancur Olson, *The Logic of Collective Action* (Cambridge, MA: Harvard University Press, 1965).

9. Terry M. Moe, *The Organization of Interests* (Chicago: University of Chicago Press, 1980).

10. The survey was conducted by Harris Interactive through the use of their Internet sample of American adults. The observations were corrected for selection effects (because people who use the Internet are

not a cross-section of the larger population) through the use of a well-developed technology that they use for many of their surveys, involving the construction of "propensity scores." Observations were also weighted to ensure representativeness by region, age, gender, race, grade level (elementary, secondary), and location (urban, suburban, rural).

11. Public Agenda, *Stand by Me* (New York: Public Agenda, 2003). The three sets of quotes and figures are from pages 46, 47, and 48, respectively. Note that these Public Agenda figures include teachers from states and districts without collective bargaining. The support percentages would be still higher if these teachers were excluded.

12. More accurately, it usually takes place between unions and administrators hired by the board. But because board members are the authorities and ultimately responsible for whatever bargain is struck, I will frame the discussion as though it is the board itself doing the bargaining.

13. On school boards, see William G. Howell, ed., *Besieged: School Boards and the Future of Education Politics* (Washington, DC: Brookings Institution Press, 2005).

14. Terry M. Moe, "Teachers Unions and School Board Politics," in *Besieged: School Boards and the Future of Education Politics,* ed. William G. Howell (Washington, DC: Brookings Institution Press, 2005).

15. Charlene Haar, *The Politics of the PTA* (Somerset, NJ: Transaction, 2002).

16. Terry M. Moe, "Political Control and the Power of the Agent," *Journal of Law, Economics, and Organization* 22, no.1 (Spring 2006).

17. Moe, "Political Control and the Power of the Agent." To clarify: both studies are presented in the same paper.

18. Moe, "Teachers Unions and School Board Politics."

19. Terry M. Moe, "Politics, Control, and the Future of School Accountability," in *No Child Left Behind? The Politics and Practice of School Accountability*, ed. Paul E. Peterson and Martin R. West (Washington, DC: Brookings Institution Press, 2003).

20. Robert L. Walker, *The Teacher and Collective Bargaining* (Lincoln, NE: Professional Educators Publications, 1975), p. 29.

21. Dale Ballou, *Teacher Contracts in Massachusetts* (Boston: Pioneer Institute, 2000); Pamela Riley, *Contract for Failure* (San Francisco: Pacific Research Institute, 2002).

22. See, for example, Lieberman, *The Teacher Unions.*

23. See, for example, Robert Chase, "The Union as a Professional Lifeline," in *Shaping the Profession That Shapes the Future*, ed. American Federation of Teachers (Washington, DC: American Federation of Teachers, 1999); Sandra Feldman, "Teacher Quality and Professional Unionism," in *Shaping the Profession that Shapes the Future*, ed. American Federation of Teachers (Washington, DC: American Federation of Teachers, 1999). In more general terms, here is how the NEA describes its mission: "NEA has a long, proud history of advocating for its members, America's children, and public schools. . . . In pursuing its mission, the NEA has determined that it will focus the energy and resources of its 2.7 million members on improving the quality of teaching, increasing student achievement, and making schools safer, better places to learn." NEA, "What Is NEA's Mission?" available online at http//:www.nea.org/aboutneaq/index.html.

24. Bess Keller, "Community Tries to Influence Teacher's Pact," *Education Week*, April 28, 2004, p. 5.

25. For evidence that teachers do indeed tend to find jobs at disadvantaged schools undesirable, and that they use whatever flexibility they have to move to more advantaged schools, see Eric A. Hanushek, John F. Kain, and Steven G. Rivkin, "Why Public Schools Lose Teachers," *Journal of Human Resources* 39, no. 2 (Spring 2004): 326-354.

26. Steven G. Rivkin, Eric A. Hanushek, and John F. Kain, "Teachers, Schools, and Academic Achievement," Working Paper No. 6691, National Bureau of Economic Research, revised 2001.

27. Terry M. Moe, "Bottom-Up Structure: Collective Bargaining, Transfer Rights, and the Education of Disadvantaged Children," Working Paper, Stanford University, February 2005.

28. Kate Walsh, *Teacher Certification Reconsidered* (Baltimore: Abell Foundation, 2001).

29. Dale Ballou and Michael Podgursky, *Teacher Pay and Teacher Quality* (Kalamazoo, MI: W. E. Upjohn Institute for Employment Research, 1997).

30. Lieberman, *The Teacher Unions.*

31. Hanushek, "The Evidence on Class Size."

32. Randall W. Eberts and Joe A. Stone, *Unions and Public Schools: The Effect of Collective Bargaining on American Education* (Lexington, MA: Lexington Books, 1984); Randall W. Eberts and Joe A. Stone, "Teachers Unions and the Productivity of Public Schools," *Industrial and Labor Relations Review* 40 (1986): 355-363; Martin I. Milkman, "Teachers Unions, Productivity, and Minority Student Achievement," *Journal of Labor Research* 18 (1997): 137-150; F. Howard Nelson and Michael Rosen, "Are Teachers Unions Hurting American Education? A State-by-State Analysis of the Impact of Collective Bargaining among Teachers on Student Performance" (Milwaukee: Institute for Wisconsin's Future, 1996); Sam Peltzman, "The Political Economy of the Decline of American Public Education," *Journal of Law and Economics* 36 (1993): 331-370; Laura M. Argyris and Daniel I. Rees, "Unionization and School Productivity," *Research in Labor Economics* 14 (1995): 49-68; Paul W. Grimes and Charles A. Register, "Teachers Unions and Student Achievement in High School Economics," *Journal of Economic Education* 21 (1990): 297-308; Michael M. Kurth, "Teachers Unions and Excellence in Education: An Analysis of the Decline in SAT Scores," *Journal of Labor Research* 8 (1987): 351-367; Lala Carr Steelman, Brian Powell, and Robert M. Carini, "Do Teacher Unions Hinder Educational Performance? Lessons Learned from State SAT and ACT Scores," *Harvard Educational Review* 70 (Winter 2000): 437-465.

33. Caroline Minter Hoxby, "How Teachers Unions Affect Education Production," *Quarterly Journal of Economics* 111 (1996): 671-718.

34. Lieberman, *The Teacher Unions.*

35. Clive S. Thomas and Ronald J. Hrebenar, "Interest Groups in the States," in *Politics in the American States*, 8th ed., ed. Virginia Gray and Russell L. Hanson (Washington, DC: CQ Press, 2004); Clive S. Thomas and Ronald J. Hrebenar, "Interest Groups in the States," in *Politics in the American States*, 7th ed., ed. Virginia Gray, Russell L. Hanson, and Herbert Jacob (Washington, DC: CQ Press, 1999).

36. National Committee on Excellence in Education (NCEE), *A Nation at Risk* (Washington, DC: NCEE, 1983).

37. See, for example, Thomas Toch, *In the Name of Excellence* (New York: Oxford University Press, 1991); Terry M. Moe, "The Politics of the Status Quo," in *Our Schools and Our Future*, ed. Paul E. Peterson (Stanford, CA: Hoover Press, 2003).

38. National Education Association, "Class Size," 2005, available online at http://nea.org/classsize. Also American Federation of Teachers, "The Benefits of Small Class Size," 2005, available online at http://www.aft.org/topics/classsize.

39. See, for example, John Gehring, "State Preschool Efforts Vary across Country, AFT Report Concludes," *Education Week*, March 5, 2003, p. 21.

40. See, for example, Chase, "The Union as a Professional Lifeline"; Feldman, "Teacher Quality and Professional Unionism"; American Federation of Teachers, *Shaping the Profession That Shapes the Future* (Washington, DC: Author, 1999); Dale Ballou and Michael Podgursky, "Gaining Control of Professional Licensing and Advancement," in *Conflicting Missions? Teachers Unions and Educational Reform*, ed. Tom Loveless (Washington, DC: Brookings Institution Press, 2000).

41. Hanushek, "The Economics of Schooling" and "Assessing the Effects of School Resources on Student Performance."

42. National Center for Education Statistics, *Digest of Education Statistics 2003* (Washington, DC: Author, 2004).

43. Ballou and Podgursky, *Teacher Pay and Teacher Quality.*

44. Hanushek, "The Evidence on Class Size."

45. Williamson M. Evers and Herbert J. Walberg, eds., *School Accountability* (Stanford, CA: Hoover Press, 2002).

46. Moe, "Politics, Control, and the Future of School Accountability."

47. Peterson and West, *No Child Left Behind?*; Evers and Walberg, *School Accountability.*

48. For detailed accounts of how the teachers unions have tried to defeat accountability proposals in the

states, see Paul T. Hill and Robin J. Lake, "Standards and Accountability in Washington State," in *Brookings Papers on Education Policy 2002*, ed. Diane Ravitch (Washington, DC: Brookings Institution Press, 2002), pp. 199-234; Frederick M. Hess, "Reform, Resistance . . . Retreat? The Predictable Politics of Accountability in Virginia," in *Brookings Papers on Education Policy 2002*, ed. Diane Ravitch (Washington, DC: Brookings Institution Press, 2002); and Michele Kurtz, "Testing, Testing: School Accountability in Massachusetts," Working Paper 1 (Cambridge, MA: Kennedy School of Government, Rappaport Institute for Greater Boston, 2001).

49. Both the NEA and the AFT publicly support standards. The AFT, in particular, has moved aggressively to be a leading voice on this score. But the fact is that both groups are opposed to any meaningful consequences. See National Education Association, "NEA 2001-2002 Resolutions," available online at http://www.nea.org; and American Federation of Teachers, *Making Standards Matter* (New York: American Federation of Teachers, 2001). For empirical accounts of union efforts to weaken standards, see Hill and Lake, "Standards and Accountability in Washington State"; Hess, "Reform, Resistance . . . Retreat?"; and Kurtz, "Testing, Testing."

50. Some of their arguments have merit and are the kinds of points that need to be taken into account in the well-intentioned pursuit of appropriate measures. But even if these issues were entirely resolved, the unions would still be against testing because it is ultimately threatening to their interests. They would simply find other reasons for carrying on the fight. See the more detailed discussion in Moe, "Politics, Control, and the Future of School Accountability."

51. For union complaints about testing, as well as arguments for relying on the subjective judgment of teachers, see National Education Association, "NEA 2001-2002 Resolution"; and American Federation of Teachers, *Making Standards Matter*. For their political activities in opposition to testing, see Hill and Lake, "Standards and Accountability in Washington State"; Hess, "Reform, Resistance . . . Retreat?"; and Kurtz, "Testing, Testing."

52. For evidence on the political activities to weaken or eliminate consequences, refer again to Hill and Lake, "Standards and Accountability in Washington State"; Hess, "Reform, Resistance . . . Retreat?"; and Kurtz, "Testing, Testing." Regarding pay for performance specifically: the national unions are opposed, but they have tried to respond to pressures for change by saying that some forms of differential pay—and thus some modifications of the traditional salary schedule—might be okay. These include extra compensation for things like additional responsibilities (e.g., mentoring), National Board certification, teaching in hard-to-staff areas, and the like. The unions do not support paying teachers on the basis of how well their own students perform. See, for example, American Federation of Teachers, "Real Incentives for Professionals: AFT Tackles Professional Pay for Teachers," *American Teacher*, April 2000. For specific examples of union opposition to pay for performance, see Linda Jacobson, "Plan for Merit Pay in Conn. Faces Union Opposition," *Education Week*, November 17, 2004, p. 20; Michelle R. Davis, "Teacher-Evaluation Plan Unlikely to Fly in Delaware," *Education Week*, September 1, 2004, p. 30. At this writing, a pay-for-performance plan is in the process of adoption in Denver with the support of the local union. But this is an unusual departure from the national pattern, and it is not nearly as big a move as it is being made out to be. It relies mainly on "performance" factors *other* than student performance, it is voluntary for all existing teachers, and it is accompanied by a huge increase in money for the additional compensation—no one will be paid less, but some may be paid more. In effect, the teachers have been bought off, agreeing to modest pay-for-performance arrangements in return for a 12 percent increase in pay for teachers as a whole. See Bess Keller, "Denver Teachers Approve Pay-for-Performance Plan," *Education Week*, March 23, 2004, available online at http://www.edweek.org.

53. See, for example, Edward P. Lazear, *Personnel Economics for Managers* (New York: Wiley and Sons, 1998).

54. For a detailed treatment of these issues, see Terry M. Moe, "The Structure of School Choice," in *Choice with Equity*, ed. Paul T. Hill (Stanford, CA: Hoover Press, 2002).

55. On the choice movement, see Paul E. Peterson, "Choice in American Education," in *A Primer on America's Schools*, ed. Terry M. Moe (Stanford, CA: Hoover Press, 2001); R. Kenneth Godwin and Frank R. Kemerer, *School Choice Tradeoffs* (Austin: University of Texas Press, 2002); and Hubert

Morken and Jo Renee Formicola, *The Politics of School Choice* (Lanham, MD: Rowman and Littlefield, 1999).

56. See the discussion and analysis in Terry M. Moe, *Schools, Vouchers, and the American Public* (Washington, DC: Brookings Institution Press, 2001). See also John F. Witte, *The Market Approach to Education: An Analysis of America's First Voucher Program* (Princeton, NJ: Princeton University Press, 2000); and Daniel McGroarty, *Break These Chains* (Rocklin, CA: Prima, 1996).

57. See Moe, *Schools, Vouchers, and the American Public.*

58. William G. Howell and Paul E. Peterson, *The Education Gap* (Washington, DC: Brookings Institution Press, 2002).

59. See, for example, National Education Association, "School Vouchers: The Emerging Track Record," available online at http://www.nea.org/vouchers; and American Federation of Teachers, "The Many Names of School Vouchers," available online at http://www.aft.org/topics/vouchers.

60. Ironically, Al Shanker, the longtime leader of the AFT, was the first to promote the idea of charter schools in a 1988 speech. See American Federation of Teachers, *Do Charter Schools Measure Up? The Charter School Experiment after Ten Years* (New York: Author, 2002). His vision was one of unionized teachers essentially running their own schools, free to try alternative approaches and curricula. But in the almost two decades since he made this proposal, the unions have done virtually nothing—even under Shanker himself—to pursue this vision. One can certainly imagine that teachers, as experts on education and schooling, would have a comparative advantage in starting and running successful charter schools. But whether these advantages can be realized when the unions are actually in charge, and union rules and interests get in the way of student learning, is another matter entirely—and may explain why the unions have done nothing to show the world that unionized schools are indeed more productive than nonunion ones. The United Federation of Teachers is currently seeking to set up a charter school in Brooklyn, touting this new development as an example of its support for the right kinds of charters. But if the UFT really supports charters, where has it been for nearly two decades? And why are unions all over the country not setting up charter schools and demonstrating their productivity?

61. On the charter movement, see Chester E. Finn, Bruno V. Manno, and Gregg Vanourek, *Charter Schools in Action* (Princeton, NJ: Princeton University Press, 2000).

62. Gregg Vanourek, *State of the Charter School Movement 2005* (Washington, DC: Charter School Leadership Council, 2005).

63. See, for example, National Education Association, "Charter Schools," available online at http://www.nea.org/charters; and American Federation of Teachers, *Do Charter Schools Measure Up?* For concrete examples of union opposition, see Christina A. Samuels, "Ohio Coalition Fighting to Keep Charter Cap," *Education Week*, April 6, 2005, p. 21; and Andrew Trotter, "Charter Resistance," *Education Week*, June 23, 2004, p. 24.

64. Diana Jean Schemo, "Charter Schools Trail in Results, U.S. Data Reveal," *New York Times*, August 17, 2004, p. 1.

65. See especially Charles Taylor Kerchner and Julia E. Koppich, *A Union of Professionals* (New York: Teachers College Press, 1993); and Charles Taylor Kerchner, Julia E. Koppich, and Joseph G. Weeres, *United Mind Workers* (San Francisco: Jossey-Bass, 1997).

66. See, for example, Jeff Archer, "NYC Unions on Hot Seat at Hearings," *Education Week*, November 26, 2003.

About the Contributors

Leo Casey is special representative for high schools for New York City's United Federation of Teachers (UFT). Prior to his stint at the UFT, he taught in an inner-city high school in the Crown Heights section of Brooklyn for 15 years, where he was named national Social Studies Teacher of the Year. Casey holds a PhD in political science from the University of Toronto, and has written extensively on civics, education, unionism, and politics.

Morgaen L. Donaldson is an advanced doctoral student at the Harvard Graduate School of Education and a researcher at the Project on the Next Generation of Teachers. She studies policy and practice that pertain to teachers' professional growth and career development, teachers unions, and current changes in rural and urban schools. A former high school teacher, Donaldson was a founding faculty member of the Boston Arts Academy, Boston's public high school for the arts.

Henry S. Farber is the Hughes-Rogers Professor of Economics and a research associate of the Industrial Relations Section at Princeton University. Farber is also a research associate of the National Bureau of Economic Research and a fellow of the Econometric Society and of the Society of Labor Economics.

Dan Goldhaber is a research associate professor at the University of Washington's Evans School of Public Affairs and an affiliated scholar of the Urban Institute's Education Policy Center. Goldhaber also served as an elected member of the Alexandria City School Board from 1997 to 2002. His research focuses on issues of educational productivity and reform at the K-12 level and the relationship between teacher labor markets and teacher quality.

Jane Hannaway is director of the Education Policy Center at the Urban Institute in Washington, D.C. Her research is most centrally concerned with the effects of structural reforms in education. She previously served on the faculties of Columbia, Princeton, and Stanford universities and received her PhD from Stanford University.

Frederick M. Hess is director of educational policy studies at the American Enterprise Institute and executive editor of *Education Next*. He is known for his work on a diverse range of educational issues, including urban education, accountability, charter schooling and school vouchers, educational politics, teacher and administrator quality, local governance, competition, and school improvement. He holds a master's of education degree in teaching and curriculum and an MA and PhD in government from Harvard University.

Paul T. Hill is a research professor at the University of Washington's Daniel J. Evans School of Public Affairs, and director of the Center on Reinventing Public Education, which studies alternative governance and finance systems for public elementary and secondary education. His recent work on education reform has focused on school choice plans, school accountability, and charter schools.

Susan Moore Johnson is the Pforzheimer Professor of Teaching and Learning at the Harvard Graduate School of Education, where she served as the academic dean from 1993 to 1999. A former high school teacher and administrator, Johnson studies and teaches about teacher policy, school organization, educational leadership, and school improvement in schools and school systems. Johnson is a member of the board of directors of the National Academy of Education.

Richard D. Kahlenberg is a senior fellow at The Century Foundation, where he writes about education, equal opportunity, and civil rights. He was previously a fellow at the Center for National Policy, a visiting associate professor of constitutional law at George Washington University, and a legislative assistant to Senator Charles S. Robb (D-VA). Kahlenberg graduated magna cum laude from Harvard College in 1985 and cum laude from Harvard Law School in 1989.

Andrew P. Kelly is a graduate student in political science at the University of California, Berkeley. His work has appeared in such publications as *Educational Policy, Education Week*, and *Education Next*. Prior to attending graduate school he worked as an education policy researcher at the American Enterprise Institute. He graduated from Dartmouth College in 2002.

Julia E. Koppich is a San Francisco–based education consultant. She previously served on the faculty of the Graduate School of Education at the University of California, Berkeley and as director of policy analysis for California Education. She holds a PhD in educational administration and policy analysis from the University of California, Berkeley.

Paul Manna is an assistant professor in the Department of Government at the College of William and Mary, where he is also affiliated with the Thomas Jefferson Program in Public Policy. He has research and teaching interests in American politics, public policy, political behavior, and applied research methods. Before becoming a professor, Manna served as a high school social studies teacher and debate coach.

Terry M. Moe is a senior fellow at the Hoover Institution, a member of the Institution's Koret Task Force on K-12 education, and a professor of political science at Stanford University. He is an expert on educational policy, U.S. political institutions, and organization theory. His current research projects are concerned with school choice, public bureaucracy, and the presidency.

Andrew J. Rotherham is cofounder and codirector of Education Sector, a senior fellow at the Progressive Policy Institute, and a member of the Virginia Board of Education. He is the author of numerous articles and papers about education and coeditor of two books on education policy. He previously served at the White House as special assistant to the president for domestic policy during the Clinton administration.

Index

A

Accountability, 2, 4, 18
  adequate yearly progress, 160, 161-162, 175-178
  collective bargaining process and, 54
  resistance to, 23-24
  standardized testing, 150-151, 154, 160-161
  standards movement and, 21, 24, 187, 189, 209-210
  union politics, education reform and, 246-249
  value-added model and, 175
  See also No Child Left Behind (NCLB) Act of 2001
Achievement of Tenure Process for New Teachers, 135-136
Adequate yearly progress (AYP), 160, 161-162, 175-178
Administrative power, 10-11, 17
  contemporary bargaining process and, 66-67, 199-200
  cooperative labor-management relations and, 211-214, 224
  impact bargaining and, 59
  industrial-style collective bargaining and, 208-209
  peer review process and, 20, 133-134
  principal-agent theory and, 162-163
  reform/structural change and, 54
  staffing decisions and, 98-100, 125-131
  teacher evaluation/dismissal, 131-134, 199
  See also Collective bargaining agreements (CBAs); Education practices; Reform bargaining; Teaching assignment issues
AFL-CIO, 9, 143, 144, 220, 226

Altomare, George, 12
American Federation of Labor (AFL), 8, 9
American Federation of Teachers (AFT), 7-10, 56, 62
  education reform and, 209-210
  historic development of, 7-9, 14-15, 142-144
  mission of, 141-142
  reform unionism and, 219-221
  See also Collective bargaining; Collective bargaining agreements (CBAs); Education practices; No Child Left Behind (NCLB) Act of 2001

B

Benefits. See Compensation
Binding arbitration, 58
Boston Plan for Excellence, 106-107
Boston Public Schools (BPS), 106-107, 129-130
Bureau of Labor Statistics (BLS) data, 54, 56, 67, 69

C

Career ladders, 136-137, 190
Career in Teaching (CIT) program, 136
Certification, 21, 137, 199
Charter schools, 251
Class size reductions, 8, 13, 14, 17, 66, 92, 123-124
Collective bargaining, 4-5
  benefits of, 8, 13, 16-17
  criticisms of, 17-19
  demand for, 10-11
  expansion of, 14-16
  federal employees and, 13
  future education practice/policy and, 258-263

historical perspective on, 186-188
new unionism and, 23-24
obstacles to, 9-10
political involvement and, 15-16
recommendations for, 263-266
reform unionism and, 5, 8, 19-23
scope of issues in, 13-14, 56
teacher organizations, development
    of, 7-9, 14-15
unionization and, 146-147
union reinvention, process of, 19-23
watershed developments in, 11-13
See also Collective bargaining agree-
    ments (CBAs); Democratic voice
    model; Reform bargaining;
    Union membership
Collective bargaining agreement costs,
    89-91
cost effects summary, 104-106
cost imposition mechanisms, 91-104
cost inequalities and, 96
district-level effects, 91-96
funding disparities, 102-104
quality teachers, disadvantaged
    schools and, 96-98
remedies to, 106-109
salary costs, 91-95, 102-103
seniority placement privileges and,
    100-102
staffing decisions, control over,
    98-100
tenured teachers and, 94-95, 98, 100
Collective bargaining agreements (CBAs),
    53-56
balance of power issues in, 62-66
bargaining process and, 56-59
contemporary issues in, 66-67
content of, 77-78
contract language, explicitness of, 79,
    82-86
contract length and, 60, 78-81
district-level practices and, 69-77
future education practice/policy and,
    258-263
impasse resolution procedures, 57-58
interest-based bargaining and, 57, 61

last-best-offer power and, 66, 68
management flexibility and, 60, 77-78
national context of, 61-62
recommendations for, 263-266
scope of negotiations and, 56, 59, 66,
    68
state legal environment and, 59-60
strike actions, decline in, 67-68, 72
traditional bargaining and, 57
union pay premium and, 60
See also Collective bargaining agree-
    ment costs; No Child Left
    Behind (NCLB) Act
Collective bargaining rights index, 41-43
union coverage and, 45-46, 47
wage structures and, 48-50
Colorado Student Assessment Program
    (CSAP), 120
Compensation, 8, 9
backloading of pay, 147
collective bargaining effects and,
    16-17, 91-93, 114-115
differentiated compensation, 53, 117
health care costs and, 67
income disparity and, 10
merit pay, 8, 18, 20-21, 23, 119-121,
    173-175
nonunion wages, union effects on,
    145
ProComp system, 61, 120-121
public-sector bargaining laws and,
    46-50
salary levels, 115-116
single salary scale, 117-119, 262-263
strike actions and, 13
teacher quality and, 116-117, 119-
    121, 152, 198-199
union pay premium and, 60, 198
Condon-Wadlin Act of 1947, 12
Contract negotiations, 14, 17-18, 22, 53
performance evaluation/dismissal and,
    131-133
reform bargaining and, 210-215
See also Collective bargaining agree-
    ments (CBAs); No Child Left
    Behind (NCLB) Act of 2001

Cost disease, 95-96

Costs. *See* Collective bargaining agreement costs; Compensation

Current Population Survey (CPS) data, 27, 34, 35, 38, 45, 46, 47, 48, 49

D

Democratic voice model, 181-182

  collective bargaining, historical perspective on, 186-188

  collective bargaining, limitations of, 185-186, 198-200

  components in, 183-185

  education institutions, change in, 192-193

  education policy, union influence and, 193-195

  knowledge-based economy and, 188-189, 191-192, 198

  power traditions and, 200-201

  professionalism, development of, 189-191, 193, 198

  retention crisis and, 195, 197-198

  school-based contracts and, 192-193

  teacher quality and, 195-200

  teachers unions and, 182-183

Denver Classroom Teachers Association (DCTA), 61-62, 76, 120, 211, 219

Dewey, John, 9

Disadvantaged schools/students, 13-14, 15, 18, 21, 23

  achievement gap and, 2, 173

  funding disparities and, 102-104

  immigrant settlement neighborhoods, 106

  incentives for teachers and, 199

  quality teachers and, 96-98, 104, 125, 128

  stabilization measures for, 106-107

  teacher assignment and, 100-102, 128

  See also No Child Left Behind (NCLB) Act of 2001; School choice; Student achievement

Discipline policy, 14, 17, 199

Dismissal decisions, 131-134, 199

Displaced Workers Surveys (DWS), 35

Due process rights, 131, 199

E

Eberts, Randall W., 17, 152, 153-154, 155

Economic environment, 2, 32, 61, 62, 89

  cost disease and, 95-96

  knowledge-based economy, 188-189, 191-192, 198

  labor market/productivity, union effect on, 145-146, 148

  school choice and, 249-252

  See also Collective bargaining agreement costs

Education policy, 4

  contract negotiations and, 14, 17-18, 22

  funding equalization, 15-16

  future collective bargaining and, 258-263

  More Effective Schools program, 13-14

  reform unionism and, 5, 8, 14, 23-25

  standards movement and, 21, 24, 187, 189

  union effects on, 148-149, 193-195

  See also Collective bargaining; Discipline policy; Education practices; No Child Left Behind (NCLB) Act of 2001; Public policy; Public-sector labor movement; Strike actions

Education practices, 229-230

  accountability systems development and, 246-249

  contract provisions/work rules and, 236-241

  education reform, union politics and, 241-252

  future practices, reform unionism and, 252-255

  local politics, collective bargaining efforts and, 233-241

  mainstream union politics and, 243-246

  school board politics and, 233-236

school choice, political issue of,
249-252, 254
union interests/organization and,
230-233
The Education Trust, 96, 97, 104, 258
Elementary and Secondary Education Act
(ESEA) of 1965, 15, 159, 160,
173, 177, 258
Evaluation approaches, 131-134
Evergreen Freedom Foundation, 77
Exit-voice concept, 147-148, 182-183

F
Fact finding procedures, 57-58
Feldman, Sandra, 22, 219-220
First Amendment protections, 55, 56
Fourteenth Amendment rights, 131
Freeman, Richard B., 31, 39, 40, 41, 42,
195, 197

G
Global knowledge economy, 188-189, 198
Government employees, 13, 27-32
See also Public-sector labor movement
Grievance process, 10-11, 85, 133

H
Health care coverage, 67
Hobson v. Hansen, 108
Hoxby, Caroline M., 152, 153, 155, 241

I
Impact bargaining, 59
Impasse resolution procedures, 57-58
Improving America's Schools Act (IASA) of
1994, 160-161
Induction programs, 135-136, 211
Institute for Teacher Union Leadership
(ITUL), 222
Interest-based bargaining (IBB), 57, 61

J
Just cause standard, 131

K
Kerchner, Charles Taylor, 23, 205, 257
Knowledge-based economy, 188-189, 191-
192, 198
Koppich, Julia, 23, 148, 257
Kurth, Michael, 151, 152, 155

L
Labor unions. *See* Collective bargaining;
Reform unionism; Union mem-
bership
Last-best-offer power, 66, 68
Lieberman, Myron, 13-14, 22, 64, 85

M
Makinac Center for Public Policy, 77
Making Standards Matter series, 209-210
McDonnell, Lorraine, 59, 66, 67, 78, 86,
123, 226
Meany, George, 9
Mediation procedures, 57, 58
Mentoring programs, 135-136, 187-188,
190, 199
Merit pay, 8, 18, 20-21, 23
career ladders and, 136
No Child Left Behind Act and, 173-
175
rejection of, 24, 119
teacher quality and, 119-121, 198-199
See also Compensation
Minneapolis Federation of Teachers, 211-
212
More Effective Schools program, 13-14

N
National Assessment of Educational
Progress (NAEP), 150
National Board for Professional Teaching
Standards (NBPTS), 21, 190,
199, 244
National Commission on Excellence in
Education, 19
National Council for Accreditation of
Teacher Education, 244
National Education Association (NEA), 7-
10, 56, 62
education reform and, 210

historic development of, 7-9, 14-15, 142-144
mission of, 141-142
reform unionism and, 219-221
See also Collective bargaining; Collective bargaining agreements (CBAs); Education practices; No Child Left Behind (NCLB) Act of 2001
National Labor Relations Act (NLRA) of 1935, 9, 32, 38, 207, 208
National Labor Relations Board (NLRB), 32, 33, 188, 225
National School Boards Association, 63-64
A Nation at Risk, 19, 22, 189, 193, 203, 209, 243
A Nation Prepared, 136
NBER Public Sector Collective Bargaining Law Data Set, 39, 41, 42
New Teacher Project, 97-98
New unionism. *See* Reform bargaining; Reform unionism
No Child Left Behind (NCLB) Act of 2001, 4, 23, 24, 159, 247
adequate yearly progress and, 160, 161-162, 175-178
collective bargaining and, 54, 87, 160, 165-168
disaggregated test scores and, 161
future challenges of, 178-179
implementation, union interests and, 164-178
policy venues, group interests and, 162-164
reform unionism and, 220, 221
salary schedules, merit pay and, 173-175
standardized testing and, 160-161, 171-173, 175
supplemental services requirements and, 176
teacher quality and, 160, 168-171
teaching assignments and, 177-178
value-added model and, 175
North American Association of Education Negotiators, 62-63

O
Oregon School Boards Association (OSBA), 167, 168, 170

P
Pascal, Anthony, 59, 66, 67, 78, 86, 123, 226
Peer Assistance and Review initiative, 133-134
Peer review, 20, 23, 53, 190, 191, 211
Performance. *See* Accountability; Merit pay; Student achievement
Policy. *See* Collective bargaining; Discipline policy; Education policy; Public policy; Strike actions
Political action, 14-16, 183, 184
Pontiac v. Spellings, 172
Poverty. *See* Disadvantaged schools/students
Preparation time allotment, 8, 17, 124-125
Private-sector labor movement, 10
collective bargaining regulation and, 38-39
employment growth, union membership and, 31-34
public-sector/private-sector comparison, 35-38
union membership rates, 27, 28, 146
Privatization pressures, 66
ProComp system, 61, 120-121
Professional development, 17, 53, 57, 134, 199
career ladders and, 136-137
induction/mentoring programs, 135-136
professionalism, development of, 189-191, 193, 198
teacher quality and, 134-135
violence management strategies and, 184
Professional Growth System (PGS), 214
Public Employee Relations Board (PERB) (California), 58
Public policy:
policy venues and, 162-163
private-sector situation and, 38-39
public-sector regulation and, 39-50

right-to-work laws, 38-39, 41, 47
union coverage, bargaining laws and, 43-46, 47
wage structures, bargaining laws and, 46-50
See also Collective bargaining agreements (CBAs); Education policy
Public Policy Institute of California, 97
Public-sector labor movement, 9, 10
collective bargaining, regulation of, 39-43
development of, 11-13
employment growth, union membership and, 34-35, 36
political activism and, 15-16
private-sector/public-sector comparison, 35-38
right-to-strike policy, 14-15
union coverage, bargaining laws and, 43-46, 47
union membership rates, 27-32
wage structures, bargaining laws and, 46-50

Q
Quality. *See* Teacher quality
Quality Educational Standards in Teaching (QuEST), 210

R
Reform bargaining, 20, 23, 147-148, 203-205
contract negotiation and, 210-215
cooperative labor-management relations and, 211-214, 224
industrial unionism and, 209-210
leadership in, 218-219
organizational capacity, development of, 215-219
recommendations for, 263-266
reframing process, expectations modification and, 223-227
scope of negotiations and, 214-215, 224-226
student achievement and, 224
See also Reform unionism

Reform unionism, 5, 8, 14, 178-179
contemporary union practices and, 23-25
future of, 223, 252-255
industrial unionism and, 206-210
interest-based bargaining and, 57
leaders for, 218-219
meet and confer approach and, 205-206
No Child Left Behind Act and, 220, 221
precursors to, 205-209
prospects for, 219-222
reinvention process, collective bargaining and, 19-23, 223-227
support for, 219-221
teacher quality and, 53
union politics, education reform and, 241-252
See also Education practices; Institute for Teacher Union Leadership (ITUL); Reform bargaining; Teacher Union Reform Network (TURN)
Retention rate, 102, 196-198
Rhode Island Federation of Teachers, 220
Right-to-strike policy, 14-15, 67
Right-to-work (RTW) laws, 38-39, 41, 47
Rochester Teachers Association, 214
Roza, Marguerite, 101, 103, 104

S
Safe Schools against Violence in Education (SAVE) legislation, 184
Salaries. *See* Compensation
School Based Option (SBO), 99, 192, 193
School Based Transfer and Staffing Plan, 192, 193, 197
School choice, 8, 18, 21, 249-252, 254
School improvement, 13-14, 15, 54, 128
See also Education practices; No Child Left Behind (NCLB) Act of 2001; Student achievement; Teacher quality
Schools and Staffing Survey (SASS), 157
School violence, 183-185

Selden, David, 11, 12
Senge, Peter M., 212
Seniority-based assignments, 126, 128, 147, 196-197, 238
Shanker, Albert, 8, 11, 12, 17, 18, 19-23, 189, 190, 209
Single salary scale, 117-119, 262-263
Standardized testing, 150-152, 154, 160-161, 171-173, 175
Standards movement, 21, 24, 187, 189, 209
Stone, Joe A., 16, 17, 152, 153-154, 155
Strike actions, 9
    decline in, 67-68, 72
    development of, 11, 12-13, 18
    interest-based bargaining and, 61
    last-best-offer power and, 66, 68
    non-wage issues and, 14
    right-to-strike policy, 14-15
    See also Collective bargaining; Collective bargaining agreements (CBAs); Grievance process
Student achievement, 4-5, 141-142
    achievement gap and, 2, 173
    curricular reform and, 8
    educational resources/practices and, 152, 153-154
    future research topics on, 154, 156-157
    labor-management cooperation and, 224
    school improvement and, 13-14, 15
    standardized test scores and, 150-152, 154
    teacher salary levels and, 152-153
    teacher turnover and, 102, 196-198
    teacher unions, development/mission of, 141-144
    union influence on, 149-154, 155
    See also Disadvantaged schools/students; Education practices; No Child Left Behind (NCLB) Act of 2001; Teacher quality

T
Taft-Hartley Act, 38
Taylor, Frederick, 187
Teacher Bargaining Organization (TBO), 12
Teacher Internship Program, 187-188
Teacher quality, 16-17, 18, 111-112
    board certification and, 21, 137, 199
    career ladders and, 136-137
    collective bargaining and, 112-114, 121, 137, 138-140, 198-200
    democratic voice model and, 195-200
    differentiated compensation and, 53, 117, 120
    disadvantaged schools and, 96-98, 100-102, 104
    evaluation/dismissal decisions and, 131-134
    induction/mentoring programs and, 135-136
    merit pay and, 8, 18, 20-21, 119-121, 198-199
    new unionism and, 22-23, 53
    pay scale issues and, 114-121
    peer review and, 20, 133-134
    professional development and, 134-137
    research efforts on, 112-114, 138
    selection process and, 148-149
    single salary scale and, 117-119
    teaching assignment issues and, 125-131
    working conditions and, 121-125
    See also Collective bargaining agreements (CBAs); No Child Left Behind (NCLB) Act of 2001; Student achievement
Teachers, 4
    evaluation/dismissal of, 131-133
    grievance proceedings and, 10-11, 85
    incompetent teachers, 8, 18, 20-21, 23
    peer review and, 20, 23, 53, 133-134
    political involvement of, 15-16
    turnover rates for, 16
    unions, development of, 7-9

working conditions of, 10, 13
See also Collective bargaining;
Collective bargaining agreements
(CBAs); Compensation;
Education practices; Student
achievement; Teacher quality;
Teaching assignment issues
Teachers Guild, 11, 12
Teacher Union Reform Network (TURN),
24, 178, 222, 253
Teaching assignment issues, 125-126
annual staffing decisions, 126
Boston Public Schools example,
129-130
delayed hiring, 130-131
No Child Left Behind Act and,
177-178
seniority-based reassignments, 126,
128, 147
tenured teachers, new assignments for,
128
transfers of staff, 126-127
See also Administrative power;
Teacher quality

U
Union membership, 7-10
employment growth factors and,
31-38
labor market/productivity and, 145-
146, 148
private-sector unions, 27, 28, 31-33,
38-39
public policy/regulation and, 38-50
public-sector unions, 27-31, 32, 34-
35, 36, 39-50
right-to-work laws and, 38-39, 41, 47
union coverage and, 43-46, 47
unionization vs. collective bargaining,
146-147

wage structures and, 46-50
See also Collective bargaining;
Democratic voice model;
Education practices; Reform bar-
gaining; Reform unionism;
Student achievement
Union security law index, 40-41
union coverage and, 44-45, 46
wage structures and, 46-48
UniServ system, 63
United Auto Workers, 12, 13, 186-187
United Federation of Teachers (UFT),
12-14, 56
democratic voice model and, 183-184
historical perspective on, 187-188
reform unionism and, 219-220
See also Collective bargaining;
Collective bargaining agreements
(CBAs)

V
Valletta, Robert G., 39, 40, 41, 42
Voucher system, 18, 19, 21, 23, 250-251

W
Wages. *See* Compensation
Wagner Act, 38, 188
Wisconsin Association of School Boards
(WASB), 167, 168, 173
Working conditions, 10, 13, 16-17, 66
class size, 123-124
facilities/resources, 122-123
preparation time allotment, 124-125
teacher quality and, 121-122

Z
Zero-sum bargaining, 57